THE LETTERS OF GEORGE GISSING
TO EDUARD BERTZ

The Letters of George Gissing to Eduard Bertz 1887-1903

edited by

ARTHUR C. YOUNG

CONSTABLE · LONDON

LONDON
PUBLISHED BY
Constable and Company Ltd
10–12 ORANGE STREET W.C.2

First published in Great Britain 1961

Made and printed in Great Britain by
William Clowes and Sons, Limited, London and Beccles

To my parents
and to Kathy

ACKNOWLEDGMENTS

ONE of the pleasures in publishing this edition of letters is the opportunity it gives to thank publicly those persons who have, in multitudinous ways, aided me in my work. In particular, I wish to acknowledge my gratitude to Mr. Alfred C. Gissing, George Gissing's son, who read the manuscript and genially answered innumerable questions; and I am also indebted to him for granting permission to publish these letters as well as quotations from other Gissing papers. I am especially grateful to him and his family for their hospitality and graciousness during my visits to them in their serene home in Les Marécottes, Switzerland. I shall not forget the Alpine hikes with Michael, nor Jane's interest in her grandfather, nor the warmth and kindness of Mrs. Gissing.

I am also grateful to Professor Gordon S. Haight, Professor of English at Yale University, under whose mentorship I first began work on this volume. His attainments in scholarship have been an example and a goal, and I can only hope that this book will be a small tribute to his skill as a teacher.

To the curators of the two major Gissing collections in the United States, Miss Marjorie Gray Wynne, of the Rare Book Room, Yale University Library, and Dr. John D. Gordan, of the Henry W. and Albert A. Berg Collection of the New York Public Library, I offer my thanks for their patient cooperation and their constant good-natured aid. I should also like to thank the Trustees of the Yale Library for giving their permission to publish the Gissing-Bertz correspondence and extracts from other letters; and I must thank the Trustees of the New York Public Library for permitting me to publish portions of the Gissing diaries. Recognition is also due to the Librarian of the City Library of Wakefield, Yorkshire, for the copy of Dr. Henry Hick's "Notes on the Life of George Gissing"; and to the Registrar and the Archivist of the University of Manchester, and to my friend Dr. Geoffrey Pilcher, of the same University, all of whom gave me tea and valuable information about Gissing's college life and records.

I wish to thank Professor Hobart Coffey, of the Law Library of the University of Michigan, who gave me a thorough account of the provenance of the letters and the history of the Dreising family. He gives place to no one in this enthusiasm for Gissing's novels. Miss Winifred F. E. C. Isaac, of 110 Grove Lane, Denmark Hill (certainly an evocative address for readers of Gissing), also an admirer of Gissing, helped me in my research; and her gentle epistolary reminders over the years have kept me conscientiously at work.

Professor Paul F. Mattheisen, of Harpur College, not only read the manuscript with rare scrupulosity but also, in spite of the pressures of his own scholarship, gave openly of his time in reading proof. His willing assistance can only inadequately be acknowledged in words.

For assistance in verifying my translations and transcriptions of the various languages in Gissing's letters, I express my gratefulness to the following friends and colleagues: Professor John Ciardi, Rutgers University; the Reverend Doctor John W. Beardslee, Jr., Professor Emeritus of the New Brunswick Theological Seminary; Professor Ernestine F. Kritsch, Douglass College; Professor John J. O'Connor, and Mr. William L. Gray, Rutgers University.

To Mrs. Anne Zimmer, who typed and retyped with acute vigilance and wariness, I wish to record my gratitude; and to Mrs. Moira W. Metcalfe, of Rutgers University, who helped in checking the manuscript and in translating, I also offer my thanks. I am obliged to Professor John F. Vickrey, of Lehigh University, who made important comments on parts of the manuscript.

For financial assistance I have a special obligation to the Rutgers University Research Council and to Dr. Mason W. Gross, President of Rutgers University, for their sympathetic responses to my requests. Their support has been generous.

Finally, I should like to thank my students and friends who, with apparent interest and some indulgence, have occasionally encouraged me to talk about Gissing.

ARTHUR C. YOUNG

Rutgers, The State University

INTRODUCTION

ON his deathbed George Gissing told his wife: "I have done a work which, I think, will not be entirely forgotten tomorrow."[1] His work has not been forgotten, for since his death there have been successive editions of one or another of his novels, especially, of course, of the durable *The Private Papers of Henry Ryecroft*. Literary histories regularly carry a paragraph or two on his fiction, and doctoral dissertations about him have not been infrequent. Yet only a decade ago, *The Western Humanities Review* published an article by Russell Kirk called "Who Knows George Gissing?" in which he pointed out how little accurate information there seemed to be about Gissing's life.[2] According to Mr. Kirk, a major reason for the lack of such knowledge is that

> ...Mrs. Grundy, whom Gissing more than once defied by name and defeated (in Pyrrhic style), exults over him now that he is dead, and fear of what that woman might say has induced people who loved him to lock up letters and choose their phrases.[3]

Since the publication of Mr. Kirk's article, a biography and several studies on aspects of Gissing's life have appeared so that the important events of his career are now known. But neither the biography nor the brief articles reveal the nature of his personality, and they often conceal, by exaggeration or by prejudice, rather than illuminate his character. The student who desires more than a register of statistics about Gissing's life cannot be satisfied, nor can the critic who wants to know how he acquired his literary skill and what he thought about his own work. So much evasiveness and subterfuge have accompanied the biographical accounts of Gissing that one courts frustration trying to sift through error, fact, and ambiguity. Still, one keeps digging for the truth about

---

[1] Gabrielle Gissing to E. Bertz, 17 January 1904, Yale.

[2] Winter 1949–50, pp. 213–22.

[3] *Ibid.*, p. 216.

Gissing, because, as Sir Edmund Gosse said in a review of *The Letters of George Gissing to Members of His Family*, "... it may well be argued that such a character as that of Gissing is not worth discussing if the truth is not told."[4] Ironically, the very volume about which Gosse wrote suffers from the zeal of Gissing's family in silently excising anything they found distasteful. There can be no quarrel about the family's right to prune as they saw fit, but the excisions are regrettable simply because they give rise to insinuation and implication, both usually more repellent than the truth. Even Gissing's friends contributed to the misinformation about his life in their reminiscences and memoirs in which they revived blurred impressions and repeated inaccuracies without admitting any haziness in their recollections.

Morley Roberts, in *The Private Papers of Henry Maitland*, simply invented when he could not remember and dramatized whatever seemed colorless in fact to him. For example, Roberts writes that Gabrielle Fleury was "partly Spanish" and that she knew her Spanish well. He also asserts that Gissing's second visit to England after his marriage to Gabrielle occurred because "... he was certainly run down and much underfed, his nerves were starved too, so he got into one of his sudden rages and practically ran away from France."[5] Although Gabrielle is not mentioned at this point, one naturally assumes that Gissing fled from her as well as from starvation. However, Gissing's letter to Bertz, dated 5 April 1903, in this volume, proves clearly that if Gabrielle were of Spanish descent she did not know the language, and, certainly in her husband's lifetime, did not study it. And Roberts's version of Gissing's flight to England seems apocryphal when one reads the letter to Bertz written on 22 June 1901. An entry in Gissing's diary for June 1901 also says that Gabrielle accompanied him, and Dr. Henry Hick of New Romney, Gissing's boyhood friend and physician, said about the trip that "The whole thing was arranged beforehand and he did not stay with me at all. There was, however, no question of his leaving his third wife."[6]

Even H. G. Wells, in his *Experiment in Autobiography*,

[4] *Leaves and Fruit* (London: William Heinemann Ltd., 1927), p. 276.

[5] Roberts, pp. 179, 199.

[6] "Abstract of Notes by Dr. Henry Hick on George Gissing's Life in Wakefield," City Library of Wakefield.

seemingly refreshed his memories of Gissing by going to Roberts's book, without being sure of what was fact and what was fiction. Although Wells does not attribute Spanish blood to Gabrielle, he does repeat, and indeed reinforce, the idea that Gissing abandoned her.

In the absence of published materials, other writers have speculated about the sources of Gissing's novels and about his attitudes towards his own books. One critic thought that *The Private Papers of Henry Ryecroft* (1903) might have had its inception in C. F. Keary's *The Wanderer* (1901), and then bolstered a supercilious comment on the former book by alleging that Gissing had confessed to a mutual friend: "I did not put my innermost thought into *Ryecroft*."[7] Actually, according to the letter of 24 October 1900, *Ryecroft* had been completed before the Keary book appeared; and in Gissing's letter for 26 October 1902, he clearly affirms his pleasure in *Ryecroft* by writing: "I suspect it contains the very best literary work I can hope to turn out." There is no reason to carp further on these matters; the point is that this correspondence between Gissing and Bertz offers reliable answers to some questions that have never been adequately answered before.

The letters written to Eduard Bertz contrast favorably with the brief, often hysterical notes which Gissing frequently sent to friends whose advice or aid he needed immediately. His letters to his brother Algernon are intimate, spontaneous, and rational when dealing with common affairs, but those written when his domestic life was in upheaval have a frenetic intensity and a tone of self-pity that are somewhat appalling. Equally disturbing are some of the notes sent to Dr. Henry Hick, to whom Gissing appealed frequently and without restraint. Still, Gissing, after scribbling an impetuous letter to one of these men, was capable of checking his despair long enough to write a calm, thoughtful letter to Bertz; possibly such discipline had become part of him as a result of his debasing experiences with his first wife, Nell, whom he had often dragged home from a pub or street where she had collapsed in an alcoholic fit. After cleaning and quieting her, he could seat himself at his desk in the next room and fill

---

[7] "John O'London [Frank Swinnerton]," "Letters to Gog and Magog," *John O'London's Weekly*, LXII (23 January 1953), p. 71.

page after page of his current novel with his small, neat writing. As the letters to Bertz indicate, Gissing never lost the power to recover control of his emotions, at least temporarily, when he had to write.

Besides providing a partial record of Gissing's life and reflecting part of his personality, these letters contain substantial information about the commercial aspect of a literary career in the last decade of the nineteenth century. For the student curious about the marketing of literature, Gissing's experiences are revealing. Although he accepted abominable contracts himself, he thought his literary agent's fumbling unforgivable and he raged at his publishers for advertising his books clumsily. However, these letters offer more than an index of Victorian publishing practices and a mere compendium of biographical data, for they tell us what books Gissing read, how he developed ideas for his novels, what he thought of the world around him, and how he evaluated his own work. In these letters Gissing speaks for himself.

When a definitive biography does appear, and if a standard edition of his works ever is printed, Gissing may emerge as a man of fine intelligence and as an artist whose skill contributed more to the development of the English novel than he has been given credit for. It is clear even now that, as Edmund Gosse predicted in 1927, "His books will continue to be read and he himself to be talked of when many more dignified and sententious authors are forgotten."[8]

This edition contains 189 letters and post cards written by Gissing to Eduard Bertz between April 1887 and October 1903. I believe that the correspondence offered here is all that remains of the many letters that passed between the two men during their twenty-four year friendship. Except for brief quotations and some paraphrased statements printed in earlier studies,[9] the contents of these letters have never been published. Bertz himself considered

---

[8] Gosse, p. 281.

[9] The excerpts were published in Jacob Korg's "Division of Purpose in George Gissing," *PMLA*, LXX (June 1955), 323–36 and A. C. Young's "George Gissing's Friendship with Eduard Bertz," *Nineteenth Century Fiction*, XIII (December 1958), 227–37; a few phrases from the letters have been quoted and some remarks recast in M. C. Donnelly's *George Gissing: Grave Comedian* (Cambridge: Harvard University Press, 1954).

publishing the correspondence in 1905, if the family and Gabrielle would give him permission. He wrote to Algernon Gissing, who was the executor of his brother's estate, asking that his own letters be sent back to him because they would be important in editing George's correspondence. Algernon returned the letters to Bertz, gave permission to publish, and commended the project as a fitting memorial for his brother.[10] Legally, Bertz could have begun his edition, but, out of courtesy to Gabrielle, he asked her if she too would agree to its publication. For over a year Gabrielle procrastinated and then said no. Her objection was not unreasonable. She feared her reputation might be soiled if a definitive edition of letters were put into the hands of what Gissing once called "the greasy citizen." She wrote Bertz:

> I have come to the conclusion that nothing wld be more desirable than yr publishing G.'s letters as much in full as possible, and with a truthful introduction by you giving all the supplementary informations you can give. But, at the same time, I can't help thinking that such a true, complete, definitive publication (for it ought to be all of that) is *at present impossible*. Do forgive me that word, and allow me to try and explain to you my reasons. As you say, to give an account of G.'s private life and *not* to mention at all our marriage is really impossible, not only for the effect on all the people who know of me, but for the thing in itself. It wld be actually *suppressing me altogether of his life*, and in consequence treating our marriage as a mere *liaison*, which wld be to inflict a real tacit insult on both of us, seeming to be ashamed of mentioning that most solemn act not only of *my* but of *his* life. And this, coming from a personal, intimate friend of his, fancy how graver in effect and consequence it wld be! I must say, *I could not bear that*. It wld be the last stroke on me, a thing which nothing cld ever redeem in the future."[11]

Bertz accepted Gabrielle's denial and packed away the letters in one of his numerous trunks, even though he had been in touch

---

[10] Algernon Gissing to E. Bertz, 18 July 1905, Yale.
[11] To E. Bertz, 7 December 1906: A. C. Young, "George Gissing's Friendship with Eduard Bertz," p. 236.

with Constable, the London publisher, who apparently had planned to bring the book out.[12]

That Bertz owned a large quantity of Gissing letters was a matter of record, but no one seems to have queried him about their contents or about what he planned to do with them, until Madame Wanda von Sacher-Masoch, the divorced wife of Leopold von Sacher-Masoch, inquired about them. In June 1909, she sent a cryptic post card to Bertz, asking if he were the German friend of Gissing, whom she had known in Paris many years before. When Bertz replied that he was that friend, Madame von Sacher-Masoch wrote again, explaining that she had renewed her friendship with Gabrielle Fleury Gissing in the summer of 1908 and that the letters Bertz owned had been mentioned. During that summer, said Madame von Sacher-Masoch, she had finally become aware that Gabrielle and her mother were vicious, grasping women who had deliberately hurried Gissing to his death. If the letters were published, the women would be exposed as amoral harpies, and Gissing's death would be avenged.[13] In his reply, Bertz admitted that he still owned the letters and that they read like a "naturalistic novel," but he insisted that he would not print them without Gabrielle's consent or until they could appear without injuring any of Gissing's family. Still determined, the woman wrote again, thanking Bertz for telling her about the letters. It was imperative to publish them, she argued, for in no other way would the reading public ever know of "the last act of his life."[14] If Bertz would not publish this correspondence, she, Wanda von Sacher-Masoch, would write a novel about the Fleury women which would rip the pearls from their crowns. Bertz, worried over the woman's insistence and threats, ceased writing, without explaining to her that the "naturalistic" letters involved Nell, not Gabrielle.

Possibly this exchange of notes awakened Bertz to the potential obloquy to which his friend's memory might be vulnerable if the entire correspondence ever appeared. At this time he must have read through the letters again, destroying the early ones written

[12] Henry A. Lappin, "George Gissing's Letters," *The Bookman*, LXV (1927), 345.

[13] Wanda von Sacher-Masoch to E. Bertz, 1 July 1909, Yale.

[14] Wanda von Sacher-Masoch to E. Bertz, 8 September 1909, Yale. My translation.

before Nell's death while Gissing was still unrestrained and incautious; when the letters were taken from the trunk after Bertz's death, there remained only one letter written before 1888. The first letter for 1888 is dated 27 September, eight months after Nell's death in a London doss house on Lucretia Street.[15] The sequence from that date seems complete except for one post card, apparently mailed between 29 November and 14 December 1889.

On Bertz's death in 1931, his property, including the library and the literary papers, went to a family named Dreising, with whom he had made his home in Berlin for many years. The library, in which there was a complete set of presentation copies of Gissing's works, was sold to a dealer, but the correspondence was tossed back into the trunk as valueless, where it stayed until the end of World War II. Then it came to light in a casual way through the offices of an American Professor, Hobart Coffey, of the University of Michigan Law Library, who met the Dreising family in Berlin during the occupation and performed an important service for them. After his return to the University of Michigan, he received the packet of Gissing letters from Frau Anna Dreising, who understood only that they had been written by some English novelist; she sent them as a gift to Professor Coffey in return for his generosity to her family. Fortunately, the professor knew and admired Gissing's novels, so that he recognized the value of the collection. He did not feel that he could accept such a valuable gift, but he did arrange to sell it for the benefit of the Dreisings, who had been impoverished by the war. Thanks to his good judgment, the letters were not sold separately but were kept together, and through the aid of Mr. Edwin J. Beinecke, a Yale Library Associate, the correspondence was added to the Gissing Collection in the Yale University Library in 1949.

A few rough drafts of letters Bertz wrote to Gissing are also in the collection, but the posted copies have not been found. According to Frau Dreising, no letters of Bertz remain in her possession, so that for the time being the majority of his letters must be assumed lost; some of them, to other correspondents, are in public and private collections. The Yale Library also owns five Bertz letters written, in 1880, to Heinrich Rehfeldt, a German friend.

[15] Nell died on 29 February 1888; the death certificate lists the cause (perhaps euphemistically, as Morley Roberts says) as chronic laryngitis. Gissing is identified on the certificate as a journalist.

2

THE TEXT

As editor of these letters I have tried to present as accurate a text as possible. I have not made any attempt to provide a facsimile of the original manuscripts, since the appearance of the text is less important than the contents. The task of transcribing has been lightened by Gissing's scrupulous writing, which is easily read even though it is minute and cramped; however, a few words here and there resisted deciphering, so that in a small number of instances I have had to rely on the position of a word in context and on common sense; such conundrums are identified by a question mark in brackets [?].

In the headings of the letters, I have silently expanded the names of the months and the numerical designation of the year. Abbreviations have been expanded within square brackets except that for "volume." In every instance, "and" is substituted for the ampersand, and the symbols for shillings and pence have been changed to their orthographic counterparts. The spelling has not been meddled with, and the few misspellings have been noted with *sic*. Gissing's orthography includes both old forms of words and the new ones that were gradually becoming standardized; he uses both *judgement* and *judgment* indiscriminately, but prefers such forms as *advertized* and *sympathized*, both of which were no longer popular in his day.

The punctuation has not been altered, because Gissing's system precludes misreading, vagueness, or ambiguity. Single and double quotation marks appear, infrequently, in the same letter, depending on Gissing's whim, and these remain without normalization. If one quotation mark of a pair was overlooked, I have mended the slip without comment. No changes have been made in the capitalization, nor has the original paragraphing been altered. Occasionally, Gissing used a dash either preceding the opening word of a sentence or following the end punctuation, an idiosyncrasy which I have not reproduced.

To save space, the headings of the letters have been placed on one line, the virgules showing what the original alignment was. The addresses from the post cards have been given in order to provide a running record of the various changes in residence Bertz made. Some of the post cards have had their stamps cut out; where such excisions have removed the date and address on the reverse side, I have restored the missing data within brackets.

ANNOTATION

My concern in annotating the letters has been to clarify the text. Since it is impossible to cater to the needs or the taste of all readers, I have charted, I hope, a summer passage with brevity as the pole star. Although I have attempted to identify, at the first occurrence of their names, all the people mentioned, some resisted discovery. Sources, and often excerpts, of literary quotations and book reviews have been given in the notes, as well as some bibliographical data on the numerous books mentioned. The names of the publishers of Algernon's, George's and Bertz's books have been given, but for the books of other authors only the date of publication has been supplied. Cross-references within the letters have been pared to the simple designation of the date of the adjunct letter, but since there is never more than one letter for any date, the reader should not be baffled in locating a reference. I have supplemented some of Gissing's remarks with quotations from his letters to other friends and from his personal diary. Excerpts from the bowdlerized 1927 edition of *The Letters of George Gissing to Members of His Family* have been used only when I could not see the manuscripts. When the original letters were available, I used them as references without calling attention to the published version.

ABBREVIATIONS

Diary.   This important document, now in the Berg Collection of the New York Public Library, consists of three parts: Volume I runs from 27 December 1887 to 7 May 1889; Volume II, from May 1889 to 14 March 1895; Volume III, from 27 March 1895 to 8 November 1902. In my notes the three parts have been treated as a single item. Only the first volume is incomplete. Gissing himself removed the pages filled before 1887, in which he had recorded Nell's disintegration.

Roberts   *The Private Life of Henry Maitland*, ed. Morchard Bishop (London: The Richards Press, 1958).

Letters   *The Letters of George Gissing to Members of His Family*, eds. Algernon and Ellen Gissing (London: Constable & Co., 1927).

Yale   Indicates unpublished letters in the Gissing Collection, Yale University Library.

GRG   George Robert Gissing.

GISSING AND BERTZ

When Gissing returned to England in 1877 after his year's exile in America, he traveled directly to Manchester, where his young mistress, Nell Harrison,[1] still lived. Together, they moved to London, which offered them anonymity. While earning a living as a private tutor, Gissing read and studied conscientiously, but he still reserved time each day for his own writing, on which his total hope for a decent career rested. Because both Nell's character and his own police record precluded him from many professions, he

[1] Marianne Helen Harrison, called Nell, was the prostitute for whom GRG destroyed his academic career when he stole money from clothes hung in the Owens College Cloakroom. According to the records of Owens College, there had been several cases of theft from the cloakroom during the winter of 1876, and the college authorities finally asked the police to help. On 31 May 1876 the police caught GRG taking some marked money from an overcoat. He was taken into custody and appeared before the Magistrates on 6 June, when he was convicted and sentenced to one month's imprisonment with hard labor. The College authorities also discovered GRG's relationship with Nell, and in the official administrative investigation:

The Principal further stated that Gissing had also been leading a life of immorality and dissipation.

The Principal added that Gissing had entered the College as an Oxford Local Exhibitioner in 1872 and had held that Exhibition for the usual term of 3 years and was now in the fourth year of studentship; that he had obtained an Exhibition in Latin of £40 per annum tenable for 2 years and another in English of £30 per annum tenable for 2 years in 1875 in the University of London, and that in the same year he had

had to find some kind of work that would not involve an examination of his past. He chose journalism not only to exploit a flair he knew he possessed but also to escape the forked tongue of Mrs. Grundy. His material, he wisely saw, lay close at hand in the working-class section of London in which he lived. But in spite of his tutoring, studying, and writing, he had time enough to suffer over his isolation. He wanted companions with whom he could exchange ideas and share thoughts. Nell could offer only the most primitive comfort, beyond which she was incapable of going. If he were to find friends, either chance or fate must pluck them out of the London multitudes.

Then on a December morning in 1878, Gissing read an advertisement in the personal columns of a London newspaper which requested an English gentleman, eager for scholarly companionship, to reply through the paper's offices. Intrigued by the tone of the notice, Gissing answered it and received a quick reply from Eduard Bertz.[2] After another exchange of notes, the young men

---

gained the Shakespeare Scholarship in the College of the annual value of £40 tenable for two years.

> RESOLVED: That the Senate be advised to recommend the Council to formally expel Mr. Gissing from the College and that the Shakespeare Scholarship which he holds be declared forfeited.

(Extract from Appendix to the Minutes of the Proceedings of Senate of Owens College. Meeting of 13 June 1876.)

After GRG completed his prison term, Harry Hick's father helped him get a job, which he held briefly before emigrating to America.

[2] GRG used this episode in *The Unclassed* (1884), in which Julian Casti, a lonely, intellectual clerk, responds to Osmund Waymark's advertisement:

> "In a morning newspaper of March 187–, appeared a singular advertisement.
>
> 'Wanted, human companionship. A young man of four-and-twenty wishes to find a congenial associate of about his own age. He is a student of ancient and modern literatures, a free-thinker in religion, a lover of art in all forms, hater of conventionalism. Would like to correspond in the first instance. Address O.W. City News Rooms, W.C.'
>
> "An advertisement which, naturally might mean much or little, might be the outcome of an idle whim, or the despairing cry of a hungry heart. It could not be expected to elicit many replies; and brought indeed but one."

I am grateful to Mr. Alfred C. Gissing for the details of his father's meeting with Bertz.

agreed on a meeting, which took place early in January 1879. On their first encounter Gissing and Bertz recognized that they had similar backgrounds and shared the same ideas. Gissing listened sympathetically when his new acquaintance talked about himself and narrated his history.

Bertz was born on 8 March 1853, the younger son of a Potsdam merchant. While Bertz was still in school, his father, like Gissing's, died. However, after a few years Frau Bertz remarried, this time to a widower named Winckler, who had seven children by his first wife, most of whom had already left home. One son, Fritz, was born to this second marriage. Although Bertz resented his mother's remarriage, he stayed with the Wincklers during his school vacations, probably because he had become fond of his half-brother. As for Winckler himself, Bertz thought him a boor and a blockhead without any good qualities, and he worried for years that his stepfather might turn his mother against him. However, as he grew older, Bertz acknowledged that Winckler made a good husband even though he was unpolished and un-educated.[3] Whether there was reason or not, Bertz did not enjoy his home life, and he was unhappy at school until he entered the University of Leipzig in 1870, enrolling as a student in philosophy and political science.[4]

From Leipzig he transferred to the University of Tübingen, where he drifted into a circle of young rebels who were dedicated members of the German Socialist Party. Under the Party's influence Bertz wrote and published several radical essays which brought him to the attention of the government's watchdogs.[5] When the government succeeded in passing its strict Anti-Socialist Laws, Bertz along with several of his University friends was arrested as a dangerous agitator. Given the choice of either renouncing the Party and being freed or sticking to the membership and being jailed with the loss of citizenship, Bertz clung to the

[3] E. Bertz to Heinrich Rehfeldt, 4 March 1880, Yale. Rehfeldt was Bertz's closest German friend. Five letters, now in the Yale Library, written by Bertz to Rehfeldt in 1880 contain the story of Bertz's association with GRG in London as well as a number of details about the refugee's private life before he was exiled.

[4] *Ibid.*

[5] Adolf Hinrichson, *Das litterarische Deutschland* (Berlin, 1891), p. 104.

Socialists, but astutely fled to France, where he received asylum
as a stateless political refugee. From 1877 to 1878 he lived in
Paris, consorting with other political expatriates and with sympathetic French radicals. Within a few months the fervid international
radicalism in which he lived smothered him; he was bored and
disillusioned, and he concluded that his intellectual growth had
outrun Socialist doctrine. Since he spoke, wrote, and read English
well and still had money in his pocket, he picked London as his
next refuge, hoping that there he could avoid the political fanatics
whom he had found distressing in Paris. In London he lived on
his savings, occasionally getting a little income as a reviewer of
German books for English publishers or as a private tutor in
German. His wish to avoid Continental and English Socialists
was granted so thoroughly that he was soon entirely alone without
an opportunity to make new friends. No London door opened to
welcome him into a respectable parlor; he knew no one. In
despair he appealed to the city at large through the columns of a
newspaper.

Although Gissing answered the advertisement in December
1878, the first occurrence of Bertz's name comes in a letter George
wrote to Algernon on 19 January 1879: "Last Friday night
[17 January 1879], according to agreement, I went with Bertz
to the Lyceum,[6] and we enjoyed ourselves immensely. He had tea
with us here before we went, and supper on returning."[7] The
invitation to tea and supper was an unusual courtesy because
Gissing rarely brought friends home to meet Nell. Not even the
ubiquitous Morley Roberts had been introduced to her. The
reason for the invitation may have been that Bertz knew nothing
of the couple's raffish history, so that Gissing did not feel self-
conscious or apologetic in letting Nell be seen by him. She was
not included in the later conversations, which were usually held
in Bertz's rooms, or in the rambles in and around London, simply
because any talk other than gossip stupefied her, and sight-seeing
walks bored her.[8] Probably Gissing preferred to go to Bertz's

[6] Henry Irving was playing in *Hamlet.*

[7] *Letters*, p. 39.

[8] A record of these conversations can be found in the opening chapters
of *The Unclassed*, in which Julian Casti and Osmund Waymark talk at
each other interminably.

rooms in order to avoid the possibility of Nell's appearing after she had been drinking. At any rate, the friendship between the two men rooted so quickly that by April 1879, Gissing felt close enough to Bertz to give him a copy of Tennyson's *Poems*, probably as a late birthday gift, to which he attached an eight-stanza dedicatory poem.[9] As their intimacy grew, Gissing must have confided to Bertz the difficulties he endured with Nell.[10] However, the most significant confidence that Gissing made at this time was the revelation that he really wanted to be a novelist, that he had written one novel already which he had destroyed, and that he had stored a half-finished manuscript in a closet. The first novel, written in 1878, had been rejected by a couple of publishers, but the new one excelled it in interest and power. Bertz asked Gissing to let him read the manuscript, and when he finished reading it, he swore that there would be no problem in finding a publisher for the book. Besides relighting Gissing's enthusiasm for the novel, Bertz also volunteered to sketch an additional chapter on student life in Germany for it. Gissing accepted the offer and incorporated the material in a long chapter, in which his heroine writes a diary on her impressions and ideas of German philosophy and teaching. When the novel, *Workers in the Dawn*, was published in March 1880, Bertz triumphantly wrote to his friend Heinrich Rehfeldt about his part in getting the book finished.[11] After the publication of the novel, one or two journal editors, apparently impressed by Gissing's display of knowledge about contemporary Germany, invited him to submit articles on the current political condition of that country; the material for the essays, which were published, came directly from Bertz.[12]

Although Bertz enjoyed the propinquity with Gissing, in February 1880 he moved to a cheap ground floor apartment in a Tottenham cottage. By staying in what was then a suburb, he thought he could reduce his expenses so that he could live without

[9] The manuscript is in the Yale Collection; see "George Gissing's Friendship with Eduard Bertz," pp. 228–29.

[10] Later, Bertz wrote to Rehfeldt about the miseries in which GRG lived (To Heinrich Rehfeldt, 4 March 1880, Yale).

[11] *Ibid.*

[12] Cf. "George Gissing's Friendship with Eduard Bertz," p. 231.

working while he studied for the doctoral examination which he hoped eventually to take at the University of Zurich.[13] But the move did not isolate him from Gissing, who twice a week took the train to Tottenham for a few hours of smoking and talking. Within seven months, however, Bertz had had enough of his voluntary rustication; he wanted the culture of London, and he wanted an opportunity to make more friends. Since Gissing had acquired a little glow of fame in some literary and philosophical circles, Bertz thought he might, on the basis of his friendship with the younger man, be able to step into the same groups.[14] But when he returned to London, he was disappointed because Gissing could not open doors for him. Neither man had a home suitable for entertaining, and Gissing could not, or would not, ask that his invitations be expanded to include Bertz. And another irritation developed. Nell, whom Gissing finally married in the autumn of 1879, grew jealous of Bertz, and slandered him to her husband, claiming that friends of hers knew definitely that Bertz was a "dissipated scoundrel whose companionship could only lead to the gallows."[15] Her jealousy disgusted Gissing, who scornfully, and with a bitter recognition of the irony of her complaints, squelched her report as obvious malice. A few months later, Nell's own public capers and private debauches became so frequent and obstreperous that Gissing, hopeless in the face of her perpetual drunkenness, sent her to live at Hastings, and once again he had to rely on Bertz's company and sympathy.[16]

There was a difference in the association this time, for Gissing, a published author, knew that people of intelligence and reputation were interested in what he had to say, without making inquiries about his marriage or his background; he had gained poise and regained his belief in his own worth. But Bertz, who had formerly been the stronger of the two, was now in an inferior role in the relationship. All his plans had failed to ripen. He had never been able to force himself to endure the pettinesses of a schoolmaster's life in any school; he could not turn up enough students to live by private tutoring; and he could not establish an income by

[13] E. Bertz to Heinrich Rehfeldt, 4 March 1880, Yale.
[14] E. Bertz to Heinrich Rehfeldt, 30 August 1880, Yale.
[15] GRG to Algernon Gissing, 3 November 1880, Yale.
[16] GRG to Algernon Gissing, 24 June 1881, Yale.

book reviewing, since he was too conscientious and thorough in his assignments, with the result that he could not crank out his articles rapidly enough to make the small payments worthwhile. His depression and frustration increased as his reserve funds dwindled. Then one day he read a prospectus advertising an ideal community, founded by Thomas Hughes, in Rugby, Tennessee, which was designed as a colony where young men and women, short of money but rich in ambition, could, with a modest investment, buy land for farming on a cooperative plan. The object was to create a kind of agricultural Utopia. Life in such a colony offered to Bertz what he had been seeking for: there he would have companionship, an income, and, above all, a sense of commitment to something more than abstract principles. After long colloquies with Gissing, Bertz bought a farm and membership in Rugby. On 27 July 1881, Bertz, with his Highland collie as a companion, sailed from England, one of the most naïve pilgrims ever to embark for these shores.

The planting season was long past when Bertz arrived in Tennessee, so he settled down in a one-room log cabin where he read away the autumn and winter, waiting to begin the cultivation of his land. Within a season, the battle between him and the soil was over, and Bertz filled his letters to Gissing with a recital of the miseries of being an unsuccessful colonist.[17] At last the Rugby authorities rescued him from the farm and placed him as a clerk in the community library, where Bertz found himself finally at rest. His letters to England spoke of his determination to stay permanently in Rugby now that he had a job that pleased him, and Gissing rejoiced to think that his friend had at last found a satisfactory home. Then, unexpectedly, the trustees of Rugby declared the community bankrupt and notified the investors that their money was gone. There were no funds with which to pay the workers, who had to shift for themselves. Bertz, having retrieved what cash he could from the sale of his land, deserted America and set out for England, reaching London early in the summer of 1883. Although he rented a room close to Gissing's place, the old relationship could not be re-established. Gissing guarded his spare time for his writing, and at the same time, he was practically restricted to his own rooms because of his wife.

[17] GRG, in turn, reported Bertz's hardships in letters to Algernon.

He had taken Nell back again, and since her health was bad and her thirst for alcohol unlimited, he had to keep watch over her constantly.

Once more Bertz had to spend most of his time alone, but he seemed to be happy in a job he had found in a London library and in establishing a home for himself and his dog. Again he picked up his studies for a while, but suddenly one day he resigned from the library and joined the Salvation Army as a fulltime volunteer worker; he announced that he had abandoned the intellectual life forever. Gissing was shocked by his friend's defection, and in a complaint to Algernon said:

> I could tell a sad story about poor Bertz. To my amazement he has drifted over to the religious revivalists, has joined Blue Ribbon Army, Young Men's Christian Association, and I know not what. Spends his days and nights at Salvation Army meetings, and the like. Whether this means weakening of the brain, I can't say: I stand and marvel, but protest has been in vain. It is shocking to think how many people take this turn. Happily I don't fear for myself: my position has long been a very clear one.[18]

Bertz stayed with the Salvation Army until the money he had salvaged from the Tennessee disaster was safely in the hands of the poor. When he discovered that he could not even afford to buy bones for his dog, he finally realized what his philanthropy had cost him. Full of despair, he turned for help to Gissing, who lent him money to live on and arranged for Morley Roberts to take over the collie. Since the German government was now offering to pardon the exiled Socialists, Bertz could have gone home, except that he no longer had sufficient money to buy passage, nor could Gissing lend such a large sum at one time. As a way of earning money, Bertz spent the winter of 1883–4 writing a boy's story, *The French Prisoners*, in the hope that some publisher would accept it. On its completion Gissing sent the manuscript, with a personal note, to the Macmillans, who bought the story for £25, enough to take Bertz home.[19] He left England on Easter Sunday, 1884, after an exile of six years.

[18] To Algernon Gissing, 2 September 1883, Yale.
[19] GRG to Algernon Gissing, 21 March 1884, Yale.

He was thirty-one years old when he returned to Germany, too old, he felt, to work for a doctorate; his one talent was literary, and out of that talent he had to construct a career. And so Bertz became a journalist, a free-lance critic and essayist, who slowly earned recognition as a careful and thoughtful writer. In 1889 he was elected secretary to the Deutsche Schriftsteller-Verband and then became the managing editor of the association's journal, *Die Deutsche Presse*. Probably in emulation of Gissing, Bertz also experimented with novel-writing, but he composed so painstakingly and his ability to concentrate was so transient, that he could never produce enough fiction to make a profit. His first novel, *Glück und Glas* (1891), sold two editions, but his second and third efforts, *Das Sabinergut* (1896), and *Der blinde Eros* (1898), attracted few readers. If any of his literary work survives, it will probably be the critical studies of Walt Whitman, whose poetry he first read during the long winter in the Tennessee cabin. Bertz published a eulogistic article in honor of Whitman's seventieth birthday and then sent the poet a copy. As a result, a correspondence began between the two men, and Whitman presented him with copies of his works. Several years later Bertz changed his opinion about Whitman's personality and philosophy, concluding that the poet's call for universal love and brotherhood arose from sublimated sexual perversion and consequently had no significance for the normal world. Bertz's first pejorative critique, *Walt Whitman: Ein Charakterbild* (Leipzig: Spohr) appeared in 1905.

Bertz naturally concentrated his study on German writers, and in particular he was attracted by Theodor Storm, about whom he published several biographical and critical essays between 1906 and 1914. There are no records of further publications after 1914, and by the time of his death on 10 December 1931, his name meant little in the literary world; modern German literary references fail to give him even a line or two. His memorial, however, can be found in Gissing's letters, even though Bertz's personality can be seen only in vague outline, like a figure in a photographic negative.

Although after Bertz returned to Germany, Gissing could do almost nothing to help him in his career, he was important in other ways. Just as Gissing felt that Bertz was invaluable to him as a representative of European culture and thought, so did Bertz look on Gissing as a link to another world. Bertz's letters encouraged Gissing, who also gave sympathy and approval when it was necessary. But Gissing did not let Bertz make him a father-confessor nor did he allow the correspondence to become gossipy or sentimental. Nevertheless, his occasional comments permit the reader to understand something of Bertz's character. Bertz was a man so sensitive to grossness and vulgarity that even the noises of daily household life irritated him. Like Carlyle, he shuddered at the sound of his neighbors' voices seeping through the walls, the banging of pots in the kitchen, and the clatter of traffic on the streets. But since he could not afford a cork-lined room, he could only move from house to house in search of quiet. Although he needed friends, those he had never satisfied him, for he found them either too gregarious or too reserved, or their flaws were more objectionable than their virtues were attractive. A cross word or a slight, either real or imagined, embittered him for days. If he lived in the country, he sighed for the city, but when he got back to busy streets and crowds of people, he dreamed of returning to the woods and fields. A hypochondriac, he delighted in listing his aches and pains in his letters and often implied that he was only a breath or two away from death. Storekeepers and landlords preyed on him, and he hated their vulgar trafficking. He had a noble idea of what man should be and despised those who did not measure up, yet he betrayed his own principles by whining and dramatizing his illnesses. As a scholar Bertz was gifted; he was well read, thoughtful, and perceptive. He did have trouble in finding subjects suitable to his aptitude, and occasionally he wasted his time by not being able to differentiate between what was valuable and what was not, as in the case of his monograph on the philosophy of bicycling, which took more time and effort than it deserved. As we glimpse Bertz through Gissing's eyes he becomes almost a caricature of a scholar, competent in his studies but narrow in his world view, uncommitted to life, petty and egotistical. Enough is said in these letters to show Bertz's dependency on his mother and his general maladjustment; he was indeed neurotic, but beyond that catch-all word we cannot go.

Gissing's own attitude towards Bertz should be mentioned. In letters to friends and relatives, Gissing exhibited a wry tolerance of Bertz, whose name crops up now and then in a slightly mocking phrase or with a word of pity. However, there were similar qualities in both men, and almost any character trait attributed to Bertz might have a counterpart in Gissing. They were in accord on politics, literature, economic theories, and philosophy; they shared similar resentments and prejudices; they exalted knowledge and manners. Only in their attitudes towards women was there a great difference. Gissing, urgent and knowledgeable sexually, looked for satisfaction almost clinically, while Bertz, accustomed to self-denial, pronounced himself an irredeemable bachelor, if not a celibate, at the age of twenty-five.[20] Except for this quirk, they were so much alike temperamentally that it is probable their friendship endured because they were separated. Gissing made only one trip to Germany to see his friend, even though, when on the Continent, he was often not far from him. Neither did Bertz seriously plan a return visit to London. Perhaps they both realized that their real worth to each other lay not in physical proximity but in the unbroken flow of letters, which warmed pleasant shadows of the past without making demands in the present.

Throughout his years as a critic and journalist, Bertz did all that he could to bring Gissing's name before the German public, which did develop some interest in the Englishman's work. Such efforts on Bertz's part also kept him alive in Gissing's mind, and they probably supplied a good deal of the impetus that kept the letters flowing. But the important thing to Gissing was simply receiving Bertz's letters for their intrinsic worth and because they kept him in touch with the Continent. In *The Private Papers of Henry Ryecroft*, Gissing honored Bertz as a faithful correspondent, saying:

I have a letter to-day from my old friend in Germany, E.B. For many and many a year these letters have made a pleasant incident in my life; more than that, they have often brought me help and comfort. It must be a rare thing for friendly correspondence to go on during the greater part of a lifetime between men of different nationalities who see each other not twice in two decades. We were young men when we first met in London, poor, struggling, full of hopes and ideals; now we look back upon those far memories from the autumn of life.

[20] E. Bertz to Heinrich Rehfeldt, 15 July 1880, Yale.

B. writes to-day in a vein of quiet contentment, which does me
good. He quotes Goethe: *"Was man in der Jugend begehrt hat
man im Alter die Fülle."*[21] (*The Private Papers of Henry
Ryecroft* [Westminster: Constable & Co. Ltd., 1903], p. 169.)

THE WAKEFIELD GISSINGS

Margaret Bedford Gissing (1832–1905), George's mother, was
the daughter of a solicitor, and as such, she was a degree higher
in the social system than her husband, Thomas Walter Gissing
(1828–1870),[22] a pharmaceutical chemist and an amateur botanist.
There is no indication that Bertz ever met Mrs. Gissing, and
consequently her name is rarely mentioned in these letters. With
her two daughters, she lived in Wakefield, a small industrial
town in Yorkshire, on a little sum of money left by her husband.
Although money was scarce in the household, she seems to have
been able to lend a few pounds to any of her sons when they
needed it. She outlived her husband and two of her sons, George
and William (1859–1880), the latter of whom is never referred to
in these letters.[23]

Towards his two sisters, Margaret (1863–1930) and Ellen (1867–
1938), Gissing acted as a surrogate father. Since he had already
left home when the girls were very young, his advice and his
orders always came through the mails. As the girls matured, he
wrote them long pompous letters about the books they should read
and the ideas they should cultivate in order to rise above other
women of their class. Nelly, the more docile of the two, accepted
his suggestions and even tried to understand his alien philosophy.
But Margaret, if she read what he directed, was not much interested in anything but piety and decent behavior. Without doubt
Gissing sought only to emancipate the minds of his sisters for
their own benefit, but from his injunctions, it seems as if he were
attempting to create women who pleased him, the model for

[21] Actually, GRG first mentioned the quotation to Bertz, asking him
for his comments on it. See Letter, 30 September 1900.

[22] GRG, searching the parish records at Halesworth, Suffolk, in 1894,
found that his father had been baptized on 27 June 1830, two years after
his birth (Diary, 26 May 1894).

[23] See Mabel C. Donnelly, *George Gissing: Grave Comedian*, for a hypo-
thesis about George's relations with his mother.

whom lived in his own mind and occasionally came to life in his novels. His sisters were to follow the pattern of the kind of woman he could converse with but whom he could never approach romantically.

Like their mother, the two girls were Unitarians, and their brother's free-thinking chilled them. In their general attitudes the Gissing women were provincially conservative and rigidly moral. The maverick son and brother's cynicism, his provocative novels, and his unorthodox alliances must have disturbed them exceedingly, yet they were always tolerant and loyal towards him. In spite of his sophistication and experience, Gissing never considered that his efforts in moulding his sisters' characters might result in unhappiness for them by making them dissatisfied with the social class to which they were bound. There is no indication that he ever thought they might want to marry, nor did it occur to him that his system of education for them might well create women from whom men of their own class fled. At any rate, neither sister married. About 1898 Margaret and Ellen opened a preparatory day-school, in which Walter Gissing, George's elder son, was a student.[24] In one sense, Gissing's plan for their education did succeed, for they were, at least, able to support themselves.

Both sisters knew about Bertz and might have met him when they visited their brother in London.

ALGERNON GISSING

Algernon Gissing, born on 25 November 1860 in Wakefield, was the youngest of the three boys in the family of five children. He attended the same school at Alderly Edge as his brothers. Having finished his schooling there, he studied law and eventually returned to Wakefield as a qualified solicitor, but after a few years, he gave up the profession, convinced that he could earn more money with less strain by writing fiction. In spite of George's warnings about the dangers of Grub Street, Algernon was convinced that his literary talent would see him through. In the autumn of 1887 he married, probably close to the time that a publisher bought his first work and probably on the strength of

[24] GRG sent a gift of £5 towards their expenses in organizing the school (To Ellen Gissing, 22 February 1898, Yale). He also paid tuition for his son.

the sale. Successful writing for Algernon meant finding a salable formula that, like a jigsaw puzzle, could be knocked apart and put together innumerable times. Fiction was a trade, and he examined the market for what was currently selling. Since he had moved his family to a rural cottage for economy's sake, he thought he might well use the country life around him, and so he settled on the pastoral romance as his province. He gradually found a slight following for his books, but he never acquired a reputation or aroused much literary interest.

The attention George's novels drew helped Algernon get his books published, and occasionally he sold more of them in an edition than his brother did. Algernon's publishers had a promotional device of their own for his books; they held one of his novels until one of George's appeared, and then, capitalizing on the other's reputation, they quickly put the inferior work into print. Although George objected to this technique, Algernon seems not to have been anxious to stop it.

Algernon lived for thirty-four years after George's death, dying at the age of 77, at Bloxham in Banbury. He was survived by his wife, Enid, and five children.

Perhaps Algernon's most valuable work is the bowdlerized edition of George's letters which was published in 1927, with Ellen Gissing as co-editor. Algernon had neither great creative skill nor exceptional intellectual energy; his novels did not grow out of a necessity to write but, more likely, from a powerful wish to clamber over the social barriers he found facing him as a result of his birth. As a writer, he could think himself outside the class structure, and in time, he could forget that his father was a shopkeeper.[25] The weaknesses of Algernon's character, impracticality, stubbornness, and pretension, irritated George, but they did not hinder the amiable relationship the brothers had.

MORLEY ROBERTS

Morley Roberts (1857–1942) first met Gissing at Owens College in 1873. The son of an Inspector of Income Tax, who had a

[25] In the data supplied to *Who's Who* (1937), Algernon gave his father's occupation as "botanist," instead of chemist; the claim is based on two tiny books the elder Gissing published, *Ferns and Fern Allies of Wakefield* and *Materials for a Flora of Wakefield* (*1867*).

comfortable income, Roberts had an easier life as a boy than did Gissing. On entering Owens College, Roberts became a classics major. He knew about Gissing, through hearsay, as the brightest scholar in the class, and eventually they became friends; to a degree, they became confidantes, but they were not as close at this period as Roberts later insisted.[26] Unlike Gissing, Roberts completed his education at Owens, and then, having had a quarrel with his father, ran off to Australia.[27] When he drifted back to England three years later, he had tucked under his belt a variety of experiences; he had worked on remote sheep stations in Australia and had been employed as a railroad gang member, and then had sailed as a seaman on merchant ships. Having temporarily satisfied his urge for vagabonding, Roberts took a clerical job with the Civil Service, in which he remained until 1884, when he became surfeited with sitting behind a desk and set out to explore the American West and the Canadian wilderness. This adventure forms the background of his first book, *The Western Avernus*, which was published in 1887, the year of his second return to England. Possibly because he could not face another desk job, Roberts set himself up as a journalist. When he saw that Kipling, a newspaper editor in India, had become popular with his lusty military verses, he decided he could exploit the same market by writing about his own rough-and-ready experiences abroad. Although Gissing tried to control Roberts's enthusiasm by pointing out the frustrations and uncertainty of such a career, nothing could stop him. Since he unhesitatingly accepted any writing assignment, Roberts began well, for he could as cheerfully write advertising for soap manufacturers as he could compose sober essays on steamships, and, while grinding out his commercial work, he also turned out poetry and fiction. A few novels, blood-brothers to Kipling's tales, sold well, but none ever created a

---

[26] GRG's closest friend was a student named Black, who knew intimately of the affair between GRG and Nell. Black was caught in the net of the College authorities during the investigation of GRG's case, and, like his friend, was expelled in 1876. Although not implicated in the thefts, Black was punished for having known about and having participated in GRG's "life of immorality and dissipation" (Owens College Records, 1876).

[27] *The Private Life of Henry Maitland*, Introduction by Morchard Bishop (London: The Richards Press, 1958), p. 10.

rush at the booksellers. The poetry had little merit. In his later years, Roberts turned away from fiction, and, becoming ponderously serious, wrote many books on economics, politics, and various branches of science; he sometimes turned out two or three books a year. In scanning the titles of his books, one sees Roberts's great flaw; he had no intellectual humility, and he presumed himself an authority in practically all fields.

Nine years after Gissing's death, Roberts published his disguised biography of his friend, *The Private Life of Henry Maitland*. Roberts's apologists have tried to give the book high literary status as a legitimate kind of biography, but it still remains an unpleasant study with all the disabilities and none of the advantages of impressionistic portrait drawing. The use of fatuous pseudonyms is objectionable, but the denigrating tone of Roberts's remarks about Gissing's character and work is even more repugnant. One senses Roberts's intense feeling of superiority over his subject.

Gissing mentions his affection for Roberts in Chapter VIII, "Spring," of *The Private Papers of Henry Ryecroft*, but he also spoke less flatteringly about Roberts's character in several novels. Roberts is the prototype of Whelpdale in *New Grub Street* and of Malkin in *Born in Exile*, and his personality informs a multitude of boisterous, gregarious characters in other novels. There is no doubt that his robustness and vigor, and even his shoddy romances, attracted Gissing, who thought him a man perfectly equipped to handle all the problems and pleasures of practical life.

When Gissing was dying at St. Jean Pied de Port in December 1903, he asked Gabrielle to send for Roberts, who responded to the telegram but unfortunately arrived after the death occurred. He was, however, a great help to Gabrielle, with whom he established a friendly relationship. In many ways, Roberts must be recognized as responsible for keeping Gissing's name alive; he saw that some of the novels were reissued and from time to time published articles on Gissing's work.

Roberts continued to publish throughout his long lifetime until a few years before his death in 1942, in his eighty-fifth year. His name, ironically enough, lives now through Gissing rather than in the heap of seventy-odd books he published.

EDITH UNDERWOOD

The exact circumstances of Gissing's first encounter with Edith Underwood will probably never be known, but the question of how and where he found her captivates his devotees. The earliest explanation comes from Morley Roberts, who, eighteen years after the event, quotes Gissing as saying that one Sunday "I could stand it no longer, so I rushed out and spoke to the very first woman I came across."[28] According to Roberts, the place was Marylebone Road, and the woman was Edith. Roberts's report, in this instance, seems to be the most accurate and satisfactory, for not only does the action seem typical of Gissing in his hysterical moods, but Roberts, at this time, was his closest friend, the one person to whom he spoke most openly. Even for Roberts the incident was peculiar enough to make it stand out in his memory, and in view of the disastrous years that followed as a result of the meeting, he probably remembered it clearly. Dr. Harry Hick, in his "Notes on George Gissing's Life," corroborates Roberts's story, and adds that Edith was the daughter of a plasterer's laborer.[29]

In another version, H. G. Wells changed the place to Regent's Park and identified the woman as a domestic.[30] The most recent theory, and the least seaworthy, is that of Dr. Mabel Donnelly, who believes that Gissing, stalking a bride, sighted Edith in an Oxford Street coffee shop.[31] It is not vital to pinpoint the London park, shop, or street nor the girl's occupation, but it is important to recognize that Gissing was simply in search of a sexual partner, not a wife, and that his fastidiousness, acquired after Nell's death, would prevent him from accepting the advances of an obvious

[28] Roberts, p. 116.

[29] The marriage entry at Somerset House gives Edith's father's occupation as "sculptor."

[30] *Experiment in Autobiography* (New York: Macmillan, 1934), p. 482.

[31] *George Gissing: Grave Comedian*, p. 136. Dr. Donnelly does not document her claim, but she probably bases her interpretation on the following Diary entry: "Day of extreme misery. Wrote nothing. In evening to the Oxford.—E.U." (25 September 1890). Dr. Donnelly also rejects Roberts's statement that GRG was merely looking for any woman and suggests that he simply went to places where he could meet marriageable girls; however, the letter to Bertz (15 August 1890) shows clearly that GRG's objective was not marriage.

trollop while it would not hinder him from approaching a decent-looking working girl. After all, such a sortie as Gissing's is not uncommon, and he had already acquired a certain experience in making sidewalk acquaintances so that his approach should not be surprising. All that we are certain of is that he met Edith and made some kind of proposition.

The entries in Gissing's diary indicate that Edith did not hesitate to come to his rooms unchaperoned, but when he proposed that she come to live with him, she refused unless he married her. He finally agreed, but she vacillated longer until he wrote to her father that if she did not appear on the specified date she need not come at all. The ultimatum had its results, and Gissing had his bride. They were married on 25 February 1891, in the Register Office of the District of Pancras, in the presence of H. J. and Florence Underwood.[32]

Although the marriage was totally utilitarian for Gissing, he was so invigorated by the physical release he gained that he even grew tender about Edith and optimistic about educating her. She could not be introduced to his family until her speech and deportment improved, but Gissing did not expect the transformation to take long. Shortly before his marriage he had written to his sister Ellen:

> I have a letter from her [Edith] to-day which has really surprised me, it is so well written and informed. I quite believe that in a year's time there will be no great fault to find with her demeanour.[33]

But at the end of the first year of marriage, Gissing had to admit that he had been too sanguine, that once again he had gambled and lost; for Edith, once compliant and eager to learn, had rebelled against the lessons and commands showered on her. She cursed her husband, bullied the maid (they came on approval and often left before their boxes were unpacked), and when she failed to score verbally, she threw crockery. Gissing's diary carefully describes the constant jangling between himself and his wife and the daily increase in her virulence. When he recognized that he could no longer control the storms under his roof, he enlisted Sarah Orme, a friend of his publishers, Lawrence and Bullen,

[32] From the marriage certificate, Somerset House.
[33] 24 January 1891, Yale.

and Clara Collet,[34] London Labour Correspondent of the Board of Trade, who had come to him as an admirer of his novels, as domestic pacifiers. But their interference spurred Edith into more frequent and fiery outbursts. Even the addition of two sons, Walter Leonard in 1891, and Alfred Charles in 1896, increased the disharmony, until at last Gissing, completely wilted by Edith's fire, fled, in 1897, from the sound of her voice and hid himself in the country. This separation was permanent (he had tried a few flights before), and Gissing no longer considered himself married. He stayed in his rooms as much as possible to avoid meeting her accidentally, but even so he harried himself with the fear that she might turn up on his doorstep, sharp-tongued and brutal. His son, Walter, whom Edith disliked, had been taken for safety to Wakefield, but Alfred, the baby, remained with her.

After his elopement to France on 6 May 1899, Gissing never saw Edith again, and the news of her commitment to an insane asylum released him from the last tie of responsibility. He was relieved, too, that Alfred was now out of his mother's hands and physically safe on a farm in Mabe. From the time of her commitment in 1902 until her death, Edith remained in an asylum, where she died on 27 February 1917 in Fisherton House, Salisbury, of organic brain disease.[35] Dr. Hick, one of the few people to say a good word or two about Edith, thought she would have made a good wife for a man of her own station. Hick also believed that Gissing should have had the courage to introduce his wife to his friends and that his refusal to do so caused most of the difficulty in the marriage.[36] But if the disease had already set in shortly after her marriage, neither she nor Gissing can be blamed for the turbulent six years they spent together.

GABRIELLE FLEURY

Gissing, like many authors, often received letters from women who had read his books and had been moved to write to him. Many of them identified themselves with Gissing's portraits of

[34] For further information, see Ruth M. Adams, "George Gissing and Clara Collet," *Nineteenth Century Fiction*, II (June 1956), 72–7.

[35] From the death certificate, Somerset House. The register gives her age as forty-five and describes her as "Wife of — Gissing, occupation unknown."

[36] "Abstract of Notes by Dr. Henry Hick."

cool bluestockings, barely touched by passion, who preferred dia-
lectics to diapers. European feminists praised his work, and then
asked for permission to translate one book or another into their
own language as ammunition in the battle to emancipate women.
And intellectual women, surfeited with vapid Victorian romances,
expressed their gratitude for his honest writing. One of these intel-
lectuals was Gabrielle Fleury, a Frenchwoman, who first wrote
to Gissing in June 1898, expressing her delight in *New Grub
Street* and asking for the right to translate it into French as an
important piece of literature.[37] Although Gissing replied that one
of her countrymen, Georges Art, who had translated *Eve's Ransom*
into French, was considering doing the book for a Paris publisher,
Gabrielle quickly understood that no irrevocable contract had been
made, and so she wrote again, saying that she was coming to
England and would see him personally, and then they could discuss
the choice of translators. The lady's determination and admiration
charmed Gissing, who agreed to meet her, if she would come to
H. G. Wells's home at Worcester Park, where they could talk
with proper chaperonage. On 6 July 1898,[38] Wells entertained both
of them at luncheon, which he described later in his autobiography:

> They lunched with us and afterwards they walked in our
> garden confabulating. She was a woman of the intellectual
> bourgeoisie, with neat black hair and a trim black dress, her
> voice was carefully musical, she was well read, slightly voluble
> and over-explicit by our English standards, and consciously
> refined and intelligent.[39]

The "confabulating" was so successful that Gissing invited
Gabrielle to Dorking, his retreat in the country, where they could
talk freely—without chaperons in the dining room. She accepted
his invitation without hesitation, and, after the day's consultation,
secured permission to translate *New Grub Street*. She also agreed
to come back to England in October for a week's holiday with him
at Dorking.

By the time Gabrielle arrived in England, on 8 October 1898, she
and Gissing had already decided to spend their lives together, and
the object of the visit was to discuss ways of getting round the

[37] Diary, 25 June 1898.   [39] *Op. cit.*, p. 489.
[38] Diary, 6 July 1898.

prickly difficulties such a union would entail. The cryptic diary entries covering her week's stay at Dorking only tell where they rambled during the day and what they read aloud to each other (Victor Hugo, Tennyson, Browning, and Poe) all night, except for the portentous notation for 9 October: "Talk all day—of the future."[40] That day's talk settled the future, and at the end of the week Gabrielle returned to France with the plan settled. The solution was simple: the couple would live in France not only to avoid any legal action on Edith's part but also to accommodate Gabrielle, whose parents were ill and needed her. Before M. Fleury died in February 1899, he was succinctly told that Gabrielle was going to marry an English author, but Madame Fleury had to be drawn into the conspiracy, which she finally accepted with the stipulation that some kind of marriage ceremony be held. At the expiration of a brief mourning period for her father, Gabrielle sent for Gissing, who met her at Rouen on 6 May 1899.[41] There on Sunday evening, 7 May 1899, he and Gabrielle had their symbolic wedding ceremony in a hotel.[42]

A brief honeymoon in St. Pierre en Port was the single opportunity the Gissings had of being together without Maman, in whose Paris flat they set up a joint household. Mme. Fleury supervised all the domestic affairs, including the kitchen, while Gabrielle aided her husband in his writing and executed her mother's orders. For a few months Gissing relished his new life even though he was not satisfied with the delicate French meals he was served. Then the matter of cooking became more important, and he and Mme. Fleury quarrelled over the kind of food that was to be served. Gissing's medical friend, Dr. Hick, says that the disagreement arose over breakfast, because Gissing wanted bacon and eggs, while Madame Fleury said they made a disgusting meal.[43] Neither would compromise, so for two years they skirmished over the daily table fare, until Gissing, hostile and

[40] When GRG revised his diary, he apparently underlined each mention of Gabrielle in red.

[41] See A. C. Young, "A Note on George Gissing," *The Journal of the Rutgers University Library*, XXII (December 1958), 23-4.

[42] The Diary reads: "In the evening, our ceremony. Dear Maman's emotion, & G.'s sweet dignity."

[43] "Abstract of Notes by Dr. Henry Hick."

underweight, wrote the famous "starvation" letter to Dr. Hick, who then persuaded him to return to England for an examination. According to a prearranged plan, Gissing stayed with H. G. Wells, whose wife, on Dr. Hick's orders, overfed him so that he put on seven pounds the first week and shortly was back to his normal weight.[44] Soon Gissing decided that he could stay no longer with the Wellses, so Dr. Hick sent him to a sanatorium in Suffolk, operated by Dr. Jane Walker, where the heavy feeding treatment could be continued. From June to the end of August 1901, Gissing remained in England, and then, rested and well-fed, he rejoined Gabrielle in Autun, where he and Madame Fleury accepted a culinary armistice.[45] There was never any doubt in Gissing's mind that he and Gabrielle would remain together regardless of any difficulties.

Gissing's four years with Gabrielle were certainly the best ones of his short life. He was as happy with her as his temperament and character would permit, and, although he swore he would die in the poorhouse, he wrote novels enough to support families on both sides of the Channel.

After her husband's death, Gabrielle visited his family at Wakefield in May 1904, where she was hospitably accepted by his mother and sisters.[46] No provision was made for Gabrielle in Gissing's will, which had never been changed from the day of its registration in Siena, Italy, in 1897, in accord with an agreement they had made. Nevertheless, Gabrielle supplemented from her own small income the pension granted to Gissing's sons by the English government. She helped Walter Gissing, the elder son, who was killed in World War I, and she and Alfred remained friends until the end of her life. Having never remarried, she lived alone after her mother's death in the Latin Quarter of Paris, still interested in the arts and writers. In April 1954, Gabrielle was injured in a street accident in Paris; she went to recuperate at the home of a relative living at Nevers, and there, within a few months, she died.

[44] "Abstract of Notes by Dr. Henry Hick."

[45] The letter to Bertz dated 24 February 1902 indicates that Madame Fleury never completely surrendered, and that she and GRG still sparred over food.

[46] Gabrielle Gissing to E. Bertz, May 1904, Yale.

The Letters of George Gissing to
Eduard Bertz

7. K. Cornwall Residences. / Clarence Gate. / London NW.

April 17th. 1887.

Dear Friend,

I can only excuse myself on the plea of work of the most tremendous description. In the past seven weeks I have written 2 vols. of a novel. I wished to get as much as possible done before my pupil[1] came back from Cannes; his lessons begin again to-morrow. So I fear the 3rd. vol. will take me almost as long as the first two.[2] The book is called:

"Clement Dorricott:

A Life's Prelude,"

and it deals almost entirely with theatrical life. So here is a new start!

I don't know whether you still see the *Athenaeum*. "Thyrza" has been advertized for many weeks, and at last is announced for the 26th. of April. You shall of course have a copy at once. Roberts's book[3] comes out on the same day.

Roberts, by the bye, has had a stroke of good fortune in another direction. He sent a number of his poems to Macmillans, and in consequence old Mr. Macmillan[4] called upon him and invited him to dinner. It is arranged that certain of the poems shall

---

[1] "[Walter] Grahame is a wonderful boy not quite sixteen yet and he will soon know almost as much Greek as I can teach him. Practically his mind is already mature. If he continues at this rate, he will be a most exceptional scholar" (GRG to Margaret Gissing, *Letters*, 13 November 1887, p. 203). Walter was a nephew of Sir Anthony Hope Hawkins.

[2] By 6 May he had finished half of the third volume. Since the story had been written specifically for magazine publication, GRG refused Richard Bentley's offer to bring it out as a book, fearing that Smith, Elder and Co., who had published the preceding novel, *Thyrza*, would think him un-gracious (GRG to unknown correspondent, ? 1887, Yale). I am indebted to Mr. Alfred C. Gissing for telling me that his father finally destroyed the unpublished manuscript.

[3] *The Western Avernus; or, Toil and Travel in Further North America* (London, 1887).

[4] Alexander Macmillan (1818–1896), who, with his brother Daniel (1813–1857), founded the publishing house in Cambridge in 1844; the firm moved to London in 1863.

appear from time to time in the "English Illustrated," and I think Macmillans will ultimately publish a volume.[5] This is marvellous good luck, what say you?

I have not seen Morison's book,[6] but certain quotations from it that I read were very nauseous. I cannot tell you how I loathe that positivism at present.[7] Morison certainly is not dead yet. I did not even know that he was ill.

Your German note has recalled to my mind certain thoughts which I have frequently had of late. You, after all these years, are the only man of *European* culture with whom I have been intimate. Of Roberts I see a good deal now, but he is almost exclusively English, and this lack in him is a great hindrance in conversation. So very much of my own culture derives from foreign literature, that I cannot be my real self when unable to refer familiarly to the foreign authors I value. Now, you it was who greatly strengthened in me the tendency to read widely, and those periods of our personal intercourse were fruitful to me in a way which I appreciate more and more as time goes on.

How sluggish-minded are the few people whom I know in England! I do not think over-highly of my own attainments, but certainly, compared with them, I am a very Casaubon.[8] I keep up steadily my reading in Greek, Latin, German, French; and I do not know a soul—save yourself—who ever reads anything but English—at all events for pure pleasure. Hence their terrible narrowness.

My brother is established in the Cheviot Hills, and is writing a novel.[9] Heaven knows what the end will be, but I cannot be

[5] Three of Roberts's poems were printed in the *English Illustrated Magazine*: July 1887; April 1888; August 1888. For the publication of the volume of poetry, see 20 July 1891.

[6] James Augustus Cotter Morison (1832–1888), *The Service of Man: an Essay Towards the Religion of the Future* (London, 1887). Until his death on 26 February 1888, he was an active member of the London Positivist Society.

[7] GRG had joined the Positivist Society on 2 November 1880. He studied Comtean philosophy, dated his letters according to the positivist calendar for a few months in 1881 and tried to convert his brother Algernon; by 1883 GRG had lost faith in positivism.

[8] Isaac Casaubon (1559–1614), the Genevese humanist scholar.

[9] Algernon Gissing, *Joy Cometh in the Morning: A Country Tale* (2 vols., London: Hurst and Blackett, 1888).

sanguine. I see not the faintest chance of his ever being able to marry. His position, at present, is not a little tragic.[10]

I have no library-subscription now, so can see no new books. It is much better, for I have only an hour and a half in the day free for reading. Homer and Shakspere take it up at present.

I am glad your lecture came off so satisfactorily; I wish to Heaven I could form any idea of what it was all about.[11] Doubtless you are now again at your regular work. According to your last letter, the novel[12] you were engaged upon should now be finished. Is it so? I hope no change of mood, or external trouble, has come in its way. It delighted me to hear that you were in good spirits. It is the same with myself, to a quite unusual degree. I hope your satisfactory frame of mind continues. Your summer visit to Rehfeldt[13] will do you good. For myself, I doubt whether I shall go anywhere this year, unless it be to Eastbourne for a week in August. By the bye, you will read much of my favourite Eastbourne in "Thyrza."[14]

Certainly you are *not* wanting in energy, but it has always been so hard for you to keep long at one subject.[15] That was greatly due to the difficulties of your life. I earnestly hope you have now finished the novel, and that you will be able to get cash for it.

So you have read 'Richard Feverel.' Yes, it is a very *clever* book, and in many ways more than clever. I think your remarks on the plot are just; but Meredith has absolutely no constructive power.[16] I wish you had time to read some others of his. "Diana of the Crossways" is full of congenial matter.

Trollope? Ah, I cannot read him; the man is such a terrible Philistine. Indeed, of English novelists I see more and more clearly that there is *only one* entirely to my taste, and that is

---

[10] See Introduction.

[11] Nor have I been able to discover what the subject was.

[12] *Glück und Glas* (Leipzig: Ottmann, 1891).

[13] Dr. Heinrich Rehfeldt, Bertz's closest German friend.

[14] Cf. *Thyrza* (3 vols., Smith, Elder and Co., 1887), Chapters VII, XVI, XXVIII, XXIX, XLI.

[15] One of Bertz's vagaries that irritated yet amused GRG.

[16] See also 2 December 1892.

Charlotte Bronte. A great and glorious woman! George Eliot
is miserable in comparison![17]

Ever yours, dear Friend,
GEORGE GISSING

Addressed: Eduard Bertz. / Holzstrasse,[18] 18. / Potsdam. /
Allemagne.
Endorsed by Bertz: Received September 29th, 1888.

[September 27, 1888][19]
An absurd and vexatious thing has happened. The Hôtel Cujas,
of which I had been told, has just been pulled down.[20] Your letter
I suppose will be returned. Will send you address soon.

G. G.

Addressed: M. Eduard Bertz. / Holzmarkt Strasse,[21] 18. / Potsdam. / *Allemagne.*

Friday Night. [September 28, 1888][22]
Am much annoyed at the contretemps which has prevented me
from receiving your letter. To-day I am established in very com-
fortable quarters, marvellously cheap. Address: Hôtel de Londres,
Rue Linné. You will see from the name that I am close to the
Jardin des Plantes.[23] With me in the same hotel is an acquaintance

[17] GRG admired George Eliot's "rare conscientiousness" and studied her
style, but he found Charlotte Brontë a more interesting and attractive
personality. One reason for his attraction to her is explained in a letter he
wrote to his sister Ellen: "Strange to think of Charlotte Brontë having
stood on the spot [Anne Brontë's grave at Scarborough], at the time, regarded by those with whom she had dealings as an insignificant stranger.
These revenges of time are very palatable to me. I think of such cases with
a sort of exultation over oblivion, a rebellious triumph over the world's
brute forces" (30 August 1888, *Letters*, p. 222).
[18] A slip. He meant Holzmarktstrasse.
[19] Postmark.
[20] He went to the Hôtel Atlantique, Rue Jean-Jacques-Rousseau, for the
night (Diary, 27 September 1888) and then moved to the Hôtel de Londres,
Rue Linné.
[21] GRG generally separated the two elements in this compound.
[22] The postmark reads 29 September 1888, but 28 September 1888 was a
Friday.
[23] The streets adjacent to the garden were named after naturalists.

named Plitt,[24] a German whom I have known slightly for a year or two, and who happened to be coming to Paris; of course we have separate rooms, but it is pleasant to have an acquaintance at hand. He is an artist, though of very slight attainments. We have *dined* this evening in the Rue de Rivoli, which must account for incoherences in this note. To-morrow I begin to think of work, but I shall of course spend many hours in wandering. Please re-post your returned letters; yours are too interesting to be missed.

G. G.

Addressed: M. Eduard Bertz. / Holzmarkt Strasse, 18 / Potsdam. / Allemagne.

Thursday. [October 4, 1888][25]

Many thanks for your letter. I have been to the P.O. to inquire about the other, and they think it must have been already returned; however, I filled up a *réclamation* and shall hear if they still have it. Before long I will write a letter; at present I am seldom at home, as you may suppose. Smith and Elder will not give me more than £150 for "The Nether World," though they are complimentary about it. "A Life's Morning" is advertized for publication in 3 vols at end of November;[26] you shall of course have a copy, but I shall dread your remarks. Never mind, if my plans are not altered, I shall then be at *Naples,* whither Plitt has persuaded me to accompany him for 3 months;[27] we shall probably leave here at the end of October. I should much have preferred Rome but Plitt has certain artistic connections at Naples, and moreover his experience of Italy will be very valuable to secure cheapness of living. I am sorry to say there is nothing but the

[24] See 7 October 1888.

[25] Postmark.

[26] Smith, Elder and Co. published the novel before 15 November 1888.

[27] GRG had decided to spend the winter in Naples before he left England, but he told his mother only that he was planning a short visit to Paris. He wrote to Algernon: "I will just hint to you (but don't breathe it to Wakefield) that there is every chance of Plitt and me going on, at the end of November, to Naples, by way of Marseilles. There we should stay (at cost of 5 shillings a week, all told, and in the healthiest suburban district) until end of April, when I should return home via Rome and Florence" (24 September 1888, Yale).

most superficial sympathy between us; but I will tell you about it soon. You have done very well to address yourself to "The Writer,"[28] though I had not yet heard of this periodical. "Englische Jugend Literatur" is an excellent subject for you. Mon Dieu! you are energetic at present. I much hope your letter has come back to you by now.

Ever yours,
G. G.

(I will write on *Sunday* next)

33 Rue Linné, / Paris.

Sunday. October 7th. 1888.

Dear Friend,

My room looks upon the courtyard of the house, and each morning, when I look out to inspect the weather, I see the upper part of the white-painted wall opposite gleaming against a sky of wonderful blue,—the effect is just such as I have seen in Italian pictures. Indeed the weather here is wonderful, a little cold but gorgeously bright. And I feel well, well; I get up without a suspicion of headache, and throughout the day am cheerful. My life is beginning.

You will have received my card, telling you that I inquired at the P.O. It is strange if the letter has not yet been returned to you.

I daresay you are wondering who this man Plitt may be, with whom I have suddenly begun to travel about. I have known him casually for two years, but so casually, and with such little real interest in him, that I do not think I have even mentioned to you his name. He came to see me at 7.K. one evening, and said he was going to Naples by way of Paris. "Mais, voilà mon affaire!" I at once cried, and in half an hour our plans were made. I wish he were an intellectual man, but then, as you know, it is my lot to live with those who are in no way sympathetic.[29]

---

[28] A monthly professional journal, published by the English Publishing Company, which failed in 1889.

[29] A few weeks after they had been travelling together, GRG wrote: "I understand the man now; he is not an *artist*, but an *artisan*, that's all. He aims merely at decorative house-painting" (Diary, 11 October 1888).

I left England before hearing of "The Nether World" from Smith and Elder. They have since written, offering me £150. It is very little, but of course I accept it; they are complimentary, and say that they hope the *small sale* of my books will improve as they get better known. Eh bien! But I am sure the sale of the *two cheap editions* of "Demos" is not exactly small.[30]

"The Nether World" will, thank Heaven, appear "early in the spring."[31] So I hope to redeem my character in your eyes very soon. I believe the book is strong.

Of course I am enjoying myself here enormously. At the Louvre, I am making serious studies, and at the same time am giving careful attention to the Parisian newspaper press; I read several papers daily, and you will understand my motives.[32] Then I go to theatres, and also to certain lectures at the Salle des Conférences, B. des Capucines, where I have heard Louise Michel,[33] "Sur le rôle des Femmes dans l'Humanité," and Francisque Sarcey[34] on "L'Immortel," the latter a treat beyond expression. What delightful appreciation! Putting aside, in a few amusing phrases, his quarrel with Daudet apropos of the subject of the book,[35] he began to examine it from the point of view of literary style, and read passages—ah! imagine *how* he read them! *Il s'extasiait* over the best things. Never yet have I heard the subjects which most deeply interest me so spoken of. It gave me courage and hope.

If I were not going on to Italy, I should ruin myself at the book-shops and book-stalls.

But Italy, Italy! Think that I am really going thither at last, a thing I never dared to hope. At the end of the present month,

[30] The first three-volume edition of *Demos* published by Smith, Elder and Co. sold for 31 shillings 6 pence; a one-volume edition brought out in November 1886 cost 6 shillings; and in May 1888 another one-volume edition sold for 2 shillings.

[31] Published in 3 vols. in April 1889.

[32] To gather material and ideas for his writing.

[33] Clémence Louise Michel (1833–1905), French writer, anarchist, and militant feminist.

[34] Francisque Sarcey (1827–1899) relinquished a professorship at Grenoble to become a journalist. He wrote for *Figaro* under the pseudonym of Satané Binet and became famous for his spirited public lectures.

[35] GRG's Diary says that Sarcey objected to Daudet's "*personal* pictures" in the novel (4 October 1888).

we go to Marseille, and thence by boat to Naples. I cannot write about that prospect. At present I am learning a good deal of Italian daily.

As for work, well I am working enough. I scarcely think I shall do any writing before I get back to England, next spring.

Henceforth, I hope never to spend a winter in England. My real life is beginning.

And you too; try and rejoice and hope. Before very long now we shall certainly have endless conversation together. Work on for the day of deliverance; for you it surely is not far away. We shall yet see Italy together; be sure of it.

The room I have taken here is very cheap; only 35 fr. a month. To be sure it is not in a very nice part, and if I had been alone I should have known how to find better accommodation at a rate very little dearer.[36] I am afraid Plitt rather despises me for my desire to have surroundings of some degree of refinement. Still, I am not sorry. I am seeing the life of the people. The shopping I have to do is very valuable as regards language. At present I have few difficulties in that latter respect.

Fellows are shouting on the Boulevards every night: "Voilà les mémoires authentiques de Frédéric III—15 centimes!"[37] Of course there is much malicious writing in the Paris papers on that matter.

As I shall not see any English papers after I leave here, perhaps you will tell me if anything notable comes out in the *advertisements* of "A Life's Morning." No reviews will be sent to me; I have done with such things.[38]

Your last letter showed me that you were striking out in hopeful directions. Do not lose hold upon these English projects, if you can possibly combine them with your other work.

[36] Plitt searched for the cheapest rooms available, regardless of their location or condition. To get a decent room for himself, GRG had to bribe Plitt by paying five francs of his rent (Diary, 28 September 1888).

[37] "A reprint, I suppose, of the extracts from F.'s journal just published in the Deutsche Rundschau, and making such an uproar" (Diary, 2 October 1888). A few months after Frederick III's death in June 1888, an intimate friend, Professor Geffcken, published excerpts from the Emperor's diary, discrediting Bismarck's government.

[38] He wanted to prevent Bertz from summarizing or forwarding reviews. After his literary reputation was secure, GRG mellowed on the subject of reviews and enjoyed receiving them. See 24 February 1902.

For the present, good-bye. I do not expect you to write very often, for it is expensive, and your time is valuable. Hold on in good cheer.

Ever yours,
GEORGE GISSING

You got the photographs, of course.[39]

Addressed: Herrn Eduard Bertz. / Holzmarkt Strasse, 18 / Potsdam. / Allemagne.

October 11th. [1888]

33 [Rue Linné]

Your letter arrived. I have received a [notice?][40] from the P.O., in which they tell me that the letter I inquired for has been returned to Berlin. I am sorry to say that Plitt is so foolish as to be seriously alarmed at my receiving letters from Germany,[41] whilst we are here. To avoid his constant complaints, I will ask you to send your next to: Stoneleigh Terrace. / Agbrigg. / *Wakefield*.[42] A needless and foolish waste of money! In Italy it will be all right, and I hope we go at the end of this month.

Certainly write for the English serials, and let me have the articles beforehand.[43] Your English remains very good.

I went and stood before Daudet's house yesterday.[44] To-night I hear Sarcey on "François le Champi."[45]

G. G.

[39] Probably of pictures and statues in the Paris museums.

[40] The tops of the letters of this word were clipped off when the stamp was cut out.

[41] Franco-German relations were under severe strain from 1887 to 1889, and Plitt became self-conscious about his German birth: "Letter from Bertz, greatly to Plitt's disgust—he being terrified lest we be seized as German spies; strange mania"; "Wrote to Bertz, on Plitt's account, telling him to send his letter to England—Bah!" (Diary, 11 October 1888).

[42] His mother's address.

[43] There is no record of publication of the proposed articles.

[44] "Daudet is doing the same work as myself; his books are arraignments of society" (To Ellen Gissing, "Day after Shakespeare's Birthday," April 1888, Yale); "Could Daudet know of me, assuredly I should not need to stand out in the street" (Diary, 10 October 1888).

[45] George Sand (2 vols., Paris, 1850).

Addressed: Herrn Eduard Bertz. / Holzmarkt Strasse, 18 /
Potsdam. / *Allemagne.*

Mardi. [October 23, 1888][46]

33 Rue Linné

Nous partons vendredi pour Marseille, en route pour Naples.
Ma nouvelle adresse aussitôt que possible.

Hier soir j'ai passé une heure au Café Soufflet, et j'y ai demandé
des nouvelles de M. Jansen.[47] Paraît qu'on ne l'y connaisse plus.

La traduction de "Demos" vient d'être mise sous presse.[48]

Attendez une longue lettre de Naples. Tout va bien, qu'il soit
de même avec vous!

Votre devoué
G. G.

Addressed: Herrn Eduard Bertz. / Holzmarkt Strasse, 18. /
Potsdam. / *Germania.*

Vico Brancaccio, 8. / 30 p. / (Casa di Luca) / Napoli.

October 31st. 1888

Dear Friend,

Thank heaven I am at last established, and well established.
A very long letter must tell you all my experiences. I am very
tired, and too full of words to speak. Indescribable what I have
seen. A word from you, if possible! Hope to stay here long. My
window looks over Posilippa [*sic*] and Vergil's Tomb. Impossible,
impossible to imagine it!

Ever yours,
G. [G.]

Vico Brancaccio, 8. / 30 p. / Napoli.

November 9th. 1888.

Dear Friend,

Your letter contains perhaps the best news I have ever received
from you. If you had reserved it until this time for the mere

[46] Postmark.

[47] Kristofer Nagel Jansen (1841–1917), Norwegian poet and novelist.

[48] The translation was done by Mlle. Fanny Le Breton, a Parisian, whom
GRG visited in October. Although she completed her translation in 1888,
she had difficulties with her publisher, Hachette, and the novel did not
appear until 1890. She published under the pseudonym "Hephell." See
6 December 1888.

purpose of heightening my enjoyment in this wonderful country, you could not have done me a greater service. I must of course have the Carlyle article;[49] send it me as soon as it appears, and, if necessary, you shall have it back. I should like to see some of the smaller writings,[50] also. The paper for "The Writer" send me and you shall have it again, with my remarks, speedily; there will be little to suggest, I am sure. Yes, your greatest difficulties are over. You are now doing the proper kind of work (in the Carlyle article) and I hope before long to read all your literary and ethical views. Your existence will soon be well enough recognized.

About my life here, what am I to say? Where begin—where end?

First of all, the material conditions. The upper portion of this house belongs to a certain Frau Häberle,[51] (she is recommended by Baedeker) and from her I have my room for which I pay 45 lire a month. It is a rather high rent, but the sanitary conditions are perfect, the quarter admirable, the service all that could be wished. A large room, with a floor of tiles, with of course no fireplace, and the window looking west, so that I get all the sunsets. By looking out, I can just see one end of Capri. Posillipo [sic] is directly in front, and beyond Posillipo I know there lies that exquisite bay of Pozzuoli, which on the whole gives me more pleasure than this of Naples.

I generally go out for my breakfast: a good caffè latte, two rolls and a piece of butter, cost 35 c. My mid-day meal consists of bread, fruit and wine, eaten wherever I happen to be. I buy grapes for 10 c. a pound (one penny a pound!) and figs at the same rate, figs just off the tree. My wine—of very good quality—costs 60 c. a bottle!

Already I have seen a good deal of the town and its immediate neighbourhood; the longer excursions (Vesuvius, Pompeii, Capri etc) must wait a little. For the climate renders much exertion

---

[49] "Carlyle als Berufschriftsteller," printed in three parts in the *Deutsche Presse*, I (4 November 1888), 356–57; I (11 November 1888), 363–65; I (18 November 1888), 372–74. See 2 June 1889.

[50] See 2 June 1889, *et passim*.

[51] "Find this [Häberlin] is proper spelling of her name; they have adopted Häberle only because other form was impossible for Italians" (Diary, 20 February 1890).

impossible. One day we had scirocco, and it prostrated me; I could scarcely walk a yard. But for the most part the weather is what *we* should call that of mid summer, almost too hot, and a cloudless sky.

Here is a sketch of one of my walks. Through the hill of Posillipo are bored two enormous tunnels, leading to the district of Pozzuoli; one of these is Roman, one—shorter—of late years, and used by the tramway. Through the Roman tunnel I walked and found myself in the village of Fuorigrotta; thence a long straight road, between vineyards and pine trees, led me to the shore, at Bagnoli. As I walked along, I noticed the thousands of various lizards that kept scampering over the walls and the ditch-sides. From Bagnoli I walked along the shore-road to Pozzuoli. Ah, what an exquisite little town! By the little port is a little public garden (planted with palms) and there I sat for an hour, enjoying the sunshine, the breeze, the shipping, the dazzling colours of everything about me. Then my walk recommenced, and I was soon at the foot of Monte Nuovo, a hill created in the 16th century by an earthquake. There I found myself upon the banks of the Lucrine Lake—of which you do not hear for the first time. Its smallness astonished me; but then it was much lessened by the earthquake. Here I had a little détour to make. I struck inland by a roadway, and in ten minutes stood by another little lake, deep amid hills. An old boatman was there, and, as I approached, he stretched out his hand towards the water and said solemnly—"Il lago Averno!" Yes, it was Lake Avernus. There I gathered some flowers, and one of them I send you.

I retraced my steps to the shore and went on again for a mile, stopping just before Baja (Baiae). To stand on the shore at Baiae— great Heavens! Ah, if I could give you an idea of the view. But no words, no colours on canvas, can avail to describe what one sees here at every turn. I shall never try.

Another day I took the tram to Torre del Greco, which is at the foot of Vesuvius and has constantly been destroyed by earthquakes and eruptions. It was most curious to examine the seashore here; it consists of black scoriae and black volcanic earth. Here is an inscription which I found on a column in the town:

"Sarà perpetua la gratitudine di questi abitanti verso i fratelli di tutta l'Italia, nei quali fu tanto viva la carità della commune patria recentemente unita, che, quando, il di VIII di Dicembre del MDCCCLXI, un crollo del soprastante Vesuvio ruinò quanto era murato, accorsero da ogni parte con ajuti si generosi che ne furono alleviate le miserie presenti e ne avanzò da fondere un asilo d'infanzia."[52]

As regards the language, there is a serious difficulty. With educated people I can make myself understood, and can understand, perfectly well; but then one very rarely has to do with a man who can be called educated, and the masses of the people speak an unintelligible jargon. The Neapolitan dialect is extraordinary. I am beginning to notice a few of its peculiarities. First of all, they cut off nearly all grammatical terminations, and almost always a final *o* or *i*. Thus, they say *"buon' giorn',"* and *"la piccol"* for "il Piccolo," the name of a newspaper; and when I ask for "un mezzo chilo di fichi,"[53] the man replies: "Un mezz' chil' di fich'?" A *soldo* (5 c.) is *un sol'*—to me a blessed word, for one seems to pay for everything either 1 or 2 soldi, rarely more. These are trifles; there are of course multitudes of words I cannot in the least understand.

I must tell you of an amusing adventure I had yesterday. In the morning I climbed to the monastery of I Camaldoli,[54] and after enjoying the view of which I dare not say a word, I made my way down to a village called Soccavo. I was exhausted, and looked out for a place where I could buy some wine. At last I turned into a tolerably decent shop (the drinking-places are awful in little villages, as a rule,) and was met by a man in spectacles, whom I at once saw to be an interesting fellow. To begin with, he spoke pure Italian, and, when he had opened my bottle of wine, he sat down by me to talk. I soon told him

[52] "The gratitude of these inhabitants will be perpetual towards their brothers from all parts of Italy, in whom the charity of the common country, recently united, was so much alive, when on the 8th of December 1861 an eruption of the lofty Vesuvius ruined as much as was built, they came to the assistance from each part with aid so generous that the misfortunes of that occasion were alleviated, and there remained enough to found an orphanage."

[53] "A half kilo of figs."

[54] Founded by St. Romuald, a Benedictine monk, in 1585 on the heights of the Appennines.

I was an Englishman, whereupon he exclaimed: "Ho dei libri inglesi,—tre libri,—magnifici!" My curiosity was excited, and at once he produced the books. What do you think they were? "Verdant Green,"[55] with illustrations; an English translation of "Paul et Virginie,"[56] and an odd volume of Hannah More's works! His chief delight was in "Verdant Green," which he understood pretty well (though not knowing a word of English) by help of the illustrations. He kept pointing to pictures of Verdant himself, whom he called "il protagonista," surely the first time that such a grandiose term was ever applied to the character!

I shall go and see this man again. He is lately married, and has a baby two months old, "Mia figlia!" he said to me with pride. We shook hands warmly on parting, and—to complete the story— the wine he gave me, and for which the price was *four pence*, made me all but drunk. By the bye, he told me that he was the president of the "Società del mutuo soccorso di Soccavo!"[57] I should like to learn a little more about that society.

When one first walks in the streets of Naples, the thing that most impresses one is the enormous size of the houses and everything about them. The *portoni* are enormous; the stair cases of vast width; the windows like those of palaces. And inside you find enormous rooms, with party-walls often two feet thick. Then the doors of the rooms are twice the size of English doors.

Let me jot down a few more of the characteristics of the town which have struck me these first days. The beautiful flocks of goats, with bells, driven about the streets morning and evening for milking; also cows occasionally, always with a calf. The frequent monks walking about, real monks; and indeed the force of the clerical element in general. The terrific uproar everywhere, every true Neapolitan taking every opportunity of shouting and roaring. The extraordinary amount of buying and selling in the narrow streets. The abundance of fruit. The abundance of donkeys and their terrific braying. The gleaming and elaborate harness of horses, and the wretchedness of the animals themselves. The multitude of barbers.

[55] Edward Bradley, pseud. Cuthbert Bede, *The Adventures of Mr. Verdant Green, an Oxford Freshman* (3 vols., London, 1853–1857).
[56] Henri Jacques St. Pierre (Paris, 1789).
[57] "Society for Mutual Aid of Soccavo."

As for the situation of the town, you are aware that it is built on the side of a high hill. I never knew any exercise so fatiguing as to walk about Naples for a few hours; perpetually you are doing hard climbing. Many of the streets are called *gradoni*, and you literally ascend by steps for perhaps a quarter of a mile. Often you find yourself on the edge of a precipice, and have to search a long time for the path by which to proceed; at the foot of such precipices are always wonderful gardens. Even the flat roofs of the houses are often used as gardens. And in the poor parts of the town, there is no describing the filthiness and narrowness and picturesqueness of the streets; I have seen streets where a cart could not possibly squeeze itself. Everywhere you think you must every moment be run over, but life is leisurely here, and drivers seldom—indeed *cannot* go very fast.

I rejoice that I have seen Naples thus soon. In a few years the character of the town will be greatly changed. The newspapers are always talking about "la sventramento"[58] which is going on, the clearing away of dark quarters and the opening up of wide roads. Yes, but it will not then be Naples. If you could see the Strada di Chiaia at 5 o'clock of an evening! It is one of the main thoroughfares, in the best part of the town, and is nowhere more than six yards broad, I think. Along this street all the carriages return from the Corso. Heavens! In the west end a whole new city is rising, wealthy, commonplace, as far as anything can be commonplace under this sky.

I am sorry to say that my companion is somewhat worse than useless. His utter lack of poetry has developed into a rather aggressive philistinism, and it is a sad fact that his society *appreciably* lessens my enjoyment of Italy. Well, we arrange our affairs pretty much apart at present, and when I leave Naples I hope he will not accompany me. Indeed he talks of *nothing* but the cost of dinner—the cost of rooms etc.—I will say no more of the matter henceforth.

I have very good news from Roberts; he has been selling several articles since I left England.

On Sunday, the Museo is free. I took the opportunity last Sunday, but I was suffering so much from the climate that I

[58] "Disembowelling."

could only just survey the rooms. The Farnese Hercules and the Bull must be studied before long. The pictures are not of great importance, but of course the things from Herculaneum and Pompeii are of enormous interest.

In a few days I think of going to Paestum, thence to Salerno, and thence to Amalfi,—I shall have to be three days from home, and perhaps can return from Amalfi by steamer.

Here is something to give you a hearty laugh. In the "Corriere di Napoli" of yesterday was a leader on American affairs, and in that leader occurs the following astounding passage,—I say astounding with reference to its last sentence:

"I poetissimi poeti che quel gran paese ha prodotto, o sono degli spiriti latini, come Longfellow, o torbide effervescenze alcooliche, come Edgardo Poe, *o la voce del sangue barbaro e della selvaggia natura, non ancora in tutto dominata, come Nataniele Hawthorne.*" [59]

Poor Hawthorne! Of whom is the man thinking? And yet the paper is pretty well informed on the whole. Surely the writer must be thinking of someone else. But it is good!

No, I don't think I shall do any writing in Italy. I have so much to see, so much to learn. At present I give three hours a day to Italian, of course reading the newspapers much. Ah, if one had time to read the Greeks and Latins here! If one had time to read history here!

The "Italienische Reise" [60] has been of great value to me, of course. Thank Heaven I brought it with me! For guide-books, it would scarcely be possible to improve on Baedeker. I bought in Paris his three vols, north, middle and south Italy, and they are my constant companions.

Oh, I must tell you. Just beyond Posillipo is the little island of Nisida. Whilst I was looking at it, I consulted Baedeker, and he reminded me that it was hither Brutus came after the murder of Caesar, and here that he was visited by Cicero; hence he set out

[59] "The most poetic poets which that great country has produced, either are Latin spirits, such as Longfellow, or turbid effervescent alcoholics such as Edgar Poe, or the voice of barbaric blood and wild nature, not yet completely tamed, such as Nathaniel Hawthorne."

[60] Goethe (2 vols., 1816–1817). GRG had bought a cheap copy in Paris (Diary, 9 October 1888).

for Greece, for Philippi. That was a thought! The coast and the islands have not changed. As I see Capri, Ischia, Nisida, so did Vergil and Horace and Cicero see them. One cannot speak about such things.

Again I must rejoice that your own period of success comes just when I could wish it. My pleasure is doubled by thinking of you in a state of happy activity. Let me have your articles.[61]

The monk at Camaldoli yesterday said to me, speaking of England, "Si dice che v'è molta nebbia!"[62] Yes, yes, "molta nebbia!" At present they have perpetual night in London, perpetual rain. Here is blue sky and blue sea; here are figs and lemons and grapes, and the oranges are ripening!

Let me hear again soon. Ever yours, dear Friend,

GEORGE GISSING

Addressed: Herrn Eduard Bertz. / Holzmarkt Strasse, 18. / Potsdam. / *Germania.*

Vico Brancaccio, 8.

November 27th. 1888.

On the evening of the 29th., at 10.40, I start for ROME.

I know very well that your articles are good, and I wait for them impatiently. Excellent news about "Glück u[nd] Glas,"—*all* goes well!

As for the Translation Bureau, pray let me have fuller details when you can.[63] Regarding Payn,[64] do not forget that he is a *member* of the firm of Smith and Elder, and therefore committed to the publisher's side; but we will talk about it. The "English Publishing Company" has an equivocal position, and must not be too much counted upon. Think of some way in which I can really be of use. Roberts's address is—4 Danvers St., Chelsea, London SW. Very gladly he will correspond with you.

A copy of "A Life's M[orning]"[65] will be sent to you, but I implore you not to speak to me about it. It is trash. Wait for

---

[61] See 2 June 1889.
[62] "It is said there is a lot of fog there."
[63] See 6 December 1888.
[64] James Payn (1830–1898), novelist and editor of the *Cornhill Magazine* from 1883 to 1896; he read manuscript for Smith, Elder and Co.
[65] 3 vols., London: Smith, Elder and Co., 1888.

"The Nether World," and, I beg, do not think I am falling into dotage.

All your prospects are excellent, and you are indeed active.[66] Doubtless Rehfeldt rejoices, among others.

The next from Rome!

G. G.

Addressed: Herrn Eduard Bertz. / Holzmarkt Strasse, 18. / Potsdam. / Germania
59 Via Margutta / Roma. 40 p.

November 30th. 1888.

I write in an exhausted state, in a Café on the Corso. Travelled all last night in 3rd. class, and no sleep. To-day could not resist the Tiber and Forum and Colosseum! I hope the above will be my address for a month. Yours ever, in weariness and bliss.

GG.

59 Via Margutta. 40p. / Roma.

December 6th. 1888.

Dear Friend,

Your letter reached me this afternoon. I took it with me to read whilst I was having dinner at a little *cucina*[67] which I frequent opposite the Palazzo Borghese. I will make a beginning of my reply at once.

First about the *Athenaeum*. Never yet have I known this paper do a generous thing, whilst the mean ones that have come under my notice are innumerable. Again and again I have said to Roberts that I was astonished at its persistency in narrow malice; he observes the same characteristic. I cannot but wonder what clique of men can be responsible for such an ignoble line of conduct. Scarcely ever do they give hearty praise to any book, save those written by two or three authors whom it is the *fashion* to praise. It must be managed by a very small corporation of very silly fellows. And, by the bye, earnestly I implore you not to

---

[66] See 6 December 1888.
[67] "Kitchen."

tell me what it says about my book.[68] Indeed, do not speak another word about the book; already your short reference has disturbed me too much, and taught me how easily my stay in Rome could be ruined. If I saw a *single* review, I might as well at once go back to London; my pleasure here would be at an end.

The idea of the translation bureau is very good, but in England there will be frightful difficulties. I am sadly afraid that the English Society of Authors[69] makes no progress at all. A man in real need—as almost all *young* authors are—cannot belong to a society; and, when he ceases to be in need, then he no longer cares to belong to it. For all that, I heartily wish both your society and theirs may prosper. Besant has taken a very strong line lately in attacking the greed of publishers, and there can be no doubt that he will cooperate with your movement. Ask Roberts to get you information. I heartily hope you may get your secretaryship;[70] I suppose it will be a demand on your time, but, on the other hand, you have been far too long a stranger to every form of active life. Above all, I prize this evidence that you are valued. It could not but be so as soon as men got to know you.

As to "Demos," you have made a little mistake. It was for "Thyrza" that I asked £20. The copyright of "Demos" includes right of translation and that I sold. But it appears that the publisher's right to demand a fee for translation only extends to the 3rd. year after publication, for Smith and Elder told Mlle. Le Breton[71] that she was free to do it, now, without charge. Hachette

[68] The reviewer praised *A Life's Morning* for excellence in incident and characterization, but added, "Mr. Gissing is somewhat prone to moralizing, and though he is always thoughtful and intelligent, and occasionally acute, he is loth to say a plain thing in a plain way, and exhibits an unfortunate predilection for ponderous Latinisms which would have irritated the late Mr. Barnes. Such affectations of style are to be regretted in a writer who holds a high view of the functions of a novelist, and is obviously animated by a sincere sympathy for all that is best in human nature" (*Athenaeum*, 8 December 1888, p. 770).

[69] The Incorporated Society of Authors was founded by Walter Besant (1836–1901) in 1884, with Alfred Lord Tennyson as president. Besant, spokesman for the group, fought for a better distribution of profits between publisher and author.

[70] Bertz had been nominated for the office in the Deutscher Schriftsteller-Verband, which published a weekly magazine, *Deutsche Presse*.

[71] See 23 October 1888.

is the publisher, and I suppose the book has already appeared. I am on the point of writing to Mlle. Le Breton, and then I shall probably have news. I should be very glad indeed to see the book translated into German, and evidently it can be done without paying anything.

As to Zola's remark about translations into French not selling, I don't understand it. Mlle. Le Breton told me that there never had been such a demand for translations of English novels. It is true that they mostly appear in feuilletons, but then I used to see the book-shops full of Hachette's series of foreign novels. The serious English books (I include novels) are no good, it's true. The *Débats* refused "Demos" because it was "trop sérieux."

£20 was of course too much for Sharp's "Heine."[72] Is the book really of much value? You had better leave it alone.

You must not have more to do with Story[73] than is absolutely necessary. He is not a man of your level, at all, indeed of very far below it. Be very careful, I beg you; it won't do for a serious connection.

The projects concerning the *Deutsche Presse* are very important. As concerns yourself, they may prove of the greatest moment. But one word. You are not exactly—thank heaven!—a man of business, and it behoves you to be cautious in pledging yourself to any journalistic undertaking. Pray understand exactly beforehand how much is to be demanded of you. You cannot become a slave in an office; your health will not allow it, and your time is too precious. An editorship is too often utter slavery. At the same time, it *may* be a delightful position. Look into it all thoroughly. It is excellent that you can count yourself all but independent. Doubtless you will do right to go to Berlin, and there, before very long, I hope to visit you. Indeed, I think the turning point in your life has come. Be strong, and utilize every opportunity. A year or two, and the past will seem very far behind you.

I told you nothing of all my doing the fortnight before I left Naples, yet it was the most important time of my stay there. I

---

[72] William Sharp, *Life of Heinrich Heine* (London, 1888). Bertz wanted to buy the translation rights.

[73] Alfred Thomas Story (1849–1934), English journalist, connected, at various times, with the New York *Herald*, Paris *Morning News*, and *Le Matin*.

made an unspeakably delightful excursion of rather more than a week. First I went to Salerno, then to Amalfi, thence to Paestum, thence back to Pompeii, then up Vesuvius, then to Castellamare and Sorrento, and finally for a couple of days to Capri!

Oh, it was all glorious beyond description. Both sides of the Sorrento peninsula are exquisite. The southern side is, almost all along, sheer cliff; a wonderful road has been made as far as Amalfi, and it often runs 500 feet above the sea, on the side of the mountain. From Salerno to Amalfi, I drove, and it is like a dream in looking back. Opposite, the blue mountains of Calabria, making one's eyes moist with joy at beholding them. And Amalfi! Heavens, what an old, old little town. To have been there is to have lived in the middle ages. It lies in a great mountain gorge, and its one street climbs up along the course of a stream. You cannot walk anywhere for five minutes without severe climbing, and to find one's way is for a stranger the most impossible of things. There is a grand old Cathedral, Norman-Lombard, where I wandered a whole morning. And the strange little port, with its fishing-boats, the huge mountains overhead, with clouds on them, a wonderful memory.

And Paestum. The most delicious of all my experiences. Ah, they are grand, those three Doric temples. You alight at a little roadside station (Pesto), and without being annoyed by guides (an astonishing thing in South Italy) you walk out onto the plain where the ruins are. All is absolute peace. A few fine oxen were ploughing a field close by, and they added to the strange antique impression. From the wife of the guardian I bought a bottle of Calabrian wine, and made a lunch in the *cella*[74] of Poseidon. Both ways an exquisite view. Westward, a strip of blue, blue sea, in the distance; eastward, a noble valley in the Apennines, rising to the rose-coloured heights: both pictures seen in a framework of Doric columns. I could have shed tears for the sadness of it. The few poor fields around are walled in with stones which once built a glorious Greek city. These columns here have echoed to the sound of Hellenic speech, and now such an intense silence. About the temples grow masses of ancanthus [*sic*] and thistles and ferns; in summer there are dangerous snakes. And

[74] The body of the temple.

5

all the columns are covered with delicate little snails,—I brought a lot of them away with me.

The ascent of Vesuvius was of course very interesting, especially as the mountain was unusually active. I ascended from Pompeii, on horseback, and with a guide. At the foot of the cone we had to dismount, and the last hour was a tough pull. For one thing, it utterly destroyed my boots. We had a struggle at one point with sulphur fumes, but soon came out of them. Inside the great crater is a cone which encloses the actual crater, and onto this cone we could not get, for it was yellow with sulphur, and fuming terribly, whilst enormous volumes of smoke rose from within. Every few minutes a great volley of stones rose high into the air, and all the time there went on a sound like that of a monstrous iron-foundry—throb, throb, throb! It made one look with foreboding at the busy little towns at the foot of the mountain.

By the bye, it is extraordinary how many Germans I meet everywhere. The Germans have conquered Italy. The Albergo del Soli, at Pompeii, a delightful place, was full of them. It is rather hard for an Englishman in my position. It is the very rarest thing that I can speak my own language. Why am I always called upon to speak German, or French, or Italian? Why the devil don't some of these people make shift to talk English occasionally [?] The Germans are not foreigners here; they live in colonies, swarms of them. But a *poor* Englishman is a foreigner in the uttermost sense of the word. For the rich it is of course a different matter. However, I get on pretty well with Italian, now that it is no longer a question of the Neapolitan dialect. Of course I always eat at Italian places, and so save much money. I am now, too, in a purely Italian house.

However, I have still to tell you of Capri. There I found roses blooming, and daisies along the roads, and butterflies and bees! I was delighted to walk about the island which I had so long gazed at, over the bay; it is splendidly rocky, and the cliffs along the shore are at times terrific. Do you remember once giving me Andersen's "Improvisatore"[75] to read? I thought of that when I was in the Grotta Azzurra. Well, that is a surprising sight. I always thought that pictures exaggerated the colour, but to exaggerate it is impossible,—such a blue I never saw.

[75] Hans Christian Andersen, *The Improvisatore; or, Life in Italy,* 1835.

And now I am in Rome. Wherever I look I see the letters "S. P. Q. R.," at the heads of public announcements, on buildings, even on dirt-carts! And a curious bit of antiquity is the custom of putting "Est Locanda," on houses to be let. The other day I wanted to have a bath, and could not, because, as they told me, the "Aqua Marcia" had failed, and Rome was practically without water. The Aqua Marcia!

I have spent much time in the Forum, which I am studying seriously. Also I have been to several of the private galleries. The Vatican I have not yet dared to approach;[76] I purpose devoting to it the whole of the coming week. At first the place put me into despair, but by degrees I am bringing order into my plans and my impressions.

Michelangelo's architecture has demanded attention these last two days, the Piazza del Campidaglio, the Farnese Palace, and a few other places; this links itself with the ruins, which are architecturally glorious. Of such buildings as the Basilica of Constantine, I had formed no conception; this in especial appals one, so vast and beautiful it is, even now. Well, I have walked on the *Via Sacra*,—think of that! If the present be indeed the paving on which Horace walked, then he must often have stumbled whilst "Nescio quid meditans nugarum, et totus in illis," (I am getting tired, and can't write Latin, you see,)[77] for it is strangely rude, of polygonal blocks, like at Pompeii.

I must continue to-morrow.

December 7th. 1888

Since the year 1871, Sig. Rosa,[78] who directs the public antiquities

[76] GRG's enthusiasm for the Vatican had been satisfied when he returned to Rome in 1898 with H. G. Wells, who later wrote that "Gissing, like Gibbon, regarded Christianity as a deplorable disaster for the proud gentilities of classicism and left us to 'do' the Vatican and St. Peter's by ourselves" (*Experiment in Autobiography*, p. 486). Wells's impression of GRG's attitude on this tour is not supported in the letters to Bertz written in 1898. GRG did not avoid the Vatican out of principle, but because he wanted the time to seek out other old churches which he had not yet seen (see 13 January 1898).

[77] "Ibam forte via sacra, sicut meus est mos, / Nescio quid meditans nugarum, totus in illis" (*Satires*. I. ix. 1–2).

[78] Pedro Rosa (1815–1891), Italian archeologist, directed the program for restoring and preserving Roman antiquities. The flora was removed to retard disintegration of the stone.

of Rome has completed a thorough cleansing of the Colosseum, with the result that all its flora, which used to be so beautiful and interesting, has disappeared. The old walls are bare. With great difficulty I have to-day found you the little flower (I know not what,) and the sprig of green which I enclose. They were growing out of chinks between the bricks.

You know that, more or less all my life, the history of painting has been one of my chief interests. Here I am studying seriously at the subject. The private galleries are rich in examples of the decadent schools, from the end of the 16th. Century onwards, and I am doing my best to see what is good in Annibale Caracci, Guido, Guercino, Caravaggio, and the rest. When I get to Florence I shall have a much more satisfactory field, for I love the early men.

St. Peter's has to be seen several times before you in the least understand even its proportions. The dome it is impossible to appreciate save from some distance. I got it finely last evening. At 4.30 I went up onto the Pincio, where, as you know, are public gardens, and a sort of "Rotten Row" for society. A good band was playing. The sun had just set, a little to the left hand of St. Peter's, and the dome stood clear out against an amber sky. Then I understood its beauty, and could compare it with all the other domes in sight.

The Capitol always delights me. There in the middle of the Piazza (which is really the middle space between the Arx and the Capitolium,) stands the glorious equestrian statue of Marcus Aurelius, the horse to which Michel-Angelo said "Cammina!"[79] A step or two, and you look right down upon the Forum, with the Palatine on the right hand. Here indeed is sacred ground. And in the Capitoline Museum there is of course endless nutriment. Especially I have been interested in the sepulchral inscriptions which abound there. Try and make out the special liking I have for the following, which I copied:[80]

"D. M.
Festibae Libertae

[79] "Walk!"
[80] GRG copied the inscriptions in his Diary and wrote of them: 1) "One imagines here a tender story"; 2) "Here is a poor little stone"; 3) "And here a voice from far off" (Diary, 2 December 1888).

Quae Vixit Ann. XXV
Ippolytus Patronus
B.M.F."

Again:

"Symphonus
Vixit Ann. I.
Menses VIIII."

Again:

"D. M.
Obelliae Fortunatae
Conjugi Carissimae
C. Julius Magnion
Et sibi."

Glorious bits of practical irony are discoverable among the ruins
of the Forum. Look here:
"Dominis Omnium Gratiano Valentiniano et Theodosio Im-
peratorib. Aug." This on a broken bit of marble, in the dirt. And
again:
"Toto orbe victori D. N. Constantio Max. Triumfatori (*sic*)
Semper Aug." Eheu, eheu, eheu!
I have arranged my life on an economical basis. In the morning
I get out and have two cups of *caffè latte*, in which—more
italico—I dip rolls of bread. This costs 30 c. My mid-day meal I
eat wherever I am,—bread and cheese, or salame, with an apple,
and perhaps a *bicchiere di rosso*,—at most 40 c. Then for dinner
I go to a good little cucina, and have soup, meat, fruit and wine for
L 1.35. The worst of it is, one has to spend so much money in
gratuities to the *custodi* at the private galleries; it really makes
a serious tax. Every Sunday certain public places are free, and of
course I shall make good use of this; but the Capit[oline] Museum
is 50 c., and I must needs go many times.
A thought on realism. In the Corsini Gallery is Salvator Rosa's[81]
picture of Prometheus Bound. On a rock lies a naked wretch,

---

[81] Rosa (1615–1673) became famous for his romantic landscapes and his
interpretations of historical events. For a developed statement of GRG's
thoughts on realism, see his "The Place of Realism in Fiction," *Humanitarian*, July 1895.

whose bowels are being visibly torn out by a huge bird of prey. Blood pours down from the ghastly wounds, and the sufferer's mouth[82] is stretched wide in a yell of agony. The background is black with horror. Well now, *why not* all this? It is a perfectly truthful representation of such an event. Yes, but it happens to be supremely loathsome, and to convey merely the impression of a galley-slave under torture. We know very well that this is *not Prometheus at all*, and there is the answer to all such nonsense.

In the same way with regard to the realistic pictures of the Madonna by Caravaggio, Murillo, etc. These are mere portraits of modern women nursing children. Next to one such by Caravaggio, in the Corsini, hangs a "Presepe" by Vandyck. Both are realistic, but in how different a way. Take away from Vandyck even his Ass and the Manger, and much more remains than a woman watching her new-born child, much more. Yet there are no aureoles, whilst Caravaggio, absurdly enough, gives one to *his* Madonna.

Dear old Andrea del Sarto is realistic enough, but he never ceases to be poetical, never. He does it by the expression of the faces, and by the imaginative grouping. His Lucrezia looks out at you from every canvas, but she is generally a Madonna likewise.

Strange, the colour of the Tiber. "Flavus" is the very word for it, to this day. It is like water very thickly mixed with yellow clay, and indeed I suppose that's what it actually is. The sun gleaming on it makes it look almost solid.

I had a fine view from the top of Monte Testeccio the other day. Far away in the north stood, clear and high, Soracte!

"Vides ut alta stet nive candidum
Soracte—?"[83]

Well, perhaps I shall still see it like that.

I don't think I shall be able to make any excursions in the neighbourhood of [Rome?]. I spent too much during that last fortnight at Naples, though I shall never regret it. And I still have Florence and Venice before me. Good that I shall be here for Christmas.

If you knew how it delights me to receive letters from you

---

[82] The word "wound" precedes "mouth" but has been scored out.
[83] Horace, *Carmen.* I. viii. 1–2.

and from England! Many thanks for telling me step by step all
your progress. But not another word of "A Life's Morning"!

Ever yours,

GEORGE GISSING

Addressed: Herrn Eduard Bertz. / Holzmarkt Strasse, 18. /
Potsdam. / *Germania.*
Via Margutta, 59. / Roma.

December 22nd. 1888

Heartiest congratulations! Did I not always foretell that some
day you would find a sphere of activity?[84] Glorious that you should
be progressing just when I too am growing most in health both
of body and mind.

I hope you got my long letter, some ten days ago. I shall soon
have much more to tell you.

On the 30th. I depart for Florence. I hope to have a month
there, and then a month in Venice, or perhaps six week in
Florence and two in Venice. Am over head and ears in painting
and sculpture. Great Heavens! The Museum at the Vatican!

It will not be safe to post to me after the 26th.

Again I rejoice at the news you send!

G. G.

Casa Nardini. / 17 Borgo SS. Apostoli. / Firenze.

January 3rd. 1889.

Dear Friend,

Yes, it is Italy still, but it is not the Italy of the South. The
views from all the heights around Florence are indescribably
lovely, and could not have been better seen than in these last
days of brilliant sunshine. The Uffizi and the Pitti are glorious,

---

[84] "Printed form from Bertz, announcing his election as Secretary of the
Deutsche [*sic*] Schriftsteller-Verband" (Diary, 22 December 1888). GRG
wrote Algernon that, "Poor old Bertz seems at last to have got his foot on
firmer ground. He has been elected Secretary (hony.) of the German Society
of Authors, and appears to have got into the thick of active journalistic
life; there is talk of giving him an editorship, etc. I confess I had given up
all hope of such things for him" (2 January 1889, Yale).

and the many churches are full of interest. But it is not Rome; it is not the bay of Pozzuoli; it is not divine Paestum, and Salerno and Capri. I have been taught in these days how intensely classical are my sympathies; if indeed I needed the lesson. Amidst the most splendid artistic work of the Renaissance, I felt a heart-ache for the Forum Romanum, and for the passionate beauty of the southern sea. At present there is but one word in my mind, and that is "Sicily!" The very next holiday I can take, I go to Sicily.[85] There one has both Greece and Rome. In Sicily, with Thucydides and Theocritus in my hands, I shall reach the supreme earthly happiness. Day after day I lament that I could not take ship from Naples for Messina. I might have done it; but it was wiser to see the north, this time. But Sicily, Sicily!

I have so much to tell you that I know not where to begin. A word or two of modern Rome. It is detestable! To live in modern Rome, at present, is to occupy a house which is in the hands of the builders and upholsterers. Not a street where there is not building and pulling-down. The whole effect is one of raggedness and dirt. The newest buildings are inconceivably ugly—even as they are in Naples; great barracks, very much like the model lodging-houses of the East-end of London! All the open fields between the Campus Martius and the Castle of St. Angelo are being built over in that style. The shores of the Tiber are squalid with ruin. It is all necessary, I doubt not; but a most regrettable necessity. Not only is modern Rome the least picturesque city in Italy, but, I should think, almost the least picturesque in the world.

Never mind; the old Rome still remains. The longer I stayed, the more passionate delight did I take in the Forum and the Palatine and the Colosseum and the Via Appia, and a hundred other glorious scenes. Did I tell you of the long walk I had along the Via Appia? I think not. The old road has now been cleared right away to the Alban Hills; in many places the paving remains, with the old wheel-ruts, though I very much doubt whether it be the Roman paving; it looks much more like medieval work. Far away on the Campagna, I sat down to eat my lunch on the tomb of somebody whose name is forgotten. And close by was another

---

[85] He never visited Sicily; his next holiday was spent in Greece.

tomb of which nearly all the inscription was legible. A delightful
inscription; I copy it for you: "Hoc est factum Monumentum
Maarco Caecilio. Hospes, gratum est quom apud meas . . . seedes.
Bene rem geras, et valeas; dormias sine cura." You notice the
very old spelling. The word after *meas* I could not read, but it is
easy to supply.[86]

I stop to say how impossible it is for me to give you anything
like even an abstract of my Roman diary.[87] When shall I see and
speak with you? Only then can I hope to tell you a tithe of what
I have learnt in Italy. I am ashamed to write these scrappy letters;
they seem to indicate such poverty of mind. I implore you not to
think that I tell you all I have to tell. It is mere lack of time and
weariness of hand that compel me to close my letters.

Of the regions round Rome I could see very little, partly because
I had not time, partly because I wished to spend my money on
other things. But one day I took a walk of 24 miles, for the sake
of visiting the site of *Veii*. Yes, I have been at *Veii*! It is a
desolate spot, right out on the Campagna, and no one would
suspect that ever a great city stood there. The height which is
believed to have been the Acropolis (the Arx) is occupied by a
poor village called Isola Farnese; in the middle ages it was a
strongly fortified position. There I found a guide who led me
to see what he called "la Grotta," that is to say, the Etruscan
tomb, which is almost the only relic of Veii. It was a laborious
walk that he took me, up and down hill, through swamps, over
fields full of splendid long-horned cattle, and at last he unlocked
a wooden door on a hillside, and then, having lighted a candle,
asked me to enter the tomb. It was only discovered in 1843, and the
interior has been left just as it was found. There are grotesque
paintings on the stone walls, and there are a number of very large
Etruscan vases. I brought away a piece of the travertine, a piece

[86] "An inscription I copied: on left hand of road, just after (or before) the
huge skeleton pyramid with mushroom base. The second word in 3rd line
I can't understand, though I copy the letters exactly" (Diary, 17 December
1888). GRG sent a translation to his sister Margaret: "This monument is
erected to Marcus Caecilius. Stranger, I am grateful when you sit down by
my resting-place. May you prosper in business and health, and may your
sleep be without care!" (*Letters*, 17 December 1888, p. 262).

[87] Simply entries in his ordinary Diary.

of stone that had never yet seen the light of day since the beginning of the world!

A desolate prospect! The background formed by the Sabine Hills, the highest of them Monte Gennaro, which is believed to be Mons Lucretilis. To the North the jagged form of Soracte. Far away in the south, the sweet forms of the Alban Hills. All around the indescribably dreary Campagna, its colour a sad brown. The shepherds who spend their days on it are wrapped in undressed skins of sheep and goats, which gives them a strange appearance. Besides the tomb, there remain one or two pieces of ruined building, and a wonderful tunnelled bridge over what we call the Crimera, and that is all.

Another day, I walked to the Pons Milvius (you know it well,) and thence along the Tiber to the site of Antemnae. But of Antemnae not one stone remains! Thence I walked on to the Mons Sacer.

How can I tell you of such things? We ought to have our long Tottenham evenings over again.[88] It is no use. One thing that constantly delighted me in walking about the outskirts of Rome was the sight of the teams of oxen. They are magnificent beasts, with glorious horns. They always reminded me of antique statuary, and indeed their slow dignified movement is strongly suggestive of sculpture. Such oxen as these did Homer see, and Vergil. I never passed a team without stopping to look at them in absolute delight. They are stilled [sic] yoked with the old juga, precisely.

When I last wrote to you, I had not ventured to go to the Vatican. Ah, how many days I have since spent there! On the right hand of the façade of S. Peter's, under Bernini's magnificent colonnade, is the entrance to the palace. Thence you go up Bernini's Scala Regia, and at last, on a small staircase, you find yourself before a little green door, on which hangs a placard, inscribed "Cappella Sistina!" There you knock, and the Custode admits you. I studied it with much thoroughness, making plans of the ceiling and the walls. No description has ever done justice to Michelangelo's work. It is beyond all description; one can

[88] When Bertz lived in Tottenham, GRG visited him twice a week: "It is a walk of some six miles. I get there at 6:30 in the evening, remain chatting till 10:30 and catch an 11 train back into town" (*Letters*, pp. 63–4).

only sit there in awe, humbly trying to grasp a little of his mighty intention.

And in this place let me say how exasperating it is to see the kind of people who constitute the mass of foreign visitors to Rome. As sure as ever the English language fell on my ear, so surely did I hear words of ignorance or vulgarity! Impossible to describe the vulgarity of most of these people. Many of them are absolute shop-boys and work-girls. How in heaven's name do they get enough money to come here? And where are the good cultured people? And how it enrages one to think of the numbers of those who *could* make noble use of this opportunity, if only it were granted them. Every day I saw people whom I should like to have assaulted. What business have these gross animals in such places? [89]

On the floor above the Sistina are the Stanze and Loggia of Raphael. Must I confess to you that Raphael has not greatly delighted me? Well, the one exception is the Loggia, where the ceiling is painted with some forty pictures of Bible history. These little pictures (for they are quite small) are exquisite beyond expression. I will copy a passage from my diary. "These pictures fill me with keenest joy. The clear colouring, the sweet, idyllic treatment, the exquisite landscape, are like so many delicious notes of music. It is the Bible made into a fairy-tale of the most touching kind. Especially that lovely picture of Jacob, with his flocks, meeting Rachel and Leah at the well. What a sweet and gentle idealism is here! The whole story becomes a pastoral; everything harsh is omitted; every severity of doctrine has vanished. We are in the land of eastern fable, and never again will eastern fable be so illustrated." [90]

[89] As he grew older, GRG repudiated these harsh, snobbish judgments: "Foolishly arrogant as I was, I used to judge the worth of a person by his intellectual power and attainment. I could see no good where there was no logic, no charm where there was no learning. Now I think that one has to distinguish between the two forms of intelligence, that of the brain, and that of the heart, and I have come to regard the second as by far the more important" (*The Private Papers of Henry Ryecroft*, "Spring," Chap. XVI, p. 48).

[90] GRG does not quote exactly from his Diary. The original reads: "They fill me with keenest joy. The clear colouring, the sweet, idyllic treatment, the exquisite landscape; it is the Bible made into a fairy-tale of the most touching kind. That lovely picture of Jacob with his flocks meeting Rachel

The Vatican is huge. Having seen the Cappella and the floor above, and having gone up yet another story, to the picture gallery, where are some 50 chef-d'oeuvres, (the Transfiguration among them,)[91] you have to descend again, and, in order to reach the Museum of Sculpture, walk *all round* S. Peter's, a mile or more! Well, I love painting, and of late I have studied it laboriously, but I love sculpture still more. I cannot give you an idea of the rapture with which I walked about these immense and magnificent galleries, crammed with Greek and Roman work. A few things I studied for hours, making many notes.

Especially the Sala Rotonda. In the centre is a gigantic vase of porphyry, and all round are busts alternating with statues. There is the Adonis as Bacchus, the Juno Barberini, the gilt-bronze Hercules, and others. But the busts. There are two of Zeus; the one, that which is believed to be the Zeus of Pheidias (called Jupiter of Otricoli,) and the other a Jupiter Serapis. Here I copy again from my diary: "The Jupiter of Otricoli is the more majestic; the latter is remarkable for a divine placidity. The former has one deep line across his forehead; one might almost attribute to him something of the care of rule, or something of pity for mankind. The Serapis is above care of all kinds: a sublime and passionless reverie possesses him: the face is unutterably bland."[92]

And in the same Sala Rotonda are three busts of Roman Empresses to which I gave close attention. These are (1) Julia Domna, the wife of Septimius Severus; (2) Plotina, the wife of Trajan, and (3) the elder Faustina, wife of Antoninus Pius. All are magnificent busts, and representing very different women. Julia Domna is the most pleasing; it is a notably Patrician face; about the fine lips there is a touch of idle scorn and pride, yet not ill-natured. Of rather slow understanding, one would say; a woman to humour and to be friends with. She would take her dignity as a matter of course, but might easily fall below it. Plotina is anything but beautiful and scarcely even Patrician; and yet one sees that

---

and Leah at the well. Those that have suffered most of damp are naturally the squares on the *outer* side all along. But most are nobly preserved, the colours gem-like in their freshness. What a sweet and gentle idealism there is here!" (11 December 1888).

[91] By Raphael.

[92] The excerpt is an exact quotation (Diary, 12 December 1888).

the bust is idealized, for all that. Very heavy features, high cheek-bones, big mouth and chin. A dull, homely woman, but conscientious; there is even a touch of anxiety on her forehead. She looks like a careful housewife, and one to be trusted in small things and great. Faustina is an intensely aristocratic type of beauty. The good-nature of Julia is here lacking; on her lips and forehead is a cold pride. She has a splendid coronet of woven hair. A woman to be afraid of, unsubduable.

(By the bye, I have forgotten all about Julia Domna and Plotina, as historical characters. Perhaps you will laugh at my interpretation of their faces.)[93]

Greatly also was I delighted with the statues of the Muses in the next hall, the Sala delle Muse. And especially I studied the two, Thalia and Melpomene. At first sight it is startling to observe how little difference there is between these faces of Comedy and Tragedy. The thoughtless observer expects a radical distinction from the first moment. But the old sculptors knew better. Thalia is crowned with ivy, Melpomene with vine. The face of the latter is stamped with silent pain. Thalia, a sweet and noble face, shows a weary sadness; she has deep, far-looking eyes. And is not this the true genius of Comedy, in the Attic and noble sense? But her face is extremely subtle. Though I must have looked at it for two or three hours altogether, I cannot now recall it as distinctly as that of Melpomene.

Eheu, jam satis!

The most interesting thing that I saw in Christian Rome was at the church of Ara Coeli, the church on the Capitol, where Gibbon tells us that he first conceived the idea of writing his history.[94]

From Christmas onwards, the second chapel in the left aisle was fitted up as a stage, with a scenical representation of the infant Christ adored by the shepherds and the Magi. The scene is most elaborate. The figures are of wood; life size; there are sheep and

[93] The character impressions are historically accurate.

[94] "It was at Rome on the 15th of October, 1764, as I sat musing amidst the ruins of the Capitol, while the barefooted friars were singing vespers in the temple of Jupiter, that the idea of writing the decline and fall of the city first started to my mind" (Edward Gibbon, *The History of the Decline and Fall of the Roman Empire*, ed. by Milman, Guizot, and Smith [London, 1925], I, pp. 85–6).

cattle in front. The Madonna holds on her lap the old wooden *Bambino* which is the chief treasure of Ara Coeli, an image supposed to work miracles, which is frequently carried solemnly to the houses of sick people; it is crowned with gold, and thickly studded with precious stones. Up above are clouds and angels and the *Padre Eterno*, and all is artistically illuminated from behind.

Now, opposite the chapel is raised a little platform, and on this platform, each day from 3 o'clock to 5, the most astonishing displays took place. Little children, almost all girls, and aged from 5 to 10, delivered recitations, in prose or verse, descriptive of the birth of Christ and all that followed. They were the children of contadini,[95] and poor townspeople, and were much dressed up for the occasion. A very few showed shyness, and their mothers with difficulty coaxed them into reciting, but for the most part these little creatures had an astonishing self-confidence. They began and ended with a bow, and their recitation generally closed with a prayer, spoken kneeling. The verses were generally in short lines of four trochees, ($\underline{\iota}\cup|\underline{\iota}\cup|\underline{\iota}\cup|\underline{\iota}\cup$) and of course very simply worded. But the mere act of memory was noteworthy, for sometimes the recitation took a whole TEN minutes, and as for the marvellous delivery, I can give you no idea of it. No English child could possibly do such a thing. In one case there was a little play acted. Two little girls acted the parts of shepherds; one began by pretending to be asleep, and was awoke by the other, who had seen the wonderful star, and heard angels singing etc. It was intensely amusing.

On three evenings I was attracted to this spectacle. One time I heard an extraordinary polemical sermon delivered by a girl of about 10 or 11. It was a justification of religion against modern disbelief. One period began: "O congiurati filosofanti!" (Comical enough in the mouth of this child.) Then she recited a list of evidences of God's power, beginning: "E tace Dio? Dio non tace; favella!" Finally she knelt, and prayed to the stage opposite: "Bambinello santissimo, che tua benedizione scenda su tutti, e principalmente su miei genitori e parenti!"[96] And so on! A great

[95] "Peasants."

[96] "O philosophizing conspirators! Is God silent? He does not remain silent; he speaks.... Most Sacred Infant, may your blessing descend upon every one and particularly upon my parents and relatives."

crowd listened to her, and at the end shouted "Brava! Brava!"
I may mention that the recitations went on without interruption,
even when Vespers were being sung at the other end of the
church.[97]

The journey hither was enjoyable, for I had the first part of it
in delight. About 20 minutes after quitting Rome, I had a
wonderful sight. The city had entirely disappeared, but there on
the far horizon, standing boldly against the sky, was a great dome,
the Dome of S. Peter's. How impressive it must be for those who
enter Rome for the first time by this line.

One thing enraged me. Just after we passed Chiusi, it began to
be dark. An hour after that, I heard a strange rumbling sound,
as if we were passing over a viaduct. And what do you think it
was? WE WERE GOING ALL ALONG THE SHORE OF
LAKE TRASIMENUS![98] And I could not see anything of it.
Alas, alas! I would have given a sovereign for daylight.

And now I must cease. This letter is all about myself, but you
know already how I rejoice in your activity—the activity which
I have always foreseen. I look forward to the day when we shall
again see each other.

I hope to remain here until the end of the month, at all events.
A line from you before long, I hope.

Ever yours,

GEORGE GISSING

Extraordinary, that Hamel[99] should so have turned up!
Capital, his being present at your election! I am delighted with
your accounts of the interesting acquaintances you have made.

17 Borgo SS. Apostoli. / Firenze.

January 20th. 1889.

Dear Friend,

It occurs to me that you might like a few rough remarks on

[97] Cf. GRG, "Christmas on the Capitol," published in the Bolton *Evening
News*, December 1889.

[98] Where Hannibal conquered the Romans in 217 B.C.

[99] Richard Otto Hamel (1835–19?), teacher, poet, and drama critic. He
and Bertz had been friends in the German Social Democrat organization,
but after the party was outlawed, Hamel denounced it and supported
Bismarck while Bertz chose exile.

Italy from the political and social points of view, now that I have been here long enough to form judgments about certain obvious aspects of the country thus considered. Of course my opportunities of observation are very limited, but I read the newspapers regularly, and keep my eyes and ears open.

But, first of all, I trust you did me [sic] not think me too abrupt in declining your offer of introduction to Frau Kurz.[100] No, I think you would credit me with sincerity. My reasons were absolutely valid. I should not do justice to myself in private society, owing, partly to my lack of practice in speaking German, but still more to my insufficient means. The Kurz's [sic] coud [sic] not possibility [sic] have presented me to any friends: I am not respectable enough in appearance. I should merely have embarrassed them, and discredited you. No doubt I shall hear from you that you understand all this.

Well now, I like the Italians, emphatically. I like them infinitely better than the French. Their faults are many and manifest; very bad ones, indeed, for they are the *vices of poverty*, and you know my opinion on *that* subject. They will cheat you unscrupulously; they will tell lies; they will abuse you behind your back if you do not give them all they expect from you. But, on the other hand, they are very easily satisfied, and *when* satisfied, are exquisitely courteous, charmingly urbane. Among themselves, they are delightful; it is a joy to watch a party of decent young Italians eating together, for example, or to go and sit in the *caffé* of an evening, or to walk among them in their parks and public gardens. To-day, for instance, I have spent a couple of hours, in the *Cascine*, which is the Bois de Boulogne, or Hyde Park of Florence. What strikes an Englishman first of all is the utter absence of anything resembling English rowdyism, whether male or female. It was the same in Rome, though scarcely, I fear, in Naples. Nowhere a giggling shopgirl; nowhere a young fellow behaving like a fool or blackguard. In dress, there is really good taste; in manners, a delightful courtesy and suavity. And one is impressed by the domesticity of the people. Here in Florence is a large *brasserie*, called Cornelio's, where great numbers of people

---

[100] Possibly the wife of Dr. Kurz, a German physician resident in Florence, who was the son of Hermann Kurtz (1813–1873), a novelist and anthologist.

go of an evening to drink, and smoke, and listen to a band. Now in England or France no decent woman would be able to go to a place of this kind. Here, on the other hand, it is the rule to see, not only respectable women, but whole family parties. The *bambini* are present in strong force: indeed the Italians are great bambino-worshippers. There they all sit together, and enjoy themselves in the most human ways. Everyone who enters, salutes gravely; also on departing. In England such places are sacred to strong liquors; here it is generally coffee that is drunk. And, by the bye, I may say that ever since I came to Italy I have not seen one drunken man, not one.

The girls and women of the labouring classes make no vulgar attempt to resemble in dress and manners those above them. A simple line of distinction is drawn by the fact that they go about bare-headed, at all times. This morning I was in the Uffizi Gallery, and noticed with much interest the numbers of low-class girls. They are fat-faced and ruddy-cheeked, cheerful but never noisy, and they come to the gallery because it is a *festa* and they really find pleasure in looking at the pictures. It was the same in Rome. In Naples I fancy the *people* care much less about art. There, their one delight is to make as much uproar as possible. Not seldom I found them insolent, and, it seemed to me, ungenerous, ignoble, malicious. On the other hand the peasant people of the South are kindly. Avaricious, of course, but very kindly.

For the first time I have felt well disposed towards soldiers. The Italians [*sic*] officers are, in appearance and manners, splendid fellows. At the restaurants in Naples I used to laugh with pleasure when I saw them come in with their clanking swords and sweeping cloaks. I made the acquaintance of one in Capri, and he did not disappoint me. The Italian officials, too, are almost invariably polite and more than polite. A Frenchman in office is generally a detestable creature, impossible to be dealt with.

And an Italian *crowd* is beyond all doubt superior to a French one. I shall never forget how disgusted I was one Sunday—a fête— in wandering among a crowd on the Place du Carrousel. The men were ignoble; the women were mostly disagreeable. I never have such impressions here. Certainly they have vile habits, for instance, that of *spitting* perpetually and in every place, in churches, in libraries, in trattorie, everywhere. But they are not essentially ignoble, and that, I sadly fear, the French really are becoming. It seems that the Italians are not so musical as they used to be. It is very rarely that one hears music in the streets, and very poor whenever there is any. In Naples, it is true, the street-organs were numberless, but since leaving Naples *I have not heard one*. I regret this, bitterly. My whole life is brightened by a little music, however poor.

The newspapers are miserable—with two exceptions. The only papers which I can read with any kind of satisfaction are the *Secolo* of Milan, and the *Corriere di Napoli*. The latter is by far the better of the two; indeed I think it rivals all but the best of the French. I get it here every day. It is publishing at present a story of Neapolitan life, called "Il Paese di Cuccagna," which is just of the kind to appeal to me. And the amusing style of these Italian journalists! The ludicrous exaggerations of language! You have heard perhaps that old Gladstone is at Naples.[101] Well, the *Corriere* has something about him every day, and always in a strain of delicious hyperbole. At Pompeii the other day he was offered a cup of tea, and he accepted it "con squisitissima affabilità"![102] But this is a trifling example.

Throughout Italy, the feeling against France is one of extreme bitterness.[103] Some of the newspapers—the *Corriere* in especial—do their very best to make things still worse and to incite the people to war. Proportionately, they are enthusiastic for Germany and all things German. Of England little is said, though the country and her affairs are always mentioned with excessive respect, but of Germany I am always reading. Here, to-day, for instance, is an article on "Bismarck and Richter,"[104] very interesting. In certain places I have been accustomed to represent myself as a German, simply because I knew I should have a better reception—and be charged less, to boot, than if I declared my nationality.

But the country is almost bankrupt. The financial difficulties of the government grow every day more serious. They are rendered

---

[101] Gladstone arrived in Italy in December 1888 and stayed in a villa at Posillipo until 8 February 1889.

[102] "With the most exquisite affability."

[103] France, apprehensive over the Triple Alliance, was trying to force Italy out of the coalition.

[104] Eugen Richter (1838–1907) led the German Liberal Party's fight against Bismarck's conservative policies.

worse by the fact that, in every town, the expenses of public administration are perpetually increasing. In Naples they are spending some millions of francs every year on what they call "la sventramento," that is the "disembowelling" of the city, the destruction of all the unhealthy quarters and the making of vast new roads. Naples will be no longer the Naples of old very shortly. Then in Rome, the process of material change is extraordinarily rapid. Yet another Rome is perishing, the Rome of Papal christianity [sic]. In every street there is pulling down and building up. The *prati del Castello*, which till recently made a great open space between the most modern part of the City and the Vatican, are now being quickly covered with huge houses, the biggest and ugliest that can be built. Amid all this, it is most significant that the *Sindaco* had to publish, at Christmas, a proclamation, stating that a great number of buildings were standing in an unfinished state, *with the work suspended*, and admonishing the contractors that they must at once remove the scaffolding, which was an inconvenience and a danger to the public!

In fact, the Italians are mad for material progress, and are going ahead beyond their means. *Mad* in many senses. Great heavens, in a lecture before the British Archaeological Society at Rome the other evening, a certain Italian official stated that the municipality of Rome is about *to build an iron bridge right over the Forum*!!! Whereupon "una esclamazione di meraviglia dolorosa è scoppiata unanime in tutta la sala!"[105] I should think so, indeed.

I am afraid the glory of Italy is gone for ever. She is trying to rival Germany and England, and will ruin all the best part of herself in the process.

Magnificent days, these last three. Yesterday I sat for several hours by the side of the Arno, reading, in glorious sunshine. And I gathered some beautiful flowers that had just come out. But before this outburst of fine weather it was bitterly cold and very gloomy.

On the 29th. I leave here. Perhaps I shall stop a day in Bologna. I have already—guided by Baedeker—written for a room in

[105] "A general exclamation of painful surprise broke forth at the same time in the entire hall."

Venice, and my address there will be: / Palazzo Swift. / Canal Grande. / S. Maria del Giglio, 2467. Don't think I have gone mad, in reading the number. It is literally correct.

I have just corrected the first half volume of "The Nether World." This time I will tell you honestly that I believe the work to be good. It is to be pub[lished] in March. I shall be desperately eager for your opinion.

A line when you are able. But I am ashamed to ask it, for you are terribly overworked. And for Heaven's sake, let me have your articles as soon as you can.

Roberts is doing "art criticism" for the Scottish Review.[106]

Ever yours,
GEORGE GISSING

Addressed: Herrn Eduard Bertz. / Holzmarkt Strasse, 18. / Potsdam. / *Germania.*
Firenze.

[January 25, 1889][107]

Much grieved by your letter. I knew you were doing too much, and I dreaded the reaction.[108] Steadily, quietly and persistently! I will write again as soon as possible. I suppose you received my letter just after posting your own.

I leave here on the 29th., and shall pass a night in Bologna. My address in Venice will be: / Palazzo Swift / Canal Grande. / S. Maria del Giglio, 2467. / Don't think I have gone mad; that is really the number.

Am correcting the proofs of "Nether World." Hope they will be done before I leave for England. Cheer up, and work less violently. Nothing is lost, only you have fallen into one of your fits of depression.

G. G.

[106] There are no "art" criticisms in this magazine, but the allusion might be to the unsigned reviews of the French periodical *L'Art,* which were regularly included in the summaries of foreign periodicals.

[107] Postmark.

[108] See 1 February 1889.

Addressed: Herrn Eduard Bertz. / Holzmarkt Strasse, 18. /
Potsdam. / *Germania.*
Palazzo Swift. / S. Maria del Giglio 2467. / Venezia.

Genn[aio] 30. 1889.

[109]Arrivato e gia stabilito! Sono venuto in gondola dalla stazione.
Ieri ho notteggiato a Bologna. Scrivo queste righe in un caffè sulla
piazza S. Marco.
Che pensi del Boulanger?[110] Diavolo!

Sursum corda, amice!
G. G.

Addressed: Herrn Eduard Bertz. / Holzmarkt Strasse 18. /
Potsdam. / *Germania.*
Venezia.

February 1. [1889]

Hearty thanks for your instrumentality in matter of "Demos."
Have just written to Frau Steinitz.[111] Yes, S[mith] and E[lder]
themselves told Mlle. Le Breton that the book was *domaine public.*
Yesterday a fine warm day. I lunched in the open air on the
Piazza San Marco. My window looks *directly* onto the Canal
Grande, and, as I write, I hear the splashing of the gondoliers'
oars. A marvellous place! How you would enjoy the intense
quietness!
I do hope you will be able to get into the country before long;
evidently this experience of headaches is decisive. You must think
it over seriously before summer comes.

[109] "Arrived and already settled in! I came in a gondola from the station.
I spent last night in Bologna. I write these lines in a café in St. Mark's
Square.
What do you think of Boulanger? The devil!"
[110] George Boulanger (1837–1891), a general in the French army, had
been deprived of his command in 1888 by the French government, which
feared his Radical Republican ambitions. On 27 January 1889, he won an
important political victory in Paris and threatened to seize control of the
country.
[111] Clara Klausner Steinitz (1852–?), wife of Berlin publisher Heinrich
Steinitz, had agreed to Bertz's suggestion that she translate *Demos.* The
translation appeared in "Ottmanns Bücherschatz-Bibliothek" (Leipzig) in
1891.

Ce diable de Boulanger! Du moins, c'est intéressant.

G. G.

Shall certainly hope to see Jacobsen's[112] work.

Palazzo Swift. / S. Maria del Giglio, 2467. / Venezia.

February 13th. 1889.

Dear Friend,

At the present moment it is hard to believe that I am not on board ship in the middle of the sea. All last night a gale was blowing; the Canal Grande became quite rough, and lashed with roaring waves against the houses. Things are but little better this morning. Sea-gulls are screaming about in front of my window, and if I look out, I see the gondolas with difficulty struggling against the foaming water. The tide is so high that it has swamped the *cortile* of our house; the Piazzo di San Marco is half under water, untraversable. If it were not for those long narrow islands, with their vast barriers of stone-work, Venice would long since have perished in some severe storm; one only recognizes the danger when one sees weather such as this.

But first of all I must tell you about my journey hither. I am glad I broke it at Bologna, and so had both parts in the daytime, for the scenery was interesting all along. Not long after leaving Florence, the railway begins the ascent of the Apennines; it follows a rising pass, and reaches the highest point at a place called Pracchia. Up to there, you pass through 22 tunnels. When the descent begins, the line goes along the valley of the Reno, which for many miles is a wild narrow gorge. The mountain streams were all frozen, and made dazzling streaks down the precipices. From Pracchia to Pistoia there are 23 tunnels, some very long: so that we had 45 in all! All the way there are little villages— strange *conglomerates* of houses, built as if to support each other against the terrible winds. On the mountains was much snow.

Bologna makes a strange impression. The narrow streets are

---

[112] Jens Peter Jacobsen (1847–1885), Danish poet and naturalistic novelist. Bertz wanted GRG to read Jacobsen's *Niels Lyhne* (1880), which had been translated into German (1888) by M. von Borch. The novel deals with the social problems of a young atheist.

made yet narrower and darker by being arcaded on both sides. Here no one need ever carry an umbrella. The architecture seems at first grotesque, if not ugly. Certainly the great square leaning tower (it leans frightfully) is a monstrosity; by its side is another square tower, greatly higher, which also has an appreciable inclination. The place may well be called *grassa*;[113] such shop-windows I never saw, such gigantic sausages, such butter and cheese and pastry! And the life of the streets is uproarious. At night there were concerts going on in nearly all the cafés. I enjoyed myself greatly.

The next morning I had just time to look in at the Accademia and see Raphael's S. Cecilia—a divine picture. A serviceable custodian also pointed out to me certain good works of the Bolognese school. By chance we spoke of Titian's "Death of Peter Martyr," which was burnt in Venice in 1867, and he told me that there are grave doubts as to whether the picture was burnt at all. It happened to be placed temporarily in the chapel which was destroyed by fire. But I suppose this story is nonsense.[114]

That day's journey was interesting in its extreme dreariness. Not a hillock until we came to the odd pyramidal volcanic mountains at Padova. We crossed the Po, a vast muddy river, considerably above the level of the plain. All day there was no sunshine. Miles upon miles of vineyards and rice-plantations. Ferrara and Padova are distant from their stations; I had only melancholy views of towers and chimneys. Then came the approach to Venice. It happened to be low tide, and the long bridge which goes over the lagoon appeared to stretch over an infinite waste of sands and seaweed. It is a bridge of stone, with very low arches. As I stepped from the landing-stage at the station into a gondola, it began to rain. But the strangeness of this mode of traversing a town was most enjoyable.

I had been led to believe that the existence of the gondolas was threatened by steamboats. This is all nonsense. It is only on the Canal Grande that steamers ply, or by any possibility *could* ply. The gondola is no more likely to perish than are the cabs of London. And to watch the gondoliers is a constant delight, so

[113] "Fat."
[114] The picture was burned; a copy, painted by Cardi da Cigola, has been hung in its place.

marvellous is their skill and the gracefulness of their attitudes. My window looks immediately onto the Canal, so that I can watch the scene at my ease.

The difficulty of finding one's way about is extreme, as you may imagine. Of the 358 canals, very many have no sidewalk, and, except in one or two instances, your way has to be *wriggled*, in and out, among the most confusing labyrinth of streets which, for the most part, will not admit more than three people abreast; in many of them, *two* people with difficulty pass each other. Baedeker's map is excellent, but, even with this, I can scarcely follow a certain direction unless I have previously *marked* the track in *ink*; otherwise the network of *calli* is too puzzling to the eyes. Of course well-to-do people never walk any distance, but always take a gondola.

It is unfortunate that the Piazza of S. Mark is in confusion, owing to drainage-works. Moreover, the Basilica and the Palazzo Ducale are both scaffolded in several parts, owing to those restaurations [*sic*] which drive Ruskin mad. Still, the spot is unique. On my first view of S. Mark's, with its five domes and its gleaming mosaics, I felt very strongly how oriental it all was. (It seems to me, too, that the prevalent type of face is distinctly oriental). The sunny side of the Piazza is crowded in the later hours of the day. The numerous cafés put out a great number of tables, and there people take their drinks joyously in the open air. A good band plays, several afternoons in the week.

Again I notice the democratic character of Italian society. Here promenade, side by side, the gentleman and the gondolier, the lady and the girl who makes wax-matches. There is no feeling in the poor people that they are out of place. And it is the more remarkable in the case of women, seeing that here the work girls have a distinct costume; they are, of course, bare-headed, and wear invariably a long shawl, which reaches the ground, generally of grey colour. Heavens! The beautiful faces that I pass every hour. They are magnificent, these Venetian work-girls! And for the most part in robust health, with red cheeks and bright eyes. Decidedly I observe more beauty here than in the other towns. They walk with much dignity; I never see them frisking about, or laughing noisily. In figure and motion, they correspond to the gondoliers, who are often splendid fellows. On the Riva degli

Schiavoni (the chief quay, and always crowded) I pass men whose heads would be magnificent on canvas.

A word or two concerning the dialect. In its pure form it is unintelligible to me; in the case of people slightly educated, it becomes a question chiefly of peculiar pronunciation. E.g: *Pesce* is pronounced *pesse*, and so with the soft *sc* always. *Piazza* becomes *piassa*, and *mezzo* is pronounced like the zz in English. Even the soft *c* becomes an *s*; they say *mi dispiasse*, for *mi dispiace*. The place *Chiaggia* becomes *Chiozza*. Gondola is *gundola*, and so on.

Each evening I have a rare treat.[115] Shortly before eight o'clock, I look out of my window. Dark below me, and dark in either direction, are the waters of the Canal; opposite rise the domes and campanile of the great church of Maria della Salute; it is just silvered by the new moon, as are also the roofs of the houses. The silence would be absolute, but that now and then comes the soft splash of a gondolier's oar, as a boat moves past with the little light on its prow. At eight o'clock booms the gun from San Giorgio Maggiore, an island close by; it makes the windows shake, and intensifies the stillness that follows. But now, looking in the direction of S. Marco, I see a gondola with four red lamps coming this way. It moors just in front of a palace on our side of the Canal; then there is the sound of musical instruments, and, a moment after, a chorus of singing voices—generally the song is "Addio, bella Napoli"—breaks forth. When this is finished, there is again a soft prelude, and all at once I hear an exquisite woman's voice, singing alone. Such a voice, I assure you, as I have only heard in great concert-halls; a glorious soprano. And the concert lasts for about a quarter of an hour. Then the four red lamps move silently away—towards the Adriatic.

February 14th.

In severe weather the suffering among poor people here (and indeed all over Italy) must be extreme. Fires they have none. You see women going about with little earthenware pots, containing glowing charcoal or wood-ashes, just to render their hands capable of work. Everything—in house and street—is constructed to obtain coolness, and therefore in winter the cold is worse than it need

[115] Cf. *Letters*, pp. 275-76, for a slightly different version of the event described here.

be for the inhabitants of these towns. I myself have suffered intolerably; indeed cold becomes more and more insupportable to me. And yet I have a great stove to take refuge before. The night before last, when the storm was raging, a number of workpeople were unable to return to their homes in Venice from the workshops on the island of Murano, and, as accommodation was entirely lacking, they lay all night in sheds and work-places, returning ill to Venice next day.

I hope I shall never come to Italy again in the winter. It is not the Italy of the other nine months of the year, only the skeleton remains. You cannot see things in the open air, for the biting wind; you cannot spend time in galleries and churches, for they are like ice-cellars. My month at Florence was all but wasted, owing to the bitter weather. At my beloved Naples I just had the end of autumn to enjoy. No, it must not be winter next time.

You have heard of the pigeons of the Piazza di S. Marco. They are always an interesting sight, but especially so when they are being fed. In the Piazza you can buy little packets of grain; as soon as you begin to scatter this, you are overwhelmed with a rush of hundreds of birds. Not only do they envelope you, but they even perch in numbers upon your hands and arm. Very pretty to see girls thus surrounded with pigeons.

Another sight I have witnessed in the Piazza. At the foot of the great Campanile takes place every Saturday the public drawing of the lottery, and it is a contemptible sight. For one thing, just think of the profanation of this magnificent building! That lottery business is the curse of the country. It is very difficult to understand how grave politicians, responsible for the welfare of their country, can deliberately foster such a scheme. I am glad to have beheld the ridiculous business, for it characterizes unforgettably the Italians' present state of civilization.

Apropos of that, how amusing it is to compare the state of mind of Gladstone with regard to modern Italy, with that of Ruskin. In his recent visit to Naples, Gladstone could not speak highly enough of the "progress" he everywhere beheld. Ruskin, on the other hand, never ceases to lament that Italy has sunk beneath contempt, and that day by day all her treasures are perishing through the bestial ignorance of their custodians. An interesting contrast between two kinds of intellect.

Despite the fact that Italy is on the point of national bankruptcy, (the deficit in the budget for the present year is *192 millions* of francs,) there can of course be no doubt as to her great *material* progress. Typical of it, for instance, is an immense cotton mill which I have to-day seen in a remote part of Venice,— I thought myself in Lancashire. But one can scarcely hope that this progress will permit the preservation of those things which have always made Italy interesting. The sky and the hills will remain, perforce, but in the next century, the Italy of antiquity and of the Renaissance will assuredly be only a tradition, supported by the evidence of a few museums and much-restored buildings. Italy has no art and no literature;[116] no signs of either coming. It is a law of nature that is being fulfilled; the great struggle needed to raise her from the abyss of the 18th. and early 19th. centuries does not leave any force *disponible* for purely intellect [*sic*] progress. For a long time she will pursue with rage a material prosperity. Her exemplar is the vulgar side of England. The Italians all wear English clothing, I mean the educated; and this typifies their general state of mind.

But there was one other little thing I wished to mention, to illustrate the prevalent spirit of gambling. I dine at a 3rd. class *trattoria*, and thus see a good deal of the habits of the people. Every evening there comes in a man with a basket of pastry. He does not sell his wares in the ordinary way, but proceeds thus. He offers to the customer a bag of marbles, all inscribed with different numbers; and the customer, putting in his hand, draws out three, at a venture. Now, if the sum of the numbers on these marbles prove to be less than 100, the customer has won, and he takes 25 centesimi of pastry for 5 c. If the total is more than 100, he has to pay the whole price.

The other evening I went to hear a lecture by a certain Professore, on "*Emilio Zola*: Vita, Abitudini, Idee." The aspect of the audience astonished me. In the first place, I had expected that there would be few people; instead of that, a very large hall was crowded. And quite half were ladies, with a large number of young girls. Moreover, there was even a boy's [*sic*] school of some kind, in uniform. Now is not this slightly astonishing, considering the subject?

[116] I.e., in which GRG had any interest.

The lecture I thought poor and commonplace. But its delivery was remarkable. If one could have watched the man and heard his voice without understanding his words, one would have taken it for granted that he was reciting a tragedy! Of course this is extremely ridiculous. He glorified Zola, as an example of all that is noble in the literary life, and worked himself up to an extravagance of passion. I laughed much. As I was coming out, I heard someone call the lecture *"potente."*

Now I must turn to matters of art. In Venice one thinks first of all of architecture, and Ruskin's divine work thereon.[117] But, alas, I must confess it freely; I do not greatly care for any architecture save Greek and Roman. Were it warm weather, I could sit in the Piazza, or by the Canal Grande, and enjoy looking at the noble buildings all around me; but there is not in me the real impulse to study them.

Ah, how different when the architecture is antique. The other day I went by steamboat out to Lido, one of the long narrow islands which protect the *laguna*; and as soon as I found myself looking south-east over the Adriatic, how I once more felt the joy of proximity to the classical peoples! Over there was fought the battle of Actium; over there lay the land of Hellas! And so it will always be. I cannot deeply interest myself in medieval history, and therefore Florence and Venice are not so much to me as they ought to be. Indeed my one thought here, these last few days, has been: If only I knew enough of the Venetian working classes to write a story about one of those magnificent girls with the long shawls and the high coil of dark hair! You see, it must either be Greece and Rome, or modern industrialism. How do you explain this? Surely it is a strange characteristic?

Therefore I cannot give much time to the superb mosaics of San Marco; they leave me cold. But some of the Venetians [*sic*] painters do interest me. First of all comes Tintoretto. I have followed him through the Palazzo Ducale, the Accademia, and several churches. He is great, powerful, richly imaginative.

You notice that I place him before Titian. Well, this is my feeling. I cannot be as enthusiastic for Titian as people commonly are. His portraits are great and magnificent—anyone can see that,

---

[117] *Stones of Venice* (3 vols., London, 1851–53).

and at all times his colouring is noble; but as a rule he fails to attract me. To tell you the truth, I suppose Titian's great qualities are mainly technical, and that only an artist can fully appreciate him. Take the celebrated so-called "Venus"—which isn't a Venus at all—in the Tribuna of the Uffizi. I cannot say it disappointed me, because I already knew the picture; but I felt more strongly than ever that its value was that of an academical study of the nude—and of colour; nothing more. The woman[118] is not—to me— even beautiful. And to speak of the "Assumption," here in the Accademia, of which you quoted Thackeray's opinion. Well, I should be sorry to have to say what I thought the greatest picture in the world; and of course on Clive's lips that is only meant for an outbreak of extreme enthusiasm.[119] But in this case I cannot be *enthusiastic*; though I can admire greatly. The picture is noble; the Virgin's figure is conceived as only those can conceive who see visions of the Ideal. *But then the subject is so deadly uninteresting to me.*

And there you have the root of the matter! The art of Christianity makes no appeal to me, because I do not feel—have *never* felt—the least vital interest in Christianity itself.

But take Giovanni Bellini, now; the master of Giorgione and of Titian himself. In the Accademia there are two pictures of his which I could gaze at for hours. One is a Madonna with SS. George and Paul; the other, the Virgin between Magdalen and S. Catherine; the figures in both are half lengths. Now here, the subject is purely arbitrary—I mean, it is so *in fact*. I care nothing for the Virgin and the Saints, but I care much for exquisite faces of ideal men and women, which express their souls to me. And Bellini's (Giovanni) type of female face is always dear to me; I always recognize it. It is more precious and significant than Raphael's (Raphael leaves me cold generally,) more so than the faces of Perugino (which I love,) more so than those of Andrea del Sarto—who is my favourite of all, for the sake of his Lucrezia.

[118] Eleonore, wife of the Duke of Urbino, is said to have posed for the picture.

[119] "They travelled Rhineland and Switzerland together—they crossed into Italy—went from Milan to Venice (where Clive saluted the greatest painting in the world—the glorious 'Assumption' of Titian") (Thackeray, *The Newcomes* [Whitefriars, 1855], II, 170).

But my remarks are valueless, for they express only individual predilections. With what contempt would Ruskin regard my state of mind in matters of art!

To-day it is sunny, and, in the sun, comparatively warm. I must go and smoke a cigar on the Riva degli Schiavoni, and watch the great ships going out or coming in, making me think of that divine land away there to the south-east, beyond the Adriatic.

Thank you much for all you have done for me, regarding "Demos." You rec[eived] my postcard. Indeed I shall always owe you much, for your help throughout my work has been constant. Yes, *I am going to use my Italian experiences for the background of my new novel.*[120]

Tell me more of Jacobsen,[121] if you discover more.

I grieve much over your troubles with regard to health. The signs are indeed too serious to be neglected; you must follow the course which allows you to work uninterruptedly, and, in that way, I trust you will suffer less.

I know not whether I shall write another long letter. My journey home will be terrible. I leave on the 27th. The first night I spend at Milan, the next at Strasburg, the next at Brussels; then, from Antwerp to Harwich. It will be high time to be at work again, but I dread the journey.

Ever yours,
GEORGE GISSING

I forgot to tell you that, at Florence, I noted Galileo's Tower, and also the Villa where Milton went to see him. Sacred ground, that! I never passed without a shudder that fountain by the Palazzo Vecchio which stands on the spot where Savonarola was *cooked*! Those memories make me curse humanity.

---

[120] *The Emancipated: A Novel* (3 vols., London: Richard Bentley and Co., 1890). Much of the story is set in Naples, Paestum, and Pompeii. The scenes described in these letters appear occasionally in the novel. In general, the Italian setting of the story is important for its effect on the characters, whose impressions and responses indicate personality traits.

[121] See 1 February 1889.

Addressed: Herrn Eduard Bertz. / Holzmarkt Strasse, 18 /
Potsdam. / Germany.

7. K. Cornwall Residences. / London NW.

March 1st. 1889.

Reached here this morning. Hope you received a little parcel
and that it will interest you.[122] I go to Wakefield for a few days,
but shall speedily be back, and at serious work.

So it is all over—alas, alas! But the memory remains, and
you shall see what I make of it.

G. G.

7. K. Cornwall Residences. / Clarence Gate. / Regent's Park. NW.

April 2nd. 1889.

Dear Friend,

What a singular and startling story, this of Mahr's death![123] If
indeed there was no other cause, then he illustrates in a unique
manner the dangers of life-long *grubbing* at a subject naturally
inexhaustible. However, I am relieved to hear that the burden
of continuing his toil is not to fall upon your shoulders; indeed,
the thing was impossible. Your visit to Ilmenau, on the other
hand, has clearly been a distinct benefit. If only you could at all
times enjoy the care of friendly people, and be thus relieved of
material annoyances!

I have never yet replied to the last letter of yours that I received
in Italy. It delighted me with the richness of its information
concerning your various work. I am very glad you possess the
whole of "Niels Lyhne," and hope I shall some day read your
printed account of it. Many thanks for your promise, now, to
send the Saxe-Coburg essay[124] and other articles; I shall receive
them with eagerness, after this long waiting.

[122] Probably a packet of photographs of paintings and statuary.

[123] Mahr, whose home was in Ilmenau, Thuringia, was working on an
obscure literary project at the time of his death; he was an old friend of
Bertz, who mentions his name in a letter to Heinrich Rehfeldt. I cannot
find any further identification of Mahr.

[124] Probably "Ein Wort für Ottilie Wildermuth," *Deutsche Presse*, II
(15 December 1889), 404–6. Frau Wildermuth wrote many stories and
novels about Swabian life. For Bertz's other articles, see 2 June 1889.

Alas, Hamel seems to be an impossible man! I cannot understand—or rather, cannot put myself into the position of—a fellow
who incessantly demands that other people shall talk of him.
With me, it becomes more and more difficult to say anything about
myself even to intimates. I suppose there is no need to have a
positive rupture with him; you will simply take your own course.

That evil of small-town life of which you speak is only too
likely to distress you, to some extent, wherever you settle. No
intellectual man who flees to the country ever wholly escapes
these annoyances. One ought, in truth, to be *boorish*; it is the
only way to keep a clear space round about one. A gentle de-
meanour is a fearful provocative of Philistine onslaught.[125]

Well, London is not a cheerful place after Venice; still less so
after my beloved Naples. On returning, I spent a week at Wakefield; now at length I have really settled down to ordinary work.
The weather helps me, for it is very mild, and every day we have
even a few hours of sunshine, a contrast to the terrible state of
things with you.

I find, by long experience, that I shall never be able to write
fiction in the morning hours. On the other hand, it is damaging
to spend all the first part of the day without a definite task, so
I have settled down to "The Frogs" of Aristophanes. This I read
until 10.30. Then I go out and walk vigorously until 12.30. Then
I visit a dirty little eating-house in Edgware Road, and have
dinner. After dinner, newspaper-reading and reflection. At 2.30
a cup of tea, and at 3 o'clock I sit down to my desk, ready to
work till 10 or 11 at night, with a break at 8 o'clock for a little
bread and butter and a cold cup of tea.

My novel[126] will deal with a tolerably large group of English
people,—some remarkable, some representative of English follies
and vulgarities—temporarily settled at Naples. I have begun with

---

[125] Of his own sensitivity to the Philistines, GRG wrote: "Strange that I,
all whose joys and sorrows come from excess of individuality, should be
remarkable among men for my yieldingness to everyone and anyone in
daily affairs.... I never dare say what I think, for fear of offending... or
causing a misunderstanding. And this has so often been the case in the
course of my life. Therefore it is that I am never at peace save when alone"
(Diary, 14 October 1888, *Letters*, p. 227).

[126] *The Emancipated*.

delight to write of that divine region. But at first, as always, it is slow and hard work; my first chapter I have written three times, and I fear I have not done with it yet. There may be a scene or two in Rome, but further north than that I shall not go.

I keep up communication with the man Shortridge, whose acquaintance I made at Pompeii.[127] I think I told you about him, about his extraordinary mode of life at the Villa Cozzolino, with his Capri wife and his children? An excellent and remarkable fellow. I have recently visited a married sister of his here at Acton, and find a very respectable household, people I shall certainly see now and then.[128]

I have not yet heard from Frau Steinitz, but shall be glad to. My brother has positively made £16 out of his novel![129] He has finished another,[130] but no arrangements are yet made. It will interest you to hear that Hurst and Blackett sold 329 copies;[131] whilst, of "Thyrza," Smith and Elder sold 400. Truly, my public is a very small one, and yet they advertize my books always in quite a special way.

[127] John Shortridge stayed at the same inn as GRG: "Here made an acquaintance J.W.S.; at dinner he was talking German—very fluently, but in a way that betrayed him as a foreigner. Something in his accent reminded me strangely of—I knew not what; of something very familiar. After dinner it came out that he was a Yorkshireman, and with a strong Yorkshire accent; there was the secret. Related to Wakefield people. Was delighted to hear I knew them. He had been in Italy seventeen years" (Diary, 20 November 1888). Shortridge was the nephew of Dr. Wood, the Gissings' physician at Wakefield. See 12 May 1889.

[128] "The day before yesterday I went out to Acton, to fulfil my promise of calling on Shortridge's sister, and very glad I am that I did so. This sister is married to a doctor, with the unfortunate name of Jolly. I was welcomed with much friendliness, and, to my satisfaction, found a refined family group. The doctor appears to have a good practice, and the house is furnished with that modern luxury which seems somehow or other to come within the reach of *all* educated people except ourselves" (GRG to Ellen Gissing, 22 March 1889, Yale). After his next visit there, he noted: "Did not see Mrs. Jolly, and the husband and sister were not particularly cordial. Shall not go again unless I am invited" (Diary, 3 May 1889).

[129] *Joy Cometh in the Morning.* See 17 April 1887.

[130] *Both of This Parish: A Story of the Byways* (2 vols., London: Hurst and Blackett, 1889).

[131] I.e., of *Joy Cometh in the Morning.*

I will send "The Nether World," by book post (three separate vols.) as soon as a card from you announces your arrival in Potsdam.

I hope this will get to Ilmenau in time to find you there. Thank heaven, you will shortly have—if not summer, at all events an end of winter. What it must be like now, among the olive-groves of Sorrento!

Ever yours, dear Friend,
GEORGE GISSING

7. K. Cornwall Residences. / Regent's Park. / London NW.

May 12th. 1889.

My dear Friend,

I fear your estimate of "The N[ether] W[orld]," as regards its acceptability with the public, is likely to be justified. Yet the few people whom I know whose opinion is worth having agree with you that this is the completest work I have yet produced. All you say about it is very pleasant to me. The note *re* philanthropy is good; I shall perhaps never again deal directly with that subject. Heavens! the labour that book cost me! Indeed each successive book is harder work. Every chapter is written several times, that the style may be as good as I can make it. I exhaust myself in toil—and the public pays no heed. Reviews I do not see, but each week I read the *Spectator*, and I notice that S[mith] and E[lder] have found no laudatory comment to add to their advertisement. Never mind, if only I can earn enough money to live upon.

You would be amused to see the catalogue of my books in the British Museum.[132] I looked at it the other day. It becomes quite an imposing list.

I am very hard at work on my new story, which I think is to be called "The Puritan,"[133] though I am not sure. The first volume well begun, but not more. I have a strong story, full of colour and passion. The scene is at Naples and in Capri! The people are a

[132] *The British Museum Catalogue* (XXI, 1881–1900, col. 328) lists: *Workers in the Dawn* (1880); *The Unclassed* (1884); *Isabel Clarendon* (1886); *Demos* (1886); *Thyrza* (1887).

[133] Published as *The Emancipated*.

curious mixture of intellectual and worldly; artists, philistines, beauties, adventurers.

The articles of yours were promised for shortly after Easter, but they have not yet come. Don't delay longer than is necessary.

I thought I had spoken of Shortridge. He is a Yorkshireman whom I met at the Albergo del Soli at Pompeii. He took me to his home, a village called Massa, just beyond Sorrento, and there I spent a night before going over to Capri. He married a Capri girl nine years ago, and by this time has sufficiently repented; they have four children, and neither these nor the mother speak a word of English. With them live the peasant father and mother of the wife; also a brother of Shortridge, a good-for-nothing drunkard, who has always failed to pass his examinations to become a doctor of medicine.[134] Shortridge has a moderate income; he is a man of bright and active brains, and I had great pleasure in talking with him. Their house is called Villa Cozzolino; it stands in a great lemon-orchard, and looks upon the gulf of Naples, the huge cliffs of Capri just opposite. The man might have done good work in the world, but fate has hampered him. He talks always of coming to England, but I doubt whether he ever will. A strong democrat, and a thoroughly good fellow. I hear from him at times.

Roberts makes a little progress. He writes novel after novel fruitlessly, but of late he has had some employment as an art-critic on the "Scottish Review." I fear he knows little or nothing of the matter, but he writes as well about it as most art-critics. His private life abounds in intrigues with women and so on; very strange adventures sometimes. We see each other once a week, and talk much. Of you we speak very frequently. By the bye, Don is flourishing, a finer dog than ever![135]

I read very little just at present; my labour is too great. In a week or two I hope to be in smoother water. I have no library subscription, and consequently see no new books. Nothing of moment seems to have come out lately.

---

[134] Herbert Shortridge failed his final examination at Edinburgh, and then came to the Villa Cozzolino, where he terrorized and mistreated his nephew and nieces. Apparently, John Shortridge cared so little for his children that he rarely interfered when they were abused.

[135] The collie Bertz had given to Roberts. See Introduction.

My brother has a new book in the press.[136] Hurst and Blackett have given him £25 for the copyright. Out of the last book he made £16. I regard it as a grave misfortune to both him and myself that he is obliged to pursue this career.[137] But his position is every day more serious.

Heavens! It is a month since the date of your letter; you will be growing anxious to hear. Indeed your secretarial burdens are very heavy, too heavy; I grieve to hear of your toiling over such repulsive duties. Are you better in health, old friend?

I hope you will have your summer holiday. I cannot expect one for myself, and it is scarcely necessary. My book must be finished by autumn if possible.

Ever yours,
GEORGE GISSING

Addressed: Herrn Eduard Bertz. / Holzmarkt Strasse, 18. / Potsdam. / *Germany.*
7. K. Corn[wall] Resid[ences].

May 21. 1889.

Many thanks for the packet. I had difficulty in finding the Eng[lish] Pub[lishing] Co.; they occupy a very little room jointly with other Companies. *The Writer* will "possibly" yet appear; but it is very uncertain.[138] If *not*, then they will communicate with you, and return the money. The man I saw (I don't know who it was,) said that they "hadn't received the support they expected."

You seem to be very active, and at all events are earning much experience.

---

[136] *Both of This Parish.*

[137] Algernon's publisher tried to capitalize on GRG's name. After his own literary reputation was secure, GRG finally objected and wrote to his brother: "It has ere now occurred to me that my growing literary repute may act injuriously upon *you.* It may create a twofold prejudice. The people who dislike *me,* may be prejudiced against your books owing to the mere name; and my readers may be disappointed when they find that your work is conceived in such a different spirit. Do you feel inclined to consult Watt on such a matter as this?" (9 January 1895, Yale). Alexander Watt was a literary agent; see 15 May 1891.

[138] See 4 October 1888.

I will look for the papers, and send them. Don't trouble to return the books till you can do it conveniently. There is no hurry.

My brother has a new novel to appear in a few months.

I have replied to Frau Steinitz, with full permission, to do as she likes.[139] Of Mlle. Le Breton I have heard nothing since my return, and feel unequal to the effort of writing to her just yet.

G. G.

Addressed: Herrn Eduard Bertz. / Holzmarkt Strasse, 18. / Potsdam. / *Germany.*

7. K.

May 24th. 1889.

Am sending you a packet of such notes etc. of yours as I can find.[140] There may be yet others, and I will look again. But to-morrow I go to Wakefield for a few weeks. I am not at all well, and this house is besieged by painters. Address Stoneleigh Terrace. / Agbrigg. / *Wakefield.* Will write soon.

G. G.

Stoneleigh Terrace. / Agbrigg. / Wakefield.

June 2nd, 1889.

Dear Friend,

I hope the packet of papers reached you safely. Probably it contains a lot of material that will be very useful to you, and which will come back pleasantly out of the past.

I have now read such of your publications as you sent me.[141] Several times, in reading, I caught the sound of your voice, in

---

[139] GRG received her letter about translating *Demos* on 13 May. After noting its arrival in the Diary, he added: "As it is in the absurd German cursive, I can't read it" (13 May 1889). "Plitt came at twelve, and took him to have lunch in Chapel Street. He read me the letter, and I find it asks my permission to curtail 'Demos' for publicn. in a feuilleton. Matters nothing to me" (Diary, 14 May 1889).

[140] Papers Bertz had left behind him in London.

[141] "In morning read German papers containing some contributions of Bertz's, and wrote him a letter about them" (Diary, 2 June 1889).

certain phrases. Of course the "Heine"[142] and "Carlyle"[143] chiefly interested me. They reminded me what a thorough grasp you have of modern English literature; I should think there are few Germans better qualified than yourself to write on this subject. You are so obviously *at ease* in your side-references; there has been no cramming to get up the matter; you know the men and women, as well as their writings; your allusions are just such as would occur to an Englishman. At the same time, we know it is not an Englishman who speaks; the freshness of handling pleasantly betrays you as looking at it all from a calm distance. The "Carlyle" seems to be admirably written; an excellent resumé of his professional life; old as the matter is to me, I read it with keen interest, always anxious to know how you would treat this or that point. And, by the bye, your translations from Carlyle struck me as good, though of course my judgement is worthless; they amused me with their easy German rendering of old Thomas's trenchant style.

The "Herzog Ernst"[144] is more difficult for me to appreciate, as I am in such ignorance with regard to the subject. But it impresses me as a most remarkably conscientious piece of work. If you get an "order" for it, I shall feel you have at least earned the reward, which, as you say, would not be amiss from the point of view of your connections. You must have studied the book very seriously. In the 2nd. part, beginning of 2nd. paragraph, I noticed: "Jeder Charakter wird durch seine frühesten Umgebungen wesentlich beeinfluszt" etc., and I thought much of your own life-history. Again, on page 122, where you say, "Ich möchte nicht behaupten" etc., many of our old talks came back to my recollection.

"Das heimische Naturleben" struck me as a very good little bit of prose. The feeling is characteristically your own, and the expression, I feel sure, is good, very good.

The remarks on style, which you append to your notice of *The Writer*, certainly hit the nail on the head. I am always

---

[142] "Heine in England," *Deutsche Presse*, I (23 December 1888), 410–11; II (1 January 1889), 4–6; II (6 January 1889), 10–12.

[143] See 9 November 1888.

[144] "Herzog Ernst II. als Schriftsteller," *Deutsche Presse*, II (7 April 1889), 115–16; II (14 April 1889), 121–23; II (28 April 1889), 139–41.

annoyed when people talk of *teaching* style. Either, as you say, a man will teach himself, or he will for ever remain style-less, for all the help others can give him in direct precept. A foolish clergyman wrote to me last year, saying he was going to give a lecture on style, and, as an admirer of my books, (mirabile dictu!) he ventured to ask me how I had "obtained my skill in diction." I'm afraid my civil answer, though civilly acknowledged, gave him small help; however, he said he should quote it in his lecture.[145]

My post-cards told you about the present state of *The Writer.* I fancy it is defunct.

Well, we have summer weather here. I succeed in working pretty well in this home of Puritanism,[146] and shall probably stay till a good portion of the book is finished. I am deeply discontented with the outer circumstances of my life, wherever it be led. I wonder whether I shall ever have a home of my own? Most probably not.

These scraps of your work have given me an appetite for more. I trust it will not be long before I receive a book. But you are working well, and your life is now that of an active man of letters. You have attained the dignity (*sine otio*) of the editor's chair. I don't like the circumstances under which Steinitz[147] has left the work to you. And I shall be anxious to hear your further speculations as to his character.

[145] The Reverend George Bainton, of Coventry, was the lecturer. Besides GRG, Bainton petitioned such authors as Hall Caine, Vernon Lee, and George Meredith for statements on the technique and development of literary style. Then Bainton published the replies he had received in *The Art of Authorship* (London, 1890). The book precipitated a controversy, carried on primarily in the Society of Authors' magazine, *The Author,* between Bainton and the contributors, who accused him of misrepresentation and breach of faith; they had assumed their answers were to be used for a lecture, not a publication. Most of GRG's reply was printed in the book (pp. 81–5), but he did not join the battle since Bainton had requested permission to publish the letter on 25 September 1888 (Diary, 25 September 1888).

[146] Wakefield had been a town of dissenters since 1651 when George Fox talked many of the citizens into the Quaker fold; in 1748 the Methodists gained many converts there as well. The remark may refer specifically to GRG's mother and sisters.

[147] Heinrich Steinitz, the Berlin publisher, was the official editor of the *Deutsche Presse*; he had delegated the editing of the magazine to Bertz.

A "scrap-cutter" has sent me the enclosed,[148] with a request for *orders*. I send it on to you; throw it into the fire when you have glanced at it. When—and if—the *Spectator* notices the book, you shall hear of it. By the bye, a 2 shilling edition of "A Life's Morning" is announced.[149]

I will return your papers very soon. At present I often work 12 hours a day, but get on slowly.

What is it like in Naples now? How looks Baiae? How would it be to wander among the verdure of Sorrento, or sit on the crags of Capri? Oh, beloved South, with its glory on land and sea, its joyous life, its music!

Ever yours, dear Friend,
GEORGE GISSING

Addressed: Herrn Eduard Bertz. / Lagow. / Regbezk. [?] Frankfurt a. Oder. / *Germany.*
Agbrigg.

July 4th, 1889.

Shall write in a day or two. Much pleased with *D[eutsche] P[resse].*[150]

Have not seen the "Athenaeum," and know nothing about the matter.[151] Could you tell me on a postcard what it was about, as I have no communication with anyone else who sees the paper.

Past the middle of my book.[152]

G. G.

[148] Probably a review of *The Nether World.*

[149] Published by Smith, Elder and Co., August 1889.

[150] Bertz had sent more copies of the *Deutsche Presse,* in which some of his articles appeared, and the German translation of *Niels Lyhne* (Diary, 4 July 1889).

[151] "A set of articles, principally on social subjects, from the pens of leading novelists, will be published shortly by Messrs. Tillotson and Son, Bolton" ("Literary Gossip," *Athenaeum,* 29 June 1889, p. 826). The contributors were to be G. A. Sala, Justin McCarthy, Mrs. Hungerford, and GRG. The reference in the notice is to GRG's article "Christmas on the Capitol," Bolton *Evening News.*

[152] *The Emancipated.*

Stoneleigh Terrace, / Agbrigg. / Wakefield.

July 7th. 1889.

Dear Friend,

It is my opinion that you are at present in a very satisfactory state. Your activity seems to be admirable, and I rejoice in the confirmation of the hope I always held, that a serious demand upon your faculties would bring out the practical ability in which you have so often declared yourself deficient. It is no slight feat to have edited this paper so successfully, with so little previous experience. And, beyond all doubt, you have made the thing greatly more interesting than it was before. There is unity in it, and I like the spirit much. No such paper exists in England; I doubt whether it ever will. Most lamentable it will be if Steinitz allows the tone to fall.

But your post-card shows me that you no longer have quite so bad an opinion of the man as at your former writing. I am very glad that he has paid something; the present he brought you is of course acceptable.

Now for a few notes on the articles.

That on the *English Authors' Society* begins with much liveliness.[153] This is your lighter manner, and a happy one. Of *Walt Whitman* you write genially;[154] no doubt it will send many readers to his works. The question of *Pay* is well treated in the "Schopenhauer";[155] here I notice the characteristic tone of your editorship. But still more strongly does it come out in your comments on *The Writer*; the obituary paragraph is a trifle savage, but I think not a bit more so than the vulgar thing deserved. How very English that paper was! Excellent in its practicalness is the *"Bühnenkritik."*[156] There is a fine impartiality in this, a reviewing of evidence which points to your historical power, a decided dignity of language. I like it much. Much also do I like the

---

[153] "Der Englische Schriftsteller-Verband," *Deutsche Presse*, II (26 May 1889), 169–72.

[154] "Walt Whitman: Zu seinem siebzigsten Geburtstag," *Deutsche Presse*, II (2 June 1889), 177–79.

[155] "Schopenhauer und die Honorarfrage," *Deutsche Presse*, II (9 June 1889), 188–89.

[156] "Warum Bühnenkritik?" *Deutsche Presse*, II (16 June 1889), 195–98.

"Volksthümlichkeit."[157] Indeed I think it the most noteworthy of these articles; heartily I agree with every word of it. Readers of journalistic matter seldom have a problem of the day put before them with this lucidness, with such avoidance of partisanship, such breadth of view. A thoroughly good piece of work. No wonder people write to you and express a wish that you could remain editor. I wish it myself; but I know at the same time that you have more important work to do. (In this last article it delights me that you insist upon the fact that the average "educated" person has no more real "culture" than the untaught proletarian.)

Comical matter in that note on the *Sprachverein*. I laughed heartily at the words: "Beamtenschulfuchserei,"[158] and "Genusz-empfänglichkeitsseite."[159]

Apropos of your remarks on the Giordano Bruno business, I have had some Roman newspapers sent me, which contain accounts of the day.[160] Very amusing things happened. Among others—one of the Cardinals went about Rome distributing gratuitous railway-tickets to all who would leave the city for that day!

I am now glad to think of you as idle and enjoying the sunshine. My own work will continue till the middle of August; if I have then finished, I mean to take my elder sister[161] to the Channel Islands, and over into Bretagne; I suppose we shall make a holiday of about three weeks. What I shall do after that I cannot say; it depends much on what I receive for my novel.

Several things have happened of late of which you will be glad to hear. First of all, Lippincotts of Philadelphia sent me a notice that they are going to publish a supplement to "Allibone," (do you know it? The largest and best dictionary of English literature,) and requested me to let them have biographical details to append

[157] "Echte und schlechte Volksthümlichkeit," *Deutsche Presse*, II (23 June 1889), 202–6.

[158] "Official pedantry."

[159] "The side which is receptive to pleasure."

[160] The newspapers were sent by Plitt, who had returned to Italy in the summer (Diary, 1 July 1889); they reported the dedication of a statue of Giordano Bruno, which had been placed opposite the Vatican, on 9 June 1889. The Vatican considered the whole affair a direct insult to the Pope on the part of the Italian government, since Bruno had been martyred in the Inquisition.

[161] Margaret, who was four years older than Ellen.

to my own name.[162] Then again, I find that Harpers have published "A Life's Morning" and "The Nether World."[163] Moreover, I wrote not long ago an article for a newspaper "syndicate" (Tillotsons, which you casually mention in the *D[eutsche] P[resse]*) called: "Christmas on the Capitol"; this was in fulfilment of a promise given in reply to a request of theirs which I received in Italy. They pay me £10. It is to be published shortly, and they have written asking me to let them print my *signature* with the article, my autograph, that is to say. I will let you have the thing when it comes out.

Again; Roberts has sent me a notice of "The Nether World" from the "Pall Mall Gazette." I enclose it. It is at all events respectful.

The other day came a note from Thomas Hardy telling me he is in town, and wishing to see me. I was sorry to be away, for Hardy interests me.[164]

Well, I think we are both of us getting something like a firm foot-hold. Heaven be thanked!

Roberts, who is now in Cornwall, has had two sea-articles in "Murray's" these last two months.[165] He cannot be very cheerful, poor fellow. I very much doubt whether he will ever do anything as a writer of novels, and as he cannot take to regular journalism, it is hard to say how he will live. Still, he has done some very good picture-criticism of late, and there may be hope in that direction.

My brother is correcting the proofs of his new book, which is to be called "Both of This Parish." I think it will be better than the last, but again in his case I am very doubtful whether novel-writing is a real resource. He and his wife and child have left Worcestershire, and are gone to live up in Northumberland. He is a singular fellow, and I don't quite understand him.

---

[162] *Allibone's Dictionary of Authors—Supplement* (Philadelphia, 1891), I, 675. The entry gives date and place of birth, school attended, a review of *Workers in the Dawn* from the *Spectator* (Liii, 1226), and a list of his novels up to 1888.

[163] He was confused about the publishers. Harpers reprinted *The Nether World* in 1889, but Lippincott brought out *A Life's Morning* in 1888.

[164] GRG met Hardy in 1886 (*Letters*, p. 190). See also 22 September 1895.

[165] "Two Voyages:" "I. A Steerage Passage," *Murray's Magazine*, V (June 1889); "II. Life in the Foc'sle," *Ibid.*, VI (July 1889).

Well, we have seen black days together, and, if I mistake not, we shall yet look back upon them from a more assured height. It rejoices me that our correspondence has never ceased, never suffered an interruption. You are of great help to me, in many ways, and I trust that now and then my letters give you an impulse in your work.

Many thanks for "Niels Lyhne."[166] I have begun the reading, and find it enjoyable. Without you, I should remain in ignorance of these new men.

By the bye, you told me you had read "Trente Ans de Paris." I got it when it first appeared, and have read it several times. But have you seen the subsequent "Souvenirs d'un Homme de Lettres"?[167] This has not yet come into my hands.

You will have received my card. I shall be glad if you tell me what the remarks in the "Athenaeum" were.[168]

My work goes on steadily and quickly. It is long since I wrote with such ease. I wonder much what you will think of this book.

Ever yours, old Friend,
GEORGE GISSING

I return the D[eutsche] P[resse]'s by this post.[169] No, I find you wish me to keep them till your return from the holidays. I will do so.

Stoneleigh Terrace. / Agbrigg. / Wakefield.

August 4th. 1889.

Dear Friend,

You probably return home to-day, so I will write a line. In a few days I will return the newspapers to you. Don't send the books until I am again settled in London.

To Allibone's I sent very brief information. That I was born in 1857 at Wakefield, that I was educated at Owens College, Manchester, and that I had published such and such books. This was all. I suppose you will scarcely need to say anything else. For your

---

[166] Jacobsen's novel. See 4 August 1889.
[167] Alphonse Daudet, *Trente Ans de Paris: A travers ma vie et mes livres* (Paris, 1888); *Souvenirs d'un Homme de Lettres* (Paris, 1888).
[168] See 4 July 1889.
[169] This sentence has been scored over.

sake, I sincerely hope that you will not have to write those articles. But certainly you are doing me a great deal of good.[170]

On receiving your letter, I wrote to Mlle. Le Breton,[171] and to my annoyance she replies thus:

"Je suis allée ce matin même chez M. Hachette, qui s'est engagé à donner Demos à l'impression le 1er Octobre. Je suis désolée de ce retard, mais vous êtes probablement plus philosophe que moi, qui ne le suis pas du tout. Enfin il faut courber la tête devant les Editeurs, qui sont les tyrans de notre époque civilisée."

I can't understand such delay. It will be too late for your purpose.

I hope to have finished my novel by the end of this new week,[172] and on the 19th. August, I hope to start with my sister[173] for London. I think I shall try Bentley with this MS., though it is very possible indeed that there are things in it which will frighten him.[174] But I want to have a change from Smith.

It delights me to hear of your correspondence with Walt Whitman. Certainly you have now all the materials for an important essay, and I shall hope to see it before long. Excellent that he has given you all his works, which cost a good deal.[175]

I wonder whether you will succeed with "Phoebe."[176] Doubtful, is it not? There is little of general interest in it.

[170] "Bertz writes that he is penning articles on me for certain German newspapers, by way of introduction to the German transl. of 'Demos.' He is spending a holiday with a doctor-friend [Rehfeldt] in the country, and is maddened by domestic life, a 'herd-like existence,' he says" (GRG to Ellen Gissing, 4 August 1889, Yale).

[171] See 23 October 1888.

[172] It was finished on 13 August.

[173] Margaret.

[174] See 21 October 1889.

[175] Bertz initiated the correspondence with Whitman: "Ich sandte Whitman einen Abdruck meiner Festgabe nach Camden, New Jersey, wo er sein Alter verlebte, und schrieb ihm dazu. Er war sehr erfreut und bezeigte mir seinen Dank auf mancherlei Weise. Aber besonders freute ihn die Aussicht auf eine noch umfangreichere Würdigung; denn sein Herz hungerte nach Beifall. Um ihr nachzuhelfen und sie in seinem Sinne zu lenken, überschüttete er mich im Laufe des nächsten Jahres mit Büchern und Zeitschriften, und zwar ausschlieszlich mit solchen, die von den überschwenglichsten Lobhudeleien strotzten" (E. Bertz, Der Yankee-Heiland [Dresden, 1906], p. VII). See 11 September 1889.

[176] Bertz was translating "Phoebe," one of GRG's short stories, which had

It is very annoying that your holiday has been so far from a complete rest. I had imagined that Rehfeldt's wife was more intellectual. No, these good housewives are terrible persons to live with, terrible! In fact, they are the ruin of all intellectual aspiration. Good creatures, to be sure; but not companions for men who *vivunt ut cogitent.* They hold the world together in decencies, but would never allow it to advance a step. Of course we have no right to abuse them; the simple fact is that we have no business in their proximity.

I shall only remain in London a day, then travel on to Guernsey, first of all.

Already I am contemplating a new book, which will probably be of English provincial life. I want to let another year go by before I again deal with London. The next book that I shall write on *that* subject is very clear in my mind; it will be terrific, if I have the power to carry out my idea.

I am sorry to see that a 2 shilling edition of "A Life's Morning" is announced.

This for the present.

Ever yours,
GEORGE GISSING.

It is so long since I finished "Niels Lyhne" that I had forgotten it still remained to be spoken of to you. Hearty thanks for sending me this book; I have enjoyed it greatly, and hope soon to read it a second time. From a study of the Introduction, I gather that Niels is, on the whole, Petersen[177] himself, even to certain physical characteristics. The book is one of the most deeply pathetic I ever read. One does not fully realize the author's purpose until the end is reached. That poor Idealist! It is a sad figure, always alone, doomed to disillusion and above all to solitude, experience after experience adding its weight of melancholy.

"Und dann endlich starb er den Tod, den schweren Tod."

That closing sentence haunted me through the night.

---

been published in the *Temple Bar* (LXX, March 1884, 391–406). The Deutsche Verlags-Anstalt, Stuttgart, accepted and printed the German translation in their "Bibliothek der fremden Zungen," after the story was printed in Joseph Kürschner's *Aus fremden Zungen* (Heft 18, 1891). See 30 August 1892.

[177] A mistake. He means Jens Peter Jacobsen.

The style is curious and interesting. Obviously the work of a young man, whose maturity was still ahead; but for all that, a work of much absolute value. I shall be very glad to hear that other books of his are to appear in the Bibliothek.

GG.

Addressed: Herrn Eduard Bertz. / Holzmarkt Strasse, 18. / Potsdam. / *Germany.*
Agbrigg.

August 16th. 1889.

Have to-day sent the numbers of the "D[eutsche] P[resse]." On Monday next I go to London, and on Tuesday to the Channel Islands. Shall not be able to give you my address, as we shall keep moving; but please write to Agbrigg, and they will forward the letter. My holiday will last about three weeks.

Have finished my book. Name, *"The Emancipated."* Shall offer it to Bentley this time.

Hope you are invigorated. Shall be anxious to hear of your work.

G. G.

Sark.

September 5th. 1889.

Dear Friend,

I have now been absent from England, with my sister, for three weeks. We have found the Channel Islands so delightful and interesting, that it has decided us to give up our proposed crossing into Bretagne, which, indeed, I find would also have involved rather too much expense. We spent nine days in a corner of Guernsey, with excursions to many parts of the island, then came over here to Sark, where we propose to remain until September 13th. After the 14th., I shall again be in London.

Do you know anything of these Islands? They have astonished me with their beauty. I knew that the climate was admirable, and I was prepared for wonders of vegetation; but I had not formed an adequate idea of the varieties of delightful scenery to be found here. The lanes of Guernsey are exquisite, dense with ferns and flowers and brambles and overhanging trees. The houses are covered with enormous fuchsias and geraniums; the gardens are full of magnolias and arbutus and gladiolus and all manner of shrubs of which I know not the name. Part of the coast consists of fine bays with smooth strands, and part of very bold cliffs, where the Atlantic waves dash up splendidly. We have had many days when not a cloud could be discovered, and when the sky was as blue as that of Italy. The shore, in such light, would often look Italian, if only there were the *purple* shadows; for this we are of course not far enough south.

This little island of Sark (six miles from Guernsey; three miles long, and a mile and a half broad,) is a marvel. Geologically it is one of the most interesting islands in Europe. It consists of various kinds of granite, with an admixture of softer stone, and under the influences of sky and sea it is gradually being worn away. The shore is terrific. Only in two or three places can boats effect a landing, and in bad weather no boat can either issue or come in, so that in winter the people here are sometimes cut off for weeks at a time. Everywhere are magnificent caverns; some capable of being examined at low tide from the shore, some only to be reached in boats. Many of these huge chasms are marvellous repertories of sea-wonders; zoophytes of all kinds abound.

I wish we could have a day or two of rough weather. At such times the scene upon these shores is tremendously grand. The sea bellows furiously in the caves, and dashes its foam five-hundred feet into the air along the granite cliffs.

There is no town, not even a village. Two small hotels exist, and a number of little houses let lodgings. We have taken rooms with a decent woman. Food is not very plentiful; with the exception of farm-produce, everything has to be ordered from Guernsey. The people are mostly bilingual; but a great many speak no English.

Being in Victor Hugo's country, I have just re-read some of his novels, unfortunately in cheap English translations, which I bought in Guernsey. "Les Travailleurs de la Mer" is superbly imaginative, but too extravagant even for romance in its demand upon one's credulity. "Quatre-vingt-treize" I think rather poor. "Les Misérables" has renewed its old impression on me; it is a great book, in many senses of the word, a great book.

I hope I shall soon hear from you. You received the numbers of the "Deutsche Presse" all right?

"The Emancipated" is in Bentley's hands. I am curious to see (1) if he will accept it at all, (2) what he will offer for it, if he does accept.

And I am very anxious to get to work again, very anxious. These holidays must not be made too long; for my part, I soon begin to rust. And then I suffer so much from the absolute lack of conversation. My poor sister is a Puritan,[178] and we can talk of nothing but matter of fact. I shall be glad to see Roberts again; he has been spending a long time in Cornwall and Sussex, but is now on the point of returning to London.

I know not what I shall do as soon as I get back. Let me hear from you, that I may help myself by sympathy with your own exertions. You are well, I trust; it seems very long since I had news of you.

Ever yours, dear Friend,
GEORGE GISSING.

Sark.

September 11th, 1889.

Dear Friend,

You will have received my short letter of the other day. To-day comes yours, from Wakefield. It is full of interesting matter, and, for me, of excellent news. If only there were not that melancholy story of your wasted holiday! Did you ever read "Middlemarch"? Rehfeldt and his wife remind me of Dr. Lydgate and *his* wife—a dolorous situation. Yes, it is suicide to contract such a marriage. And Rehfeldt, poor fellow, *cannot* treat his friends as he would wish to. I heartily wish you could have found real rest somewhere. It is so long from one summer to the next.

I cannot be glad that you give up all your really important work to labour at my books. But it is vastly kind of you. Indeed, you are the cause that my books are beginning to have sympathetic readers in Germany; but for you, this would perhaps never have

---

[178] Margaret's piety irritated him more than her lack of conversation. Her reading habits ordinarily did not please him either, for when he relaxed with Ovid, she busied herself with "some dirty little pietistic work" (Diary, 25 August 1889).

happened. It is admirable that Schweichel[179] also will give me a notice; you and he cannot but assist me enormously. But you are the prime mover; I am indebted to you beyond expression.

Whether Farrar's article[180] concerns me or not, I do not know; this is the first I have heard of it. If it does, then it is more than a help; it would be simply priceless, in the *Contemporary*, and by so popular a man. Probably you know by this time. But I shall be enraged if you have spent money on a false supposition.

Now about Walt Whitman. I perfectly understand the modifications in your feeling and judgment. As you know, I myself have no genuine sympathy with his optimism, though I can take pleasure in it, as I can in any other manifestation of *strength*. The point of which you speak in detail is important. I do not go so far as the writer in the *Gentlemen's*;[181] these passages do not strike me as "disgusting"; but, on the other hand, I am inclined to think that Bucke's[182] enthusiasm makes him wilfully blind to this writer's meaning. In fact, the passages in which Whitman speaks in this way of male friendships awaken no sympathy in me; it is my habit to regard such language as a tender exaggeration. Far *truer* to me would it sound if he talked of hearty grasp of hands. I have always felt, indeed, that some of Tennyson's language in "In Memoriam" went beyond my sympathy.

But would this be so to a member of the Latin races, of to-day? I am doubtful. Is it not—this feeling of most Englishmen—strongly Anglo-Saxon?

[179] George Schweichel (1821–1907), novelist and journalist. "One [letter] from Bertz, with news that a German novelist, Schweichel, thinks of writing an article on me in the *Neue Zeit*" (Diary, 11 September 1889). *Neue Zeit* was a weekly review published in Stuttgart.

[180] Frederick W. Farrar, "The Nether World," *Contemporary Review*, LVI (September 1889), 370–80. Farrar, the Archdeacon of Westminster, was a cultural and religious leader in London society. His article discussed the misery of the London poor. See 21 October 1889.

[181] "Elsewhere he speaks of the sick, sick dread of unreturned friendship, of the comrade's kiss, the arm round the neck—but he speaks to sticks and stones; the emotion does not exist in us, and the language of his evangel-poems appears simply disgusting" (Arthur Clive, "Walt Whitman, the Poet of Joy," *The Gentleman's Magazine*, XV NS, December 1875, 713).

[182] Dr. Richard Maurice Bucke (1837–1902), Canadian physician; a close friend of Whitman, he wrote the eulogistic biography, *Walt Whitman* (Philadelphia, 1883).

Well, I have told you what I think about it. I suppose you are obliged to deal with the point?[183]

I pass to your questions concerning the translator's difficulties in "Demos."

A *bloater* is only the finest kind of red-herring. It is always eaten cooked. Indeed, I know of no fish whatever that is eaten in England without having been put on the fire. The bloater is considered rather a vulgar dish. Unfortunately I do not know the word *Bückling*.[184]

Yes, I think *Fachwerk* will do for "half-timbered." The style of building which you describe is often used in old English mansions.

A *pram* is vulgar for a *perambulator*, a child's carriage. The man is warned, lest he should tumble over it in the dark.

Yes, *black-band* is a kind of metal, but for my life I could not tell you what kind.[185] If I were in London, I would look into a technical dictionary for the German word. Indeed, I will do so when I get home, and let you have a card.

I must know more of these men—Schweichel, Zapp,[186] Alberti,[187] etc. When I am established in London, and if I get well paid for my novel, I shall try to get hold of some of their books. You would of course let me know if an article appears in the *Neue Zeit*; but on no account are you to buy it for me; I cannot continue to tax you in this way. Simply let me know, and I will order the number.

Heavens! how it must have brought back old days, to re-read "Workers" and "The Unclassed."! [*sic*] Not for any consideration would I open those dreadful books! All I have ever written seems to be apprentice-work; I fear to examine it. And there is so much of my suffering in it! Yes, yes; you and I have both a share in that literature of struggle and misery. What man but yourself can

---

[183] Bertz thought that Whitman's poetry was shot through with homosexual suggestions. After mulling the problem over for many years, Bertz published two deeply critical character studies, *Walt Whitman: Ein Charakterbild* (1905), and *Der Yankee-Heiland* (1906).

[184] A smoked herring.

[185] A variety of iron ore.

[186] Arthur Zapp (1852–?), German novelist, dramatist, and philologist.

[187] Konrad Sittenfeld (1862–1918), pseudonym, Konrad Alberti, actor, novelist, and editor of the Berlin *Morgenpost*.

completely understand the books? It makes me both sad and happy to look back into the fog, and to discern our figures looming there. Well indeed, thrice well, that we came together in the wilderness! No one will ever take your place in my regard, for no one can live *with* me as you did. Eheu!

The weather here is still glorious; cloudless skies day after day, as blue as in Italy. Sark is a rarely beautful island, full of magnificence and loveliness. I am very glad to know it.

We leave on Saturday morning, (the 14th.) go to Guernsey, and there catch another steamer for Southampton, where we arrive about 6.30. London at 9.45. My sister will stay with me till the following Wednesday, and then go home to Wakefield.

All good be with you!

Always affectionately yours,
GEORGE GISSING

Addressed: Herrn Eduard Bertz. / Holzmarkt Str[asse] 18. /   *Potsdam. / Germany.*

October 7th. 1889.

Bentley has paid £150 down; the agreement is that there shall be another payment of £50 if 850 copies are sold; and yet another of £50, if 1000 copies are sold. This is fair enough. Hope the book will be published about the end of the year.[188]

I intend at present to leave England as soon as proofs are finished. I shall probably go to Marseille, and thence by sea to *Athens*. Let me hear from you soon.

Ever yours,
G. G.

7. K. Cornwall Residences. / Regent's Park. / London NW.

October 21st. 1889.[189]

My dear Friend,

May your labour on my "twenty volumes" soon come to an end! You can imagine how very eager I shall be to see the results of it.

Frau Steinitz wrote me a line not long ago, merely saying that

---

[188] *The Emancipated* was published in March 1890.
[189] The Diary notation, "... to Bertz," is dated 20 October 1889.

she continued to be pleased with "Demos," and was getting on well with her translation. I did not think she expected a reply; but her note was gratifying to me.

Yes, I have read Farrar's article. To tell you the truth, it struck me as a little insulting; the tone was so very much *de haut en bas*. Only an English cleric would be capable of writing about a book, and never once mentioning the author's name.[190] I don't like to think of the matter.

The proofs of "The Emancipated" are coming in slowly; I fear I shall not have done with them till the end of November. I am not displeased with the book, so far.

I have just corrected the proofs of "Christmas on the Capitol," for Tillotson. You shall have a copy when it appears. For that, I receive £10; it is only the ordinary magazine rate of payment. Of course I should never dream of writing a *story* for a newspaper syndicate; the kind of stuff they publish, and the way they advertize it, is too ignoble.

Already I am working hard at my next book, which I think will be called "The Head Mistress."[191] I do not mean that I am writing; only reading, and making notes, and reflecting. The book will deal with the "female education" question—in my way; the scene is in a provincial town. And I fancy it will be written in a manner rather different from my usual one; I am growing dissatisfied, in some degree, with my old *method*. Something I have learnt from Jacobsen. But what that "something" is, it would not be very easy to describe. My own mind is not yet quite clear on the subject. But I can no longer write—as I used to—with slight preparation; I grow more and more laborious in my preliminary study. An awkward change for a man who has to earn his living; still, it is better to follow one's ideal—as you say—and earn less money.

As soon as the proofs are off my hands, I shall start for Paris; thence direct for Marseille; and there take boat for the Peiraeus—

[190] "Of the author of 'The Nether World' I know nothing, and his previous novel, 'Demos,' has left no strong impression on my mind. But his present work is so sombre and earnest in its terrible realism that it will not easily be forgotten by any serious thinker" (*Contemporary Review*, LVI, Sept. 1889, 370).

[191] A few months later, this subject was discarded.

going either by the Messageries Maritimes, through the straits of Bonifacio and Messina; or else by one of Fraissinet's coasting vessels, which would make the voyage long, but interesting. No, I cannot spend much time in Greece; for it will be rather expensive; I doubt whether I shall be there more than a month. I shall try to see Attica, nothing more. No doubt my companions—as in South Italy—will be Germans; they abound at Athens. I have bought Baedeker's "Griechenland," an admirable guide.

For the first time for long you speak of paying a visit to London. How glad I shall be when you do so! Some day we will have a tremendous meeting here: vast drinking and smoking, talk to the small hours, laughter roof-shaking!

Well, I am not quite so solitary as of old. Lately I have been making, through Roberts, the acquaintance of quite a number of painters and sculptors; not men of any great mark, (except perhaps Lee, the sculptor,)[192] but of course interesting to me. Then I have come into personal relations with Miss Edith Sichel, who wrote the article—you remember—in "Murray's."[193] She wrote to me about "The Nether World," and the other day I went to see her at her country home in Surrey. Curiously, she lives there with a sister-in-law of Miss Thackeray.[194] Miss Sichel is about eight-and-twenty, of Jewish face; distinctly intellectual. She belongs to a circle of wealthy and cultivated people, who have personal acquaintance with all the leaders in literature and art. At the end of this month she will be back in town,—she and a younger sister inhabit a flat,— and I shall then again see her. Well, her Murray article was not very significant, and as yet I cannot say that she strongly interests me. But at present it is my business to make acquaintances.

[192] Thomas Stirling Lee (1856–1916) had been exhibiting statuettes, busts, and medallions in the Royal Academy from 1878. Lee, Morley Roberts, Alfred Hartley, W. H. Hudson, and GRG gathered in one another's rooms a few nights a month for informal dinners and discussion. Lee visited only occasionally, but the other men formed what Morley Roberts called the "Quadrilateral," and thought of the group as a kind of fraternal organization (Diary, 5 October 1889).

[193] Edith Sichel (1862–1914) published many articles on literary and social problems in various periodicals; her study of GRG and Walter Besant, "Two Philanthropic Novelists," appeared in *Murray's Magazine*, III (April 1888), 506–18.

[194] Emily Ritchie, whose brother, Sir Richmond Ritchie, married Anne Thackeray.

Naturally, this becomes easier for me now that, wherever I go, my name is tolerably well known. *I cannot stand obscurity.*

(By the bye, Bentley made no kind of moral objection to "The Emancipated." If it had been by an unknown man, he would have objected—I am sure—to twenty things in it, as you will see.)

Your own intercourse with men of mark is highly satisfactory; it must have been an agreeable morning with Fontane[195] and the rest. (Yes, I must get some of those books out of a foreign circulating library.)

I wonder what sort of biog[raphica]l articles you are going to write for Frau Steinitz? Should like to hear about that paper again.

What a tragedy, that of poor Mahr![196] For a man's work to kill him, and then to be judged valueless! A dolorous business.

Your toil over official letter-writing will never do; but I expect you will find strong opposition when you wish to resign.[197] They will not so easily dismiss a valuable man. But you must act with due regard to your own objects in life.

Ever yours, dear Friend,
GEORGE GISSING

7. K. Cornwall Residences. / Regent's Park. / London. NW. /
November 4th. 1889.
Dear Friend,

I have got done with the proofs much sooner than I expected. So I shall leave England this day week, early on the morning of the 11th. That will enable me to catch Fraissinet's boat at Marseille on the morning of the 13th.

Will you, then, send your papers on the unworthy "G[eorge] G[issing]" to *Poste restante, Athens,* where I hope to be on the 18th of Nov[ember]. You shall have a card from Athens directly I get there. This present week will be a time of hurry for me; I hate the preparations and leave-takings, and so on.

Did I not tell you of my making acquaintance with Miss Sichel?

[195] Theodor Fontane (1819–1898), drama critic of the Berlin *Vossische Zeitung*, poet and novelist.
[196] See 2 April 1889.
[197] From the secretaryship of the Deutscher Schriftsteller-Verband.

It has just come to my knowledge that she inherited from her father—£20,000.[198]

Your strictures on my work are very true. Invention is the weakest of my various weak points, and I shall strive hard to remedy this. The "two-women" point is curiously English; it occurs everywhere in our fiction. I will keep clear of that, as much as possible. Your promised list of dangers to be avoided will be most welcome and valuable; pray do not forget to send it.

"The Emancipated" simply means the English people who have delivered themselves from the bondage of dogma and from the narrow views of morality that go therewith. It is written in a less continuous way than my other stories, being really a succession of scenes and sketches of character. Of course your copy shall be sent to you. It will not be out till the next year—early, I hope.

Yes, you are right about Farrar. But he needn't have been so particular in repelling the suspicion that he "knew anything about me."

I send you a proof of "Christmas on the Capitol." It is to appear in some hundreds of newspapers about Christmas week. You need not return the sheet.

I too have just been reading a book that professes to depict the future of humanity,—"Looking Backward,"[199] by Ed. Bellamy. It has almost created a sect in America. The ingenuity of the man in working out details is most remarkable and plausible. But I feel —as you do—that these men postulate too great a change in human nature.

Most admirable, the suggestion that you should become part-proprietor of a periodical, and, if possible, its editor. How perfectly are you adapted for surveying the literature of England, for instance! I do hope to hear more of this project. It would put your mind at ease in a way you have never hitherto known. And what sterling work you would do! What a sphere of influence you would soon make for yourself! Press on this undertaking, I beg of you.

---

[198] Later in the week, GRG again visited Miss Sichel and found that she "interested me; for some reason her face pleased me more than when I first saw her down in Surrey. I half think she is beautiful" (Diary, 9 November 1889).

[199] Published in Boston, 1888.

No, do not get too far away—in any case—from centres of civilization. I understand the temptation. But of course all this will depend on the magazine project.

"Crime and Punishment" is a marvellous book; I rejoice that you have read it. What psychology! What realism! On the whole, I am deeply in sympathy with Dostoiewsky. Try to get the one of his books called in French—I think—"Humiliés et Offensés."[200]

I beg you to convey to Frau Steinitz my respectful thanks for her conscientious labour on "Demos." I consider it most valuable that the book should appear in German from the hands of a translator who has made her work a task of satisfaction.

Well now, of course you shall hear from me, at length, when I have seen Athens. I shall, as before, be very anxious to have a word from you in my lonely wandering. Yes, lonely indeed. I suffer more and more from my solitude.

I have persuaded Roberts to publish a volume of his poems *by subscription*.[201] I think he will easily get a sufficient number of names, and it is to be hoped that the book will appear next spring.

Do you think there would be time for me to receive the parcel of books[202] *this* week? No, I fear not. If there is any kind of doubt about it, please keep them still.

All good be with you, my dear Friend! Let me have your critical comments. I write far too much, but I can't help it; perhaps some day I shall earn enough to enable me to take more time.

Ever yours,
GEORGE GISSING

Addressed: Herrn Eduard Bertz. / Holzmarkt Strasse, 18. / Potsdam. / *Allemagne.*

November 20th. 1889.

Dear Friend,

Your postcard reaches me to-day. My address for a month will be: / Hôtel de la Couronne. / Athens. / Will write very soon; of

---

[200] Edouard Humbert did the French translation in 1884.

[201] The subscription scheme failed, but Roberts finally persuaded a publisher to bring out the volume called *Songs of Energy.* See 16 December 1891.

[202] Algernon's *Joy Cometh in the Morning* and Roberts's Western Avernus. Bertz had had the books since July 1888.

course have much to say. Am distracted by the necessity of speaking French, Italian, German, Greek, English with incessant alternation,—the Greek, you can imagine, is limited!

Shall eagerly await your article. Do not over-toil yourself. A terrible north wind [has] been blowing here for three days. There is snow on Parnes, and Hymettos looks black and threatening.

Ever yours,
G. G.

Friday November 29th. 1889.

Hôtel de la Couronne. / Athens.

Dear Friend,

I begin to be a little anxious about the "Deutsche Presse." One has small confidence in the post here. But other things have reached me, so I will hope that you delayed to post the copies. It takes a terrible time for letters to pass between here and "Europe" —for the Greeks talk of going to "Europe." Occasionally it takes a fortnight from England. This being the case, I do not advise you to write to me *here* after receiving this letter; but, if you will, you may address a line to me "Post restante, Naples." Living here is decidedly expensive, especially, of course, because of the difficulty of the language; I shall not be able to hold out more than a month altogether, so that my departure will be *on or before December 19th.* I then go to Naples; but, I fear, only for a short time. Yes, the language is a great difficulty. I am in a purely Greek hotel (by choice, of course,) and the waiters etc. only speak a minimum of French and Italian. I think of Italy, in comparison, as if it were my native country; *there* I can speak freely and with pleasure; there I have confidence in myself. But I will add a few words later on about Modern Greek.

The voyage from Marseille was very enjoyable; it took six days, one day of stoppage at Genoa. Ah! how glorious is that scene, as you sail up the Gulf of Genoa! Surely it comes close after Naples. I wandered about the town a little (in the company of two French-speaking Greeks) and at night went to the opera—an astounding entertainment! Resuming our voyage, we were soon far from land, and it was with difficulty that I descried the bold outline of Vesuvius far away on the horizon. Before daylight, on the

following morning, I went up on deck, where a wonderful sight
awaited me; we were just passing close by Stromboli, which was in
splendid eruption; I shall not easily forget the fiery mountain, the
flushed clouds, the bright silver moon, and the blue-black depths
of sky, star-sprinkled.

Then came the straits of Messina. It was glorious weather, and
the beauty of the view in all directions cannot be described. For
a long time Etna was veiled in mists; but when we had got well
out to sea, behold there rose before us a magnificent mountain,—
vast, snow-capped, Etna itself. I never received such an impression
of hugeness in a mountain; all the other Sicilian hills, and the
mountains of Calabria, looked very small at the foot of that
glorious shape. All day long it was visible, and whilst there remained a glow of sunset (what sunsets they were!) I could see,
at a great distance, the towering mountain. It made me think of
Dante's Mount of Purgatory.

Just as we got well into the Ionian sea, the weather changed.
A fierce wind blew from the Adriatic, and the sea became very
rough indeed. Nevertheless, I enjoyed it. Then came the first
sight of Greece. We drew near, and there before me was Sphak-
beria, with the harbour of Pylos! Great heavens—to behold such
places! I rejoice that I know my Thukydides pretty well. Then
rose the snowy peaks of Taygetos, which shelters Sparta. No words
can give you the faintest idea of the evening that followed; such
light, such colour, are not of this world, as we northerners understand it. The mountains seemed to become translucent; heights
and distances had no significance; such scenes must be the despair
of painters. I think it was more marvellous than anything I have
seen in southern Italy.

We sailed up the Saronic gulf in the teeth of Boreas—a terrible
wind. But the sky was bright, and when I was once established
in Athens I did not mind a little cold and discomfort. Since then,
however, we have had the finest weather conceivable. Indeed, it
is decidedly hotter than I like; a little more, and I should not be
able to walk about at all. I see clearly that, if one comes to the
south at any season but winter, one must be prepared to spend
a great deal of money in vehicles; walking would be quite out of
the question. The sun is terrific; it smites on your back like a great

fire. The light is so brilliant that it pains the eyes; I have tried in vain to read in the open air.

Modern Athens, for a town which has grown in less than fifty years, is handsomely built and even of considerable extent. In some of the public buildings they are reviving the old custom of colouring and gilding the marble; but they are not so bold in this as the old Pericleans. I cannot say that the effect pleases me, and, with all reverence, I shall never be able to believe that the painted Parthenon was the perfection of taste. But there is one feature of the town which so astonishes at first sight that one has eyes for nothing else. With the exception of a few trees and shrubs, absolutely *not a blade of green growth* is anywhere to be seen. The open spaces are like waste building-ground; as barren as a high-road; I speak literally. The river Ilissos is about *one* foot broad, and all but disappears; the river Kephisos *does* disappear, its little stream of water being all absorbed by the olive-wood and currant-gardens in the Attic plain. The result of this state of things (combined with little or no rain) is that one lives in a cloud of dust. It is the duty of a waiter, at every hotel, to *dust* you as you enter. The discomfort of course is great. In old times things must have been very different; for the channels of the Ilissos and Kephisos are very broad and deep, and there are traces of many little streams connected with them.

The streets show very curious costumes, the commonest being the Albanian, which you doubtless know. One feels the Oriental atmosphere everywhere. Excepting the dirt, Athens is not like an Italian town; the houses are low, and there is an absence of colour. The character of the people does not appeal to me. I see very little liveliness, and a great deal of hard business. Politeness is the exception. The voices are very harsh, and modern Greek sounds disagreeable. I think with regret of the universal *melody* of Naples. In Naples every costermonger cries his goods melodiously.

In one of the finest streets stands the house of Schliemann;[203] on the front of it is written: ΙΛΙΟυ ΜΕΛΑΘΡΟΝ.[204] A very beautiful house it is, too; along the top are copies of old statues, and in

---

[203] Heinrich Schliemann (1822–1890), German merchant turned archeologist, who discovered and excavated the site of Troy.
[204] "Palace of Ilion."

front of each story is a beautifully painted marble loggia. Fortunate man!

The Museums are of purely archaeological interest; everything is fragmentary. Still, I ought to except the collections of sepulchral monuments, some of these reliefs being very beautiful indeed.

Now for the language. I am making no attempt to learn modern Greek—beyond the few necessary phrases. There is no difficulty in reading it; the newspapers are quite intelligible. But in the spoken language, the stumbling-block is *accent*. You know that in England we wholly neglect accent in ancient Greek, and pronounce solely by *quantity*. What is your practice in Germany? Now the use of the accents makes words unintelligible which are otherwise quite familiar. I am doing my best to understand this matter. I asked a Greek on board the boat to read me some Homer; he did so, and in a manner which left no music of the verse whatever. I believe that *one* reason of this was, that the man had *no ear* for the rhythms. Think of our modern verse. It is almost the exception, even with us, for *accent* and *ictus* to coincide; yet we have no difficulty in preserving the metre. And I believe I am beginning to be able to read Greek verse with the accents and at the same time preserving the metre. Very often indeed you will find lines where accent and ictus coincide perfectly; in Aristophanes it is especially frequent. But I have discovered (doubtless others have remarked it long ago) that the *later* Greek poets are far easier to read with accent than the earlier. In Homer it is rare for accent and ictus to coincide; in Apollonius Rhodius it is—I believe—rare for them *not* to do so. What does this mean? Was it a change in pronunciation, or were the later poets more *mechanical* than the earlier? But, on the whole, I am convinced that the solution of the whole problem lies in remembering the fact that we moderns have just the same phenomenon in our versification. Read a passage of Goethe, and recognize what I mean. First *scan* it methodically; then write it out with an indication of the accents necessary in good reading. Very seldom indeed will accent and ictus coincide.[205]

At Rome one reads Horace; at Athens one reads Aristophanes. It is with joy that I recognize how easy he is becoming to me. I read him, and other poets, for several hours daily.

[205] See 5 March 1891 for a letter GRG sent to the London *Times* on this subject.

What shall I say of ancient Athens? Let me copy from my diary a description of a sunset the other evening.

I was standing on the Mouseion, which is now, from a late monument, called the hill of Philopappos. The sky was all but cloudless; never yet had I seen the mountains far and near in such distinctness. To the south stretched the Saronic gulf, between Attica and Argolis, with the island of Aegina rising to a bold peak in mid distance. Westward I looked to the Piraeus, which is only three or four English miles away, (beyond a brown and dusty plain,) and above that stood the island of Salamis. The water on which the battle was fought is clearly distinguishable, even the little island of Psyttaleia, and the hill which is called Xerxes' throne. Moving my eyes northwards, I saw the Acrokorinthos, the mountains of Megaris, and, lastly, the great range of Parnes, northern boundary of the Attic plain. Eastward, in the distance lay the cone-shaped Pentelikon; nearer, the desolate and many-valley'd Hymettus, and nearer still Lykabettos and the Akropolis.

Keeping my back to the sun, I looked at the Akropolis; it stood in golden splendour; temples, bulwarks and rock, all of the same warm amber-colour, as if all were but one structure. As the sun sank, the shadow of the hill on which I was standing gradually rose upon the Akropolis, which little by little lost its glory. I turned, and saw the red sun disappear behind the Argolic mountains. A few minutes of cold sky and earth, then began the afterglow. The western sky glowed with yellow warmth; the zenith and the east became a profound azure, and again the Akropolis took its golden colour, though deeper than before.[206]

How it helps one to understand the Greek writers! For instance, whenever I am on the Akropolis, I have but to look westward, and there I see the white road winding away to Eleusis, the Sacred Way of the Mysteries. At a very little distance lies a hill, among the olives of the Kephisos, which is no other than Kolonos; you see the white-gleaming of the monument of K. O. Müller,[207] which

---

[206] The two preceding paragraphs are variations of the version in the Diary, 25 November 1889.

[207] Karl Otfried Müller (1797–1840), professor of archeology at Göttingen, whose excavations on the sites of ancient Athens and Delphi stimulated the study of Greek antiquities.

stands there. The proximity of Salamis, I have mentioned. Look north, and you all but see De Keleia, thus realizing an important part of the Peloponnesian War. On the side of Pentelikon you see the quarries from which the temples were built. Greek literature becomes a different thing.

Indeed, I shall scarcely henceforth think of Greek as a dead language. How can I, when I have heard the newsboys shouting about the streets every morning—"'Η 'Ακρόπολι-ι-ις!"[208] which is the name of a newspaper.

Very, very little of old Athens remains, putting aside the Acropolis. There is the glorious Theseion, most perfect of existing Greek temples; and indeed it makes a wonderful impression; but the rest is mere crumbling stone and marble. The Acropolis itself I am studying carefully. You know that Pheidias's great frieze ran round the wall of the *Cella* of the Parthenon. Now I find what I have always suspected concerning it; it is *impossible*, and must always have been impossible, to see this frieze properly. Not only have you to break your neck with looking upwards, but you look into comparative gloom, which must have been still worse when the temple was roofed. This troubles me. I am convinced that the frieze has been far better seen in the British Museum than it ever was on the Parthenon.

And cannot one make the same objection to the ceiling-paintings in Italy? Who ever was able to see the pictures in the Sistine Chapel as they ought to be seen?

— —

My life is one of solitary study. I have no acquaintances, and evidently shall not be able to make any. Of course I sometimes feel a great loneliness. No one can imagine what I have lost by making these journeys without a sympathetic companion.

I have not yet had a line from England, and it seems a long time, though of course it is not really so. I feel disposed to ask you whether your life has undergone any great change since I last heard. In any case, I fear you have begun to suffer from wintery weather. I shall be very glad indeed to hear from you. Doubtless I shall have done so long before you receive this letter.

You know the difference in the Greek calendar. To-day it is here the 17th. of November only.

[208] "The Acropolis."

Well, I will send this for what it is worth, and hope it may reach you safely. I wish I had more confidence in the post.

By the bye, if you receive this *before the 10th of December*, perhaps there would be no danger in sending a postcard to my address here.

Ever yours, dear Friend,
GEORGE GISSING

Athens.
Dear Friend,

December 14th. 1889.

After an interval of magnificent weather, hot and bright as the best of an English midsummer, we are again tormented by the violent winds which are evidently a characteristic of Attica. Impossible to walk about in such a gale. And unfortunately I have had a sore throat for more than a fortnight; cannot get rid of it. Evidently I shall not do so till I reach Italy. As my time here is now drawing to an end, I will write you a little more about Athens. I shall leave Patras by an Italian steamer on the night of December 17th. By December 20th. I hope to be in Naples.

But first—you received my card,[209] in which I mentioned the *Deutsche Presse?* Well, I need not say that the article pleased and gratified me enormously.[210] I can quite understand the approval with which it has met, as a piece of literary work. You have omitted no single point which I could have wished to see mentioned. Of course it is the writing of a friend, but then there has never been a lack of the other kind of criticism.

A sad example of modern degradation is seen in the Cemetery here. The monumental marbles are in wretched taste, and often very pretentious. Vulgar portraits of the dead people are very

---

[209] The post card is not in this collection.

[210] E. Bertz, "George Gissing, ein Real-Idealist," *Deutsche Presse*, II (3 November 1889), 357–59; II (10 November 1889), 366–67; II (17 November, 1889), 374–75. The Diary records receipt of the papers: "At last a letter from Bertz, inclosing the 3 numbers of the Deutsche Press (3rd, 10th, 17th Nov.) in which he criticizes (or rather eulogizes) me: 'George Gissing: Ein [sic] Real-Idealist.' Very good of the old fellow. He tells me my name is getting known to a literary circle there" (4 December 1889).

common, and in one instance I saw the bust of a man, in relief, with the *stud* in his shirt-front carefully *gilded*.[211] But the worst indication of an utter loss of the old noble habits of thought with regard to death and burial is seen in the fact that, on the wooden cross at the head of the grave, it is quite the common thing to paint a *skull* and *cross-bones*, a revolting practice. The heading of the inscription is generally the pure Attic: ΕΝΘΑΔΕ ΚΕΙΤΑΙ.[212]

A painted notice in the Cemetery interested me by having its words written without intervals, precisely as in the old inscriptions and manuscripts. What is the habit of mind that leads to this practice? I suppose it is a literal reproduction of the way in which we talk.

The town swarms with soldiers. This continental curse of militarism! Most of them are very young fellows, and anything but imposing. They are of low stature, thin, badly shaped; their faces are small, bony, ignoble, of dirty complexion. Their intelligence must be very elementary. Most of them look hungry, and have obviously been brought up on miserable diet. I know not what type of Greek they represent. But indeed it is the rarest thing to see a man or woman whose face is not ignoble. I suppose the old races have in truth been utterly supplanted by successive invasions of barbarism.

I have had a little intercourse with a young Greek named Parigory, who came in the boat from Marseilles. He came here to see me lately, and was civil—he speaks French—so that I at length invited him to dinner, and we spent an evening together. He is tolerably well educated, but knows little of the antiquities of Greece. He is, in fact, *uninteresting*, and that, I fear, is the fault of all the Greeks.

Alas! alas! The Piraeus is a great busy manufacturing town, and has huge mill-chimneys which vomit fumes. From every point of view, its smoke is an eyesore in the exquisite landscape looking

[211] In GRG's *Sleeping Fires* (New York: Appleton and Co., 1896), Louis Reed says: "There's a marble life-sized medallion of a man in his habit as he lived, and, by Jove, if they haven't gilded the studs in his shirtfront" (p. 15). Many of the observations on Greece recorded in these letters appear in the novel.

[212] "Here lies."

9

towards Salamis. And Athens will soon be the same; already it has several high chimneys.

The most delightful walk I have had was to Eleusis. I started early in the morning and followed the old Sacred Way, which is still the high road. After passing over the plain, it goes through a pass in the range of Aigaleos, and immediately one looks down upon the Bay of Eleusis, a glorious picture. To the right is the wide Thriasian Plain, in front the great mountains of Megaris, with little Eleusis at the foot of them, and to the left you see Salamis. There was a strong wind, and the waves were rolling up magnificently. There are no dwellings to disturb one's impression. Returning, I kept to the shore, all round the base of Aigaleos, opposite Salamis. It is a wild, stony mountain, on which only pines and lentiscs grow. The smell of the pines blended with the odour of the sea. And so I came right round to the point where Xerxes placed his throne.

From all points, the view of Athens is grand. At a distance of many miles you see its hills rising nobly, and on the Acropolis there gleams the marble Parthenon. How well I understand now that passage in the Oedipus Coloneus where Oedipus asks what town it is that his daughter beholds at a distance![213] But one cannot conceive what the view of it was like when all the old buildings and statues were in their places.

About half the old city is now mere barren ground. Look at any map of Athens you happen to possess, and you will see, west of the Acropolis, a ridge of hills; they form three eminences, divided by valleys: the Hill of the Nymphs, (now the Observatory,) the Pnyx, and the Mouseion, (now called, from a late monument, the hill of Philopappos). These hills rise abruptly on the side of the town, but on the other side have a long, slow declension to the plain. As I said, they are barren, and barren in the Attic sense of the word, that is to say, a stony wilderness and desolation. All over their surface crops up the red-and-blue limestone. Now the interesting point is, that, wherever this stone is uncovered, it is seen to be carved artificially into square hollows, and corners and steps, and so on. Evidently, every inch of the ground was covered with habitations, and the rock, wherever possible, was allowed to remain as paving, or staircase, or wall of house. Extraordinary

[213] Sophocles, *Oedipus Coloneus*. I. 1-13.

how complete is the destruction of every trace of building over this vast area.

The practice of using the native rock as much as possible is beautifully illustrated on the Acropolis itself. The surface of [the] hill was never *paved*. The rock is simply cut into terraces, and, for pathways, quite roughly levelled; in one place there is an ascent of *nine* steps, about thirty feet long, carved directly out of the stone. The result of this is that the temples and statues must have seemed to *grow* out of the Acropolis itself, and form part of the living rock.

And in walking about it, among the innumerable fragments of ruin, one sees here and there broken bits of iron bombshell, which have been allowed to remain ever since that fatal year 1687.[214] The name of Venice suffers much from the event of that year.

Within the Parthenon, on the marble walls, one sees fading pictures of saints, with aureoles about their heads, relics of the time when the Parthenon was a church. Strange thoughts these excite!

After all, I shall have seen only Athens and its immediate neighbourhood. I shall not even get to Marathon. My sore throat forbids me to be out either early in the morning or late at night. And then, the expenses of travelling are great. The accommodation, too, in the country is of a terribly primitive description; I dare not face it in solitude.

Well, it is something to have seen Athens. For the present, I must be content. You know that the scene of Aeschylus's "Emenides" [*sic*] lies at the foot of the Areiopagos, by the well sacred to the Eumenides themselves. This well still exists; it is in the farthest recess of some huge, wild rocks that are heaped about the foot of the hill. One goes in search of it with enthusiasm; but what does one find? The whole locality is simply a vast *lieux d'aisance* for the public. The air is poisoned, and you cannot step without treading in human ordure. Well, we know the habits of the South, but in this instance it is nothing less than a gross disgrace to the town. Such a place to be subject to such defilement!

I have just read Lucian's "Dream" and "Charm" and "Timon." And now I am busy with Plato's "Symposium."

[214] When the Venetians bombarded Athens, which was held by the Turks, a shot exploded a powder magazine in the Parthenon, destroying it.

If you could imagine the glory of some of the sunsets I have seen here! Vain to try and describe them. The effects on land and sea are such as I could never have conceived.

They are very careless in their transliteration of foreign names into Greek. For instance, I find to-day, in the course of *one* article the following forms of Schliemann's name: Ελεῖμαν, Ελῆμαν, Ελεῖμανν. And of Bötticher[215] the following remarkable forms: Μπαίτιχερ, Μπαίττιχερ, and Μπαίτχερ. You know, by the bye, that they represent the sound of B by Μπ, and that of D by Νῖ; seeing that β is pronounced like a German *w*, and δ like an English *th*.

— —

I broke off this patchy letter to go with young Parigory to a class at the University. A professor was lecturing on the "Philoktetes." It gave me much delight, and made me think of the many generations of old Romans who came to Athens to hear Greek teachers; here too am I, *ultimus Britannus*, after all these centuries, listening to Sophokles from Greek lips. The room was very full (about 300 attended) and up to the last moment before the lecturer's entrance a great many were *smoking*. The professor was an ugly man, dressed in every-day clothes; he placed his little ordinary hat on the desk, and began at once to read a passage of the play. Then he paraphrased it into modern Greek, and last of all he gave critical comments, largely due to Dindorf[216] and Hermann[217] and other Germans, whose names he of course mentioned. I was surprised that I could frequently understand what he said. As for his reading of the verse, it confirmed the opinions I have formed, and which I expressed to you in my last letter. He did not read it with the same attention to the metre that *we* are accustomed to give, but still I think the metre was preserved. The difficulties he had to explain to the class were very numerous, and, curiously enough, just the same as would be dwelt upon in Germany or England.

To follow the lecture, I bought a copy of the "Philoktetes,"

[215] Paul Anton Bötticher (1827–1891), known also as Paul de Lagarde, a German Orientalist, who translated many Greek, Chaldean, and Arabic texts.

[216] Either Ludwig August Dindorf (1805–1871), or Wilhelm Dindorf (1802–1883), both German classical scholars.

[217] Johann Gottfried Hermann (1772–1848), German classical philologist.

so that I shall now read this, as soon as I have finished the "Symposium." My object is—to read Greek like [sic] we read modern languages, fluently at sight; a thing, you are aware, which very few men can do, even with lucid authors like Plato. I shall very soon reach this end, I think.

So this is the last letter from Athens. My education slowly progresses; in a few years I hope to be a decently cultivated man. But I have still much travelling to do. I think Germany will come next;[218] I want to know Berlin, Dresden and Vienna, particularly. After that, if I live, I shall have a look at Spain and read Don Quixote *in situ*. Ah! how much time one wastes in learning vocabularies. The old Greeks were free from this necessity, and think what that implied.

At the bookseller's, I see a lot of Tauchnitz[219] novels put aside with a paper on them "Die Königin." I am sorry for the Queen's taste; there was some shocking English rubbish—Miss Braddon[220] etc.

And so, once more, with heartiest congratulations on the time of freedom which approaches for you,

Ever yours,
GEORGE GISSING

Your letter just received. Many thanks for the printed form. Indeed I doubt whether you ought to yield to any solicitations.[221]

Your information about the Greek accent question is very useful. In modern Greek not only are y and l and v pronounced like German *ie*, but *also* the diphthongs ei, oi and ui—an extraordinary fact. It is called *Toticism*. Yes θ is pronounced like English *th* in *thing*; and δ like that in *that*. υ after α, ε and η is pron[ounced] like Germ[an] *w*; therefore αὐτός = awtós but ου is the German *u*. And β is like *f*.

I must decidedly read the books in which this subject of the ancient pronunciation is discussed.

[218] He did not visit Germany until 1898, and then only briefly.

[219] Christian Bernhard Tauchnitz (1816–1895), a Leipzig publisher, who reprinted books for English readers on the Continent in his "Collection of British and American Authors."

[220] Mary Elizabeth Braddon (1837–1915), a prolific author of popular romances. Translations of her work were widely read in Germany.

[221] Bertz did not want to run for re-election for the secretaryship of the Schriftsteller-Verband.

You are very right about the effect of white marble in the Greek sun. Even now, one can scarcely look at the temples, in sunshine, so extreme is their brilliancy. I think here is the explanation of the painting.

Without doubt, we shall see Italy together. Before long, I hope to have a permanent abode near Naples. At present I think I shall stay there a month. I hope to spend a few days with Shortridge at Massa Labrense.

Do not trouble about the abridgement of "Demos." The newspaper publication matters nothing. I am told that it has recently been republished, in extenso, in the "Manchester Weekly Times," and that big advertisements of it were posted all over the walls of the town. I do not altogether rejoice at this.[222] But I earnestly hope that your work on my behalf has not been in vain. Indeed it cannot have been, from the more important point of view.

G. G.

Addressed: Herrn Eduard Bertz. / Holzmarkt Strasse—18 / Potsdam / Germania.

December 23rd, 1889.

Sunlight, warmth, uproar, music,—Napoli, Napoli! I have much to tell you about the journey. Were driven back onto the shore of Dalmatia by bad weather. Arrived here two days ago. Am going to send you a photograph,[223] which I hope will arrive safely. Established at my old quarters: / 8 Vico Brancaccio (30. p.) / Napoli. / Much comfort. Weather excellent just now, but the smoke of Vesuvius (old scoundrel) has begun to blow inland. Hope you have my last long letter from Athens.

The streets very lively with Christmas arrangements. Shall shortly go over to Massa for a day, to see Shortridge.[224]

Ever yours,
G. G.

[222] Because of the scandal attached to his name when he was at Owens College.

[223] A view of the Acropolis, which GRG had bought in Athens (Diary, 10 December 1889).

[224] "This morning a postcard from Shortridge, asking me to come. Left by the 11:35 train for Castellammare. There made a bargain for carriage to Massa,—4 francs. A wretched little horse in a beggarly carriage,—tattered and crusted with the mud of ages. . . . Reached Villa Cozzolino at 3 p.m." (Diary, 31 December 1889).

Vico Brancaccio, 8. (30. p.) / Napoli.

January 8th. 1890.

My dear Friend,

What a wonderful man you are! In the midst of all your manifold occupations, you find time and inclination to be far more active on my behalf than I ever could be myself in the same matter. To think of your writing to Tauchnitz![225] Well, it was a good idea, and good will come of it, no doubt. Thank you much. I should be very glad if the edition of Walt Whitman were put into your hands in consequence of this correspondence.[226] But now indeed you must take a rest from troubling about the affairs of the "Engländer George Gissing." You have more than enough to do for a long time. Leave further writing until I myself have written more.

I am sorry if you think that Wendlandt's[227] indiscretion will hinder the speedy publication of "Demos." But on my own account it does not trouble me. I know that for some years yet the sale of my books will be small and difficult. You have done very much to help me on, at all events.

Your letter is very full. The list of books you have to review strikes me with awe, and I am not a little indignant to think that you are to receive such small payment. Still, your *standing* will be improved. Indeed you must now be well known in literary circles, and before long we shall laugh over all your old doubts and despairs.

Yes, yes, I foresaw that you would be overcome in the matter of re-election to the Secretaryship. But the arrangements are better, and indeed I think you have done very well to be so practical. Also the project of removing your abode seems to solve a difficulty. I shall be glad when you are safe in the suburb.

---

[225] "Bertz sends copy of Deutsche Presse, in which is a reference to my work again. He says he has written to Tauchnitz, asking him to print my name in future on 'Demos'; Tauchnitz, in agreeing, mentioned that he has got 'Nether World' for eventual publication" (Diary, 6 January 1890). The first London edition of *Demos* had been published anonymously. There is no record of a Tauchnitz edition of *The Nether World*.

[226] Bertz was not asked to edit any of Whitman's work. Johannes Schlaf edited *Grashalme* in 1897.

[227] Wilhelm Wendlandt (1859–19?), German journalist. The mysterious indiscretion apparently was not serious.

Let me know of anything that Legerlotz[228] writes to you on Greek matters. Of course I make no pretence to critical knowledge.

I grieve to hear that sentence about Rossetti's pictures. Well, both his pictures and his poems have had a very great influence on my life and thought. I look back to the days when I first knew him as to a dawn of beautiful imaginings.

As you mention Salvatore Farina,[229] I have purchased one of his books, and shall at once read it. I am also reading a lot of books concerning Neapolitan life, studying the dialect a little, and so on. I know not whether it will all lead to anything.

But I have never yet told you about my journey from Greece, which was very interesting. If only it had been good weather. All day it blew a furious gale; at Corinth one could scarcely stand. At that place, it was curious to see the canal across the Isthmus, which is all but finished; the railway goes right over it. I am glad to have seen a specimen of this kind of engineering. Then we went on along the northern coast of the Peloponnesus, through old Achaia, a country covered with olive woods and currant gardens. The view opposite, across the gulf, was glorious; if only there had been sunshine. First the great mass of Helicon, deep in snow, and then the vaster heights of Parnassus! They were both visible for hours, and just at sunset a tender rose-tint spread over the snow of both mountains. The peaks of Parnassus unfortunately I could not see, for clouds.

At Patras I went at once on board the Florio-Rubattini steamer, and we sailed at midnight. Alas! It was dark when we passed Ithaka; I would have given much to see that island. When I went up on deck, at sunrise, we were just opposite Actium, off the Ambrucian gulf. The island of Leucadia lay south, and in the north gleamed the great snowy mountains of Epirus. I had strange thoughts, you may be sure.

We reached the harbour of Corfu very early, and lay there all day. It was as hot as an English summer. I sat on deck reading the Philoctetes, and enjoying the magnificent landscape. About midnight we again started.

I went up early next morning, thinking we must be near Brindisi. But to my surprise I saw we were approaching a great

[228] Gustav Legerlotz (1832–?), German scholar.
[229] Salvatore Farina (1846–1918), a novelist known as the "Italian Dickens."

bay on a wild mountainous shore. It turned out that the sea was too rough to cross, and so the Captain, afraid, had gone back to the Turkish coast, and here we were in the harbour of Avelona. Great was the indignation among the passengers. But the steward told me that the ship was only safe in the very calmest weather, so perhaps it was as well to wait a little!

All day long we waited. It seemed absurd, for the sky was cloudless. A magnificent sunset! We had to send a boat ashore to buy provisions, and so got some Turkish bread to eat. Meat, we were told, cost only 40 c. the kilo! And all other things were proportionately cheap.

Well, we crossed the Adriatic in the night (it only took six hours) and next morning I saw the flat coast at Brindisi. Glorious sunrise, and again a cloudless sky, indeed rather too hot.

I took the train at once. I had the choice of going either *via* Foggia, or *via* Taranto, and I chose the latter, although by the former route I should have seen Cannae. But I was tempted by the names of Metapontum and Tarentum! A desolate, fever-stricken coast, but very beautiful in the broad sunshine. At Meta-pontum we struck north for Salerno, and then entered country familiar to me. At 11 at night we reached here, with a carriage full of roaring Neapolitans.

In the train I had made the acquaintance of a Greek,[230] who spoke Italian. He was on his way to Buenos Ayres. As he had to wait a week for his ship, he came to live at this house, and we got on very well together. A good, simple fellow, who had never seen any town bigger than Athens! Naples astounded him!

I have just spent a week with Shortridge at Massa. That amazing household is more amazing than ever. It is a splendid opportunity of studying the life of the lower Neapolitans. The family live in dirt and discomfort and misery,—all this in the midst of glorious scenery, there at the extremity of the Sorrento promontory, with the cliffs of Capri opposite! Mrs. Shortridge was a Capri girl,

[230] Alexandre Panagópoulos. "Had noticed all through the journey from Patras a young Greek who travelled 2nd. class on the boat, but did not take his meals at the table. On reaching Naples, I determined to speak to him, as felt sure he knew nothing of the town and would be at a loss for a hotel. Addressed him in Italian, and he responded readily. Found he spoke a little English. I liked his face, and found his character cor-respondent" (Diary, 19 December 1889).

and does not speak a word of English, though she had been married fifteen years. Neither do the children, four girls, (a boy has died) who are growing up without learning even to read and write. The curse of the household is Shortridge's brother,—once a medical student in Edinburgh—who is drunk every day, and (happily) is dying of consumption.[231] Shortridge says he has resolved to emigrate to Connecticut next summer; but I doubt if his character has still enough strength for such a decided step; of course he proposes to take all the family with him, including his wife's father, old Raffaele, who lives in the dirty kitchen and does menial work,—he is a totally uneducated peasant. Heavens! what terrible food I had to eat![232] But the wife, poor Carmela, is not *bad*; only foolish, and animal-like, and—Italian. She took me into her confidence one evening, and lamented the misery of her life. She says that Shortridge, in his rages, sometimes threatens her with knives; I think it is very likely true, for he is a passionate fellow. She almost made me cry, telling of her sorrows in the foolish sing-song Caprese dialect. Such a situation I never knew, as that of the whole establishment at Villa Cozzolino.

We have had some bad weather. One storm was fearful; for 36 hours it thundered and lightened and rained in torrents. All the steep streets of Naples were converted into mountain streams.

But alas, alas! An incredible thing has happened. The idiotic municipal authorities have actually (from Christmas-day) forbidden the street-organs in Naples! I speak seriously when I say that this greatly diminishes my pleasure here, and affects me deeply.

They also tried to stop the explosive bombs at Christmas, but this was found to be impossible. All Christmas night the uproar was like that in a besieged city. Many people were injured. At the windows they burned Bengal lights, and the fire dropped onto your head as you walked below. No one went to bed. The people gorged themselves with gigantic eels, the regular Christmas dish, and broccoli[.]

[231] Herbert Shortridge died about two months later (Diary, 5 April 1890).

[232] "A vile dinner. Food bad, and piggishly thrown onto table; think I never saw such slovenly ways. A disgusting form of maccherone, mixed with sugar, raisins, pigne, gravy, etc. This is a regular Capri dish at Christmas" (Diary, 31 December 1889).

Now the weather is once more superb. When I wake in the morning, I raise my head, and there is sunshine making every thing a rich gold; in the sky not a cloud. These, too, are nights of full moon. After dinner, I walk along the bay; the sea and sky are both a profound blue. Thank heaven, some blackguards come to play and sing in front of the great hotels; I hear every night "Santa Lucia," and "Addio, bella Napoli." But I miss the organs sadly. Naples, the old Naples, is vanishing day by day; I notice the process even in a year's time. The next thing will be that Vesuvius will become extinct!

I have decided to stay here till February 4th., and then go home by sea, taking a steamer of the Orient Line, which calls here on its way from Australia to London. So I shall see Gibraltar, and also the Bay of Biscay, by Jove, in winter!

What about the "Influenza" with you? Poor Roberts has had it, and has been seriously ill for a fortnight or more; has had to go home to be nursed. I hope you will not be troubled. We have got it here at last, but it seems to be a very mild form.[233] It would be disagreeable to find myself prostrated; but they are good people here in the house, and it is better to have it here than in the atmosphere of London.

All good be with you throughout 1890. Strange that we have lived to see this year. Shall we see 1900? Chi lo sa?[234]

Again my warmest thanks to you for all your kind activity. You shall hear from me again before I go.

Ever yours affectionately,
GEORGE GISSING

Addressed: Herrn. Eduard Bertz. / Holzmarkt Strasse. 18. / Potsdam. / Germania.
Naples.

January 31. 1890
The ship is expected to arrive here, on its way from Australia, on the 6th February; so I have only a week longer.

[233] The influenza epidemic of 1889–90 began in Siberia in October 1889, reached Berlin and Paris by November, and by December was pandemic in Italy, Spain, and England.
[234] "Who knows?"

I have a letter from a certain Miss Nolte,[235] of Bremen, asking permission to translate "The Nether World." I think I had better warn her that there is no chance of getting it published.

I hope for the sake of the Steinitz's [*sic*] that "Demos" may be sold; but on my own account, pray do not trouble for a moment. I so fully understand the difficulties. My reputation is still entirely local, and the books themselves do not appeal to the public. I am sure your "Glück u[nd] Glas" ought not to remain unpublished; but, as you say, the difficulties are just the same. I feel with you on that point.

Glad to hear of your new address. Yes, I hope to see you there.

Am very much annoyed that Bentley has postponed "The Emancipated" so long. Of course my new book is beginning to trouble me. I have had the Influenza, and feel in very low spirits.

Ever yours,
G. G.

Addressed: Miss E. S. Gissing / Stoneleigh Terrace. / Agbrigg. / Wakefield. / Inghilterra.[236]

Naples.

February 15th. 1890.

You will be surprised to receive this. Your letter, addressed to England, has just reached me. When I ought to have been sailing from Naples, I was lying ill in bed, with congestion of one lung. Attended by an excellent German doctor, a most delightful fellow. Am quite well again, and sail on the 20th. February.

---

[235] Not identified.

[236] GRG put the wrong address on this post card, sending it to Ellen instead of Bertz. She forwarded the card with the following note:

Dear Herr Bertz,

I fancy that my brother has made a singular mistake and has sent to me a card intended for you. There being no means of letting him know of this (as you will see he was to sail on the 20th.), I am sending the card to you—as I feel sure—it is to you that it belongs. I hope that your address is still the same—as I find my brother gave me this address in 1888.

Ellen Gissing

No, no, I have done nothing rash in reference to Fr. Nolte, and of course did not speak of Fr. Steinitz's difficulties.[237] That was a purely private matter. Delighted to hear of your editorship.[238]

Have decided to come to Germany as soon as I have finished my new book, and to remain there until I have a decent command of the language. Perhaps you will not be sorry to hear this. Hope to be in Berlin by the beginning of October.

Am interested by the Münchener Allge[meine] Zeitung. Shall try to see it.

The almond-trees are in full blossom here. Am living in a circle of Swiss and Germans. Interesting acquaintance with a certain Herr von Usedom, a professor who is on leave of absence from Germany, owing to his suffering from cataract. Has been a teacher in England, and is a cultured man.

Ever yours,
G. G.

Nearing Gibraltar.[239]

February 22nd. 1890.

Dear Friend,

I am suffering from an old affliction, the *circumfluence* of English people. No, I don't like them; and just as little do they like me. After my society at Casa di Luca this ship is most depressing. We have some hundreds of people on board, but I foresee that I shall not make a single acquaintance.

About Casa di Luca I must give you more detailed information. The place is recommended in Baedeker, and only Germans go there as a rule.[240] At present there are some ten or twelve Germans and German-Swiss regularly living there, and a constant coming and going of tourists. Among the residents is one Alfred v. Usedom, a teacher in a school at Wiesloch bei Heidelberg, a man of fifty, who is waiting till his eyes can be operated for cataract. He speaks English very well, and we soon found each other very sympathetic. He is a

---

[237] I.e., in finding a publisher for the translation of *Demos*.
[238] Of the *Deutsche Presse*. Steinitz's name was still carried on the masthead as the editor.
[239] He had sailed from Naples on 20 February 1890 (Diary).
[240] GRG tried to avoid pensions and hotels used by the British.

thoughtful, philosophic fellow, with a tendency to see good in the present and devote the past to oblivion. He and I used to have lunch alone together daily, in the house; a habit I got into in consequence of my illness. Then, at dinner, there were generally seven or eight of us. After Usedom, the man who I like best is one Hugo Fink, a horticulturist;[241] during these last days his *Braut* has come from Germany, and they are going to be married at once, after an engagement of eight years. The young lady has a room in the house, and takes her dinner with the company every evening. Fink is just beginning to study English, so that I was able to help him. He has taken a house some forty miles from Naples, and will go there after the marriage.

What good fellows they are, all of them! And how impossible to find such a circle of Englishmen in any part of the world! The English are fools in the matter of foreign travel. They will not abandon the least of their English habits; they must live in grand hotels or pensions; they know not what is meant by sociability. Talk to the average Englishman when he returns from travelling, and you find that he has been all the time exclusively with English people. He seldom makes any attempt to speak a foreign language, and he turns up his nose at foreign dishes, foreign habits, etc. Fools! Fools!

The house is kept by Frau Häberlin, a Swiss, but at present she is away, starting a new pension on the Lago di Garda, in Catullus's country. In her absence the place is conducted by a niece of hers, Laurence Häberlin, a girl of eight-and-twenty. A good, admirable girl! She speaks the *four* languages with fluency; she is an excellent housekeeper; she has brains enough for five ordinary women; she has heart enough for half-a-dozen. With her lives another aunt, an oldish woman who has a disease of the spine. Those two aunts are her only relatives.

She is not good-looking; no, she is even *very* plain; but I like her more than anyone I have met for a long time. During my illness she attended to me with the greatest kindness, and we have become very good friends. As I tell you, she may be considered

[241] Fink probably worked for the Zoological Station, founded by Dr. Dohen, a German naturalist, in 1872 as a center for the study of the plant and animal life of the Mediterranean Sea area.

very well educated, and there is a moral strength and dignity in her which delights me. Well—

Then I must mention Dr. Malbranc, who came to me in my illness. One of the nicest fellows I ever met! In the best sense of the word a gentleman, and impressing one as admirable in his profession. A man of the bright German intelligence, but absolutely without pedantry. He has a large practice among foreigners in Naples (speaks the four languages admirably) and also among the poorer Neapolitans. I am going to send him a book of mine; for, though I saw him three days before leaving, and he promised to send me his bill at once, he never sent it at all.[242] Miss Häberlin tells me that this is just like him.

In short, I feel as if I had left my home to wander about the world. Naples is more to me than ever.

You say that I have never given you a definite notion of Shortridge. Well, he is not, strictly speaking an educated man. As a boy he ran away to sea, and he has since been in every quarter of the world; yet he still preserves the Yorkshire dialect in his speech. He has a bright intelligence and a vast store of miscellaneous information; speaks a very fluent (but rather bad) German, and Italian in the same way. But the man is a born artist. He has portfolios full of beautiful sketches and drawings. His marriage, and his roving temperament, have been the ruin of him. Every day things get more wretched in his wretched house. He is passionate, and, I am afraid, sometimes beats his wife. Those poor children of his! I know not what will become of them.

Tonight there is soft and beautiful lightning, from time to time, in the southern sky, away over Africa. To-morrow morning we are due at Gibraltar, and I shall see Africa itself.

February 25th.

We reached Gibraltar at 12 o'clock to-day, and stayed there three hours. It is an immense rock jutting out into the sea. The weather was rainy, and the top of the rock was covered with great

---

[242] "Went to see the doctor and pay him. Name is Malbranc, but a German; address 145 Via Amadea, Chiaia. Seems to be an excellent fellow. Talks almost perfect English. Think I shall send him a book of mine when I get home. Charged me only 5 fr." (Diary, 31 January 1890). GRG sent a copy of *The Nether World*.

black clouds. Opposite lay Africa; huge wild mountains. "Arida nutrix leonum."[243] I thought of Jugurtha and Hannibal and many another story.

Saw a good "water-spout." A point of the sea's surface seemed to be boiling; it sent up great volumes of steam, which ascended to the clouds in the shape of a long tree-trunk, expanding at the top. It moved along and crossed the front of the ship.

So now begins the rough portion of the voyage. Farewell to the Mediterranean!

February 26th

I write with difficulty. We are rolling about in the Bay of Biscay, with a stiff N.E. wind. Hope to be at Plymouth to-morrow morning, and at London the morning after. Shall post this as soon as I arrive.

The other morning the ship's parson happened to have a talk with me, and he evidently observed my name written on a book I was reading. The next morning he approached me with a grin and began: "I hear you are a celebrated author." He explained that someone in the first class had heard him mention my name and at once recognized it.

This has a symbolical significance. It is my fate in life to be known by the first-class people and to associate with the second class—or even the third and fourth. It will always be so.

But the fact of recognition was satisfactory.

Ever yours, dear Friend,
GEORGE GISSING

7. K. Cornwall Residences. / Regent's Park. / London. NW.

March 26th. 1890.

Dear Friend,

I understand very well your extreme busyness just at this time. You shall have at all events a few lines on your arrival in the new abode, where I wish you a hopeful and active time, and where, I trust, I shall actually see you before very long.

Fräulein Reuter's letter rejoices me, as you can understand.[244]

---

[243] Horace, *Carminum* I. xxii. 15–16.

[244] Bertz forwarded a "copy of a letter he has rec' from German authoress, Frlle. [*sic*] Gabriele Reuter, of Weimar, in enthusiastic praise of 'Demos' " (Diary, 24 March 1890). Fraülein Reuter (1859–1941) wrote novels about the

English women do not write in that way; I have never yet had serious appreciation from one of them, though I should have been so glad of it. From my heart I thank her, be she old or young, beautiful or not.

"The Emancipated" is just published, and I will send your copy in a few days. Unfortunately, there are a few stupid misprints, and one blunder on my part, which I have corrected. Bentley expresses himself hopefully about the book. We shall see. At all events it will be a new kind of work to those who know me only from my other books. You, of course, will find nothing for which you are not prepared.

Yes, I understand your feeling with regard to what happened at your grandfather's funeral. Of course that disregard of a dead man's wishes is absolutely wrong, and revolts one, especially in a matter such as this. But the consistent agnostics still are so isolated in the world; so seldom they have absolute sympathizers among their immediate friends and relatives.[245]

By the bye, I have just re-read the "Memoiren einer Idealistin,"[246] and with even more satisfaction than in the first case, I admire that woman greatly; she is a noble and pathetic figure. Above all, how strictly just she is! I am impressed by numerous points in which she resists—or does not even feel—a natural temptation to exaggerate. How I should like to have known her! Where and how and when did she die?

I am also re-reading, very carefully, "Niels Lyhne." In the original, the style must be very delightful; what colour it has! I wonder whether there are yet any other of his things in Reclam's Series.[247]

I have begun another book.[248] Alas, the money-question does not allow me to pause as long as I should like between one and the

emancipation of women; her most popular novel, *Aus guter Familie*, dealt with the problem of society's superfluous women, the same subject GRG investigated in The Odd Women.

[245] Possibly a religious service was held at the old man's funeral.

[246] Malwida von Meysenburg (1816–1903), (Leipzig, 3 vols., 1885).

[247] Jacobsen's *Sechs Novellen*, a collection of short stories, was also published by Reclam.

[248] He had begun the new book on 3 March (Diary). No name had been given to the story, but part of it was to be set in Sark and Guernsey (*Letters*, p. 308).

next. Did I mention to you that I am going to take my sisters to Paris for 10 days in the middle of April? I want to get about half the first volume done before then. After that I think I shall go to Wakefield, like last year. In London, the solitude soon becomes intolerable, solitude as complete as it was when I published my first book. You were here then; and now I have one friend in Roberts;[249] but no general society either then or now. What man, whose work was so well known as mine, ever—at my age—lived such a life?

The weather is very oppressive; still like mid-winter. Heavens, what it must be in Naples now!

Very right you are to resolve on having all your time free henceforth. The way is cleared before you, and you have now only to produce. It rejoices me that the years have brought you a wholesome accession of hopefulness.

An organ is playing under my windows, and I forget my miseries. You do not quite understand my attitude with regard to street-organs. My liking for them is purely personal; I do not resist their abolition *on principle*; I rage when they disappear, simply because *I* need their help so much, in my chronic depression.[250] Blessed be every organ grinder! To them I owe all that I have done.

There is nothing new in English literature, absolutely nothing. The dead level at which we stand just now is very noticeable. The "leading novelists" have taken their commercial rank, and nothing is to be expected from them. In poetry there is absolutely no activity. Now that Browning is dead,[251] Tennyson alone remains to represent it, and of course his work is done.[252] Swinburne

[249] Roberts needed the stimulation of new experiences and exciting friends; he was not able to give GRG the kind of intellectual companionship Bertz had once provided. In his Diary, GRG wistfully wrote: "In afternoon came Roberts, but only stayed until 8:30. I suspect he gets a little tired of my exclusively intellectual talk" (5 April 1890).

[250] GRG once wrote to his sister Ellen, "Do you know, I have frequently contemplated getting a barrel-organ man to play in my room for so much an hour? But perhaps the other people in the house would object" (3 April 1889, Yale).

[251] He died at Venice on 16 December 1889. GRG thought his own prose character studies followed Browning's poetic technique.

[252] See 3 November 1892.

has fallen into meaningless verbosity,[253] and there is no one else whatever.

Poor Ruskin, alas! is said to be hopelessly insane.

Ever yours, old Friend,
GEORGE GISSING

Addressed: Herrn Eduard Bertz. / Albe-Strasse. 5. / Friedenau bei Berlin. / Germany.

7. K. Cornwall Residences. / Regent's Park. / London. NW.

April 15th. 1890.

On Thursday I go with my sisters to Paris, for ten days.[254] On returning, I think I shall go at once to Wakefield, and remain there till my book is finished. You received "The Emancipated"? No hurry. I hope you are settling down.

Ever yours,
G. G.

The French "Demos" is at last on the point of publication.[255] A 3rd. edition of "The Nether World."[256]

Stoneleigh Terrace. / Agbrigg. / Wakefield.

May 25th. 1890.

Dear Friend,

Your letter makes a painful impression. It is deplorable that you should be involved in all these petty quarrels. But I suppose you really have shaken yourself clear of the most annoying of those people, and will soon be calmly occupied with your own work. I heartily hope so.

I have quite made up my mind concerning the visit to Germany. As soon as I can sell my next MS., I shall get rid of my furniture, store away my books, and set forth for Berlin, there to pass the winter. But there is one thing I want to say with emphasis. You must not apprehend that my coming will in the least interfere with your regular way of life. My own habits are those of solitude,

---

[253] For GRG's opinion of Swinburne as a candidate for the poet laureateship, see 15 January 1896.

[254] They left for Paris on 17 April.

[255] See 23 October 1888.

[256] Published by Smith, Elder and Co. for 2 shillings 6 pence in September.

and it would be anything but my wish that you should think it needful to take trouble on my account. If it were possible, I think I should like to find a house where I could eat with the family, just for the sake of the language. But there will be time enough to think of that. Don't be anxious about me; some day we shall just meet each other, and resume the conversations of London as if nothing had intervened.

Many thanks for the *Deutsche Presse*. The notice in it is kind, and I am grateful.[257] But it has occurred to me, do you quite follow my *satiric* intention throughout this book? I think you must do so, and yet it seemed to me that you regarded the "emancipated" characters rather too seriously. From the extracts which Bentley appends to his advertisements, I see with some pleasure that certain of the reviewers begin to recognize humour in my writing.[258] It has always been denied, rather to my annoyance, hitherto. But I have no doubt that you also remark the point. Do not for a moment suppose that I want you to write to me at length about each book. The thing would become burdensome, and we know each other well enough to do without it.

I have received a copy of the French "Demos." I am sorry to say the translation is very poor, even a little vulgar. Do not get the book, on any account.

Roberts has a novel in the press, called "In Low Relief."[259] He is contributing an article each month to "Murray's," and so may be considered a thriving man.

An incident in our social life has given me much amusement just lately. You know, of course, that Stanley[260] has just come to England, and is the "lion" of the Season. Now it is announced that he is going to be married to a certain Miss Tennant,[261] in a

---

[257] "Long letter from Bertz, and a 'Deutsche Presse,' with short notice of 'The Emancipated' " (Diary, 11 May 1890).

[258] "Mr. Gissing's book is clever and amusing. 'The Emancipated' (3 vols.) is a work of genuine interest, full of careful character-studies and subtle touches of humour" (From the *Morning Post* as quoted in the *Athenaeum*, 14 June 1890, p. 760).

[259] *In Low Relief: A Bohemian Transcript* (2 vols., London, 1890).

[260] Henry Morton Stanley (1841–1904) had just returned from the ill-fated Emin Pasha Relief Expedition, organized in 1887.

[261] Dorothy Tennant, daughter of Charles Tennant, sometime M.P. for St. Albans. She married Stanley on 12 July 1890.

month or so. Well, Miss Tennant is a very clever and delightful young woman, a familiar friend of all leading people, a light of London society, and so on. Her personal acquaintance with Stanley dates from *three weeks ago*. The situation is vastly interesting. Stanley, I quite believe, is a conscious humbug, a rather brutal adventurer who cares for nothing so much as for notoriety. It is significant that he remained at Cairo until—the beginning of the London season, that he might return with full flourish of drums and trumpets.[262] Now you see the dramatic aspect of this marriage between him and such a person as Miss Tennant. I should like to work out the subject.

My own life is so absorbed in labour that I have really nothing of personal interest to tell you. But I follow all your movements carefully. The restoration of your citizenship is, I think, a satisfactory measure.[263] It removes one anxiety from you.

Yes, I know I shall have a great deal to do in relation to the newest German literature. Throughout the winter, I probably shall not need to write, and all my time will be given to German studies. I look forward to rummaging in your library.

This is a poor letter, but I will write again soon. I am taking to heart your remarks on the necessity of "condensation."

Ever yours,
GEORGE GISSING

Agbrigg. / Wakefield.

June 22. 1890.

Dear Friend,

It won't do. I shall never be able to make myself at home again in England. The days are infinitely wearisome to me, and I work only in the hope of getting away very soon.

Have you yet seen "Le Journal de Marie Bashkirtseff"?[264] I am

---

[262] The *DNB* says that Stanley remained in Egypt after the expedition in order to renew his strength (*Second Supplement*, I, 391).

[263] Bismarck's Anti-Socialist Law expired on 30 September 1890, but before this date, many minor political offenders had obtained full pardon.

[264] Marie Bashkirtseff (1860–1884), a young, aristocratic Russian painter, had held a high position in Continental society in spite of her youth. Her *Journal* (2 vols., Paris, 1887), published posthumously, aroused much excitement in Europe and England.

reading it, a wonderful and delightful book, and the cosmopolitan atmosphere of it puts me into feverish unrest. It is absurd that I should be mouldering here in a Yorkshire village; it is scandalous waste of life, when already I have wasted so many years.

I am nearly half through my new novel, of which I know not yet the name.[265] It is difficult work; more ambitious in scheme than anything I have done yet.

By this, you are, I hope, quietly at work on your own tasks. I do not urge you to write; you need all your time. I myself am very little able to write letters; on Sunday only can I spare the time for a short note now and then.

Bad weather; scarcely to be called summer. That helps to depress me. But the worst of all is that I am in the wrong world. Heaven be thanked, the time draws near when I shall be able to flee from this provincial air.

Roberts urges me to live abroad altogether, and I believe he is right. I cannot make friends, not even acquaintances, in England; and the small success of my books embitters me against the country. Yes, I shall move about on the Continent, and hope some-day to find a wife there, which will never happen in England. Yet perhaps it is still less likely on the Continent. I don't know; I am so much more myself, when abroad. In the society of people here I am stiff and awkward and contemptuous. Abroad, I do not expect people to recognize me as an author, and consequently I am able to be simply a man.

Well, we will shout together once more before long, and talk over all the old London days. Do you know what? My *London* life is in the past; I cannot *live* in London now, and I think never shall again. But it was invaluable to me. I have not yet made half the use of it that I shall be able to.

I want to drink wine, to talk and laugh, to feel that I am living, and not only a machine for producing volumes. I want to hear music, above all things.

If only I live a few months more!

My brother has a new book just published, called "A Village

---

[265] He worked on this novel until 29 June and then "absolutely determined to abandon my story, and commence a new one, for which an idea suddenly flashed upon me" (Diary).

Hampden."[266] It is certainly better, but not very much. He and his wife and child live in a little village, in the heart of England, and are all in good health and spirits, Heaven be praised! But I fear for their future.

All good be with you! Don't lose patience with me. I shall do something some day.

Ever yours, old Friend,
GEORGE GISSING

Addressed: Herrn Eduard Bertz. / Albe-Strasse. 5. / Friedenau bei Berlin. / *Germany.*
Agbrigg.

July 15. 1890.

Dear Friend,

Many thanks for the parcel. The Catalogues are welcome.[267]

I am in miserable health and spirits, getting on very badly indeed with work.[268] I hope things go better with you.

Marie Bashkirtseff's Journal is in 2 Vols. f. 3.50 each. Concerning Amiel's,[269] I forget the form and price. Marie is enormously written about here just now. I think you must soon hear of her in Germany.

Heaven knows when I shall have done my book![270] Not, I fear, before October.

The weather is frightful; we are having no summer at all.

Abundant thanks for your long, good letter, which is full of interest.

Ever yours,
G. G.

[266] Three vols., London: Hurst and Blackett, July 1890.

[267] "Bertz has returned Alg's 'Joy Cometh,' and 'The Western Avernus,' which I lent him long ago. Also sends a Tauchnitz Catalogue, in which my name is at last attached to 'Demos' " (Diary, 12 July 1890).

[268] "Feeling terribly wretched. The struggle to get my story clear driving me almost to madness" (Diary, 15 July 1890).

[269] Henri Frédéric Amiel, *Journal Intime* (Geneva, 1882).

[270] This was the novel begun on 30 June, which he had hoped to complete by the end of August. On 4 July, he wrote in the Diary: "In morning did 3 pp. In afternoon a rush of inspiration. Decided to re-write from beginning these last days' work, to rename all my characters, and to call the book 'Storm-Birds.' Wrote 1½ p. of Chap. 1" (*Letters*, p. 309).

Stoneleigh Terrace. / Agbrigg. / Wakefield.

August 15, 1890.

My dear Friend,

Since last I wrote to you, I have been ill in body and mind, all but on the point of madness.[271] As one result of this, I have destroyed nearly all the work of the summer, and practically must write my story again![272] This is a frightful catastrophe; it destroys all the plans I had made for the winter. In a day or two I return to London, and must work as hard as I can to get my work done before my lease of 7.K. comes to an end.

This solitude is killing me. I can't endure it any longer. In London I must resume my old search for some decent work-girl who will come and live with me. I am too poor to marry an equal, and cannot live alone.[273]

With this pleasant news, I say good-bye for the present. Heaven knows when I shall see you.

Ever affectionately yours,
dear old Friend,
GEORGE GISSING

[271] He suffered more from loneliness and isolation than he did from his inability to get his novel clearly thought out. In August, he met a Wakefield girl, Connie Ash, and imagined he had fallen in love with her. She spent one evening with the Gissings, and then a few days later GRG and Margaret stopped at Connie's home to give her a copy of *Thyrza*, in return for which they were invited to dinner. The Diary says: "Met Mr and Mrs Ash, Connie, younger sister Gertie, a pretty, dark girl, and boy Norman. Had much music. Gertie plays the mandoline. Connie sang a good deal, and beautifully. I am in love with her, and there's an end of it. —Wrote to Nelly about her" (11 August 1890). He went again to Connie's on 14 August, but after this date her name is never mentioned.

[272] He dropped "Storm-Birds" entirely, and on 23 August "Made a beginning of a new novel, a jumble of the various ones I have been engaged on all summer. Wrote 2 pp. but in evening saw that they are no good. Am on the very verge of despair, and suffering more than ever in my whole life. My brain seems powerless, dried up" (Diary, *Letters*, p. 310).

[273] Henry Shergold in "A Lodger in Maze Pond" (1894) speaks for GRG when he says: "Perhaps it is my long years of squalid existence. Perhaps I have come to regard myself as doomed to life on a lower level. I find it an impossible thing to imagine myself offering marriage—making love—to a girl such as those I meet in the big houses."

7. K. Cornwall Residences, / London NW

September 6. 1890.

Dear Friend,

We are both unhappy creatures, and it will be miraculous if either of us ever attains to much peace on this side of the eternal silence. I can neither send you good news of myself, nor write in a way that you will find cheering, though assuredly I had better be silent than increase your troubles. However, I have been thinking over your new resolve,[274] and it *may* be for the best. Understand, it is only the consideration of your health that enables me to say that. But I am obliged to believe that you do, indeed, feel the necessity of lessening the strain of intellectual exertion. Now a temporary change of view may have results which you do not foresee; successful production of the kind at which you now aim may enspirit and strengthen you to other efforts. But, in any case, you are clearly right to turn to an easier kind of work whilst your health so seriously troubles you. And this will not *necessarily* be an inferior kind of work; by no means. The personality of the author is everything, occupy himself on what he may. That you can do good work of the kind you propose, I am well aware. So, on with it! I hope to hear soon that you have found rest in the new determination.

I am glad you do not grieve over my changed plans. When my book will be finished,[275] I cannot say; that depends on wholly unaccountable variations of health and mood and impulse. But my tenancy of 7. K. comes to an end with this year, and of course I have no thought of renewing it. Perhaps I shall go and live in some very poor part of London, to get fresh material.

By the bye, did you see the advertisement of the new issue of my books, in the Athenaeum of a fortnight ago?[276]

I live alone, as usual, and dare not, as yet, make any effort to change this state of things; my financial position is too shaky.

[274] I.e., to confine himself to writing children's stories.

[275] This was the novel called "Hilda Wolff," which he began on 23 August. He completed the first volume and then stopped work on it. On 17 September he began a new story, "Victor Yule," which later developed into *New Grub Street* (Diary).

[276] *Demos, A Life's Morning*, and *The Nether World* were advertised, at 2 shillings 6 pence each, in Smith, Elder and Co.'s "Popular Library of Cheap Editions of Standard Works" (*Athenaeum*, 23 August 1890, p. 269).

I shall see what can be done when the book is finished. But you are quite right in what you say: a continuation of my present miseries would be fatal. Marriage, in the best sense, is impossible, owing to my insufficient income;[277] educated English girls *will* not face poverty in marriage, and to them anything under £400 a year is serious poverty. They remain unmarried in hundreds of thousands, rather than accept poor men. I know that my danger, if I become connected with a tolerable girl of low position is very great: I am weak in these matters. But then, reflect: there is no *real* hope of my ever marrying any one of a better kind, no *real* hope whatever! I say it with the gravest conviction.

I have now been here seventeen days, and have not conversed with a creature except my servant Mrs King. Roberts is away at the seaside, and there is no one else living in London whom I care to see. A strange result, after all these years of not wholly unsuccessful work.

We are having fine and hot weather, after a wretched summer. In all probability much the same is the case with you, for I notice that atmospheric conditions are pretty uniform over the face of Europe. The London parks are now at their best; yesterday I happened to walk through the alleys of Regent's Park, and was astonished at the gorgeous display of flowers. The same at Battersea, where I rambled in great misery last Sunday.

One of my ideas, I may tell you, is to live for brief periods in a succession of boarding-houses. In any case I should see people in variety, and I might make useful acquaintances. The expense would scarcely be greater than what I am accustomed to. Boarding-houses have not been much used in English fiction. But the system is spreading here, and it offers a suggestive field.

I see that Paul Bourget[278] is just married. Is it not comical to think that a man who had published, in English, books such as his would have no kind of chance of finding an English wife? He would not be admitted to general society. The man has a wonder-

---

[277] In 1890, he earned £150, but by 1892 his yearly income was up to £274-14-3 (GRG, Account of Books, Yale).

[278] Charles Joseph Paul Bourget (1852–1935), French poet, critic, and novelist. His early naturalistic studies made him famous, but after 1889, he became increasingly conservative and questioned the value of naturalism in literature.

fully keen and analytic mind. I am not enthusiastic about him, but admire his powers greatly.

My brother's last novel has received some good notices. It is distinctly an improvement. The scene of one he is now writing is laid on the borderland between England and Scotland, with which he is very familiar.[279] Poverty distresses him, but his wife is satisfactory, and their little girl is a beautiful, healthy child.[280]

Well, your letter closes on a key, if not hopeful, at all events resigned and energetic. Before long, no doubt, I shall hear that you have published something new. So I too will go on without more grumbling.

Ever yours, old friend,
GEORGE GISSING

7. K. Cornwall Mansions.[281] / Regent's Park NW.

October 25th. 1890.

Dear Friend,

Your last letter was very kind and thoughtful. I cannot answer it properly, for I am physically ill, and gravely troubled in mind.

About three weeks ago, I began a novel, to be called "New Grub Street."[282] I have finished the first volume, and *must* complete the thing before Christmas, for I am all but penniless.

I have made the acquaintance of a work-girl who will perhaps come to live with me when I leave this place, at Christmas.[283] But everything is dark and almost hopeless.

I must consider nothing but mere physical needs. I feel weak and miserable, and can only recover something of my old self by the change of life I have referred to. Otherwise, there is nothing before me but lapse into mental and bodily ruin.

I wonder how you will struggle through the winter. I have already begun with colds etc, and shall have a bad time of it.

[279] *A Moorland Idyll* (3 vols., London: Hurst and Blackett, 1891).

[280] Enid, born on 11 November 1888.

[281] The name of the block of flats in which GRG lived was changed to Cornwall Mansions. He objected to the genteel pretension in the change, and, after this one instance, used "Residences."

[282] It was begun on 6 October and completed on 6 December (Diary).

[283] Between the 6th and the 24th of September 1890, GRG met Edith Underwood, who was to be his next wife.

What a good thing it was that I took those two opportunities of seeing the south of Europe! Perhaps I shall never again have enough money to enable me to leave England. The failure of my last book[284] has made it very doubtful whether I shall get much for this next, and of course in my condition it is impossible to write with much energy. I may have to fall back upon teaching, though I scarcely know how I should obtain pupils, for I have no longer any intercourse with well-to-do people.

Perhaps this is taking too dark a view. In a few months I may recover something of my old energy. We shall see.

I hope all goes well with you. I shall not be able to write a decent letter till my book is finished, but anything from you will be very welcome.

Ever Yours,
GEORGE GISSING

Addressed: Herrn Eduard Bertz. / Albe-Strasse, 5. / Friedenau
        bei Berlin. / *Germany.*

7. *K. Corn* [*wall*] *Residences.* / *London NW.*

December 30. 1890.

I am waiting miserably to hear what the publishers offer for my new book.[285] As soon as ever it is settled, I shall depart from here, and take up my abode at Exeter (Devonshire) for perhaps a year. You shall have my address as soon as possible.

The weather is extremely severe, and I suffer much from it. With you I fear it is the same. I have nothing cheerful enough to tell you to occupy a letter.

My best wishes for the new year. We enter upon the last decade of the century.

Ever yours,
G. G.

---

[284] *The Emancipated.*

[285] "Letter from Smith and Elder. They think 'New Grub Street' clever and original; but fear it is too gloomy. Offer £150. I wrote at once accepting (eheu!)" (Diary). The book was published in April 1891, and by June 1892 three editions of the novel had been issued. He lost money by selling the copyright unconditionally.

24 Prospect Park. / Exeter.

January 23. 1891.

Dear Friend,

After miseries and difficulties unutterable, I am at length established in a comfortable abode, where I hope to have some degree of peace for a year or two. I have removed all my furniture to Exeter, and am attended to by the people in whose house I have taken rooms. After the frightful experiences of this hideous winter in London, I feel the need of a long rest in this happier climate. Here I see the sun rise every morning; a wonderful thing. I am within ten miles of the delightful Devonshire coast, and promise myself many long walks when the spring weather comes on. Exeter has good libraries, so that I shall not feel out of the world.

But I have not yet told you of my latest dealings with Smith and Elder. I have sold them "New Grub Street" for the same price as my last two books brought—£150. You see, I make no advance. At the same time I have disposed of all my rights in "Thyrza" for £10, (a ludicrous sum,) so that now we shall see a cheap edition of that book added to the others. "New Grub Street" is dull and unhappy; the wonder is that I succeeded in writing any book at all during those weeks of uttermost misery. I suppose it will be published in April.

Perhaps I shall revive in this pure air, but I still feel capable of no exertion. I shall be as solitary as ever, for the people in the house here are illiterate, though decent. Perhaps it may be useful for me to join a society called the Devon and Exeter Institution, which has a reading room and excellent library. But I may tell you that I am corresponding with that girl in London—her name is Edith Underwood—of whom I have already spoken to you. Our relations are as yet platonic. She lives with her father, brother and sister; the family is a respectable one, and if anything is to come of our connection it will have to be marriage.[286] The girl is

---

[286] Three terse entries in his Diary record the progress of the affair: "In evening to Edith's: saw her father, and told him that I wish Edith to come to me at Exeter in a month's time" (9 January 1891); "Letter from Edith, saying marriage can be shortly. Replied that the day must be Feb. 25th., or *never*" (13 February 1891); "Married to Edith Underwood at Register Office, S. Pancras. Drove in fog to Paddington, and caught the 11:45 for Exeter" (25 February 1891).

peculiarly gentle and pliable, with a certain natural refinement which seems to promise that she might be trained to my kind of life. You shall hear more of this.[287]

But I must speak of your affairs, as it is very long since I wrote to you at greater length than a post-card allows. In re-writing "Glück und Glas," you have indeed shown yourself capable of a great effort; I know too well what that kind of thing means. I do hope you may now be able to dispose of the story. You do not write uncheerfully, and if the savage winter has not dealt too hardly with you, I trust you are still working on at something in the same mood. The change of abode which you propose ought to be of great benefit to you, if the drawbacks which you have before experienced do not again afflict you. But I think it likely they may be outweighed by the advantages.

Perhaps you have noticed from the literary advertisements that Roberts's book "In Low Relief" has had considerable success. He is now engaged to write a series of articles on "Great Steamship Lines," for "Murray's Magazine."[288] Indeed, he is doing so much miscellaneous work, that I think he will drift into regular journalism. "In Low Relief" has, in my opinion, great merits, but the book is a literal transcript from life; he has merely reported a story in which he played the principal part. What is your opinion about work of this kind? To be sure, such reporting can be good or bad; *his* is decidedly artistic. But I find that he has no impulse to *invent*; he can only handle actual occurrences. This is realism, but of a peculiarly restricted species. It differs greatly from that of Daudet, who declares that he introduces nothing into his books of which he has not had personal experience, but who still combines and constructs.

I earnestly beg you not to think that I am growing lax in correspondence. Heaven forbid! For I have no other correspondent to whose mind I address myself so freely, and with such confidence of being understood. But I have been so wretchedly ill; often I have thought that my day of mental effort was over. Let me have a line from you presently. The accounts of Berlin weather have been so miserable that I have now and then felt uneasy about you.

[287] In spite of this statement, GRG avoided any further mention of his marriage until after his visit to Potsdam in April 1898.

[288] Five articles were published between January and June 1891.

Do you ever see an English newspaper? There has been furious discussion concerning General Booth's society-saving project.[289] Huxley seems to have demolished the affair in certain letters to the *Times*.[290]

My brother has finished a new book.[291] He is at present in Northumberland, but will shortly come down to Gloucestershire again.

What of Ibsen's new play?[292] Here it is abused. But so are most things original.

All good be with you. Believe me the same as ever, yours affectionately,

GEORGE GISSING

24 Prospect Park. / Exeter.

March 5. 1891.

Dear Friend,

You have probably received a copy of *The Times* which I posted to you. A letter of mine therein (occasioned by correspondence which has been intermittently going on of late,) will cause you to smile.[293]

---

[289] William Booth (1829–1912) was the founder of the Salvation Army. He was campaigning for a fund of £100,000 to finance farm and city colonies in England and abroad for unemployed workers and social outcasts. The public discussion arose from Booth's insistence that he alone have control of the fund with complete freedom in its administration. The newspapers seem to have encouraged the controversy. The full program was outlined in Booth's *In Darkest England and The Way Out* (London, 1890).

[290] Thomas Henry Huxley (1825–1895) suggested that a board be set up to supervise expenditures. After consulting Ernest Hatton, Chancery Queen's Counsel, for a legal opinion, Huxley published a letter in the London *Times* quoting Hatton's statement that "Booth can 'give away' the property simply because there is no one who has any right to prevent his doing so" (22 January 1891, p. 7). The letter discouraged many of Booth's supporters.

[291] *A Moorland Idyll*.

[292] *Hedda Gabler*. Edmund Gosse's translation appeared in January 1891. For the first performance of the play see 15 May 1891.

[293] Entitled "The Pronunciation of Greek," the letter was printed on Wednesday, 25 February 1891 (London *Times*, p. 13). It was a formal

Aided by the glorious weather of Devonshire, I am already at work on a new book, which I think is to be called: "Raymond Peak."[294] The scene will be in a large Midland town, in London, in Sark, and then in Exeter. I think I have some strong ideas.

I will confess to you that I am pleased with the proofs of "New Grub Street": it is certainly a much better book than I thought. A short book, too; which is an advantage.

"Thyrza" I have corrected and greatly abbreviated; I hope the thing is improved. But indeed that old book remains very unsatisfactory to me. When they mean to bring out the cheap edition, I know not.[295]

The explanation you give me concerning Rehfeldt's wife is very gratifying. I heartily hope you may have much more comfort at Frankfurt. As you say, Rehfeldt's experience among the people ought assuredly to be of very great use to you. The description of the lodging you have taken there sounds well.

This novel of yours greatly excites my curiosity; I do hope you will very soon manage to get it printed.[296] As for the "New Yorker Staats-Zeitung"[297]—surely that is very doubtfull [sic]; I don't like to think of your appearing there first of all. Persevere with the German publishers. One can hardly believe that a work of such recognized merit will for ever go begging.

Doubtless you have noticed the great vogue lately attained by Ibsen in England. Popular he of course is not, and endless ridicule is thrown upon him, very often of the most disgusting kind. A complete translation of his works is in process of publication,[298] and

---

version of the subject discussed in GRG's letter for 29 November 1889. A copy of the *Times* had been mailed to Bertz on 28 February (Diary). GRG "rejoiced to get that letter into *The Times*. Not only did it mean that my name has weight with the editor; but it was also an excellent advertisement for me on the eve of the new publication [*New Grub Street*]" (To Ellen Gissing, 7 March 1891, Yale).

[294] Finally called *Born in Exile* (3 vols., London: A. & C. Black, 1892).

[295] Smith, Elder and Co. brought out a one-volume, six shilling edition in June 1891.

[296] *Glück und Glas.*

[297] A German language paper published in New York City.

[298] The fourth volume of the translation of Ibsen's dramas, edited by William Archer and Walter Scott, had just appeared.

from time to time his plays are acted. For my own part, I grieve that they are *plays*. More and more I dislike the conditions of theatrical exhibition. It is of necessity an appeal to the mob; consequently there is much of degradation in it. I doubt whether I shall ever again visit a theatre in England. The contiguity of the vulgar crowd, its base comments, its unintelligent applause, all are hateful to me. I much wish Ibsen had put his thoughts into narrative form. The mob cannot be effectively educated, in our day, by theatric exhibitions; for one reason, because our current journalism has abolished the sense of reverence. It is my belief that the multitude was never more remote than now from true culture. Men and women of truly cultured feeling are more and more withdrawing into privacy, dreading the clash and clang of sham education and brutal unidealism. We have to recognize that the progress of our time is purely material; spiritual growth may perchance be its result hereafter, but we shall not live to enjoy such fruits.

Heaven be thanked, springtime approaches. I shall think of you in your new and happier surroundings, and ardently hope that you may work with quiet self-satisfaction. In very truth, what more can we hope for?

I see the Americans have at length passed the Copyright Bill. But it seems to be a very imperfect measure, and, though my books are reprinted in the States, I know not whether it will enable me henceforth to get a better price.[299]

Needless to say, you shall have "New Grub Street" as soon as it is published. I will send it by book-post in three volumes. I quite think you will read it with amusement. Yes, I was right to go back to Smith. He has a solid commercial interest in my books, and he advertizes them well. I shall never again willingly leave him.

Yesterday I was looking all through my bundles of "notes." Heavens! I have material for all the rest of my life.

---

[299] Before the Copyright Law was passed in 1891, only authors who were residents or citizens were protected by law. The extension of copyright laws gave the foreign author equal protection, if his government reciprocated, but the printing had to be done in the United States. The new law did not help foreign authors financially.

I am in vastly better health and spirits.[300] May you soon be able to say the same.

Ever yours, old Friend,
GEORGE GISSING

Addressed: Herrn Eduard Bertz. / Villa Frühlingsfeld / Fürsten-walder Str. 26. / Frankfurt a. d. Oder. / *Germany.*

April 8. 1891.

24 Prospect Park. / Exeter.

I am sending you, by book-post, the 3 vols. of "New Grub Street." May they find you reasonably well settled in your new abode!

Here we have the warmth and brightness of spring. I spend a good deal of time in the open air, and have begun to botanize, geologize, etc. In the meantime I have written more than half the first volume of "Godwin Peak," a study of a savagely aristo-cratic temperament.

Alas! why give yourself such trouble about "Phoebe"? The other little story of which you speak I have long since lost.[301] But I hope to do some short things before long.

You shall soon hear at length.

"Thyrza" is announced as you will see in 1st. vol. of "New Grub Street" for a 6 shilling edition. I have greatly shortened, and I think, improved it.

Offer for me the greetings of a friend's friend to Dr. Rehfeldt.

Ever yours,
G. G.

Roberts has gone (on literary business) to Lisbon and Madeira.

---

[300] As a result of his marriage. Cautiously, GRG praised his bride: "Edith, as you know, is uneducated, but I am more than satisfied with her domestic management. She has many very good qualities, and most dis-tinctly improves. I feel sure Katie [Algernon's wife] would not find it impossible to see a little of her now and then" (To Algernon Gissing, 6 November 1891, Yale).

[301] Bertz wanted to translate another short story.

24 Prospect Park. / Exeter.

April 26. 1891.

Dear Friend,

You have been treated abominably in the matter of your lodgings. It will be both a grievous trouble and an expense to have to move again so soon. One marvels at the selfishness commonly exhibited by people where a very little trouble (or trifling self-denial) would enable them to behave humanely. Your landlord ought to have been able to apprise you of what was happening before you had begun to remove your goods; I suppose he deliberately calculated on a small gain at your disadvantage. This matter of a dwelling-place is very troublesome for people in our position; we are for ever at the mercy of ignoble creatures, and are forced to live in their hateful proximity. Surely there ought to be *Colleges* for unmarried intellectual men (or even for married of small means,) where we could dwell much as students do at the University. Some such plan is realized in the London "Inns of Court," originally devoted to Barristers and students of Law, now much used by men of letters and the like. But here again one never has quite satisfactory attendance. The life of a Fellow at Oxford or Cambridge is, I should think, almost ideal. He has his man-servant, his meals either in private or at the public table, an atmosphere of culture and peace. Who will advocate "Literary Homes"? Besant is just founding an Authors' Club,[302] but this of course does not meet the need.

Well now, it is unnecessary for me to say how your remarks on "New Grub Street" rejoice me. As all my acquaintances agree in loud praise of the book, I suppose it is not bad. I wrote it in utter prostration of spirit; no book of mine was regarded so hopelessly in the production. This experience encourages me; if I could write tolerably *then*, I am pretty sure to be able to produce under any circumstances likely to befall me.

Your objection to the consensus among my characters on the subject of money is quite just. The fault arises from my own bitterness. As for the truth or untruth of the point of view itself, I know decidedly that a man has to be of much native strength

[302] The Club, organized as a stock company, was to have dining rooms, card rooms, and dressing rooms; it was to be limited to 600 members who had to demonstrate that they had intellectual ability and were "clubbable."

if he can arrive at anything like development of his powers in the shadow of poverty. Happily, the strength is sometimes given.

Grub Street actually existed in London some hundred and fifty years ago. In Pope and his contemporaries the name has become synonymous for wretched-authordom. In Hogarth's "Distressed Author" there is "Grub Street" somewhere inscribed.[303] Poverty and meanness of spirit being naturally associated, the street came to denote an abode, not merely of poor, but of insignificant, writers. That it could be confined to the sense of poverty is, however, proved by one of the most humorous passages in Sam Johnson's Dictionary. He defines "GRUB STREET: Originally the name of a street near Moorfields in London, much inhabited by writers of small histories, dictionaries, and temporary poems; whence any mean production is called *grubstreet*." Then he adds the quotation:

Χαῖρ᾽, ᾽Ιθάκη, μετ᾽ ἄεθλα μετ᾽ ἄλγεα πίκρα
᾽Ασπασίως πὸν οὔδας ἱκάγομαι—[304]

Is not this delicious? Poor old Sam, rejoicing to have got so far in his Dictionary, and greeting the name "Grub Street" as that of his native land! (I have never seen this joke alluded to, though several others which the Dictionary contains are commonly mentioned.)

At present the word is used contemptuously. You know that I do not altogether mean that in the title of my book.

The reviews, as usual, I do not see. But I notice that they are spending much more money than usual in advertisements. By the bye, it is good to have my book[s] advertized all together at the end of Vol I.[305]

I am very glad that Rehfeldt affords you such welcome companionship. Intercourse with the children will for you, I know, be a very good thing; I trust it may give you many an hour of quiet

---

[303] The "Grub Street Journal" is mentioned in Hogarth's "The Distressed Poet." Cf. *The Works of William Hogarth*, ed. John Trusler (London, 1824), I, 85–6.

[304] "Hail, O Ithaca! Amidst joys and bitter pains, I gladly come to thy earth."

[305] Smith, Elder, and Co. held the copyrights to *Demos*; *A Life's Morning*; *The Nether World*; and *Thyrza: A Tale*, all of which were advertised in *New Grub Street*.

satisfaction. The delay about "Glück und Glas" is horribly irritating. How does *any* man get a first novel published in Germany?

You have perhaps heard that a new English publisher (Heinemann)[306] has begun a series of reprints for Continental circulation, in rivalry of Tauchnitz. He declares that he will aim higher than Tauchnitz does. It is an interesting fact that Tauchnitz's most popular authors are decidedly the trashiest; I fear the English people resident abroad do not represent the best intellect of their country.

In this glorious spring weather I botanize for an hour or two daily. This, and a little study of Geology, is refreshing my mind and extending my vocabulary.

Heartiest thanks for your encouragement. Remember that you were my first—very first—favourable critic. When I read to you the MS. of "Workers in the Dawn,"[307] we did not foresee this endless series of 3-vol. novels. I suppose you possess them all?[308] Alas! there will be many more.

The first vol. of "Godwin Peak" is finished. More news shortly.

Ever yours, dear Friend,
GEORGE GISSING

24 Prospect Park. Exeter.

May 15th. 1891.

My dear Friend,

This is indeed most excellent news that you send me! Heaven be praised that I shall at length read "Glück und Glas"! May it not be regarded as of good augury that you are a new publisher's first venture?[309] Capital! I cannot rejoice sufficiently.

I am also glad to hear that you have disposed of "Phoebe." How can you speak of the cash? That is of course yours; it is little enough, and you have had trouble enough in earning it. It rejoices me that I am indirectly the means of putting those few coins in your pocket.

[306] William Heinemann (1863–1920) also published translations of important European authors in his International Library Series under the editorship of Edmund Gosse.

[307] See Introduction.

[308] See Introduction.

[309] Victor Ottmann (1869–?) had just established a publishing firm in Leipzig and a literary journal, *Das litterarische Echo*.

I can understand that you see very little of Rehfeldt. A doctor has *no* leisure. But hold out, for you seem to be working very well. I hope the paedagogic work will shortly be finished. That must be very interesting, and I am convinced that it will have uncommon value.

"New Grub Street" seems to be more like a literary success than any other of my books. There is a mad East-end parson (an avowed atheist, by the bye,) whose acquaintance I made some time ago;[310] he persists in notifying to me in frequent letters all reviews of importance. Not only am I well reviewed, but positive articles are devoted to the book. There was one occupying a whole column the other day in the Illust[rated] London News.[311] Then, I have just been casually referred to in a *leader* in the Daily News —which means a good deal. We shall see whether all this has any financial results—to the publishers. Dash it all! I ought to get more than £150 for my next book.[312]

About a third part of the 2nd. vol. of "Godwin Peak" is now finished. It is most laborious work, involving no little research. But I feel that I grow stronger in management of material.

Summer has now set in; glorious days! I can't find much time to walk, but each day I get to the Public Reading-room, where I see the London daily papers, and one or two magazines. At present I have no means of getting new books, but I must soon take a subscription somewhere, for I find it absolutely necessary to dip now and then into contemporary work.

May 17th.

I am sending you two numbers of the *Saturday Review*, which will afford you amusement. In the earlier one is an article headed

[310] Charles Anderson, of St. John's Vicarage, Limehouse. GRG met him early in 1889 (To Algernon Gissing, 13 June 1889, Yale). According to Morley Roberts, "This Henderson [Anderson] had, I believe, read 'The Under World' [*Nether World*] or one of the books dealing with the kind of parishioners that he was acquainted with, and had written to Maitland [GRG]. In a way they became friends, or at any rate acquaintances, for the clergyman too was a peculiarly lonely man. He occasionally came to 7.K [Cornwall Residences], and I myself met him there. He was a man wholly misplaced, in fact he was an absolute atheist. Still, he had a cure of souls somewhere the other side of the Tower, and laboured, as I understood, not unfaithfully" (*Roberts*, p. 143).

[311] XCVIII (2 May 1891), 571.

[312] *Born in Exile*, the next one, brought him only £150.

"New Grub Street," and after having read it, with its marked vein of personal satire, you will be surprised to read the review of my book in the next week's issue.[313] More important than either is the mention of my name on p. 551—the kind of thing I have never yet seen.[314] Altogether, these passages will give you an idea of the progress I have been making just this last year or two.

I must ask you to return me these papers, as I wish to send them to Wakefield. Pray forgive me the trouble.

My brother has been in bad health of late, and has gone with his family to live in Jersey. A new novel by him will appear in July. His publishers have had it in their hands since January, but it is their policy to keep his books and publish them at a short interval after one of mine![315]

Ibsen's "Hedda Gabler" has been rather remarkably acted at a series of matinées in London. It was a distinct success, the theatre each day being crowded with intellectual people. Now that it has been put on in the evening, the result is complete failure.[316] Worse

[313] The first article attacked GRG's gloom and pessimism: "Even in Grub Street the fog sometimes lifts, and in the window gardens of the natives you may see blossoming the herb Pantagruelion. But it never blossoms in the windows of those who are unlucky enough to think that they are neglected and under-estimated. This is the besetting sorrow or besetting sin of artists of all kinds in and out of Grub Street" (*Saturday Review*, LXXI, 2 May 1891, 525). The second article praised the complexity of the characters and the terrible realism, and said GRG "had produced a very powerful book. He is full of clever touches on literary and social matters, and estimates to a nicety the literary pabulum which the general public enjoys" (*Saturday Review*, 9 May 1891, 572). The Reverend Charles Anderson had notified GRG of these reviews (Diary, 14 May 1891).

[314] The article, "American Servility," answered a complaint, printed in an American magazine, that American authors leaned too heavily on English aristocratic life for literary material. GRG was mentioned as one of several English authors, including Kipling, Meredith, and Stevenson, who were successful in America yet did not rely on the peerage to glorify their pages (*Saturday Review*, 9 May 1891, 551).

[315] Algernon's *Moorland Idyll* appeared in July, three months after GRG's *New Grub Street* was published.

[316] *Hedda Gabler* was produced for the first time in England on 13 April 1891 at the Vaudeville Theatre; five matinees were scheduled (*Athenaeum*, 28 March 1891, p. 418). Because of its success, evening performances were given starting in the first week in May; the play closed in the first week of June (*Athenaeum*, 6 June 1891, p. 742).

than idle to present anything original to the mob of London play-goers. They are the support of vulgar playwrights, and the ruin of those few capable men who are misled into writing for them. An example of the latter kind is Robert Buchanan,[317] once a poet of some distinction and a fair romancist; little by little he has been lured on by popular successes on the stage, until now there is no characterizing with sufficient contempt the meanness of his productions. Heaven be thanked that I have an instinctive loathing of theatrical audiences.[318]

Work on with your psychology, old friend! Use the spring sunshine!

> Ever yours,
> GEORGE GISSING

Addressed: Herrn Eduard Bertz. / Villa Frühlingsfeld / Fürsten-walder Str[asse], 26 / Frankfurt a. d. Oder / *Germany.*

July 6th. [1891]

I have come to a very quiet seaside place to finish my book. Address for a few weeks will be: / c/o Mrs Elston. / Stonington Villas. / Old Church Road. / Clevedon. / It is in Somerset (opposite Cardiff) and here, in 1792, Coleridge occupied a cottage.

Shall soon write to you at length. Hope all is well, and that you already have the proofs of "G[lück] u[nd] G[las]."

> Ever yours,
> GEORGE GISSING

Clevedon.

July 20th. 1891.

Dear Friend,

The treatment you have experienced would excuse any amount of grumbling and cursing. I do heartily wish that some end of

---

[317] Robert Williams Buchanan (1841–1901). He claimed that he had either to write popular plays or to starve (Harriet Jay, *Robert Buchanan* [London, 1903], p. 114).

[318] However, in 1884 GRG had written to his brother that he was working on a play to be called "Madcaps" and that he meant to have a play out before he was thirty (*Letters*, p. 137), and a Diary entry for 26 June 1898 says: "Idea of another play floating in my mind," so that the "instinctive loath-ing" must have been quiescent from time to time.

your wanderings could be hoped for. The internal troubles which afflict you are in themselves quite bad enough; you have an absolute need of a *quiet permanent home*. Only by thus fixing yourself will you obtain the leisure to do such work as you are capable of. It seems to me that you should not think of the proximity of friends so much as of literary conveniences. You want a modern library, and will always want it; intercourse with friends, on the other hand, is not *always* indispensable to you. When you are obliged to move, try your very best (alas! you have done so) to find an abode with reasonable promise of "fixity of tenure." This would be your salvation.

Never mind that "Glück und Glas" is behind you; its publication is to come, and people will judge it merely as a piece of literary work. You thought well of it, and, I am convinced, with reason. To see it printed and sent forth will give you the stimulus of work accomplished. I want to read it, very much indeed.

And also the other stories you are about to write. For let us take it as decided that you henceforth do your best to earn a satisfactory living as a writer of fiction. That is, I quite believe, your one hope of an income—things being as they are. Write as soon as a subject is very clear to you. Pray do not trouble about the next after that; let us have one at a time. You *can* write stories, and you *must*. *Frisch zu!* Let them not be too long.

I, for my part, am just going to write a tale in one volume. Yesterday I finished "Godwin Peak," which is not wholly bad, though some parts ought to be worked out more carefully. The next short book I am going to put into the hands of a certain literary agent[319] who is highly recommended by Besant, Grant Allen, Kipling, and so on, and so on. I shall tell him to get as much as he can for it—and then with much curiosity await the result.

In a week's time I leave Clevedon, and go westward along the coast to a picturesque little seaport called Watchet, where I may stay a week or two. Then back to Exeter.

It is a curious thing that at Exeter I am greatly better off for periodical literature than ever I was in London. I belong to an informal Society, which has a Reading-room supplied with all

[319] Alexander Pollock Watt (?–1914), originator of the concept of the literary agent, conducted his business from Hastings House, London.

the weeklies and monthlies. Now in London I could never find such a resort. To enjoy it, you must pay a heavy subscription to some club or other. We have also a decent library, which contains, I find, a copy of "The Nether World." They get a decent supply of new books from time to time.

I have seen Andrew Lang's article, of which you speak. It was written in reply to a long paragraph of Besant's, on the same subject, in the June *Author*.[320] This latter I have with me, and herewith I send it to you. The July number is at Exeter, and you shall have it when I get back.

You will notice how very imperfectly Besant has understood the book. His description of Reardon is ludicrous. Then again, you will find that Lang makes a mistake which proves that he has not read the story with anything like serious attention.[321] These things are natural enough. Such overworked men *cannot* read books with close thought; they only skim even those which they think interesting.

I shall always be grateful to you for your toil in the matter of "Demos." When it *does* get published, I only hope it won't fall flat.

I do not yet know Kipling, but from what I hear he seems to be distinctly a *clever* young man. (You know he is only about 24.)[322] Now that you have spoken, I shall read "The Light That Failed" as soon as possible.

Have you seen notices of the book by *Charles* Booth, on the economical state of the London working-classes? The 2nd. part is just pub[lished], and it is universally held to be a serious treatise, of permanent value. Well, I find that in his first vol. he spoke of "Demos" as one of the few works of fiction which would be of any

---

[320] Andrew Lang, "Realism in Grub Street," *Author*, II (1 July 1891), 43–4; Walter Besant, "Notes and News," *Author*, II (1 June 1891), 15. Both articles discussed *New Grub Street*: Lang argued that such realism was needlessly pessimistic and humorless; Besant praised the book for its verisimilitude, and in the next issue of the magazine he used the title for a column of literary gossip.

[321] Lang said that he wished he knew Mr. Yule, who was going to write an essay on Diogenes Laertius (*Author*, II, 43). It was Edwin Reardon, not Yule, who planned the classical essay (See *New Grub Street*, Chap. XII).

[322] Kipling was 26 years old.

use to a man wishing to study London work-folk.[323] This is gratifying.

I am benefiting by the air. My work finished, I shall now be lazy for a short time.

Roberts's vol. of poems will be out in the Autumn.[324] I shall send you my copy to read, some day.

May your five weeks in Rehfeldt's abode be a time of comparative rest!

Ever yours, dear Friend,
GEORGE GISSING

Addressed: Herrn Eduard Bertz. / Oder Strasse 42. I. / Frankfurt a. d. Oder. / *Germany.*

24 Prospect Park. / Exeter.

August 7. 1891.

I did not know of the Tauchnitz edition.[325] Would they not send me a copy if I asked? Don't buy one, I beg. Yes, I shall think of a third short story before long; the little volume of which you speak is a temptation.[326] Herewith I send *The Author*. Don't trouble to return them; they are valueless to me. I am thinking of a removal to Bristol, for new experience; will write to you as soon as I have arranged about "Godwin Peak." I deplore the state of your lodgings, and wonder how you will ever manage to live there again. I hope and trust that your *five years* may yet be fruitful.[327]

Ever yours,
G. G.

---

[323] "Something may be gleaned from a few books, such for instance as 'Demos'; something perhaps may be learnt from the accounts of household expenditure in the preceding chapter" (Charles Booth, *Life and Labour of the People in London* [2nd. edit., 1889], I, 157).

[324] *Songs of Energy.*

[325] Bertz had sent a post card telling GRG that Tauchnitz had published *New Grub Street* (2 vols., Leipzig, 1891) in his "Collection of British Authors" (Diary, 7 August 1891).

[326] Bertz probably urged him to publish a collection of short stories.

[327] A reference to Bertz's years in exile.

1. St. Leonard's Terrace. / Exeter.

August 27. 1891.

Dear Friend,

I have decided not to go to Bristol, as the expense of moving would be very great; moreover, a day or two that I spent in that town gave me a distaste for it. I am now established in quite a different, and a much pleasanter, part of Exeter; indeed the district is very beautiful; rich in gardens and sightly houses. Though still in disorder, I sit down to write to you, for I have news, and disagreeable news, to send.

I sent my new novel to Smith and Elder as usual, and in a fortnight's time Payn[328] wrote to tell me that, as his holiday was beginning, my MS. would have to lie aside for a month. He added that my demand for £250 could not possibly be granted; that Smith would give *at most* £150. Thereupon, I withdrew the MS., and sent it to the best literary agent, a certain A. P. Watt, highly recommended by Besant and Co. I told him of the correspondence with Payn, and said that I wanted to find out the real market value of a story from my pen.

Well, Watt sent the novel to Chatto and Windus, and now I hear from him that (though he had asked £200 for the British rights) they will not give more than *£120!* This he considered impossible, so he has passed on the MS. to Longmans.

The outlook is gloomy, like the weather. I should perhaps have done better if I had let S[mith] and E[lder] do as usual. But I have gained knowledge. I know that my books have still no solid market-value, and that I must continue to work for small sums.

Walter Grahame, (my old pupil,) who is now on the Continent, tells me that Tauchnitz "in his Magazine" has a very complimentary notice of "New Grub Street." What "Magazine" is referred to, I wonder?[329]

I shall write to Tauchnitz for a copy of the novel, in a day or two.

Don't lament about "Demos"; I myself shall grieve if any German publisher brings it out and loses by it. The idea of *your*

[328] James Payn.
[329] The *Tauchnitz Magazine* was an "English monthly miscellany for Continental readers."

giving time to the translation of my novels is preposterous; *you* have far more serious work to do, and work of your own. May you have health and strength to labour for many years!

Capital, that "Glück und Glas" will appear in a cheap little volume! I look eagerly for it. If only it were in my power to help you as you have helped me! But I know not a single editor, as you are aware.

Your material surroundings are wretched. Removal is terrible, and to you more so than to men in general. I dread to hear that you have begun the miserable undertaking yet once more.

As yet I am quite uncertain about the subject of my next book. But as soon as my affairs are in order, I must sit down and think.

Oh no, I didn't write to the *Author*. I have sent you the last number. I dare say you have found amusing matter in this periodical.

All good be with you. I shall soon receive your novel, thank heaven!

Ever yours,
GEORGE GISSING

Addressed: Herrn Eduard Bertz. / Fürstenwalder Str. 26. / Frankfurt a. d. Oder. / *Germany.*

1 St. Leonard's Terrace. / Exeter.

September 9. 1891.

Very many thanks for the Photograph; I am sure it is excellent.[330] The publisher's announcement reached me, and I await the volume anxiously. [331]

I have heard from Leipzig; a very courteous letter.[332] *Six* copies of "N[ew]G[rub] S[treet]" are on their way to me. You shall hear as soon as I have news about Longman's reception of the MS.

My brother's last book[333] has been very favourably reviewed. But I am afraid my name may prejudice some people against

---

[330] Bertz had sent a photograph of himself, which had been taken to accompany his biography in Ottmann's *Das litterarische Echo*. GRG recorded the arrival of the picture and remarked, "Poor old fellow!" (Diary, 7 September 1891).

[331] *Glück und Glas*. The advertisement had arrived on 30 August (Diary).

[332] From Tauchnitz.

[333] *A Moorland Idyll*.

him; the mass of readers don't distinguish initials. I read that Daudet is suffering from a long and miserable illness. I should think this is the first unhappiness he has ever known since his boyhood. What a brilliant life!

Ever yours,
G. G.

1. St. Leonard's Terrace. / Exeter.

September 21. 1891.

My dear Friend,

The last three days I have given almost continuously to your book. I suppose it is about the length of an English 3-vol. novel, and it astonishes me that it can be published so cheaply.[334] The type is excellent. I see that four thousand copies are already printed; may they be speedily sold.

For decidedly it is a book that ought to go forth among men, in this time of ours. I knew very well that it would be. It impresses me as a noble piece of work, full of mature thought, of great ethical significance, and artistically good.[335]

Were I criticizing it merely as a work of art, I should make certain objections. I should say, for instance, that *coincidences* are rather too frequent, and tend to weaken the air of realism. But then, it is sufficiently clear that Realism was not your first aim, and therefore I attach slight importance to this objection. I mean to say, you did not think first and foremost of imitating

[334] *Glück und Glas*, containing 365 pages, sold for 1 Mark.

[335] Bertz's novel tells the story of Felix Lubrecht, a sensitive young man who is supported by his uncle, Dr. Groch, a wealthy Epicurean. While on a military training tour, Felix stops at a boarding house where he meets Martin, the son of the landlady, Rosalie Autenrieth, a summer boarder, and Lotte, a servant in the house. Felix has an accident, his uncle comes to visit him and then falls in love with the beautiful Rosalie, who marries the old man in order to get his money. Shortly after the wedding, Dr. Groch dies and Rosalie cheats Felix out of his inheritance, forcing him to earn his own living. He tries to become a journalist but cannot sell his work. As a result of his experiences as a destitute man, he joins a Marxist group, which preaches brotherhood and financial equality. Then Felix develops a fatal disease, and his socialist friends abandon him. By accident, Martin and Lotte find him and take him back to the boarding house, where Martin talks Felix back into orthodox religion and calm acceptance of death.

the material conditions of life: what you desired was to be psychologically and ethically true. Criticism must discern the author's
purpose. Your book is an amplification, an illustration from life,
of that admirable text: *Nur diejenige Bildung hat Wert, die sich
in Kraft umsetzt.*[336] And as such, the work could hardly have
been better done. The thing is a whole, excellently planned and
rounded. Stage follows stage in natural development. No hurry;
a complete command of the material. It impresses and affects me.
I admire the ripeness, the precision of your views.

Yes, and your artistic skill. There are beautiful and strong scenes.
The interest rises, always rises, and culminates finally in that
tragi-comedy at the grave—a scene full of movement and vigour,
of irony, of emotion, of eloquence, of life-criticism. That was a
good idea, the portrait of Felix as St. John. Indeed, you have been
skilful in combining spiritual meaning with picturesqueness, and
with the activity of life. Capital, the picture of military service,
and very good indeed the chapters dealing with Felix's experiences
in the newspaper office. Then, you have no lack of humour. The
Autenrieth family are very distinct, and I think quite real; and
the Kantorin is a living person, with her mixture of goodness and
stupidity and pigheadedness. Frau Wick amused me, as you may
imagine.

About the women. I liked Rosalie better in the early than in
the later scenes; in the hammock she was very living indeed. It
is from the point of her marriage that I feel doubts. For instance,
I don't think she would have been unamiable on the marriage
day; I don't think she would have gone on to Paris alone, and so
on. Then: are you sure that she would have been annoyed when
the young musician killed himself on her account? It seems to
me she would greatly have enjoyed being so talked about. And
would Society have looked askance on her in that same matter?
Why? Who knew that she had deliberately encouraged the man?
However, of the vigour of this character there can be no kind of
doubt. I *see* the creature all through.

Lotte—well, I am not quite sure. I know by dire experience

[336] "Und lassen Sie sich noch dies eine gesagt sein: Nur diejenige Bildung
hat Wert, die sich in Kraft umsetzt, die den eignen Charakter sittlich stählt
und gegen die Welt festigt, und die sich als That für das Wohl der
Menschheit wieder verausgeben läszt" (*Glück und Glas*, 1891, p. 341).

how fearfully difficult it is to manage such a person. It seems to me that she should have had rather more of human imperfection. I felt that you did not care very much about her, yourself. Yet, after all, there *are* such girls, fortunately. Very likely I am corrupted by my realistic propensities; and it is quite certain that some of my own girls and women err on the side of goodness. It is easy to tell an author that his women don't please one's critical sense, but damnably hard to sit down and represent the women one has in mind.

Your thoughtful and mature men are admirable. Their talk never becomes wearisome, though it is so full of instruction. Take for example pp. 268–9; that is good matter for an essay, and yet it is *not* an essay, but talk.[337] Talk of the very best kind, however. English novelists have always been afraid of it—partly because of a deficiency in themselves, and still more because of the low intelligence of those readers upon whom they chiefly depend for support.

Felix is well managed, from first to last. What a curious thing that you and I were both busy at the same time with the problem of a weak but idealistic nature exposed to the miseries of poverty![338] It is delightful to me to see how *different* our men are, though they illustrate a similar state of things. Felix Lubrecht and Edwin Reardon both enlist the reader's sympathy, but in such very different ways. There is, moreover, a slight note of severity in your treatment of Felix; one feels that you are rather hard upon his failings here and there. Well now, this was, I suppose, inevitable, seeing that you oppose him to strong and noble characters. Reardon, on the other hand, has the *beau rôle*; opposed to him are only worldly and ignoble people. Yet I must repeat that our sympathy never really deserts Felix. And because you have made him actual. He *is* there, and we understand him. *Comprendre, c'est pardonner.*

I like the book, and I shall read it again some day. You will of course let me know what the reviewers have to say about it. Of course I cannot remark on the style, but it strikes me as

---

[337] Felix Lubrecht and Martin Gugelhopf discuss Socialistic philosophy, which the former defends and the latter derides.

[338] *New Grub Street* was being written while Bertz was working on *Glück und Glas.*

singularly pellucid—in places melodious. Witty, too; as, for example, where you represent Groch at dinner, and speak of *die fleischgewordene Idee des Feinschmeckers.*[339] These things must be commented upon by Germans, and I want to hear their opinion.

By the bye, you have given a very discreet, and ingenious translation of those lines of Catullus:

> Nunc in quadriviis et angiportis
> *Glubit* magnanimos Remi nepotes.[340]

Did you purposely alter the true meaning of that word *glubit?* Doering's note on the passage[341] is, I find, very much to the point. The *glubit* has always spoilt for me those beautiful and pathetic lines.

What am I to say about the tendency of the book? Well, I most heartily agree with it—at bottom. But most of all it pleases me because in it I see an assurance that you yourself are in the mood of strong and courageous work. Your last letter was very welcome. I do indeed think that your way is now clear before you. Get over that accursed removal, and set to work as soon as may be upon a new novel. You could not do better than to use your late horrible experiences. The artist makes all such miseries subserve his higher ends. I think "Glück und Glas" will make your name widely known, and that you will write with much more confidence. I can't see that this book is in any sense an immature production. You may become more realistic, in the common sense, but I don't think you will abandon this ethical standpoint.

In last Saturday's Athenaeum you will see the advertisements

[339] "Dr. Groch belustigte sich über diese schwülstige Schilderung, als endlich zwei Kellner ehrerbietig die fleischgewordene Idee des Feinschmeckers auftrugen, während der Koch sich in der Thür zeigte und einen bewundernden Blick auf seinem Meister ruhen liesz" (*Glück und Glas*, p. 56).

[340] Catullus, *Carmen.* LVIII. 4–5. Bertz translated these lines as, "An den Ecken und in den Seitengäszchen / Schröpft sie jetzt des Remus groszmütige Enkel" (*Glück und Glas*, p. 312).

[341] "Glubit, vox obscena e palaestra Veneris.—*magnanimos*, per ironiam; Romani (*Remi Nepotes*), qui magno animo res gerere debebant in latis campis, nunc libidinis exercendae causa levi et pusillo animo in angiportis reptare solebant" (*C. Valerii Catulli Veronensis Carmina*, ed. Frid. Guil. Doering [Altonae, 1834], p. 71, 5n).

of a new firm, Lawrence and Bullen.[342] They announce two books by Roberts, and one by his brother, which he is editing.[343] I hear also that Cassells are going to bring out a collection of short stories by him.[344] So you see he is progressing.

For myself, I still hear nothing more about "Godwin Peak." I am uneasy, and cannot do much work. But I must soon have my mind at rest, surely. It will be too bad if my money difficulties begin again at this time of day.

I know you are overladen with business, so don't write until you are quite settled. It rejoices me that things begin to look brighter for you. The worst of your life is over; perhaps even your health will now improve.

> Ever yours, dear old Friend,
> GEORGE GISSING

1. St. Leonard's Terrace. / Exeter.

October 18. 1891.

Dear Friend,

I trust your disturbance is now quite over, and that you sit at ease in the comfortable house of which you speak. It must be a vast improvement. And indeed you have every cause to be cheerful just now. The appeal from *Daheim*[345] is of course good and significant. Probably your connection with Ottmann will be very fruitful in happy results.

Many thanks for the German "Phoebe," and the copy of Tauchnitz's Magazine. I read the former through, and was pleased with it—especially the end. You have done me a service, as usual. The review of "New Grub Street" is, as you say, mere

---

[342] Arthur Henry Bullen (1850–1920), an expert in the literature of 16th and 17th-century England, founded the publishing house in partnership with H. W. Lawrence.

[343] Morley Roberts, *Land Travel and Sea-Faring: Adventures at Sea and in Australia*. His other book was *Songs of Energy*. Morley edited Cecil Roberts' *Adrift in America: Work and Adventure in the States* (*Athenaeum*, 19 September 1891, p. 375).

[344] Morley Roberts, *Reputation of George Saxon, and Other Stories* (London, September 1892).

[345] A weekly periodical published in Leipzig.

puffery, and not worth attending to.[346] And who *can* be interested
in such a Magazine as that? Such a collection of poor, twaddling
stories! But the English people on the Continent are very low
in intelligence; I have had many proofs of it.

I shall be very glad indeed if "Demos" really does appear
in the same series with "Glück und Glas."[347] That again would be
a result of your indefatigable zeal on my behalf.

Concerning "Godwin Peak" I have no news, but something
cheerful has happened, for all that. The new publishers, Lawrence
and Bullen, who publish Roberts's new books, have written to
ask me for a novel in one volume. They offer me one shilling on
every 6 shilling volume sold, and, what is better, will pay £100
on account, when they publish. These terms are very liberal
indeed. Accordingly, I have got to work, and am writing a book
called "The Radical Candidate."[348] They are highly pleased with
the title. The thing will take me about a month more, and will be
the length of the ordinary 2-vol. novel. I am writing quickly, and
with satisfaction; I think the book won't be bad, but it *may*
give some offence to the extreme philistine wing.

What do you know of the *Freie Volksbühne*[349]—or some such
name—at Berlin? It corresponds to the *Théâtre Libre* of Paris.
I have seen it mentioned in connection with an Independent
Theatre, which has been started in London. These London people
(headed by that rather offensive young man, George Moore,) have
acted Ibsen's *Ghosts*, and Zola's *Thérèse Raquin*;[350] but the latter
has now passed to the stage of an ordinary theatre. I have no
sympathy with this movement. It is futile, because they [*sic*] are no

[346] "Letter from Bertz. He sends a copy of Germ. periodical, 'Aus
Fremden [*sic*] Zungen,' with his transl. of my 'Phoebe.' Also the 1st no. of
the Tauchnitz Magazine, which has a very laudatory notice of 'New Grub
Street'" (Diary, 12 October 1891).

[347] Both books were published in Ottmann's "Bücherschatz Bibliothek."

[348] The title was changed to *Denzil Quarrier: A Novel* (London: Lawrence
and Bullen, 1892).

[349] According to the *Athenaeum* for 26 September 1891, p. 426, the Freie
Volksbühne had nearly 4000 members and had given twenty-two performances during the year.

[350] George Moore (1852–1933) and J. T. Grein (1862–1935) had organized
the Independent Theatre for the production of foreign plays in London.
Their initial venture was Ibsen's *Ghosts*, given at the Royalty Theatre in
March 1891. *Thérèse Raquin* opened at the Royalty on 9 October.

English dramatists, absolutely none. It is not the age for acted drama; the public is too gross.

I wonder whether I might ask you to send me Reclam's ed[itio]n. of "Hedda Gabler"? I will see if I can send you some book in return. I have not yet read the play, and it is incessantly spoken of. In English it costs 5 shillings, so that to purchase it is out of the question.

A 6 shilling edition of "New Grub Street" is announced for Oct 26th. So the scoundrels are willing to risk a new edition after all.[351]

Your new address has a pleasant-sounding name, fresh and airy.[352] It would rejoice me greatly if I could some day see you there. Who knows? But I seem to stand in a more dangerous position, financially, than for several years. It will be rather serious if I can't sell "Godwin Peak." Yet I think there is good work in the book, and it cost me infinite trouble.

We have had a savage gale blowing pretty much all over England for more than a week. Much damage and discomfort. But it is now over, and to-day the sun shines gloriously in a very blue sky. I wander about the lanes now and then, and gather blackberries.

I do wish I could have done with 3-vol. novels, and publish henceforth in a rational way. But I fear the money-question will forbid it. We shall see the results with Lawrence and Bullen.

Ever yours, dear Friend,
GEORGE GISSING

Addressed: Herrn Eduard Bertz. / Berg Strasse, 52. / Frankfurt a. d. Oder. / *Germany*.

1. St. Leonard's Terrace. / Exeter.   November 19. 1891.

I ought long ago to have thanked you for the books. Was very glad of them indeed. Have been working very hard to finish "The Radical Candidate," which is now in Bullen's hands. Shall now write a few short stories; one is already done.[353]

---

[351] The copyright had been sold to Smith, Elder, and Co.

[352] Bergstrasse.

[353] "I am writing short stories to make up a future volume. One I finished last week, 'A Casual Acquaintance'; and I am now engaged on 'A Victim of Circumstances.' Several more are in my mind" (GRG to Algernon Gissing, 24 November 1891, *Letters*, p. 324).

Ottmann sent me his *Echo*, but has not written, so neither have I. Would he expect me to do so? Probably not. Sorry your portrait did not turn out better, but I can't agree that it makes you look ugly.

Your recent experiences will make better material when you look back from a greater distance. That is my own experience.

I am reading "G[lück] und G[las]" again, and shall think over all you say. Rejoice that it sells so well, and that some noticeable reviews have appeared Your new title very good indeed![354] You will make something excellent of that idea. Go steadily ahead.

No news about "Godwin Peak." I fear that book will have to come back to me and wait. It is a serious matter.

Ever yours,
G. G.

1. St. Leonard's Terrace / Exeter.

December 16. 1891.

Dear Friend,

This year which is drawing to a close will have been important for you. I am getting anxious to hear whether any more noteworthy reviews of Glück u[nd] Glas have appeared, and also what progress you make with the planning of your next book. Perhaps you have even begun to write "Die Brille Spingas."

I have heard nothing more about "Demos." You, at all events, will let me know if it actually comes out.

I think I have already told you that my one-volume book is finished. The title "The Radical Candidate" was finally objected to, as not being attractive; thereupon I substituted the name of the hero "Denzil Quarrier." You will see a mention of the book in the gossip column of the current Athenaeum.[355]

Lawrence and Bullen have arranged for an American edition, to be sold at a dollar; also for an Australian. A Continental edition will probably be brought out by Heinemann and Balestier. In

---

[354] "Die Brille Spingas."

[355] "Mr. George Gissing has completed a new novel, 'Denzil Quarrier.' It will be published by Messrs. Lawrence and Bullen" (*Athenaeum*, 12 December 1891, p. 802).

each case I shall receive half the profits. But profits will not be large; I don't think much of the book.

A. P. Watt is still trying to sell "Godwin Peak," but as yet unsuccessfully. You will conclude that the story must be very bad indeed. But I don't think it is; I believe it rather strong. Possibly the reluctance of publishers is due to the subject; a man pretends to study for the Church, solely to gain certain personal ends.

I have not yet begun another book, but shall do so before long. A story is glimmering vaguely in my mind.

I wonder whether you have German translations of Dostoieffsky? Several of his books are in English, and rather well done. The more I read of him, the more I want to read; he appeals to me more distinctly than the other Russians, and more perhaps than any modern novelist. I bought not long ago two stories: "The Friend of the Family," and "The Gambler." They are extraordinary, like all his work; the reading refreshes me.

Of any other reading I have done very little of late. I am always peeping into the Greeks, but in a desultory way which leads to nothing.

Three "enormous reputations" have been made in England during the past year or so: Rudyard Kipling, Hall Caine, and J. M. Barrie.[356] These are fortunate men; I wish my receipts from literature were one quarter of what each of them earns. With "Godwin Peak" on hand, it begins to be doubtful whether I can henceforth count on as much as hitherto.

I am sorry to say that Roberts's Poems have attracted no attention whatever. It appears that the publishers take no interest in them, and really only published them to please Roberts.[357] I hope the other books—travels and tales—will be more successful. But what hope is there for any but either very base or very extraordinary books in such an outpouring of printed matter as now

[356] Kipling published *The Light That Failed*; Caine, *The Scapegoat*; and Barrie, *The Little Minister*. All these books were immediate popular successes.

[357] According to GRG, Bullen, the publisher, answered a query about the volume of poetry with, "Sh, we only printed them to please him! We didn't mind losing fifteen or twenty pounds. We shan't sell any" (To Algernon Gissing, 7 November 1891, Yale).

comes forth every week? It is dreadful to look at the lists of new volumes in literary papers. I seriously think that, but for money, I should cease producing altogether. It is a distinction *not* to write. Every month some new firm of publishers start operations; every month appear new periodicals of every species; the arts of advertising fill one with increasing disgust. I am tired of it all—tired of the useless struggle. Remember, I have now been producing for about 10 years. Do you recall that evening when I came to you at South Tottenham and gave you a copy of "Workers in the Dawn"?[358] How long ago it seems! But those were delightful evenings!

No doubt I shall hear from you before long. The weather here is so mild that birds' nests with eggs in them have been discovered.

Ever yours, old Friend,
GEORGE GISSING.

1. St. Leonard's Terrace / Exeter.

January 15. 1892.

Dear Friend,

I felt sure that you were too quick in discouraging yourself with regard to "Glück u[nd] Glas," and now this second letter confirms me. It rejoices me that you have such valuable reviews. Geib's treatment of you was unkind and unjust,[359] and you ought not to have allowed it to weigh for a moment. The book is a good book, and will be followed by a better. *Don't waver*; go on with your work; you *can* write novels which are by no means "pot-boilers," and I see no reason why you should feel any distaste for what is a distinct branch of art.

I have heard from Ottmann. He asked me for my photograph, and I sent the small head and shoulders (which you have)—*not* the dark profile, which would not come out well in a woodcut. I don't care much about this kind of thing, and it was not worth

---

[358] On the flyleaf, GRG wrote: "To Edward Bertz, Dear Friend, A public dedication of this book might prove a doubtful compliment; a private one I trust you will accept as a faint expression of my regard. Ever your affectionate George R. Gissing, London, May 19/80" (As quoted in the *Clique*, 16 May 1934).

[359] Otto Geib, an old friend of Bertz, probably wrote an unfavorable review of *Glück und Glas*.

while having a new portrait taken. The one I sent is supposed to be a fair likeness.

He also sent me the number of the *Litterarisches Echo* containing your review of the *"Cis-Moll-Sonate."*[360] Of course I read it with interest, but with the knowledge that it was written against the grain.

Yes, he undoubtedly made a mistake as to the price of your book. An enormous number would have to be sold to yield anything like a decent profit. For a full novel (newly pub[lished]) English publishers find it impossible to go below 3 shillings 6 pence, and even then the profits are small. They will be small even on my "Denzil Quarrier," to be published at 6 shillings.

You will be glad to hear that Watt has at last sold "Godwin Peak." Mess. A and C Black (very solid publishers who are just beginning to extend their business) have bought the British rights for £150. Out of this I have to pay Watt 10 per cent, so that my hope of getting *more* through him is frustrated. The book will not be pub[lished] before next October. Before then, I shall revise it.

As soon as Thomas Hardy's new book comes out on the Continent ("Tess of the Durbervilles") pray read it. I have not yet done so, but the reviewers are unanimous in a huge chorus of eulogy. They call it a "great book," and from all I hear I believe it deserves the name. It is glaringly unconventional, and earns its applause in the very teeth of a great deal of puritanic prejudice. Hardy is a nobly artistic nature. I am glad and proud that he has yet a future of growth before him. Do read the book.

I shall be anxious to see "Victoria Schulze." Either you or Ottmann will send it me. As for what you tell me about your autobiographic sketch, how can I be other than delighted to know that you have thus recorded our friendship.[361] This association has stood the test of a good many years now, and it will last until there are no more years to count. By the bye, I quite agree with the *Deutsche Romanzeitung*[362] as to your humour. Of course

---

[360] Dagobert v. Gerhardt, pseud. Gerhard v. Amyntor, *Die Cis-moll-Sonate* (Leipzig, 1891).

[361] The autobiographic sketch and "Victoria Schulze" were printed in Ottmann's *Das litterarische Echo*.

[362] The *Illustrierte deutsche Romanzeitung*, published in Berlin.

you are partly unconscious of possessing it; quite right that it should be so. It blends with your sadness, as all true humour has ever done. True humour cannot, however, be *cultivated*. Only hit upon sympathetic *situations*, and your treatment of them will never lack the humorous sub-note.

At present I am only reading, but I must sit down to my desk again before long. I walk a good deal, and am in reasonably good health. Snow and frost here, but day after day a bright blue sky.

Roberts's volume of short stories,[363] just pub[lished] by Lawrence and Bullen, contains some good things. But it has a lot of American tales for which you would not care at all.

> Ever yours, dear Friend,
> GEORGE GISSING

Addressed: Herrn Eduard Bertz. / Bergstrasse 52. / Frankfurt
a. d. Oder. / *Germany.*

1 St. Leonard's Terrace / Exeter

January 18th. 1892.

Hope you have received my letter already. Delighted to hear of your cheerful mood. All goes well with me. Am revising "Godwin Peak," of which I shall change the name. To a new task very soon.

> Ever yours,
> G. G.

1. St. Leonard's Terrace. / Exeter.

February 16. 1892.

Dear Friend,

I have to-day sent you a copy of "Denzil Quarrier." If you don't care much for it, just make a cross at the head of your next letter, and never mind further comment.

The past week I have spent down in Cornwall, chiefly at Penzance. A fine district, and a delightfully warm climate, though very humid. I walked a good deal, and have benefited by the holiday. Now for very serious work again.

---

[363] *King Billy of Ballarat, and other Stories* (London, 1892).

Whilst at Penzance, I received a letter from a certain Adele Berger, of Vienna, asking permission to translate my next novel. She has already translated "New Grub Street," (having *bought* the right from Smith and Elder) and it is actually being published in the *Pester Lloyd*.[364] I am read by those "qui profundum Danubium bibunt"! Eja!

In reply, I referred her to Lawrence and Bullen, apropos of "D[enzil] Q[uarrier]." Moreover, I begged her to send me just one copy of the *Pester Lloyd*; for I am highly curious to see how my novel looks, above all, to see how she has translated the title.

Before going from home, I gave a month's hard work to the revision of "Godwin Peak," and, I am sure, greatly improved the book. It now represents an important feature of my life; I shall be eager for its publication. The title decided upon is: "Born in Exile"—the significance whereof I dare say you will guess.[365] A. and C. Black, who are to publish it next October, say they are well pleased with the name.

The book I now have in mind is to deal with the great question of "throwing pearls before swine." It will present those people who, congenitally incapable of true education, have yet been taught to consider themselves too good for manual, or any humble, work. As yet I have chiefly dealt with types expressing the struggle of natures endowed *above* their stations; now I turn to those who are *below* it. The story will be a study of vulgarism—the all but triumphant force of our time. Women will be the chief characters.[366]

What progress with your own work? I do hope you are still as cheerful as when you last wrote. Do not allow small reverses to depress you. Try to work steadily on.

I think I told you of my correspondence with Ottmann. Probably he will be sending me a copy of the German "Demos."

Lawrence and Bullen have done very well with the business arrangements concerning "D[enzil] Q[uarrier]." It is to be pub [lished] by Macmillan in New York at 1 dollar; in Australia; and

---

[364] Her translation was printed serially in the *Pester Lloyd*, a Budapest daily paper, under the title *Ein Mann des Tages* (*Letters*, p. 325).

[365] Referring, of course, to himself.

[366] Eventually this became *The Odd Women* (3 vols., London, Lawrence and Bullen, 1893).

by Heinemann and Balestier on the Continent. The latter have given 25 guineas. Of all foreign profits (after the £105 is repaid) I am to receive half. They have written to ask that I will give them a chance of publishing my next book, and this I shall of course do, for they have behaved generously. Already their name is well known; I am astonished at the number of books—mostly expensive—which they have already published.

Who in heaven's name *buys* all the books that come forth? This is an endless mystery. Day by day new publishing firms appear, and the weekly issue of books is appalling. There must be thousands of people who are accumulating huge libraries, yet I don't know one of them.

You will see from the Athenaeum that Mrs Ward's new book[367] promises to repeat the success of "Robert Elsmere." I have not read it; indeed I have no means of seeing the newest books. Her method is *precisely* what mine was when I wrote "Workers in the Dawn." Of course she has a mature mind, and wide knowledge; but artistically I believe she is at the very point I had reached, after study of George Eliot, some ten years ago. Her books are enormously long, and she develops with great labour the intellectual advance of every character.

I have been much rejoiced by that news from Vienna. You, also, will be glad, I know.

We are progressing towards spring. May you work well, and be physically at ease!

Ever yours, dear Friend,
GEORGE GISSING

Very interesting, this attempt of the Emperor's to revive religious education.[368]

Afternoon

Your letter has just arrived. I am delighted to hear of the new edition of "Glück und Glas," and of the invitation from the

---

[367] Mrs. Humphry Ward, *The History of David Grieve* (2 vols., London, 1892).

[368] Clause I of Emperor William's Elementary Education Bill stated: "The work of the elementary schools is to conduct the religious, moral, and patriotic training of the young, as well as to instruct them in the general knowledge and proficiency required in civil life" (London *Times*, 9 February 1892, p. 5).

Verein. Yes, you are going ahead, and will continue to do so. Let me hear more of your novel as it progresses.

I have laughed over those ludicrous mis-translations.[369] It is a pity, but pray do not trouble yourself for a moment. Someday, if it seems necessary, the worst errors can perhaps be corrected. But remember that no one will give such thought to the matter as you do. As you say, the readers about whom I need care will read me in English.

Yes, Stead is an ass.[370] I forbade my bookseller to send me the second part of the "Ghost Stories." But one gets a great deal of information out of the Review of Reviews; I often find it profitable.

Shall wait eagerly for the *Echo.*

G. G.

1. St. Leonard's Terrace. / Exeter.

March 17th. 1892.

Dear Friend,

I have to thank you for a long letter, for Zapp's play, and for the *Echo.*[371] It is high time I acknowledged these things.

First, of your "Victoria Schulze." I think it a capital little combination of pathos and humour. Probably it will confirm those critics who have compared you with Dickens. Of course *I* understand well enough how impossible it is to make such a comparison. Intellectually, you are a century ahead of Dickens. Indeed, such phrases are profitless, and never agreeable to a writer; they only mean that the critic is rather shallow and

---

[369] "Letter from Bertz, saying that the German transl. of 'Demos' is ludicrously bad" (Diary, 16 February 1892).

[370] William Thomas Stead (1849–1912), a journalist who founded the *Review of Reviews. Real Ghost Stories* and *More Ghost Stories* came out as extra numbers of the journal.

[371] "Rec. from Bertz a new issue of Ottmann's 'Litterarisches Echo,' containing his 'Victoria Schulze,' and a short biography of him, in which it is said: 'Schon im Beginn seines Aufenthalts in London, [*sic*] hatte er das Glück, den englischen Romanschriftsteller George Gissing kennen zu lernen, mit welchem ihn seitdem die herzlichste Freundschaft verbindet.' Bertz's life reads strangely; sounds very varied and adventurous. How would *mine* read, if truly written?" (Diary, 14 March 1892). The play was probably Arthur Zapp's *Auszerhalb der Gesellschaft: in 4 Aufzügen* (Berlin, 1891).

decidedly lazy, though he may mean well. Still, I repeat that this little story is a delicately humorous bit of work; in places it all but brought tears to my eyes, and at the end it left me with a feeling of contentment. You will doubtless write more short stories.

How interesting your biography is! Strangers must think that your life has been strangely varied. Reading it thus, I felt that familiarity had half spoiled for me the decided picturesqueness of your experiences. Ah, but it is only a skeleton! Do you know what I hope? That you will some day write a full autobiography— or at all events autobiographic chapters. It would be profoundly interesting, and need not include anything too painful to yourself. Remember how many distinguished writers have only begun their serious production at the age which you have now reached.[372] It is to be hoped that you have a long spell of work before you, and that the autobiography will some day be a natural thing.

Many thanks for the very kind reference to me. I read it with great pleasure.

The review of "Glück u[nd] Glas" is sympathetic. But surely Felix ought not to be called "dilettierender Geistesproletarier"— an unhappy phrase. I notice that Spillmann calls attention to the passage which I myself spoke of: "Nur die Bildung hat Wert" etc.[373]

Do allow yourself to be encouraged and enspirited by this appreciation. Indeed, I think you are feeling much better than of old. Go on with "Menschenangesicht."[374] The subject is naturally suggested by your practical knowledge of actors. As for the title, I am unable to judge, but is it specific enough?

Adele Berger has sent me three cuttings from the *Pester Lloyd*. Unfortunately, she has had to call the story "Ein Mann des Tages," but hopes to find a better title when it appears in book form.[375] The translation seems to me very good; certainly it is very conscientious. Take the following passage, which seems to me a satisfactory test:

"Der Nebel wurde dichter; sie sah zu den Fenstern auf und

[372] Bertz was 39 years old.
[373] See 21 September 1891.
[374] No record of publication.
[375] The German translation never appeared as a volume.

bemerkte, dasz sie trüb gelblich waren. Dann entdeckte ihr Auge einen über die Galerie schreitenden Beamten und in ihrer grotesken Stimmung, ihrer höhnischen Verzweiflung kam er ihr wie eine verlorene Seele vor, die verdammt ist, ewig suchend durch endlose Regale zu wandern. Und die Leser, die an den Radiuslinien dieser Pulte saszen, was waren sie, als unglückliche Fliegen, in einem ungeheuren Netz gefangen, dessen Kern der grosze Zirkel des Katalogs war? Es ward dunkler und dunkler; den hohen Büchermauern schienen sichtbare Stäubchen zu entsteigen, die die Dunkelheit noch verstärkten"—u.s.w. (Vol. I. p. 195.)[376]

Now shall I tell you how the French translator[377] of "Demos" would have rendered this passage? Thus:

"Il faisait de plus en plus sombre. On n'y voyait guère. Marianne souffrait d'un profond abattement."

Absolutely! I have compared that chapter of "Demos" of which you speak, and it is disgraceful. No translation at all; simply a rough sketch of the *contents* of the chapter, such as I might have scribbled out before sitting down to compose.

(By the bye, when you write again, will you kindly let me know the proper way to address a letter to this Adele Berger? I mean, the form of name. Should it be Frau Adele Berger—or how?)

Well, well! We must remember that such a translation as your "Phoebe" is the rarest of things—a rendering by one who is himself an artist in fiction.

I am now correcting the proofs of "Born in Exile." I should not wonder if they publish this spring, after all. My brother's new book is just out.[378]

Now for "Denzil Quarrier." I am glad indeed that you had nothing worse to say of it. Strangely, it has been very well reviewed; the *Times* gave a prominent notice the other day.[379]

[376] Cf. *New Grub Street*, Chapter VIII.

[377] Fanny Le Breton. See 23 October 1888.

[378] *The Masquerader* (3 vols., London: Hurst and Blackett, April 1892).

[379] The review said the novel was a "satire upon the working of representative institutions in the borough of Polterham," but added that "politics, after all, are only the accessory of a story of more than usual psychological interest—a story which leaves the solution of more than one of its problems to the imagination" ("Recent Novels and Tales," London *Times* [12 March 1892], p. 5).

People seem to think it psychologically interesting. I wish you could have liked Eustace Glazzard. I thought the man painfully human.[380] However, it is very good that you think I am progressing in the matter of form.

Yes, I am inclined to think that the purely impersonal method of narrative has its advantages. Of course it approximates to the dramatic. No English writer that I know (unless it be George Moore) has yet succeeded in adopting this method. Still, I shall never try (and you do not wish me) to suppress my own *spirit*. To do that, it seems to me, would be to renounce the specific character of the novelist. Better, in that case, to write plays.

Zapp's drama (which shall soon be returned to you) has a strange resemblance to "D[enzil] Q[uarrier]"—very strange. But I cannot like it. It seems to me rather crude—as you hint. After reading it, I sympathized with nobody—though trying to do so.

Remarkable, by the way, how English opinion is progressing in the matter of subject for fiction. In a very laudatory notice of "D[enzil] Q[uarrier]," the *Saturday Review* says: "A bolder subject would better suit this writer."[381] That would have been extraordinary a few years ago. They tell me that not a single paper has objected to the theme. Indeed, after Hardy's "Tess," one can scarcely see the limits of artistic freedom.

Certainly my position improves. I am told that, recently, a lecture was delivered before the London Ethical Society on "The Novels of George Gissing."[382] Of this I heard nothing at the time, but it is very important. I don't even yet know who the lecturer

[380] Denzil Quarrier, the hero, confesses to his best friend, Glazzard, that his marriage is bigamous. When Quarrier runs for election to Parliament, his opponent turns out to be Glazzard, who betrays his friend by telling of the illegal marriage in order to win the contest. Glazzard, a completely unsympathetic character, is really more painful than human to most readers.

[381] "A bolder theme may possibly suit this author better, and good honest work may be always expected from him" (*Saturday Review*, LXXIII, 5 March 1892, 276).

[382] "Rec. copy of the 'Queen' for March 5., in which I find report of the lecture ment. by Nelly. It was delivered (date not given) by a Miss Clara E. Collet M.A. Very poor report; can't make out what the lecture really was—except that she maintained the 'healthiness' of my mind" (Diary, 19 March 1892). Miss Collet later became GRG's friend; see Introduction.

was. The Society is not contemptible; I used to attend its lectures occasionally.

Roberts often inquires about you. He is always ill, but does a great deal of work, and decidedly improves. Some things in "King Billy" are very strong.

After all, my new book will not be what I said. I am still groping about. But I am glad to tell you that a short story called "A Victim of Circumstances" has been accepted by "Blackwood's Magazine." It isn't worth much. You shall have it when it comes out.[383]

I now understand your *Lotte*[384] better. A curious pathos about that episode in your life. Yes, it would be interesting to go to the parsonage; do, if possible and if you are sure that no depression will result.

It rejoices me to see your portrait again.[385] All goes well, be sure!

Ever yours, dear Friend,
GEORGE GISSING

1. St. Leonard's Terrace. / Exeter.

May 1st. 1892.

Dear Friend,

A May Day which does not dishonour its reputation tempts me to sit down and write to you. There is warm sunshine and still air. Birds are loud about me. May it be the same at Frankfurt!

A and C. Black are behaving to me with much decency. The other day they sent me a printed list of some 200 periodicals, requesting me to mark those to which I wished a copy of "Born in Exile" to be sent for review; also, to let them know the addresses of private persons to whom I wanted copies sent. Accordingly, you will receive the book direct from the publishers, and, I hope, very soon; for the Athenaeum of yesterday mentions it as already published.[386]

Heinemann and Balestier have not sent me a copy of "Denzil

---

[383] Published in January 1893 (CLIII, 69–86).
[384] The heroine of *Glück und Glas*, who apparently had a counterpart in real life.
[385] Printed with his autobiography in *Das litterarische Echo*.
[386] *Athenaeum*, 30 April 1892, p. 564.

Quarrier,"[387] but do not on any account obtain one for me, thanks.
Roberts has got "King Billy" from them, and I shall presently
send them my address.

As yet, I hear nothing from Ottmann. Doubtless he is waiting
until all three vols.[388] are published; then he will probably send me
a copy. But we must not trouble him. The poor man is struggling
with financial difficulties, and such a position always demands
consideration.

As to the title "Menschenangesicht," of course you are right.
A foreigner cannot judge of these niceties.

It pleases me very much to hear your good opinion of Roberts's
book. It has been reviewed very favourably. I think "Mithridates
the King" is a really remarkable bit of work, and "Father and
Son," which you refer to, could not easily be surpassed as an
example of the horror to be extracted from scientific suggestions.

Those letters from old comrades prove how very widely your
book is being read. I should think your next production will be
welcomed by a public of considerable extent.

I, unfortunately, have not yet made a serious beginning with a
new book. The subject is pretty clear before me, (it will not be
quite what I suggested to you,)[389] but I cannot think of a good title,
and, for the first time, this fact seems to delay me. I want to deal
with the flood of blackguardism which nowadays is pouring forth
over the society which is raised by wealth above the lowest and yet
is not sufficiently educated to rank with the highest. Impossible
to take up a newspaper without being impressed with this fact of
extending and deepening Vulgarity. It seems to be greatly due
to American influence, but there can be no doubt that the ground
is prepared for it by the pretence of education afforded by our
School-board system. Society is being *levelled down*, and with
strange rapidity. Democracy scarcely pretends to a noble aim;
it is triumphing by the force of its appeal to lower motives. Thus,
I am convinced, the gulf between the really refined and the
masses grows, and will grow, constantly wider. Before long, we
shall have an Aristocracy of mind and manners more distinct from
the vast majority of the population than Aristocracy has ever

[387] Published in Leipzig for "The English Library."
[388] Of *Demos*.
[389] See 16 February 1892.

13

been in England. It will not be a fighting Aristocracy, but a retiring and reticent; scornful, hopeless.

My brother's latest book has been respectfully treated. It is not strong, but there is some good writing in it, and the fresh moorland spirit is really refreshing. If his next production is still better, I will see that you have a copy of it. It was of course useless to trouble you with mere apprentice work. I think he may in time develope [sic] a style which will be a distinct improvement upon that of William Black.[390]

I am reading Lucretius, steadily, and have got through more than half. It requires an effort of the mind, but the reward is undeniable.

Two German novelists are attracting attention in England just now: Ilse Frapan[391] and Sudermann.[392] Do you know much of them? It seems to me that "Glück und Glas" might very well be translated to form a volume of Heinemann's International Library, which you will have seen advertized in the Athenaeum. I wish I had the time to do this. I suppose you would not care to draw Heinemann's attention to the book, in the hope that he might select it for translation?

I notice that it is more than a month since the date of your letter to which I am now replying. You are well, I trust, and have been busy.

> Ever yours, dear Friend,
> GEORGE GISSING

1. St. Leonard's Terrace. / Exeter.

May 20th. 1892.

Dear Friend,

I have to thank you for two long and profitable letters.[393] I must try to answer them with corresponding care.

In judging the tendency of "Born in Exile," it is probable that you have been misled by the fact that the character of Godwin

---

[390] William Black (1841–1898), Scottish journalist and novelist, whose novels combined actual travel experiences and fictitious adventures.

[391] Ilse Levien (1852–1908), pseud. Ilse Frapan, psychological novelist.

[392] Hermann Sudermann (1857–1928), novelist and playright.

[393] The letters had arrived on 11 May and 20 May (Diary).

Peak is obviously, in a great degree, sympathetic to the author. But you will not find that Peak's tone is to be henceforth mine— do not fear it. Indeed, it seems to me that the tone of the whole book is by no means identical with that of Peak's personality; certainly I did not mean it to be so. Peak is myself—one phase of myself. I described him with gusto, but surely I did not, in depicting the other characters, take *his* point of view? To a certain extent you admit this. I understand very well the fear that has been excited in you, for you are well aware of those parts of my character on which Roberts has laid stress.[394] No, I hope to be more and more objective in my work; I hope to, and mean to. Already I have begun my new book, and herein you will see how I regard the pursuit of money and ease as it affects the mass of the London population; you will see, moreover, that I am very far from over-rating the moral worth, the value as individuals, of what we call the educated classes. Indeed, your first letter set me to work, after long delay. As usual, I have to thank you for impulse and encouragement. I am trying to do precisely what you hoped I should—that is to say, to present the other side of the shield. Your suggestions greatly helped to clear my mind.

"Born in Exile" was a book I *had* to write. It is off my mind, and now I go on with a sense of relief. No, no; you and I are not going to part so widely—don't think it. This new book will appeal strongly to your sympathies.

To tell you the truth, I was disappointed with Roberts's article. I don't think he understands my work in the very least!

You must not think of sending me anything in return for the *Review*. On no account! Already I am indebted to you for several things. Let us wait awhile, and we shall be able to exchange gifts more frequently.

Your valuable suggestions concerning the title for the German "New Grub Street" I at once submitted to Adele Berger, and I hope to hear her opinion of them. It was unlikely that Ottmann

---

[394] The reference is to Morley Roberts's article, "George Gissing," published in the *Novel Review*, I (May 1892), 98–103: ". . . he has been consistently hopeless; consistently careless of criticism; consistently pathological. For he is of the order of realists whose work, whether they know it or not, is neither more nor less than the study of disease in one form or another" (p. 99).

would accept that second book of mine—in any case, until he knew whether the first was going to sell. I am very glad indeed that the "Demos" is after all not so painfully bad. No doubt I shall receive a copy very shortly. Let Ottmann take his time.

But I thought you had had that photograph of me long ago.[395] Unfortunately, I have not another copy to send you.

Of course it pleases me very much that it is to be *your* article which Ottmann reprints,[396] with the additional paragraph. Most certainly there is no man living who has followed my work as you have, no one who understands it anything like so well. And I think I may say that no one else will ever take half the trouble that you have done to arrive at a just estimate of my literary personality. Here in England, people know very little indeed about me; I suppose the critics, en masse, entertain a ludicrously distorted idea of what I have done, and what I have tried to do. Shall I ever be the subject of a serious study in one of the leading periodicals—as Meredith and Hardy and Marion Crawford[397]— and all the rest of them—have been again and again? It is doubtful: probably not before my death. And yet I was told by Mlle. Le Breton that her acquaintance, the editor[398] of the *Edinburgh Review*, insisted to her on the importance of my work. It is true that there are occasional little signs of spreading recognition, but this affects only a small, very small, section of the public.

It will interest me greatly to see what you one day make of "The French Prisoners" in German.[399] Probably you would change the *phrase* rather than the *spirit*. The book remains very clear in my mind; it is no insignificant predecessor to "Glück und Glas"; indeed, an intelligent critic would divine the later in the earlier work.

I have received two copies of "D[enzil] Q[uarrier]" from Heinemann and Balestier.

May you receive from Ottmann the sum for which you venture to hope! Oh, you ought to have very much more than that! But

[395] I.e., the picture GRG had sent to Ottmann.

[396] "George Gissing, ein Real-Idealist"; see 14 December 1889.

[397] Francis Marion Crawford (1854–1909), American novelist living in Italy.

[398] Henry Reeve (1813–1895), editor from 1855 to 1895.

[399] A boys' story, in English, which Bertz wrote in 1884. See Introduction.

it is to be hoped that the book will continue to sell. Undoubtedly it has been far more than a common success. I wonder very much indeed what sort of school that can be in Lancaster! I thought at first that the man must have chosen it for a German text-book, but, on reflecting, I see that the book as a whole would never do even for older schoolboys. The thing remains a mystery.

Yes, if you *could* establish your health in the manner proposed it would be an enormous blessing. Follow the plan, by all means, if possible.

Many thanks for information about Ilse Frapan and Sudermann.

The search for a satisfactory subject for a new book is terribly worrying. At times it has made me ill. Combined with your abominable toothache, it must have driven you to distraction. In years gone by, I suffered wretchedly from my teeth, but it is now long since they troubled me; I hope your heroic remedy will at length give you ease. After all, Rehfeldt is certainly a use and comfort to you now and then. Of course he must have very little time to spare for social pleasures; the life of an active doctor is a thought that frightens me, as often as I contemplate it. To accept it with resignation, one must surely be of a very positive mind.

Let me beg you not to postpone very long the commencement of some new work. I want you to write a good deal yet. The subjects ideally adapted to one's mind and mood are of course very few; they occur only in moments of happy inspiration. One has often to struggle vehemently with what seems uncongenial matter—and indeed there comes a reward from such struggle. One's powers grow in the process.

I can't find a title. It must wait unfound for the present.

By the bye, Rudyard Kipling's book of ballads[400] is most remarkable work. Try to get it if H[einemann] and B[alestier] publish it. But it will require all your knowledge of English to read with complete understanding. I have only seen extracts.

Ever yours, dear Friend,
GEORGE GISSING

---

[400] *Barrack-Room Ballads and Other Verses* (London, 1892).

1. St. Leonard's Terrace / Exeter.

June 19th. 1892.

My dear Friend,

Yesterday I received from Ottmann two copies of the *Echo* containing your "G[eorge] G[issing]" article.[401] I have ready [*sic*] the article with no little satisfaction. Roberts, you see, has not the critical faculty; you, on the other hand, possess it in a very high degree. I am convinced that it is a great advantage for me to be introduced to German readers by such a study as this of yours; your serious writing calls for serious attention. Roberts thinks well and kindly of my work, but his tone is altogether too journalistic to influence people of the better sort. I like very much what you have added to the earlier essay. Indeed, as I have often said, my obligations to you are very great—not easily to be acknowledged.

The portrait has come out very well, I think, though the expression is somewhat altered—perhaps for the better.

In the advertisement of "Demos," I see that *Erzählung* has been altered to *Roman*—a good thing.

It is good news that the 3-vol. edition of "Glück und Glas" is going through the press. I shall be very glad to see what sort of illustrations are put on the cover. They will be better, I hope, than those which figure on the cheapest issue of my books—mere "railway" pictures.

Those days of warmth and comparative quietness must have been very grateful to you. It is hard indeed that one's work must always be performed under conditions more or less unfavourable. We are always being told that the struggle against adverse circumstances is for the good of our art, and that with prosperity comes relaxation of effort. It is so, undoubtedly, with some men, but chiefly with those who have nothing very particular to say. You, I am convinced, would work all the better for being at ease in your mind as regards material difficulties, and most assuredly I should do so.

Probably you received the *Daily Chronicle* review of "Born in

[401] "Have rec. Ottmann's *Litterarisches Echo* for June, which contains my portrait and Bertz's article on me. Acknowledged this to-day; wrote also to Bertz and Alg" (Diary, 19 June 1892).

Exile," posted to you by my brother.[402] It was the paper which got lost on the way to you, before. The writer at all events gives a very fair and full account of my book. I believe this is as yet the only favourable notice. I saw one in the *Saturday Review* which surpassed in abusive misrepresentation anything I have come across, concerning my own work, of late years.[403] People dislike the story and the characters. I can't help it.

My work goes on very slowly, and with perpetual alterations. Just now I must be rather out of sorts, I suppose. In a short time you shall hear at greater length of what I am trying to do.

Ever yours, dear Friend,
GEORGE GISSING

1. St. Leonard's Terrace / Exeter.

August 7. 1892.

Dear Friend,

It is long since I heard from you; but I hope this means that you have been busy through the bright months.

Yesterday I received from Ottmann the new *Echo*, in which was an announcement of the new edition of "Glück und Glas," with extracts from the best reviews. It all read very pleasantly.

A short time ago, a curious thing happened. I received a letter from a man at Croydon who signed himself "G. T. Gissing."

---

[402] "By an extraordinary combination of mishaps, a copy of the Chronicle which I sent to Bertz has been lost on the way. If you still have yours, would you put it carefully into a wrapper, and address to: Herrn Eduard Bertz...." (GRG to Algernon, 4 June 1892, Yale).

[403] "There is plenty about theology, geology, and all sorts of other 'ologies' and 'isms' in Mr. Gissing's pages; for his characters, when gravelled for lack of matter, have a simple habit of asking each other, in the manner of the American interviewer, 'Well, what do you think of such an one,' or 'What is your opinion of this, that, and the other?' and away go their tongues at score, making free with the contents of Mr. Gissing's commonplace book. It is all very well to quote, as does the author of *Born in Exile*, 'Oui, répondit Pococurante, il est beau d'écrire ce qu'on pense; c'est le privilège de l'homme,' but he should remember that what is 'beau' to the writer may be anything but 'beau' to the reader, and that if it be the privilege of one man to write, it may be, at least, equally within the rights of the others to skip" (*Saturday Review*, LXXIII, 11 June 1892, 688).

He wrote to say that, during his absence from home, a Mr. Steinitz had called, and had left a letter and a parcel, both addressed to "G. Gissing." There was evidently (he continued) a mistake, for he saw that "the well known novelist" was intended. Well, I wrote back, and got the letter and parcel. The former was from Frau Steinitz, who said that a cousin of her husband's, passing through London, would leave with me a copy of the German "Demos."

Now it is a very strange thing that Steinitz should have gone to Croydon. The letter he had to deliver was addressed to me at 7. K. Cornwall Residences—to which address, by the bye, my unknown namesake wrote. I can only suppose that Steinitz, on finding I had removed, consulted a Directory, and discovered the name of the man at Croydon.

Well, I wrote to Steinitz—he having left his address at Croydon. He answered, but without explanations, merely asking if he could see me. I wrote again, explaining to him that Exeter was a very long way from London, and that, moreover, I was just on the point of going for a holiday to the north of England—whence I am now returned. I concluded by asking if I could be of any use to him in London. But I have not since heard.

Of course I replied to the letter of Frau Steinitz.

I have looked through the German "Demos," and see that it is translated pretty closely. Of course your remarks on that subject suffice to me. I am very glad that you think it passable.

The summer has, for me, been all but wasted. I have begun several stories, but in each case only to destroy what I wrote. Now, after a holiday, I am again making a beginning, and I think with better hope. I must get a book done so as to have some money before the end of the year.

Did you receive, at last, the *Chronicle* review of "Born in Exile"? On the whole, the book has been respectfully received. The *Times* gave it about a third of a column.[404] But of course these people do not pretend to like it. I am getting a very solid bad-reputation for gloominess and misanthropy.

[404] The review praised the novel for "close thought and carefully-drawn character," but found GRG deficient in humor, pathos, picturesqueness, and stirring narrative (London *Times*, 1 July 1892, p. 18).

Indeed I feel very envious as to what you have been doing all this time. As likely as not, there will be a letter from you before this has had time to reach Germany.

Politics have ruined this season for the publishers, and I fear there is no very cheerful outlook; now that the Home Rulers have obtained a majority, there are sure to be perpetual uproars in and out of Parliament for the next year or two.[405] However, I suppose a quiet person here and there will continue to read books.

Have you seen Daudet's "Rose et Ninette"?[406] I know it only by English reviews, which declare it to be quite unworthy of him. Yet he is comparatively a young man, and with his regular life he ought not to have broken down so soon. Perhaps the sufferings of childhood and youth are now telling upon him.

Nothing whatever that interests me has appeared in England. I have just glanced through "David Grieve," and I think it is better than the reviews led me to expect. But of terrific length— longer, I should think, than a novel of Thackeray. It would certainly interest you, for the ethical features of the book are noteworthy. I don't in the least agree with the people who cry out that religion and morals may not be discussed (by the characters) in a novel. Anything whatever may be discussed that *is* discussed by actual men and women.

It is said that Mrs Ward received in all, for this novel, the pretty sum of £20,000. Ye gods!

Poor old Bismarck![407] If only one had knowledge of the world sufficient for the treating of great subjects; what a study would there be in a man such as Bismarck! Well, I will envelope this and post it, in the hope that it may bring a reply.

Ever yours, dear Friend,
GEORGE GISSING

[405] Gladstone and his supporters, who advocated Home Rule for Ireland, won the general election of 1892.

[406] Published in Paris, 1892.

[407] Bismarck, retired from the Chancellorship since 1890, expounded his views from his retreat, Friedrichsruh, through letters, articles, and speeches.

Addressed: Herrn Eduard Bertz. / Bergstrasse, 52. / Frankfurt
    a. d. Oder / *Germany.*
1. St. Leonard's Terrace / Exeter.

August 30th. 1892.

Dear Friend,

Many thanks to you for this book. I heartily wish your name
had been added as the translator; but I see that in no case is a
translator mentioned. Doubtless this reprint is good for me. By the
bye, what poor stuff, that story of Maupassant's.[408]

Your verses please me very much. The thought is a very happy
one, and delightfully expressed. You are far from having abandoned poetry! It is inherent in your nature, and appears in all
your work.

I rejoice that you write so hopefully, in spite of Ottmann's
rascally behaviour. The fellow must be very shameless, but I cannot think you will lose in the end. I suppose these men put off paying until the last possible moment. Still, you want the money, and
at least ought to receive an account. The reviews of your book have
been remarkable. Get on with another; success has come to you.

Yes, Ottmann sent me a cloth-bound copy of "Demos," and I
acknowledged it.

My sister[409] has already read "Glück und Glas," with much
satisfaction. But if you care to send a copy, I will gladly present
it to her, from you. Roberts, alas, does not read German—a foolish
neglect on his part.

My slow work has brought me nearly to the end of Vol I of
a new book. It deals with the women who, from the marriage
point of view, are *superfluous.* "The Odd Women," I shall perhaps call it.

"La Débâcle"[410] I have not yet seen, and fear I shall not.
"L'Immortel"[411] will amuse you, but it is far from being one of
Daudet's best.

All good wishes to you.
Ever yours,
GEORGE GISSING

[408] "L'Enfant"; printed in the *Bibliothek der fremden Zungen* in which
Bertz's translation of GRG's "Phoebe" appeared.
[409] Margaret.
[410] Emile Zola (Paris, 1892).
[411] Paris, 1888.

Birmingham.

November 3rd. 1892.

My dear Friend,

You have indeed a calamity to report. I grieve over it exceedingly. It is an extreme instance of ill fortune that this thing should have happened just when you had a reasonable prospect of profiting by the great success of your book. One feels disposed to rage against fate—were it not so idle. I can only be glad that you do not allow the blow to depress you, and that you speak so earnestly of the work before you. Surely *someone* will take up the great business which Ottmann has started?[412] The stock (especially in the case of your book "Glück und Glas") cannot be worthless, and some man will continue the sale of these publications. I shall be very anxious to hear what sort of assistance you receive from the Verband. This is a juncture which ought to prove the value of such a society. In any event, you are one of Ottmann's legal creditors. I suppose it is vain to hope that he will in future be actuated by a sense of honour? Yet his interests may somehow prove to be identical with yours, in the long run.

Do not say that you will *devote* yourself henceforth to historic fiction. Of that you cannot be sure. I am convinced that you will write most excellent historic stories; and, as you say, there is undoubtedly a good public for that kind of work; but that will not occupy you exclusively, I am sure. You will write modern stories as well. Just at present the fate of "Glück und Glas" has disgusted you; but this impression will pass away. Go on with the Luther book[413] by all means; in fact, do whatever you feel strongly inclined to do; and, above all, lose no more time than you can help. In the rush of authors nowadays, it is vastly important to keep one's name frequently before the public.

You see that I write from Birmingham. I have been spending a fortnight with my brother in Worcestershire, and now I am here to look about me for the purpose of getting new material. In a few days I shall be able to send you a fixed address, but as yet I have no abode.

Before leaving Exeter, I finished my novel, which is called "The Odd Women." It is to be published very shortly by Lawrence and

[412] His publishing business had failed.
[413] *In Luthers Heimat*, a boys' story. No record of publication.

Bullen,[414] who will pay me 100 guineas in advance of royalties. I am glad to make this kind of arrangement, as I am sure I shall profit by these books (to a small extent) in years to come. Smith and Elder are certainly deriving a good annual sum from those five books of mine which they hold.[415] Wherever I travel, I see those books, in one or other edition, on the bookstalls and in the shops. Of the cheap edition of "New Grub Street" they have obviously printed many thousands. It is a grievous pity that I could not afford to keep an interest in these publications.

Frequent references in periodicals prove to me that I am becoming pretty well known. My title "New Grub Street" has even been accepted for popular use, witness the fact that a column of reviews in the *Graphic*[416] the other day was headed "In New Grub Street." A monthly paper called *The Bookman* stated, not long ago, that it was known that "Mr Thomas Hardy has a special admiration for the writings of George Gissing."[417] In view of Hardy's great popularity just now, this was a valuable advertisement.

So much about myself. Your "Mancherlei Mär"[418] will, I am sure, be full of interesting things. I repeat: try to get it done before long. Publish it whilst your reputation is still fresh. You have suffered many blows of fate, but all the more likely that your day of success and quiet is drawing near. Work steadily on with the short stories and with "Junker Georg."[419] I am sorry to hear of your having to spend so much time over that translation from Björnson.[420] You need all for your own productions.

I suppose you have read much about Tennyson since his death.[421] Well, we have lost our one indisputably great poet; for my own

---

[414] Published in 3 vols., in April 1893.

[415] *Demos, Thyrza, A Life's Morning, The Nether World,* and *New Grub Street.*

[416] Possibly the *Daily Graphic*, a London paper.

[417] "The opinions of novelists on novels are always interesting, whether one agrees with them or not. Mr. Hardy is known specially to admire the writings of George Gissing" ("News Notes," *Bookman*, III, October 1892, 6).

[418] No record of publication.

[419] Another boys' story.

[420] Björnstjerne Björnson (1832–1910), Norwegian poet, dramatist, and novelist. There is no record of any translation of his works by Bertz.

[421] He died on 6 October 1892.

part, I agree with those who think him a worthy successor of Theocritus and Virgil. He had not much to say, but his utterance is consummate, the very perfection of language. His place among the Immortals is far more certainly assured than that of Byron—perhaps than that of Shelley. You say that "In Memoriam" wearies you. Yes, but read his shorter poems—"Oenone," "Lucretius," "Guinevere," "Locksley Hall," and all the lyrics; read "Maud" and perhaps "The Princess." (I should have mentioned "The Lotus Eaters.") No poet ever wrote more musically, or with greater command of picturesque, suggestive language. Remember that his best work belongs to a past generation. He is not of to-day—any more than Keats is.

You shall hear again from me very soon. You know well how sincerely I sympathize with you in this wretched calamity. But you do not need encouragement, for you have done fine work, and will do finer.

Ever yours, dear old Friend,
GEORGE GISSING

1. St. Leonard's Terrace / Exeter.

December 2. 1892.

My dear Friend,

I have been away from home for five or six weeks, partly living with my brother in Worcestershire, and partly getting materials for a new book in the so-called Black Country—the region to the west and north of Birmingham, a veritable Inferno, flaring at night with the chimneys of iron-works, and blasted by coal and iron mining.

It is not my purpose to deal with the working-class of that district. I shall use it as picturesque background to a story of middle-class life, insisting on the degree to which people have become *machines*, in harmony with the machinery amid which they spend their lives.[422]

---

[422] The title was to be "Gods of Iron," "meaning machinery, which is no longer a servant but a tyrannous oppressor of mankind. One way or another this frantic social struggle must be eased. I have a few people who work their way to an idea on the subject that the intellect of the country must proclaim for Collectivism, but by no means for democracy unrestrained" (GRG to Algernon Gissing, *Letters*, 28 February 1893, p. 332).

At present I am correcting proofs of "The Odd Women," which will come out early next year. It is to be, as usual, in three volumes. The publishers advance me a hundred guineas. The royalty is 3 shillings on each 3-vol. copy sold, and 6 pence on each of the subsequent 3 shilling 6 pence edition. But I have ceased to hope for larger sums of money from my books.

A short story of mine (of which I spoke to you long ago) called "A Victim of Circumstances" is to appear in the January number of Blackwood's Magazine. Of course you shall have a copy. The payment for it, to my astonishment, is as much as £20.

I wonder whether you have yet anything to report concerning Ottmann's affairs. In all probability you have thought very little about the matter. We artists cannot afford to trouble ourselves much about pecuniary questions, provided always that there is daily bread. I hope to hear that you have been progressing with new work. Above all, I trust that you have been able to adhere to the subject you took up. There is nothing more wearying and distressing than a failure of one's confidence, time after time, in a scheme of literary work. I know it myself only too well. Again and again and yet again I have begun a novel; only to write a few chapters and throw them aside as useless. Many, many months have I thus wasted. If I had confessed to you all such failures, you would have feared for me very often. But I have to keep most of my miseries to myself.

After all this time, I am returning to you Zapp's play, by book-post. Have you heard anything of him lately?

Probably you have seen that our Society of Authors has elected Meredith as President in the place of Tennyson. I suppose there can be no rational doubt that Meredith is the strongest literary man, all things considered, at present among us. I do not feel enthusiastic about his novels, but I recognize his great power of characterization, and the profoundness of his intellectual glance.[423]

---

[423] In 1885 GRG's opinion of Meredith's novels was markedly different. Of *Diana of the Crossways* he said: "The book is right glorious. Shakespeare in modern English; but, mind you, to be read twice, if need be, thrice. There is a preface, which is a plea for philosophic fiction, an admirable piece of writing, the English alone rendering it worthy of the carefullest pondering. More 'brain stuff' in the book, than many I have read for long" (*Letters*, p. 156). When he reread *Evan Harrington*, GRG

He has done fine things in poetry, too; but his latest verse[424] is more obscure than the worst of Browning. Obscurity in poetry is a contradiction in terms. However deep the thoughts, it must be pellucidly expressed.

Roberts has joined the Society for the benefit of its "authors' agency." He tells me that he never sells his own stories nowadays; the agent[425] does everything for him, and, it seems, decidedly to his profit. He is producing a great deal, and the demand for his work grows. Roberts is essentially a popular man. He has thorough sympathy with the *robust* human being. And naturally enough he is called an imitator of Kipling. Yet he does not in truth imitate; it is only that his experience has lain in spheres similar to Kipling's.

I shall not send you good wishes for Christmas, for I know you will have no merriment. Neither shall *I* be jovial;[426] we are independent of that kind of thing. My good wishes to you, old friend, are, as you know, perennial. One of the latest memories of my life will be of the evenings we spent together in the years long ago, in Chelsea and at South Tottenham, and in other places. They have a glow in my mind.

Ever yours,
GEORGE GISSING

1. St. Leonard's Terrace / Exeter.

January 15th. 1893.

Dear Friend,

I ought before this to have thanked you for sending the new edition of your book—alas! only two volumes. The illustrations

---

declared: "It is incomprehensible that Meredith is so neglected. George Eliot never did such work, and Thackeray is shallow in comparison" (*Letters*, ? October 1885, p. 170).

[424] *Empty Purse, with Odes to the Comic Spirit* (London, October 1892).

[425] William Maurice Colles was the literary agent for the Authors' Society. For GRG's association with Colles, see 29 September 1893.

[426] On the last day of the year, GRG summed up the whole of 1892 as "on the whole profitless. Marked by domestic misery and discomfort. The one piece of work, 'The Odd Women,' scribbled in 6 weeks as the autumn drew to an end, and I have no high opinion of it. Have read next to nothing; classical studies utterly neglected" (Diary).

are not, of course, worthy of the text; but one does not expect that. They might have been much worse. I lament yet again over your disaster. But there is the hope that your next production will make a new issue of "Glück und Glas" imperative.

The other day I sent you a copy of the January *Blackwood*. The story called "A Victim of Circumstances" is mine. Unfortunately, it is Blackwood's rule to publish fiction anonymously, so that I get little good from appearing in his famous magazine. However, he invites me to write again; and the payment is high—£20 for that short story. I wonder whether you will care for it at all?

Doubtless your winter is terrible. Here in Devonshire it has been freezing very hard; the one consolation is frequency of sunshine. I hope your health has not been disturbed by the weather, and that writing progresses.

I am now correcting the last sheets of "The Odd Women," and I hope it will soon be out. By the bye, the title means "Les Femmes Superflues"—the women who are *odd* in the sense that they do not make a match; as we say "an odd glove." The book of course explains this. It doesn't read badly, I think.

Lawrence and Bullen have purchased the copyright of "The Emancipated" from Bentley, and mean to bring out a cheap edition.

For the last four weeks I have been working hard at a new book, that of which the scene lies in and about Birmingham. It will be considerably stronger than anything I have written of late. I am very glad indeed that you like the subject. On the whole, it will be a hopeful book. The principal characters find their task in vigorous social work of the higher—the intellectual—kind. I have some good female types, I think.

I am glad indeed to hear that Rehfeldt proves such a helpful friend to you. How very curious I shall be to discover how you have dealt with this Luther subject! I have high expectations, for I know how thoroughly you grasp a theme of this kind. Why, of course a book for boys may be a work of art; but yours will be more than ordinary boys' literature, in every sense. I entirely appreciate your delight in the historic atmosphere. The restfulness of it is divine.

Now I must answer your question about Don,[427] as at length

---

[427] Bertz's collie.

I am able to do so. The good old fellow is dead. Here is an extract from Roberts's letter to me.

"He had ailed for some time, and had been attended by a Vet. at 5 shillings the visit. But he got worse and worse, so at last he went into hospital altogether. He came back for a week, but had to go to hospital again, and there he died suddenly, in the night. I don't think he really suffered much; in fact I am sure of it, or he would have been mercifully put out of life. This life of his had been one of high rank, and I believe his notion was that he was the cause of the Universe. Whether he remembered Bertz it is impossible to say, but the girls frequently asked him 'Where's Bertz?'—whereupon he always barked. He was wept by everyone, the whole street was grieved; our own people really cried. At all events, the good old chap could not have had a better home these last ten years."

I gather that this death took place not long ago. Roberts does not mention the date, and he is so busy that I seldom get a letter from him nowadays. I hope the news will not distress you, for indeed you knew that Don drew near to his end. How well I remember him in the old days!

All good wishes for this new year, old Friend. May it see the publication of your Luther book, and a settlement of the fate of "Glück und Glas."

Ever yours,
GEORGE GISSING

Addressed: Herrn Eduard Bertz. / Bergstrasse, 52. / Frankfurt a. d. Oder / *Germany.*

[January 23, 1893] [428]
Many thanks for letter. Roberts, I am sure, will be glad to hear from you. His address is / 35 Tavistock Place. / London W. C. / Have finished Vol. 1. of new book, and am now writing short story for Blackwood.[429] Excellent news about your "G[lück] u[nd] G[las]"![430]

G. G.

[428] Postmark.
[429] "Minstrel of the Byways."
[430] Bertz had been able to buy back the copyright of *Glück und Glas* from the bankrupt Ottmann.

14

1. St. Leonard's Terrace. / Exeter.

March 11th. 1893.

My dear Friend,

With the sunshine of spring about me, I must write and ask how you have weathered the winter. Here in Devon it has been wonderfully mild; a great deal of calm, clear weather, and greatly to my advantage. In about three weeks, I hope to have finished my book. I think of calling it:

"The Iron Gods"

a name you will understand. Do you care for the title. On the whole it is a cheerful book, the last volume progressively so; the only book of mine of which this could be said.

Here is an account of the arrangements for the foreign publication of "The Odd Women." For their Continental issue, Heinemann and Balestier have given 35 guineas; for their Colonial, they have purchased 1500 copies, in sheets, these sheets to be supplied by Macmillans from New York. The American issue is to be at a dollar.[431] When the book will be out, I don't know, but I suppose very shortly.

I have just received 7 guineas as my share of the American sale of "Denzil Quarrier" up to the end of June 1892. Better than nothing.

It seems to me I was very lucky when I made acquaintance with Bullen. His firm is rapidly making a repute for the publication of high-class and expensive books, *éditions de luxe*, and so on. Bullen is a scholar, and has just published an edition of Anacreon. In his last letter to me there was a passage which excited my astonishment, as it will yours. He writes: "We count it a privilege to publish your books. If we lose money in reissuing your early works, it will not trouble us; the pleasure of seeing them collected would atone for any loss. And yet we fancy that they may some day be profitable." Did ever author receive such a letter from a publisher before?

They deal with me in the most open way, mentioning every detail of publication, things of which Smith and Elder never spoke a word. This, of course, is encouraging.

[431] Published in Macmillan's "Dollar Novel Series."

Roberts tells me that he is going abroad. But he has ceased to send me any particulars of his life and work. That is inevitable, when a man has taken to the journalistic side of literature. But I am not without hope that he may still find patience to produce a solid book.

If you can send me any verse that you write, you know how glad I should always be to see it. The *variety* of your work has always seemed to me, from one point of view, very enviable. I wish I could do something more than write 3-vol. novels.

Let me know how it goes with Luther. That story you tell me of him is very grotesque. Yes, these are the things disclosed when one comes to grub into history. But one must not take too much account of them. The brain is dependent upon the stomach, but it is *not* the stomach. Like Malvolio, let us "think nobly of the soul,"[432] and wish that men had more of it.

Apropos—the incredible things that happen. A socialist member of the London municipal government, a man who wrote verse, and talked enthusiastically, and had earned the respect of distinguished people, (he is five and twenty,) has just been *convicted of robbing a prostitute of three shillings*, and sentenced to eight months' imprisonment.[433] Here is a psychological problem! He doesn't seem to have been particularly poor. Personal acquaintance with the man might help one to a solution, yet all who knew him refused, before the trial, to believe his guilt[.]

It is such a morning as I have seldom known in England. A sky of profound blue, without a speck of cloud. Only the faintest breeze. I hear the clucking of fowls, and the twittering of birds in the trees about. Divine weather! Where is my Homer? Let us have a page of the Odyssey.

Ever yours, dear Friend,
GEORGE GISSING

[432] *Twelfth Night* IV. ii. 59.

[433] Frederick Henderson, a member of the London County Council, was charged with stealing the three shillings from Ada Gray, a woman whom he had met in a public house and then accompanied to a brothel, where the theft occurred (London *Times*, 28 February 1893, p. 3). He was found guilty and was sentenced to four months' imprisonment at hard labor (*Times*, 10 March 1893, p. 9).

1. St. Leonard's Terrace / Exeter.

April 16th. 1893.

My dear Friend,

Your last letter makes me gloomy. I grieve that you are fallen again into this deep melancholy. But it will not hold you long. Even now, I try to hope that you have recovered courage to work again.

It is good that you have got back the copyright of "Glück und Glas." Won't you correspond with publishers about it? It is a wise thing to be *active*; the mere expectation of letters helps to keep one lively.

And how I wish you could write another novel which would follow up the success of "Glück und Glas." Indeed, that is what you *ought* to do. You know how easily you would find a good publisher—not a man of straw, like Ottmann. Why—oh why—waste the precious years? Do make use of the success you have achieved.

I have often meant to ask you: *Did it never occur to you to write a novel of English life.* Now, why not use your very exceptional knowledge in this direction? You could make a remarkable book. There is no reason why you should not write with the *most absolute freedom*. Adapt your experiences. Don't be withheld by fear of giving offence to me, or to any other English acquaintance; as far as I am concerned, I simply am incapable of such feeling, as I think you know. Think over this suggestion, I beg of you: I believe it may be fruitful.

The "Sabinergut" may be a good idea,[434] but I think an English book would be still better. You could plan it and write it in a few months.

Yesterday (Saturday) I posted to you a copy of "The Odd Women." Don't feel obliged to read it at once.

At Easter I spent a week in London, and saw my publishers. They are young, enthusiastic men,[435] evidently with a good deal of money. Their *éditions de luxe* of old books are having a most profitable sale.

Before long, I shall go back to London for good. I want the streets again.

[434] Based on Bertz's experiences in Tennessee. See 26 August 1893.
[435] Lawrence and Bullen.

The Editor of "The English Illustrated"[436] has asked me for a short story of low life. I think I have a good idea for it.[437]

Roberts has suddenly disappeared from all his friends. He *may* have gone to Africa, but no one knows. It is some eccentric freak of his. By his extraordinary behaviour of late he has made himself the talk of a large section of London society. Some men declare that he is mad. But I fancy it is only affectation: he wishes to be talked about.

Sursum corda! You will write more cheerfully next time.

Ever yours, dear old Friend,
GEORGE GISSING

1. St. Leonard's Terrace / Exeter.

June 2nd. 1893.

My dear Friend,

As usual, you have read my book with sympathetic kindness, and speak of it as is your wont. And after all I doubt whether we are greatly at variance in our views of the woman question. My demand for female "equality" simply means that I am convinced there will be no social peace until women are intellectually trained very much as men are. More than half the misery of life is due to the ignorance and childishness of women. The average woman pretty closely resembles, in all intellectual considerations, the average male *idiot*—I speak medically. That state of things is traceable to the lack of education, in all senses of the word. Among our English emancipated women there is a majority of admirable persons; they have lost no single good quality of their sex, and they have gained enormously on the intellectual (and even on the moral) side by the process of enlightenment, that is to say, of brain-development. I am driven frantic by the crass imbecility of the typical woman. That type must disappear, or at all events become altogether subordinate. And I believe that the only way of effecting this is to go through a period of what many people will call sexual anarchy. Nothing good will perish; we can trust the forces of nature, which tend to conservation.

---

[436] Clement King Shorter (1857–1926).
[437] "Lou and Liz," *English Illustrated Magazine*, X (August 1893), 793–801.

Now I really think that your own views point to much the same kind of thing. Of course the whole question is vastly complicated: for instance, the democratic question cannot be separated from it. But my own hope is that the world will some day be reconstituted on a basis of *intellectual aristocracy*. I believe that, relatively speaking, there must always be much the same social distinctions as now exist. All classes will be elevated, but between higher and lower the distinction will remain. I should be content to see the working-class woman about as reasonable as the present *bourgeoise*, which of course would imply a considerable advance.

One talks so scrappily on these huge questions. It can't be helped.

And, in the meantime, I have done with *questions*. I am going to write a novel, pure and simple. My Birmingham story will lie over, for the present. At Midsummer I go to London, and there I shall set to work upon a vigorous book, of which the scene will be in Camberwell. It will be a reversion to my old style, *without* the socialistic spirit,—indeed, I hope without any spirit but that of art.[438]

"The Odd Women" has been well reviewed. Most writers insist upon its "absorbing" interest. This is a pleasant surprise to me.

Believe me, I *do* take your troubles *au sérieux*, but I always try to write hopefully, because I am sure it is better to do so. Indeed your loneliness is very monstrous, very harmful; and yet I can quite understand how difficult it is for you to keep hold upon people of the world, and *un*worldly people are so seldom met with. What, it is really *six* years since you wrote "Glück und Glas"! But in the meantime, you have not been idle. I think it probable that you will still find some way of using the Luther material. And certainly you are write [*sic*] in applying yourself to that which is congenial; only in that way is anything good to be done. Now, finish this book *Mancherlei Mär*. And *Junker Georg*, too, by all means. I am so strongly convinced that you have only to *finish* in order to *succeed*. It was so in the case of "G[lück] u[nd] G[las]," and so it will be with these other things.

[438] The summer passed before he began to make progress on the new novel, which was first called "Miss Lord of Camberwell," and then was changed to *In the Year of Jubilee*.

I shall let you know the date of my removal. I have already taken unfurnished rooms in Brixton, near to a very fine free library recently opened. And my study is to be of South London, for a time.

A short story of squalid life is to appear in *The English Illustrated*.[439] It was written to order. I don't think it will be out till the August number.

Hic incipit vita nova! I have been rusting.

Ever yours, good old Friend,
GEORGE GISSING

Addressed: Herrn Eduard Bertz. / Bergstrasse, 52. / Frankfurt a. d. Oder. / *Germany.*

Exeter

June 20th. [1893]

Please address in future: / 76 Burton Road. / Brixton. / London S. W. / Terrible weather: heat and drought. Will write soon.

G. G.

76 Burton Road. / Brixton. SW.

August 24th. 1893.

My dear Friend,

I did not wish you to have the trouble of sending these reviews back; they are of no importance, but I thought I would let you see the kind of thing that is written about me nowadays.

Doubtless you received my story "Lou and Liz." Not long ago I was asked by the editor of the *Illustrated London News* to write a short story for the Christmas number,[440] and I did so. He professes himself much pleased with it, and now wants another, to be published shortly. So you see that editors are beginning to come to me.

Moreover, there is scarcely a week passes but I receive a letter from some stranger with reference to my books. I have had elaborate invitations to people's country houses, and so on. And

---

[439] "Lou and Liz."

[440] Clement K. Shorter was the editor for whom GRG wrote "Fleet-footed Hester," Christmas Number, 1893, pp. 26, 29, 30, 33.

did I tell you that I was invited to the annual literary dinner given by the Lord Mayor?[441]

And yet I remain in poverty, for my books will not sell. Roberts, by short stories alone, which for the most part appear in newspapers, is now making some £500 or £600 a year. By the bye, he has just been to Zürich, as a delegate at the Socialist Conference. But I don't think his Socialism goes very deep.

That reminds me of what you say about your vote at the election. I heartily sympathize with you, and approve what you did. What thoughtful man can look forward cheerfully to being ruled by a Socialistic Government such as would nowadays be constituted? No, no; it is better to battle on.

You are indeed very right to reduce that burden of correspondence. Conscientious you always have been, in a degree attained by few men; but your time and strength are too precious to be given to what you feel mere task-work. I, too, abominate the necessity of writing to people in whom I have no vivid interest; in fact, you are the one and only person with whom I keep up regular communication by letter, and may it be very long before this letter-writing ceases!

Ah, if you could get into better health! Of course so much of your nervous illness is due to solitude and the consequent unhealthy conditions of life. It is bad and wrong, for instance, to have to eat alone. The food does one little good. I keep hoping that some better arrangement will yet suggest itself to you, but of course I too well understand the money difficulty. All that you tell me about your relation with the Rehfeldts is deplorable; I understand it perfectly. It seems to me, after all, that your idea of storing away your impedimenta for a time might be a very good one; they *have* weighed heavily upon you, beyond a doubt.

How glad I am to hear that you have taken up Italian, and have even gone so far as to get a Baedeker! Now, cling to this resolve. Get a novel written, and sell it—as you most assuredly can. I wish I had your abundance of plots at command: *that* is really wonderful! Yes, I have always thought that the *Sabiner-*

---

[441] "The day before yesterday, I had a card of invitation from the Lord Mayor to dine at the Mansion House on July 1st to meet representatives of art and literature. Of course refused" (To Algernon Gissing, *Letters*, 13 June 1893, p. 333).

gut was a very fruitful subject. Do stick to it; after *Glück u*[*nd*] *Glas* a novel from you is absolutely expected and demanded. The scene will be original; your treatment of the theme is bound to be highly interesting. Now, *do, do* write this book! I should so heartily enjoy reading it.

Don't write to me again until you feel that you really have time. I want to hear that you have got a solid bit of the work finished. Of course you may write on such a subject quite freely, and if, as you say, it offers itself to humorous treatment, why so much the better.

I have read "Docteur Pascal," and don't much care for it. There seems to me a great unreality about the book. "L'Argent" I have also read, and in some respects that is wonderful.[442] In others, again, it strikes me as lacking vitality.

Xenophon's "Oeconomicus" is my latest reading in Greek. A delightful little dialogue—so fresh and sweet. It is like a breath of air from Hymettus.

I have not altogether laid my Birmingham book aside, but short stories are disturbing me at present. And, after all, I may perhaps publish a London novel first. But of this you shall hear.

Lawrence and Bullen have in the press a cheap edition of "The Emancipated."[443]

I fear the hot weather has troubled you. But autumn is coming on, a good season for work.

Ever yours, old friend,
GEORGE GISSING

76 Burton Road / Brixton. / London SW.

September 29th. 1893.

Dear Friend,

I am greatly pleased at receiving the 3rd. Vol. of the second edition of "Glück und Glas."

The story of your going up to purchase the copyright, armed with £75, is very amusing. I am delighted that it ended so well. It is a bit of comedy in literary life. Reissner's[444] payment of £60

[442] Emile Zola, *Le Docteur Pascal* (Paris, 1893); *L'Argent* (Paris, 1891).
[443] Published in November 1893 for 6 shillings.
[444] Carl Reissner, a Dresden publisher, printed the second edition of *Glück und Glas*.

down was very satisfactory, a proof of his faith in the book. In reserving to yourself the copyright you act, of course, very wisely. I only wish I had the courage and the foresight to refuse to sell those novels of mine out and out to Smith and Elder. They would now have been a source of income[.]

Well now, you have every encouragement to go on with your *Sabinergut*. If *Der Igel*[445] gets accepted by a paper, all the better; but of course that need not in the least affect your progress with the other. The subject of *Das Sabinergut* is sure to attract a good deal of attention. I should not hesitate for a moment out of consideration for Hughes.[446] You are not writing calumniously. The Rugby affair is historical, and anyone with adequate knowledge is more than justified in making literary use of it.

For my own part, I am growing less thin-skinned in this matter of literary scruple. It is an age of vulgarity, and the terrifying examples before our eyes make us fear to exercise even a legitimate freedom. But if one's spirit be not vulgar, it is surely safe to obey the dictates of literary instinct. The Rugby episode was certainly a most interesting bit of human experience, and I should think you entirely within your rights if you dealt with it under the slightest of disguises. Of course I do not mean that it would be well to present Hughes and others in their actual person, merely disguising them by a pseudonym; but all the facts of the situation may surely be retained.

Yes, it would indeed be very fine if you could come to England next spring. In that case, I should do my best to provide for a period of holiday, that we might enjoy ourselves together. And I should have much to tell you.

In the meantime, we are exchanging portraits. Yours, in the group, I am very glad to have; it strikes me as certainly good. This which I send you of myself I have had taken because the editor of a new weekly illustrated, *The Sketch*, has asked me for it, to be used "at some future date." This man—his name is Clement Shorter—now edits three periodicals, the *Illustrated London News*, the *Sketch*, and the *English Illustrated Magazine*. By

---

[445] A boys' story. There is no record of publication.

[446] Thomas Hughes (1822–1896), English reformer, jurist, and novelist, founded Rugby, the model community in Tennessee, in 1879. See Introduction.

his invitations, he has induced me to think more of short-story writing. In addition to that which is to appear in the Christmas number of the *Ill[ustrated] Lond[on] News*, he has accepted two, for use elsewhere.[447] He wrote asking me for three in a batch, stories of 6000 words each, for which he would pay 12 guineas each. But I found I was being imposed upon; they tell me that the least I ought to accept is 3 guineas for 1000 words. So I told Shorter that the payment was insufficient, and we are still discussing that point.

It has led to my visiting the Authors' Agency, which is attached to the Authors' Society, but not inseparable from it. The director, Colles by name,[448] received me with great cordiality, and told me, among other things, that Besant is an admirer of my books. Well, he is going to act as my agent for short stories, and I left with him no less than *five*. We shall see what success he has.

So I am entered upon the commercial path, alas! But I shall try not to write rubbish.

No, I see no more literary men than in the old days, and am not likely to. This last week I have regretted my isolation, because I should so much have liked to set eyes on Zola. His reception in England has been very remarkable.[449] The other day someone wrote to the *Times*, to draw attention to the fact that only a year or two ago a London publisher was *imprisoned* for issuing Zola's works.[450] And in truth the change of opinion is strange enough. All the papers now speak of him with high respect—even the most conservative. And, most comical of all, he is received by "le Lor' Maire"!

Speaking of the *Times*, I saw a notice in its columns the other day of a book by an East-end parson called "The Social Problem." They quoted, with praise, a long passage, and to my amazement I saw that half of it was simply stolen, all but verbatim, from

[447] "Muse of the Halls." *English Illustrated Magazine*, XI (December 1893), 313–22; "Our Mr. Jupp," *ibid*. (March 1894), 631–38.

[448] GRG visited Colles, "a fat, red-faced, vivacious man, and great talker," on 22 September (Diary).

[449] Zola came to England in September 1893.

[450] The letter, signed "Inquirer," was printed on 27 September 1893 (London *Times*, p. 3). Henry Vizetelly (1820–1894) was the publisher who had been imprisoned for three months in 1889 for publishing Zola's novels, even though they had been expurgated in the translation.

"The Nether World." Of course I at once wrote to the *Times*, and my letter attracted a good deal of attention. The parson replied that I was very hard upon him, seeing that he had merely meant to *quote* from my "excellent book." This reply occasioned comments in all the evening papers, of a facetious tone. And next day a third person wrote to the *Times*, a *printer*, saying that *he* was responsible for the "omission of quotation marks and of certain names." Of course this made the matter more ludicrous. An evening paper had a paragraph headed "Marvellous Confession of a Printer," and others followed suit.[451]

On the whole it was a very good advertisement for me.

Now do keep it clearly before your mind that you *can* earn money if you like. Finish your book as soon as possible, and see the result. Of course you must get into a less depressing sphere, and money alone can help you to do so. Money—remember—means *health* as well as liberty.

I have not read *Bel Ami*,[452] though I have heard so much of it. But I will get hold of it somehow before long.

Rehfeldt has fallen victim to a hobby, with a vengeance.[453] Surely it will not absorb him very long. I always thought him a man superior to that kind of craze. But how many people get drawn

[451] On 7 September 1893, the *Times* (p. 3) reviewed *The Social Problem: Its Possible Solution* (London, 1893), by the Reverend Arthur Osborne Jay, of Holy Trinity Vicarage, Shoreditch. GRG's letter, dated 7 September 1893, was printed under the lead "Borrowed Feathers": "As I read his words they sounded oddly familiar to me, and on referring to a book which I published some years ago [1889], 'The Nether World,' I discover the explanation of this bewilderment. Was it, peradventure, Mr. Jay's purpose to honour me by quoting from the 'Nether World,' and has he, perchance, forgotten to insert the usual signs of quotation? At all events, in the 28th chapter of my novel occur the following lines..." (*Times*, 9 September 1893, p. 13), and the full quotation from the novel follows. The Rev. Jay replied: "Mr. Gissing is a little hard on me for honouring myself (not him, as he suggests) by ending one of my chapters with a quotation from his excellent book, 'The Nether World.'... the printer's carelessness is responsible for the omission of the commas" (*Times*, 11 September 1893, p. 3). Then the printer, W. C. Hunt, wrote: "I am responsible for the omission of certain commas of quotation, and also for leaving out some names" (*Times*, 13 September 1893, p. 10).

[452] Guy de Maupassant (Paris, 1885).

[453] He had become interested in genealogy.

into it. *Antiquam exquirite matrem*[454]—et patrem; the dictate has still a strong hold over men's minds.

Of course I shall send you copies of my stories as they appear. But most of them will be very Londonesque.

Well, enough for the present. All good things befall you! Work on, and let me hear more of *Das Sabinergut*.

> Ever yours, dear Friend,
> GEORGE GISSING

Addressed: Herrn Eduard Bertz. / Bergstrasse, 52a. / Frankfurt a. d. Oder / *Germany*.

76 Burton Road / Brixton / London SW.

October 10th. [1893]

1) The daughter of *Sir A. B.* is plain *Miss B.* Only if the daughter of a duke, marquis or earl could she be called "Lady Maud."
Sir A. B's wife is *Lady Bunting* (never the Christian name with it.)
2) A tennis *racket*.
The Baronet himself is always addressed as *Sir Austin*.
3) The ball is light and elastic, so as to spring about. I don't know what is inside it—but of course not feathers. Rejoiced to hear of arrangements (or likelihood of them) with publisher. Yesterday I sent you a newspaper, with something amusing. Don't trouble to return it.

> G. G.

76 Burton Road / Brixton / London SW.

November 19th. 1893.

Dear Friend,

Once more the terrible season is upon us. I am looking forward to winter in London with horror, but there is no choice; work presses upon me, and it is work of a kind that can only be done here. I have begun to take cod-liver oil, and shall continue it till next summer; it supports me and warms me.

I am so sorry for that foolish mistake of mine concerning the "feather" ball; I might have understood you.

[454] Virgil, *Aeneidos*. III. 96.

Now for the other question. The guest of Sir Austin's would address his wife as "Lady Bunting," so indeed would *all people*. "My lady" (by the bye, this is never written in *one* word) would only be used by a servant to a lady of the *nobility*. I observe that you speak of the Baronet as if he belonged to the "noble" class, but he does not; he is merely a gentleman. The nobility begins with Barons, i.e. Lords. It is better I should mention this, as you may have mis-used the phrase in your book.[455]

I am far from disapproving of your making use of these titled people. All that is needed to deal with them is a knowledge of life among educated English people; which you possess.

The account you have given me of the book interests me very much. I am sure it will be a worthy successor of "Glück und Glas," and not impossibly even an advance upon that book in several ways. Your subject is excellent. Of course I now understand that Hughes's personality is the essence of the book; I did not know, before, that he figured as the central character.

The suggestion of a removal to Dresden or its neighbourhood must be very tempting. And yet I can understand your obstacles. In any case, cultivate friendly relations with this respectable publisher.[456] It will be of the utmost benefit to you to know that a trustworthy man is waiting for your new book.

Yes, let me hear more of the new reviews of "Glück und Glas." Its success must give you strength to go through with the labour of this new novel, labour so severe owing to your fine artistic conscientiousness. Indeed, I cannot tell you how I appreciate your strong assiduity, your resolve to give only of your best. Heaven forbid that I should do other than encourage it! But, all the same, I shall be very glad of the news that you have *Finis* in view.

In about a week's time, I shall be sending you certain short stories. As a matter of course, I send you everything of mine that appears, but pray do not take much trouble in criticizing these short productions. You know they are really pot-boilers.[457]

A joke—wasn't it?—Zola's reception in England! But I am sorry to say that none of the leading authors took a part in his

[455] *Das Sabinergut.*
[456] Carl Reissner.
[457] GRG's total earnings from the sale of *The Odd Women* and six short stories amounted to £193. 12. 6 for 1893 (Account of Books, Yale).

welcome. It was in the hands of a lot of new and young men, who are members of the Authors' Club, and who constitute a marvellously organized society for mutual advertisement.[458]

You see that a new edition of "The Emancipated" is out. I have not got a copy of it yet. Possibly I shall send you one, some day, for the book is greatly revised.[459]

I think of you toiling, and send you all my sympathy.

Ever yours, dear Friend,
GEORGE GISSING

76 Burton Road / Brixton SW.

January 19th. 1894.

Dear Friend,

I sympathize deeply with you in this toil of rewriting. It is the curse which always lies upon my own work: sometimes I re-write chapters six or seven times, until I hate the very thought of them. But I have no doubt that you are improving your book, and I rejoice to know that you make such progress with it.

For my own part, I have done a good deal of work these last few months. I have written six short stories for the "English Illustrated,"[460] as well as getting on with "Miss Lord of Camberwell."[461] These stories will appear at intervals. Some of them are not bad, I think.

Also, I have been asked—perhaps I told you—to write a Serial for the "Illustrated London News."[462] The agreement for this is

[458] The Authors' Club gave Zola a testimonial dinner on 28 September at the Hôtel Métropole. The newspaper account mentioned the attendance of such writers as Frank Harris, George Moore, Jerome K. Jerome, and Fred Villiers (London *Times*, 29 September 1893, p. 8). Moore was probably one of the chief organizers of the affair.

[459] A copy was sent to Bertz on 18 December 1893 (Diary).

[460] "Muse of the Halls," (December 1893), pp. 313–22; "Our Mr. Jupp," (March 1894), pp. 631–38; "The Honeymoon," (June 1894), pp. 895–904; "Comrades in Arms," (September 1894), pp. 1230–37; "The Pessimist of Plato Road," (November 1894), pp. 51–9; "Midsummer Madness," (December 1894), pp. 55–63.

[461] *In the Year of Jubilee.*

[462] *Eve's Ransom* was published in weekly installments from 5 January to 30 March 1895. Lawrence and Bullen brought out a one-volume edition in the same year.

now completed. I am to receive £150 for the *serial* rights of a story as long as one of my volumes. But the publication probably cannot begin till next year. These things have to be arranged so long in advance.

Other evidences of progress in public favour continue to reach me. This last week I have had two requests, from editors of periodicals, for biographical details; and from a town in Scotland comes the news that a "Philomathic Society" has chosen "Demos" for the subject of its debate on one evening. You will not be sorry to hear all this, I am sure. For a few weeks my brother has been staying with me. He, also, makes a certain progress, though as yet it brings no pecuniary advance. However, he is quite content to live an extremely simple life in the country; a very small income would suffice to him.

On the whole, I am glad to know of your decision to go back to Berlin. Probably this is wise, for you have suffered a great deal from provincial conditions. Whilst I write, you are doubtless engaged in the hateful task of hunting for rooms. That is one of the curses of modern existence. May you find an abode which promises some degree of comfort!

The winter with us has been extraordinary. Thus far, there has only been one week of snow and frost. It is now like a warm spring, with daily sunshine, and very little necessity for fires. Perhaps we shall suffer the miseries of winter when spring ought to be here in earnest.

I cannot say that life gives me much more satisfaction than of old. Society I shall never have; to that I am practically reconciled.[463] There is nothing before me but steady work. The worst of it is, I have been suffering from headaches, which interrupt me now and then in my daily tasks. Of course you are quite right in your

---

[463] Before marrying Edith and moving to Exeter, GRG had written to his sister Ellen: "Of course I shall have no society here. My ambition now is to make my name known, whilst personally I remain unseen and unheard of. In a time when every man of any shadow of distinction does his best to keep always in the sight of the public, one may reasonably find solace in the thought of winning reputation whilst remaining in quiet corners. We shall have to see whether I can keep my mind active without the help of congenial minds. I have the feeling of being deserted by all who ought to be my companions: but then these miseries are useful in giving a peculiar originality to my work" (*Letters*, 20 January 1891, pp. 312–13).

comments on the practice and theory of such men as Zola and Besant. The least defect of health, and the least domestic trouble, puts an end to that machine-like regularity. Nor do I think such regularity a very desirable thing. An artist, after all, should live very differently from a mechanic.

Hearty thanks for your opinions of my three stories. I believe you are right in thinking "The Day of Silence"[464] the best. These minor efforts are doing me good with the public; they make my name better known, and enable me to ask higher prices.

By the bye, I am now a member of the Society of Authors. It is just as well to join in this movement, and I did not like to withhold my yearly guinea, since I have been making use of the Syndicate which is attached to the Society.

My book may possibly be finished in two months. I am tired of it; it has been on hand too long.

Ever yours, dear Friend,
George Gissing

76 Burton Road / Brixton / London. SW.

March 25th. 1894.

Dear Friend,

I head my letter with a lie. I am not writing in London, but at Eastbourne; but it is not worth while to give you the address here, as I shall be back very soon.

"Miss Lord" is finished. And, having made that announcement, I must speak of your own triumphs over many difficulties. Indeed you have worked splendidly, with really notable energy, and I have every confidence in the result. Your removal to Berlin can, I should think, have nothing but good effects upon you and your work. Of course you are glad to be back again amid the roar of civilization. One cannot—at all events, you and I cannot,—live for ever away from it, however much we enjoy quietude when it comes as a change. Civilization, roar as it may, signifies the possibility of human intercourse, a prime need of intellectual life, as of the vulgarest. I was pleased with your postcard, written, it seemed, in good spirits. Ah that packing! A fearsome business. But perhaps it will be long before you have to grapple with it again.

I sent you, to the new address, a number of the *English*

[464] *National Review*, XXII (December 1893), 558–67.

15

Illustrated, with a story of mine in it.[465] Next month I shall have another in the *National Review*.[466] And so one's life goes.

The serial story for the *Illustrated London News* has to be finished by the end of June, and I am not yet clear even as to plot and characters. It will be rather a hard bit of work, I fear. But sometimes I write best when pressed for time.

I am now reading Balzac's "Physiologie du Mariage,"[467] a most remarkable book. It gives one a great idea of old Balzac's mental vigour. Though much of it is, by his own confession, "Plaisanterie," yet I believe there [is] very valuable matter in it.

But for months I have been able to read little or nothing. Alas! my Greeks and Romans lie untouched upon the shelves. As Thomas Hardy once said to me "Novel-writing makes one so illiterate." When not actually writing, I am laboriously thinking about writing.

By the bye, did I ever speak—nay, I fear, I fear, that I never did, of your treatment of the "verwunschene Prinzessin" in "Der Bär."[468] Be assured this is not because I neglected to read it and think about it. Your telling of the story strongly brought to my mind those fairy tales you used to read me in the good old days— tales I have never forgotten, and probably never shall forget, so graceful were they, and so full of delicate imagination. You have, I believe, a very distinct faculty for that kind of writing, and I shall think it a pity of pities if you do not some day publish the collection of which you have sometimes spoken.

I took it for granted that you meant me to keep "Der Bär." But if that was a mistake, pray let me know when next you write, and I will return the copies forthwith.

Since my last writing you have completed another twelve-month of existence. It is sad work, sending good wishes on these recurrent occasions. The one good thought at present is, that you are working, if anything, with increase of vigour.

Yours ever, dear old Friend,
GEORGE GISSING.

[465] "Our Mr. Jupp."

[466] "A Capitalist," XXIII (April 1894), 273–84.

[467] *Physiologie du mariage, ou Méditations de philosophie éclectique sur le bonheur et le malheur conjugal* (Paris, 1830).

[468] A children's story.

There is a new (a 1 vol.) edition of "The Odd Women," and also a new reprint (3 shillings 6 pence) of "Born in Exile"—to my great surprise.[469]

Addressed: Herrn Eduard Bertz. / Wormserstrasse 8. III / Berlin.
          W. / *Germany.*

84 Old Church Road / Clevedon / Somerset.

June 10th. 1894.

Please address for the present to above.[470] I am toiling to get my story done for the *Illust[rated] London News.* Wretched weather. Hope you are nearing the end of work.

G. G.

84 Old Church Road. / Clevedon / Somerset.

June 24th. 1894.

Dear Friend,

Midsummer Day, and yet we have had very little of Summer. The sky cannot get clear of clouds; there is no pleasant warmth; the winds rage. Yet one's labour goes on in the old way. I am now only two or three days from the end of my Serial,[471] and after that I shall take a much-needed holiday—perhaps read a good deal of Greek. This neighbourhood suits me very well. It is full of old historic associations, and I cannot live with any pleasure in a place which has nothing of the kind. The older I get, the more do I value and depend upon by-gone days. It is surprising how very little genuine interest I have in the movements of our time. To be sure, I study them to a certain extent, but my real pleasure is in things ancient.

You have been working very hard indeed. This book—so soon to be completed, I hope—will have taken a great deal out of you. Of course I am not altogether sorry that you have been obliged

---

[469] Lawrence and Bullen published *The Odd Women* in February 1894 for 6 shillings; A. and C. Black reprinted *Born in Exile* in the same month.

[470] Walter, GRG's son, suffered from bronchitis and had been ordered to try a change of climate.

[471] *Eve's Ransom*, begun on 4 June 1894, was completed on 29 June (Diary).

to rearrange your hours of writing, for the long vigils certainly injured your health. I can understand but too well the horrible efforts this change must have cost you.

"Die Grenzen der Erziehung"[472] is a very attractive title, and I should be very glad to hear that you meant to get the thing finished as soon as your novel is really off hand. It would not, I suppose, be a very long book? Should you have any hope of publishing it— or *part* of it—in a periodical? One would think there must be sections of the study which would be welcome in serious reviews.

It is decidedly encouraging that the publishers do not forget to inquire about the progress of your work. Pray take this to heart, for there is much probability that your next novel may be a financial success. Trust publishers for fore-seeing that kind of thing; they have the *flair*. Have you any idea what "Daheim" would pay? Something substantial, I hope.

Your solitude is, I fear, inevitable. Serious literary toil compels solitude. I know, as regards myself, that I shall *never* have society; my methods of work do not allow of it, any more than your own. To be sure, it is grievous that Rehfeldt does not at least keep up a pleasant correspondence, but, as you recognize, a doctor's life tends to self-absorption. I suppose that genealogical hobby of his is actually necessary as a relief among his professional exertions. One can only regret that he did not select a hobby in which you could have interested yourself—something less narrowly personal.

Berthold Auerbach's letters[473] I know only by name. It is unfortunate that I have so long been out of connection with good libraries. But, alas, my time for reading is so limited. At present I now and then get through a chapter of Plutarch's Lives of the Gracchi; the Greek refreshes me.

Your meetings with old acquaintances interested me much. Very curious that story of the loss of the MS. of "Demos."[474] A great joke if it really got onto the stage, in some form or other.

Of course you were right to accept election into the Committee

[472] No record of publication.
[473] Berthold Auerbach, *Briefe an seinen Freund Jakob Auerbach*, ed. Jakob Auerbach (2 vols., Frankfurt a. M., 1884).
[474] The "old acquaintances" might have been the Steinitzes. Frau Steinitz, the translator of *Demos*, must have known about the manuscript's history.

of the Verband.[475] Work for them you cannot, but it is well to have your name thus recognized. By the bye, the Authors' Society made me one of the "stewards" at their annual dinner. I did not attend, as I am afraid of crowds.[476]

What an odd thing that you did not know "Santa Lucia" by name! At Naples I never heard it sung, but I did on the Grand Canal at Venice. Ah, those days! Eheu, eheu!

The name of my serial is not yet determined upon. The novel will be out in October, I think.[477] I am going to revise the MS. presently. Of course it does not satisfy me.

I see it mentioned that the widow of Fritz Reuter is just dead.[478] Women are tenacious of life, and a great deal of nonsense is talked about their sufferings.

Yours ever, dear Friend,
GEORGE GISSING

Addressed: Herrn Eduard Bertz. / Wormserstrasse 8. III. / Berlin W. / *Germany.*

[September 13, 1894][479]

I shall be writing to you very soon, and moreover I have a copy of the *English Illustrated* for September to send.[480] In the meantime, I announce a new address: Eversley. / Worple Road. / Epsom. / Here I am near London, and yet thoroughly in the country. Beautiful scenery and fine air. Hope all is well with you.

Yours ever,
G. G.

---

[475] Deutscher Schriftsteller-Verband.

[476] According to Morley Roberts, GRG could not attend many social functions because he feared to be absent from home for any length of time lest Edith injure the child in a fit of temper (*Roberts*, p. 155). This allegation is corroborated by a statement of Arthur Peachey, the long-suffering husband of Ada in *In the Year of Jubilee*, which was written between January and April 1894. Peachey never "left home without dread of perils that might befall it [his child] in his absence" (New York: Appleton and Co., 1895, p. 218).

[477] It came out in December 1894.

[478] Luise Kuntze Reuter (1817–1894), widow of Fritz (1810–1874), German novelist who is credited with making "Platt-deutsch" a literary language.

[479] Postmark.

[480] Containing "Comrades in Arms."

Eversley / Worple Road / Epsom.

October 2. 1894.

My dear Friend,

That you have reached the end of your book is indeed good news. The revision is a matter of comparative ease; at least I find it so in my own case. I am highly curious to see what you have made of this matter.[481] That to *you* it should now seem monotonous is very easily explained; you have worked at the book so long and so hard. But I think it very likely indeed that anyone who comes fresh to the story will find it particularly interesting. The book will not fail, be assured; the high probability is that it will enhance the reputation which you already owe to "Glück u[nd] Glas."

I am grieved to hear that you think of again moving at Easter. These frequent goings from place to place, with the burden of all one's good[s], are terribly trying; I fear they work upon the nerves, and have a tendency to shorten life. For you it is rather difficult to find a permanent abode, seeing that you need both the country quietude and the proximity of intellectual society. Here at Epsom I think I have all the quietude I need, yet London is very near. Is there no such place within easy reach of Berlin? Ah, if it were but possible for you to find a permanent home! How it would rest your mind.

I have sent you the *English Illustrated*, and I suppose shall soon be sending something else. People keep asking me for short stories.

I am not altogether discontent with my new novel, which will now soon appear. Did I—or did I not—tell you that the name we have finally decided upon is:

"In the Year of Jubilee"?

Of course it has a satirical significance, and I hope you will not be dissatisfied with my picture of certain detestable phases of modern life.

My admiration and liking for Kipling has [*sic*] greatly increased.[482] The volume of stories of which you speak contains

---

[481] I.e., of Bertz's life in Rugby, Tennessee.

[482] Later, GRG despised Kipling for his imperialistic and militaristic stories. See 11 December 1899.

admirable work.[483] Especially good is "The Disturber of Traffic"—
a strong effort of imagination. Full of realism and poetry, combined, is "Love o'Women." He's a wonderful man.

Morley Roberts has just been *round the world*. He called upon
Stevenson at Samoa, and had a pleasant talk with him.

The other evening I dined with the Editor[484] of the "Illustrated
London News" at one of the biggest clubs. We were a party of
five—editors—mainly, included [*sic*] the editor of the New York
"Critic."[485] Oddly enough, I find that people talk a good deal
about "The Unclassed." Lawrence and Bullen want to republish
it, but I don't know whether to let them. What think you?

L[awrence] and B[ullen] are doing pretty well with cheap
editions of "Denzil Quarrier" and "The Emancipated," especially
in Australia, where 1200 copies of the former, and 750 of the
latter, have just been sold. The same Australian firm have agreed
to take 1500 copies of "In the Year of Jubilee."

With much appetite, I am now turning to foreign books—
chiefly Italian novels—for a week or two.

I shall presently be able to send you—I think—a number of a
weekly illustrated paper, with my portrait and a notice.[486]

Hold up, dear Friend! I am glad you have been on a visit to
Potsdam. Get your book off hand, and confidently await the result.

Yours ever,
GEORGE GISSING

Eversley. / Worple Road. / Epsom.

November 24. 1894.

My dear Friend,

It is high time that I wrote in reply to your last letter. My days
have been passed in hurry and confusion; the months go by, and
I am astonished to find the end of another year so close at hand.

[483] Rudyard Kipling, *Many Inventions* (London, 1893).
[484] Clement K. Shorter.
[485] "The party consisted of Robertson Nicoll (of the Bookman and British
Weekly), Massingham (political editor of Chronicle), a lawyer whose name
I didn't catch, and an American, Gilder, connected with New York Critic.
Very pleasant evening" (Diary, 26 September 1894). The American, Joseph
Gilder, had been co-editor with his sister Jeannette of the New York *Critic*
from 1881 to 1885, after which she became the sole editor.
[486] *The Sketch*. See 29 September 1893.

For you it has indeed been a year of hard work, for hardest of all is that terrible reshaping and rewriting of books. I hope to hear that the novel is at length finished, or all but so.

No, no, I have never desired that you should spend your time and strength in translating my paltry short stories. You have much better things to do. Don't give a thought to it, I beg.

The notice in the "Athenaeum" gave the title of my story wrongly. It should have been "Eve's Ransom."[487] This is now advertized to begin on the 1st. of January, but I am sorry to say that there is a great difficulty about the illustrations. Do you remember the illustrations of Dickens by Fred Barnard?[488] The same man is engaged to draw for this story of mine, but he, poor fellow, has become a hopeless drunkard; not yet incapable of work, but never to be depended upon. Yesterday I went to see him, and found him in dreary lodgings near Regent's Park. He was in a state of lethargy, and could not converse. I fear the *Illust*[*rated*] *London News* will have to give the work to someone else.

"Boomed into fame"[489] is damnable! But the growth of vulgarity in editors and publishers makes one surprised at nothing.

This same vulgarity is only too apparent in the generality of writers now-a-days. I dined the other evening at the Authors' Club, a dinner in honour of a new man, who has become celebrated at a bound—Anthony Hope.[490] Well, the company struck one as consisting of respectable shopkeepers. Not one interesting figure among them. By the bye, I sat near to Besant, thus seeing him for the first time. I should not have sought conversation with him, but a man who introduced us made it necessary. Besant was obviously unwilling to talk. He makes an impression of absolute nullity; the most commonplace of celebrities that I ever met.

[487] The immediate publication of *In the Year of Jubilee* (October, 1894) was announced instead of *Eve's Ransom* (*Athenaeum*, 24 November 1894, p. 695).

[488] Frederick Barnard (1846–1896) illustrated the "Household" edition of Dickens's novels (1871–1879), and published a collection of *Character Sketches* (1880) drawn from the novels. Barnard lived at 105 Gloucester Road, Regent's Park.

[489] I.e., brought to the public's attention by concentrated, planned publicity.

[490] Sir Anthony Hope Hawkins (1863–1933), pseud. Anthony Hope, whose *The Prisoner of Zenda* (1894) made him famous.

Several publishers have of late asked me for novels. But I see no reason for leaving Lawrence and Bullen. And indeed I cannot work quickly enough to supply all these people.

"In the Year of Jubilee" will be out in a few days, and of course you will receive a copy.

Doubtless you received the *English Illustrated* for November, containing my story "The Pessimist of Plato Road." There is another in the December number,[491] and you shall have it very soon.

Thanks for what you say about "The Unclassed." Yes, we have gone far in the direction of liberality since those days. Books are published now which, fifteen years ago, would never have found a publisher daring enough to undertake them. If "The Unclassed" is re-issued, I shall of course write an explanatory preface, as you suggest.[492] I am beginning to have a literary past; in meeting the young writers of to-day, I feel a veteran. And how strange a thing it is when, in walking about the streets of London, I pass the streets where I lived in those days of misery! Of course *that man* and *I* are not identical. He is a relative of mine, who died long ago; that's all.

I agree with you in seriously doubting whether you ought to move away from Berlin, again. It seems to me that it is merely the situation of your abode that ought to be changed. Evidently you live amid insufferable disturbances, and it surely cannot be impossible to discover a quieter neighbourhood. Once your book off hand, you will be very glad to spend a little time in free enjoyment of museums and galleries and intercourse with artists. It is clearly my opinion that you should do this, as a mere duty to body and mind, as soon as ever your work is finished, quite without reference to the fate of the book. When the last page is written, simply take a town-holiday, and do, *do* try to enjoy it. Remember that life slips away so fast, and, in defiance of everything, follow for a brief time the motto of *Carpe diem*. Never did man better deserve a holiday. And you are not one of those who want to spend a lot of money; you can enjoy yourself, even as I can, at very small expense.

[491] "Midsummer Madness."

[492] Lawrence and Bullen published the new edition in November 1895. No preface was written.

When you have taken this rest, think of the future; but not till then. Of course you will be all the better able to see a course before you. As you say, your state of mind at present does not allow of clear vision forward.

We have just had the first frost of the season. I dread the cold weather, for it generally disables me from writing. I know that you, too, have no liking for it.

I like to hear of your reading Don Quixote late at night. A wholesome companion!

Ever yours, dear Friend,
GEORGE GISSING

Addressed: Herrn Eduard Bertz. / Wormserstrasse 8. III / Berlin W. / *Germany*.

[December 2, 1894][493]

I am much grieved to hear of your illness, but hope it is nearly over by now. Yesterday I posted "In the Year of Jubilee," but don't trouble to write about it till you feel quite well.

I went to town yesterday, and found myself in one of the most terrible fogs. I could not live for a week in that atmosphere; a few hours all but made me ill.

Yours,
G. G.

Eversley. / Worple Road / Epsom.

December 30. 1894.

My dear Friend,

The picture I have had of you in my mind all these days is a very cheerless one: I earnestly hope it no longer answers to the reality. Your attack of eczema must have been very serious, and I marvel that you were able to do any work at all. For my own part, I yield at once under physical trouble—indeed under almost any kind of trouble. A mere cold stops my work immediately: it has, indeed, delayed this letter, until I am now too late to let you receive my greetings and good wishes on New Year's Day.

[493] Postmark.

But, though late, the wish is genuine and hearty: may you have a much better year than the last! May your book be speedily published, and be recognized for all the good which I know it contains!

During my enforced idleness,[494] I have been reading widely in recent publications. But before I speak of this, let me thank you for your kind letter about my own novel. The fault you have to find with it seems to be recognized by all capable judges. Yes, the last volume is not of a piece with what comes before. Still, I am glad, as always, that you find some good things. The satire on sham education seems to please you, and I also thought it fairly good.[495] I wish I could do something that satisfied me (and you) all through.

Ibsen's new play[496] I have not yet seen. Among the things I have read is the latest volume of Goncourt's journal.[497] Now, the more I read of Goncourt, the more I dislike the man. He seems to me radically ignoble. He talks with incessant complaining about his lack of success with the crowd—a matter for lamentation to no serious man who (like Goncourt) has the means of livelihood. His journal is very largely made up of pictures from the familiar life of Daudet, and the odd thing is that he shows, quite unconsciously, how far Daudet is his superior; he shows it by reporting things with which, avowedly, he cannot sympathize. Daudet is obviously a man not only of much wider sympathies, in life and literature, but of truer culture. "Il veut faire"—says Goncourt—"Maintenant une oeuvre où il mettra de lui ce qu'il a de bon, de compatissant: son [sic] pitié pour les misérables, les déshérités, les routiers."[498] That is something quite beyond Goncourt. Then, how noteably [sic] it contrasts with Goncourt's narrow (bitterly narrow) modernism to find Daudet quoting Theocritus and Virgil. And this again: "Daudet est pour le moment tout pris, tout absorbé, tout dominé par la lecture des Entretiens d'Eckermann

---

[494] The whole family was suffering from colds (Diary, 28 December 1894).

[495] *In the Year of Jubilee*, Part the First, Chap. II.

[496] A copyright performance of Ibsen's *Little Eyolf* (1894) was given at the Haymarket Theatre on 8 December 1894.

[497] Edmond Goncourt, *Journal des Goncourt—Mémoires de la Vie Littéraire* (vol. VII, Paris, 1894).

[498] *Journal des Goncourt*, VII, 272.

avec Goethe.'"⁴⁹⁹ But for these glimpses of Daudet, the Journal would leave a very sour taste in the mouth.

So, Stevenson is dead.⁵⁰⁰ I think, now as ever, that his merit is much exaggerated. But he was a most interesting personality.

Do you ever see the *Revue de Paris?* It has been publishing some profoundly interesting letters of Balzac's.⁵⁰¹ Altogether, I think it the most interesting of the French periodicals.

We are having, so far, a strange winter in England. No frost, no snow; much sunshine; many flowers in bloom. But I cannot much enjoy it. My health is good, but I am always in low spirits.

Next week begins the publication of "Eve's Ransom" in the *Illustrated L[ondon] News*. After all, a new artist had to be found to illustrate it;⁵⁰² poor Barnard fell into hopeless depths of drunkenness. Of course you shall have the story when it comes out in book form.

Roberts is wandering about the world again. I see him once or twice a year. Of late I have made the acquaintance of a new poet, John Davidson.⁵⁰³ His recent volume "Ballads and Songs" has had a great success, and indeed it is remarkable. But as a rule I see no one, and life contains little satisfaction.

Surely I shall now hear of your recovery from illness. I wish it for my own sake, as well as for yours, for I am gloomy in thinking of you.

> Yours ever, dear Friend,
> GEORGE GISSING

Eversley. / Worple Road / Epsom.

> January 31. 1895.

My dear Friend,

One word of very heartly [*sic*] congratulation on the completing of your severe task.⁵⁰⁴ Indeed, it has been a task of no common

---

⁴⁹⁹ "Daudet est, dans le moment, tout pris, tout absorbé, tout dominé par la lecture des *Entretiens* d'Eckermann avec Goethe" (VII, 297).

⁵⁰⁰ He died on 4 December 1894. For further remarks on Stevenson, see 6 December 1896.

⁵⁰¹ "Lettres à l'Etrangère," *Revue de Paris*, December 1894 to March 1895.

⁵⁰² Wal Paget illustrated the serial.

⁵⁰³ GRG met Davidson (1857–1909) at the Grosvenor Club on 25 April 1894 (Diary).

⁵⁰⁴ The revision of *Das Sabinergut*.

severity. The end of it—that terrible toiling under conditions of ill health—distresses me to think of. I am convinced that very few men could have gone through with it. You have given me an example of positive heroism in the pursuit of artistic perfection[.]

But now—your *health*. Postpone everything to the care of that. Most undoubtedly the disease was, if not absolutely caused, at all events made worse by the nervous strain to which you have been subjected. At whatever cost, you must now get restored, for life is intolerable under such an affliction. I am sure your Mother will insist on somehow helping you. Rest, rest; medicine and ointments cannot avail you unless your nerves find repose.

The necessity of another removal is miserable, and will be worse if you are still suffering in body. Don't dream of writing to me until you feel stronger.

I send a new *English Illustrated*;[505] let it be acknowledged at some future time.

Yours ever, dear Friend,
George Gissing

Eversley, / Worple Road, / Epsom.[506]

February 24. 1895.

Dear Friend,

I have positively been deterred from replying to your letter by the fear that all I have to say may merely excite your impatience. You have suffered a severe blow, and it is idle to try and disguise the fact. Yet there is something I wish to urge upon you in your mood of depression. You say you are "no artist," and that you must seek to live by artificial work. Now, in the first place, it has been very decidedly proved that you have *great* artistic ability; without it, such a book as "Glück und Glas" could never have been written. On the other hand, I know that you are totally unfitted, by temperament, to make a living out of the art that is in you. Therefore it is that I feel so uncertain whether I ought to encourage you to go on with this most laborious—indeed suicidal—work: work that is made so dreadful by your harassing conditions. Moreover, I think it very, very doubtful whether you

---

[505] Containing "The Poet's Portmanteau," XII (February 1895), 3–10.

[506] The address is engraved. From this date, all the Epsom addresses are engraved on the paper except for the following letters: 27 August 1895; 28 May 1896; 9 October 1896; 10 May 1897; 16 June 1897.

can do what we call "pot-boiling" work. I don't think it is in you to persevere on that low level, long enough for pecuniary success.

No. To my mind it seems a very strange thing that no other mode of existence, and of subsistence, should be discoverable. I think you ought not to look to fiction as a means of living. Have you really cast about to find other kinds of literary work? It strikes me as monstrous that a man of your wide culture and interests should be excluded from forms of production such as support thousands of men. I feel so sure that you might write what would be acceptable to editors, without all this agony which is inflicted by your conscientiousness in fiction. Among the vast multitude of German periodicals, is there no hope of finding a place for the kind of literary articles which you could write with far more satisfaction to yourself than mere "pot-boiling" stories?

I am well aware that your ill-health is a grave embarrassment. But it is obvious that *this* will improve only when your mind obtains rest. Now is it really impossible to do a little light work of the kind that editors, all the world over, are glad to accept? Not profound, not erudite, essays: but a skimming from the surface of your wide knowledge. You have not yet found out all the money-making possibilities that lie in you, that may legitimately be used. For the mere sake of change, try something of this sort.

In the meantime, it is more than likely that your book will get published, in one form or another. And suppose it issued as a volume, how do you know that the sale may not equal that of "Glück und Glas"? But, my poor fellow, you are ill; and in thinking of this I feel how vain it is to utter even well-founded encouragement. I can only say what I sincerely think, and beg you to consider the matter.

Perhaps—alas!—you have too often considered it. But I *know* you can live by your pen, and *easily* and not unpleasantly.

With us, the winter seems to be over at last. I hope the worst of it is also over with you. It shall not be long before I write again. How gladly should I hear that your confounded ailment showed signs of disappearing![507]

Ever yours, dear old Friend,
GEORGE GISSING

[507] The eczema.

Eversley, / Worple Road, / Epsom.

March 26th. 1895.

My dear Friend,

You will wonder why I have been so long without writing. For three weeks I have suffered severely from colds and other ailments. Yesterday I returned from a visit to the seaside, but it has done me little good. Next week I must go away again.

And now I have received your sad note. I am much grieved at the death of your young brother;[508] his age seemed to promise the security of manhood, and I can quite well understand how your mother suffers under the blow. Between you and her there has been a growth of tenderness for some years, and this misfortune will, I am sure, hold you yet more closely together. You must have been in a sad state of disorder and distress this last week, and I fear it will have exercised anything but a good influence upon your health.

But the summer is now before us, and I hope it will have blessings for you. You are better housed; your book will presently be published; and you will have the society of your mother more frequently. When I feel able to say more, either about you or myself, I will write again; just now I am reduced in strength from a slight attack of bronchitis, and the weather does not allow me to leave the house. My journey home yesterday was imprudent, I am afraid. Alas, you are not alone in feeling the loss of youth![509] I too am very often reminded that the years of best energy are gone and will return no more.

Ever affectionately yours,
GEORGE GISSING

Eversley, / Worple Road, / Epsom.

May 9. 1895.

My dear Friend,

If you had mentioned this matter before sending the money, I should have begged you to forget all about it—as indeed I

---

[508] Fritz Winckler, Bertz's half-brother, who was about twenty-two years old when he died. After the boy's death, Bertz returned to his mother's home in Potsdam.

[509] Bertz was forty-two years old; GRG was thirty-eight.

myself had done. The money I earn is small compared with the literary reputation I have somehow managed to achieve; but still it is sufficient for my present needs. However, as you have been able to repay the sum without inconvenience to yourself, so be it, and many thanks to you.[510] Those old days were bad enough for both of us; but never forget that *my* debt to you was a great one, inexpressible in cash. But for your companionship I might have sunk to miserable depths.

Now, I want to say a word or two about the way in which you regard these obligations to your mother. I can well understand that you contrast her grief for the dead son with her seeming lack of sympathy with yourself, and that the contrast embitters you. But I venture to prophesy that, as time goes on, your relations will much improve. Mere indebtedness to your mother for material help ought not, I think, to trouble you in the least. I hold that the parent's responsibility to the child extends through the whole of life. There can be no doubt that your mother gives this help in a spirit of perfect willingness, even of satisfaction—yes, whatever the superficial appearance of things may be. It is not as though you were a *burden* to her; this would be a very different matter. Between parent and child all mere worldly possessions should be in common, so long as no injustice results from the behaviour on either side. You are no spendthrift; you work steadily and well; moreover, you have very great natural difficulties to contend with. I maintain that you ought to look upon the freedom from pecuniary stress as an unmixed blessing, and to feel perfectly free to work in your own way. It is by doing the best work that is in you that you respond to your mother's perfectly natural assistance. If, under the circumstances, she did *not* assist you, it would be a very wrong state of things.

It is most unfortunate that again you are so tormented in the house. I know not what remedy you will ultimately discover for this great difficulty. Unless you can have a little house of your own, it seems all but impossible to escape the contact of troublesome people.

I agreed with all you said about "Eve's Ransom," except, per-

---

[510] "Astonished to receive from Bertz the sum of £27—a debt due to me for more than ten years. Wrote to him" (Diary, 9 May 1895). The money had been lent to Bertz to help him through the winter of 1884.

haps, concerning the title. I have a liking for ironical titles, and this is one of them (like "In the Year of Jubilee," and "A Life's Morning.") To be sure, Eve was not worth it all; therein lies the sting of the story. But, after all, the book was written for a newspaper, and, moreover, when I was in bad health. It certainly is not one of my best.

I am glad to hear your opinion of Tourguéneff on re-reading. Yes, I quite concur with it. He is a great fellow, and most later work pales before his.[511] By the bye, a complete English translation of him is just coming out,[512] but I have not seen a volume yet.

You must let me have "Guten Morgen, Vielliebchen,"[513] when it comes out. You know how I always liked your childrens' [sic] stories.

Your paragraphs in the Almanach I have read carefully. No 1 has a noteworthy application to myself. "Das grosse Glück" will never come to me, and I lose a vast amount of "Kleinen [sic] Freuden" through mere forgetfulness of the truth you state. No 2 is admirable: a genuine parallel, and perfectly worded. By the bye, both of these apophthegmata might very well have been done in verse. The former a couplet, (elegiac, if you like,) the latter a quatrain.

I am rather overburdened by the demand for short stories. This work is not altogether congenial to me, but it is the only kind that brings in much money. My books don't sell; though perhaps they may some day. The second edition of "Eve" is only a second thousand, and my royalty is 1 shilling a copy.[514]

Try, dear old boy, to be less introspective. Alas, if you could but have better health! There is the root of the matter. I repeat that the mere money matter ought not, now, to have the slightest weight with you.

> Yours ever,
> GEORGE GISSING

[511] "He was, without doubt, the greatest living writer of fiction. . . . I possess two letters, on matters of business, which he wrote to me from Paris. They are of course valuable and will become more so in course of time" (GRG to Ellen Gissing, *Letters*, 14 October 1883, p. 135).

[512] Translated by Constance Garnett and published by William Heinemann in 1895.

[513] No record of publication.

[514] Published by Lawrence and Bullen in April for 6 shillings.

Eversley, / Worple Road, / Epsom.

June 23. 1895.

My dear Friend,

By this, you will no doubt have received two magazines—Chapman's and the Eng[lish] Illust[rated].[515] My delay in sending the former was due to a great deal of troublesome business I have had to get through. The editors are really worrying me with demands for sketches and short stories, and as I work very slowly—far more slowly than of old—I am in constant fear of not being able to meet my engagements. Then again, hardly a day goes by but I receive some sort of invitation—either to lunch or dinner, or to stay at people's houses. All this kind of thing is pleasant enough, but ruinous to work. I feel unable to refuse *all* invitations, and lose many an hour with people I don't much care about. Thus it is that I see no chance of getting to work on a long book, though I much wish to do it. The small stories are, for the most part, poor stuff, but they keep me alive. My long novels simply *will not* sell; they disappoint everyone connected with them.

It is strange how many letters I get from women, asking for sympathy and advice. I really can't understand what it is in my work that attracts the female mind.

After this explanation of my difficulty in writing, I turn to your good news about your novel. The sum you receive is small enough for the author of "Glück und Glas"; but I suppose this is partly explained by the lapse of time, and partly by the severer nature of this new book. In any case, let us be glad that the work is to see the light. Every act of publication includes all sorts of possibilities, and, for my part, I think one ought to indulge hope as much as possible, seeing that hope in itself is pure gain. I shall read this novel with eager interest, as you know. "Der Igel" and "Vielliebchen" will also be very welcome.

I deplore the wretched circumstances amid which you have to do your work. Those noises would certainly drive *me* frantic, and you, I am afraid, suffer even more than I should. But how sorry I am that you will not go to the Black Forest. Are you

---

[515] "His Brother's Keeper" appeared in *Chapman's Magazine* in June 1895; "In Honour Bound" was printed in the *English Illustrated Magazine*, XIII (April 1895), 79–88.

quite sure it is impossible! That would do you an immensity of good. Remember you are an invalid, and consider that any small sum spent in travelling will certainly be repaid by new health and vigour. I think it a most grievous thing that you cannot go.

At present, whenever an odd half-hour is granted me, I am reading the history of the church in the 4th Century. Remembering this, you will understand how it amused me to read of the Emperor William's doings at the Canal the other day, when he laid a stone: "Im Namen des dreieinigen Gottes"[516]—I suppose that would be the German. "In the name of the triune God." Merciful powers! Are we still using such words as these! It is really a most striking and astonishing thing: especially to one fresh from Arius and Athanasius.

By the bye, have you any idea where one can get a copy of Libanius "Pro Templis"?[517] I don't want you to bother about it, but there *might* be a handy edition in Germany.

I made the acquaintance of Grant Allen[518] the other day. He is, personally, a most delightful fellow. Of course he ought not to be writing fiction at all (apropos, "The Woman Who Did" has for some time been bringing him £25 a week,) but devoting himself to science. He has an astounding memory, and can talk with accuracy on any subject that comes up. Yes, I like him very well. Quite devoid of affectation, and bringing with him the air of the Surrey moorlands, where he lives.

[516] The keystone of the North Sea Baltic Canal was laid by the German Emperor on 21 June 1895, at Kiel. According to the London *Times*, "His Majesty gave the stone three vigorous strokes with the hammer, accompanying the action with the words: 'In memory of the Great Emperor, I christen this canal Emperor William's Canal—for the welfare of the German Empire—for the prosperity of all nations'" (22 June 1895, p. 9). I do not know where GRG read the account to which he refers.

[517] Libanius (A.D. 314–393), Greek rhetorician and sophist.

[518] Charles Grant Allen (1848–1899), Canadian born scientist and writer, and sometime professor of mental and moral philosophy in Jamaica, whose most famous novel was the controversial *The Woman Who Did* (1895). GRG met Allen at a house-party given by Edward Clodd on 21 May 1895 at Aldeburgh: "Grant Allen I liked much better than I had expected. He is white-haired, and all but white bearded (a little sandy remaining) though only 47. Very talkative, and, with me, confidential about his private life. . . . Thinks there never was a man Jesus: his whole story a slowly perfected mythus" (Diary, 6 June 1895).

Not once in six months do I see Roberts. Poor fellow, he is involved in a troublesome love affair,[519] and his doctor tells him he has serious disease of the heart.

I wish to heaven you could go to the Black Forest!

Yours ever, dear old Friend,
GEORGE GISSING

Eversley. / Worple Road / Epsom.

August 27. 1895.

My dear Friend,

For the last month or so I have been chiefly at the seaside, on the east coast. I cannot say that I enjoyed it much, for the weather was very bad; but I suppose it has done me good. As usual, I suffer so much from the necessity of getting to work again that I wish I had never broken off at all. The machine needs to be kept constantly going; in my case, it rusts very soon indeed.

It is now a year since I finished my last novel, yet I am by no means ready to begin another. I have a lot of short stories to write for the *English Illustrated*, and other editors are constantly demanding that kind of thing. But I must close my ears to these applications. Only on a large canvas can I do work worth doing.

You doubtless received a newspaper I sent you, with the report of a Dinner in the country, at which I had to make a speech.[520] But for this horror, it was a grand evening. I renewed my acquaintance with Meredith and with Hardy. Meredith, who lives only 7 miles from here has asked me to go over and see him, and I

---

[519] Possibly with Alice Selous, whom Roberts married in 1896.

[520] Clement Shorter invited GRG to be his guest at the Omar Khayyám dinner, held at the Burford Bridge Hotel in Mickleham on 13 July 1895. Edward Clodd "began the speeches by a toast to Meredith, who briefly replied. He said it was the first time in his life he had spoken publicly—strange fact. Then [Louis Frederic] Austin gave 'the guests' in a capital speech. Hardy replied, very shortly, just mentioning that twenty-six years had passed since he first met Meredith, which was in a back room of Chapman and Halls. Then my name was shouted, and there was nothing for it. I told the story of Meredith's accepting 'The Unclassed' for Chapman, and my interview with him, when I didn't know who he was. . . . Meredith grievously aged; very deaf, and shaky, but mind clear as ever. As he came

shall certainly do so before long. He is now about 70, and gets very shaky.[521]

I have made a good many new acquaintances this last year, including newspaper editors—the kind of men whom authors generally exert themselves to know. In my case, it is mere wisdom to maintain the *distant* attitude which has become one of my characteristics in the eyes of the reading-public. I am looked upon as more or less of a recluse, and it is well known that I never sought the favour of influential people; and these things certainly serve me. Happily, I can now meet men in a very independent way. It is known to very few how poor I still am; most people think my books have a *large* sale, and, as the way of the world is, they treat me with great respect. I suppose the sale of the books is really increasing a little; but unfortunately the popular ones are those that belong to Smith and Elder.[522]

That fearful suffering of yours from the noises of the house *ought* to be put an end to. Whether you manage it or not, I shall keep in mind that promise of your mother's, to establish you in a cottage of your own in the spring of next year. This would probably be the greatest kindness she could do you; it would be *your* part to consider very carefully about the position of the dwelling, and all such matters.

I ought to have thanked you long ago for your kind information about Libanius etc. I have had no opportunity yet to make use of your notes, but I shall do so when my next interval of leisure comes. It is unfortunate that I cannot now *divide* my mind, as I used to do, between the ancient and the modern world. Each has to take its turn. But I am in no danger whatever of losing interest in my old studies, just as little as I am in danger of being dragged into time-wasting society.

---

round the tables on entering, someone mentioned my name to him, and he said 'Mr. Gissing! Ah, where is Mr. Gissing?' And we shook hands. Then he sat at the top of the table, talking with Clodd and Watts. On going, I went to shake hands with him, and he asked me to go to his house some day. With Hardy I talked a little, and he asked me to write to him" (Diary, 13 July 1895). See W. Robertson Nicoll, *A Bookman's Letters* (London, 1913), pp. 5–6, for a similar version of the dinner.

[521] Meredith, 67 years old at this time, was living at Flint Cottage, Box Hill, Mickleham.

[522] See 3 November 1892.

Your account of Zapp reminds me of several men I know, I mean in his literary circumstances. The extent to which novelists are becoming *mere* men of business is terrible. Besant (you have heard that he is now *Sir* Walter, together with Sir Henry Irving etc.)[523] has of course much to answer for in this matter; though I cheerfully admit that much is owing to him for his efforts to improve the payment of authorship. However, I was glad to hear that a man like Zapp thinks you have not been badly paid for the novel. It makes me decidedly hopeful that you may receive even more for the next.

Your letter ends hopefully, and for that I am heartily thankful. We shall probably see each other before our heads are grey.

> Yours ever, dear Friend,
> GEORGE GISSING

Eversley, / Worple Road, / Epsom.

September 22. 1895.

Dear Friend,

I am glad to have your portraits, and yet more glad, in looking at them, to think that you are no longer suffering so severely from so many kinds of doubt and difficulty. This last letter makes me full of hope for the time to come. It is a great thing to be able to count upon the annual M. 1200,[524] and I see that this has to some extent given you tranquillity of mind. And is it absolutely *certain* that you will have to "give up much which you had hoped some day to enjoy." For my own part, I know that, in favourable circumstances you would produce good fiction, which would eventually be much better paid for; at the same time I cannot abandon the hope that your more congenial work will also have a measure of material reward. It is right, very right, things being as they are, to work "as you feel drawn by inward impulses." You have abundance of matter for really important books and essays. Go ahead!

[523] Besant had urged that eminent writers be recognized with titles of honor, and was himself knighted for his literary achievement in 1895, on the recommendation of Lord Rosebery. Henry Irving (1838–1905), the first actor to be knighted, had declined the honor in 1883, but accepted it in 1895.

[524] From his mother.

Poor old Morison![525] There was a man who at all events might have done much more than he did; but *he* was ruined by luxury. He had not the divine ardour which becomes lord over circumstance. He was one of those who have to answer for the wasted talent. In your case there is no such fear. You have done wonderfully in spite of terrible difficulties; and kinder circumstances will lead you to do much more.

Well, I am working one [*sic*], but doing little that I care for. The *Autonym* story is finished, and also a poor little book for Cassells, called "The Paying Guest"—a frothy trifle for a popular series.[526] And I am writing more short stories.

Pray keep the *Humanitarian*.[527] I have another copy.

I went to call on Meredith one afternoon, and he invited me to dinner a week after.[528] He has a beautiful little house, with a large garden, where he has lived for twenty years. The books that lie about, are precisely such as I shall be reading, if I live to his age— Greek plays, Mommsen,[529] Dante, and so on. He is a man of high culture, and most liberal mind. His philosophy is wonderfully bright and hopeful. A scholar, he yet thinks the best of Democracy, and believes that emancipated human-kind will do greater things than the old civilizations permitted. There is a fine dignity about him, and I feel proud to sit in his room.

Last week I accepted an invitation to go down to Dorchester, and stay for a couple of days with Thomas Hardy. Now Hardy is a man of far less intellectual vigour and distinction than Meredith. Born a peasant, he yet retains much of the peasant's views of life. He evidently does not read very much, and I grieve to find that

[525] James Morison (see 17 April 1887). He was a brilliant scholar whose special interest was French history during the reign of Louis XIV, about which he had planned a definitive historical study. Wealthy, active, and gregarious, he never found time to carry out his scholarly plans.

[526] *Sleeping Fires* (December 1895) was written for Fisher Unwin's "Autonym Library," and *The Paying Guest* (January 1896) was published in "Cassell's Pocket Library."

[527] Containing GRG's article, "The Place of Realism in Fiction" (July 1895).

[528] "In afternoon went over to Box Hill, and called on Meredith. Found him sitting in the little drawing-room, unoccupied, smoking cigarette" (Diary, 12 September 1895).

[529] Theodor Mommsen (1817–1903), German historian and classical scholar, author of numerous works on Roman law, history, and archeology.

he is drawn into merely fashionable society, talks of lords and ladies more than of ordinary people. Most unfortunately he has a very foolish wife—a woman of higher birth than his own, who looks down upon him, and is utterly discontented. They have no children, and they travel about a good deal, but not to much purpose. I admire Hardy's best work very highly, but in the man himself I feel disappointed. To my great surprise, I found that he did not know the names of flowers in his own fields! A strange unsettlement appears in him; probably the result of his long association with such a paltry woman.[530] Essentially, he is good, gentle, and poetically minded. But he sadly needs a larger outlook upon life—a wider culture.

Herewith comes a portrait of myself,[531] in return for yours. It will amuse you to hear that I am now "for sale" in the shops of London photographers!

Oh, I had almost forgotten. At the urgent request of my publishers, I have revised "The Unclassed" for republication.[532] About a third of the book is cut away, and I shall write a brief preface. If the thing had been utterly forgotten, I should never have reprinted it; but reviewers frequently make mention of it. So let it, in a better form, be added to the list of my books. Of course you shall have a copy.

Yours ever, dear old Friend,
GEORGE GISSING

[530] The invitation to spend a weekend at Max Gate followed GRG's conversation with Hardy at the Omar Khayyám dinner. He arrived at Hardy's home on 14 September and stayed until 16 September, and "on the whole enjoyed it. The drawback was Mrs. Thomas [Lavinia Gifford]—an extremely silly and discontented woman, to whom, no doubt is attributable a strange restlessness and want of calm in Hardy himself" (GRG to Algernon Gissing, 22 September 1895, Yale University Gazette, XVII, January 1943, 52).

[531] This photograph, now in the Yale Collection, was taken by Russell and Sons, 17 Baker St., London. It is inscribed: "To My Friend Eduard Bertz. Sept. 1895."

[532] Published by Lawrence and Bullen, November 1895, in one volume. For a comparison of the original with the revised text, see Joseph J. Wolff, "Gissing's Revision of The Unclassed," Nineteenth-Century Fiction, VIII (June 1953), 42–52.

Eversley, / Worple Road, / Epsom.

November 12. 1895.

Dear Friend,

I am sending you a copy of the new edition of "The Unclassed." Of course the book is painful to me, on several accounts;[533] but I have made it, in this form, less crude and absurd. It is possible that "Isabel Clarendon"[534] may some day re-appear. I agree with you in thinking it not altogether a bad piece of work.

My two little things: "Sleeping Fires" and "The Paying Guest" will soon, I think, be out.

Nothing could be more pleasant to me than the news that you have improved in health. Of course, as you say, the physical improvement has followed on mental calm. If now I always receive from you such hopeful and energetic letters, a great support will be added to my own life. If indeed you make a whole book out of the Essay on Cosmopolitanism,[535] it will be a work of some note. But I suppose you would in any case try to publish it serially at first?

The difficulty about obtaining expensive books is very troublesome. The fact is, very few men can read to any advantage out of their own study. I have long ceased to make any use of the British Museum—save for an occasional rapid reference; I can do nothing there; there comes only headache and distraction of thought. Like you, I earnestly desire the means of purchasing a lot of books.

You must give careful consideration to your mother's proposal that you should live in her house. The relief *might* be great; though of course there will be a few things on the other side. Lodgings become more and more detestable as the democratic spirit grows. Of course the whole question of domestic service is one of the gravest of our time, and I hope to write a book about it.[536] I have immense material.

[533] Perhaps because the novel grew from GRG's experiences with Nell, his first wife. Ida Starr, the heroine of the novel, who saves herself from a life of prostitution, reflects the hope he once held for his own wife.

[534] Three vols., London: Chapman and Hall, 1886. The novel has never been reprinted.

[535] No record of publication.

[536] Instead of a novel on this problem, he wrote a short story, "The Foolish Virgin" (*Yellow Book*, VIII, January 1896, 11–38), in which the heroine, friendless and poor, makes a reasonable life for herself as a domestic helper.

I grieve for your loneliness, but try to believe—indeed you do believe—that it is really preferable, for the wise man, to all but a very few forms of companionship. Intellect and character in any case tend to solitude; associated with poverty, they are all but universally *condemned* to it. Ah, what a wonderful life you would lead if you had but a few miserable hundred pounds a year! And what a life would be mine in the same case! It maddens one to think of this.

Your Essay reminds me that I have just been reading Bourget's "Cosmopolis"[537]—or trying to read it. I found the book *very* dull. Not so his "Sensations d'Italie,"[538] and yet that might be more interesting.

What think you of Suderman's "Es War"?[539] Good stuff in it, I think. The fault seems to me a tendency to melodramatic situation—due, I suppose, to Sudermann's habit of play-writing.

I think of you with hope. Quiet, congenial work will be the very best cure for many of your ills. You have been worried almost to death.

Ever yours, dear Friend,
GEORGE GISSING

Addressed: Herrn Eduard Bertz. / Gr[osse] Weinmeisterstrasse, 28 / Potsdam. / *Germany.*

Epsom

November 28. 1895.

Many thanks for inquiry. Fisher Unwin writes to the papers to say that his firm is distinct from that of the printers, and that his publications will not be affected.[540] Hope to send "Sleeping Fires" very soon. Am clearing the way for a new book.

[537] Paul Bourget (Paris, 1893).

[538] Paris, 1891. For a discussion of the possible influence of Bourget's book on GRG's *By the Ionian Sea*, see Samuel V. Gapp, *George Gissing: Classicist* (Philadelphia, 1936), pp. 128–29.

[539] Stuttgart, 1894.

[540] Bertz feared that the publication of GRG's *Sleeping Fires* might be delayed by a fire at Unwin Brothers' Printing Works, Chilworth, which had completely destroyed the plant on 23 November 1895 (London *Times*, 25 November 1895, p. 6). T. Fisher Unwin's letter appeared in the London *Times* on 26 November 1895, p. 6.

Delighted with cheerful tone of your letters. Hearty thanks for little story,[541] of which I shall write again.

G. G.

Eversley, / Worple Road, / Epsom.

December 18. 1895.

My dear Friend,

I have read your letter with great and painful indignation, and rather than postpone my reply, I write briefly, in necessary haste. It is a monstrous thing that you should be subjected to these forms of physical suffering—the root of your mental misery. The whole thing is a question of food. You must not only *eat*, you must have *meals*, properly cooked and properly served. I do not care what the difficulties are. Now that in one essential respect your prospects are brighter, it is your absolute duty to take some step which will assure you a healthy mode of living. You must at once take counsel with your mother, and contrive a change. Of course you have starved yourself, and worse than that; you have often eaten unwholesome food. It is preposterous to talk of postponing the change until next spring; by that time you may have got beyond recovery. Rehfeldt is certainly behaving with unkindness; but the main help cannot come from him. Do make a frank explanation to your Mother of the grievous condition into which you have fallen, and allow her to suggest something practical. You do not want medicine; you want *good food*. This is the first and the last word. Do not tell me it is impossible; I cannot believe it.

I grieve that you should have troubled to write about that paltry little book of mine, which, I agree with you, falls short in the closing scenes.[542] I, too, am in anything but good health, and cannot just now do anything up to the mark. Your little fairy tale I read with sincere pleasure, for it reminded me of those others you used to read to me in German, long ago. It has the true lightness and playfulness of touch. You have a very distinct faculty for that kind of writing, which you would doubtless have developed more fully had grievous circumstances permitted.

The publishers, as so often, show very little regard for decency.

[541] Not identified.
[542] *Sleeping Fires*.

It would cost them a penny to send you that prospectus, and they grudge it. Of such is *not* the kingdom of heaven.

I grieve exceedingly for your sufferings. Do, *do* give ear to me, and scorn every consideration save the question of obtaining three good meals every day. In this bitter season to go unfed or ill fed, when one *has* an alternative, is to commit suicide. It is not as if you were at a distance from any relative. Your mother is bound to give effectual help in such an extreme case as this.

Why on earth should you be ashamed to tell me of such things? It makes me miserable, but only because I sympathize so strongly.

Whilst you are in this weak state, do not dream of writing me such long letters. Let me know very briefly what you do, and how your health goes on. As to ultimate arrangements, I advise nothing; but for the present, it is obvious that you cannot continue to live in comfortless solitude.

Christmas wishes would be absurd. Not so a good wish for the year to come. You have it in your power to make some satisfactory change, and of course you will do so.

Affectionately yours, dear old Friend,
GEORGE GISSING

Eversley, / Worple Road, / Epsom.

January 15. 1896.

Dear Old Friend,

These international frenzies I regard with such utter contempt that I should never have mentioned them in a letter to you.[543] The so-called civilized world is of course full of rampant barbarians— most of them reckless of everything in the furious chase after wealth and power. More likely than not, they will bring about terrible things in the immediate future. Be it *our* part to live in quiet hostility to all such baseness.

The one thing in politics at present that strongly moves me is the position of Armenia.[544] It is the strongest possible satire on the

[543] Britain herself was involved in three major difficulties: she was disputing the Venezuelan boundary with the United States; she had to resolve the hostility against her in South Africa; and she along with other powers was trying to hold down the riots in Armenia.

[544] The great massacres had begun in Constantinople on 1 October 1895, apparently by order of the Sultan of the Ottoman Empire, who planned to wipe out the Armenians.

state of the world, that Europe can look on whilst damnable Orientals repeat the horrors of the Middle Ages, *recognizing* that it is withheld from interference by motives entirely selfish. Were the leading nations really civilized, they would of course rise together on an instant impulse, and stamp out this disgrace of the modern world.

Well now, I am very glad to hear that your health is improving. I thoroughly understand the grievous difficulties you find in living (or even dining) under your mother's roof; but you *must* not relapse into carelessness about diet. No change of air will avail, unless you are eating a sufficiency of good, well-cooked food. You know this, and, by whatever means, you must act upon the knowledge.

Of course removal is a terrible business. If you really go straight into another apartment, see that it does not involve a loss of your proposed holiday.

It is very amusing with regard to my two little books. Roberts tells me that "The Paying Guest" is utter rubbish, whereas "Sleeping Fires" is very good. And there is much diversity of opinion among people who speak to me on the matter. For my own part, I am disposed to think with *you*, and, as always, I am very glad that you feel able to praise the one story.[545] But the fact remains that I am very tired of short things. I must get to a solid book once more. Thank heaven, I have begun to shape my ideas.

I received the announcement of your book,[546] with its very unsatisfactory portrait. I wish they would be quick and let you have proofs; to get them off hand would certainly be a relief to you. In the meantime, you will of course feel a good deal of uncertainty as to your next piece of work; for one thing, you of course ought not to work very hard at any thing until your health is in a much better state.

Of late I have been occupied in a singular way—making a little study of physiology and of botany. To the latter I have felt a good deal attracted of recent years, and it is probable that I shall pursue the study—though of course within modest limits.[547] This change

---

[545] Bertz preferred *The Paying Guest* to *Sleeping Fires*.

[546] *Das Sabinergut.*

[547] T. W. Gissing, GRG's father, also studied botany. See *The Private Papers of Henry Ryecroft*, "Spring," Chap. XXV, and Introduction.

of thought has, I believe, helped to give a better tone to my mind.

I continue to make new acquaintances. If I were to accept all the invitations I receive, I should dine in town about once a week; but I am afraid of excessive distraction. Most of the London editors are now known to me, and I find some of them tolerably sympathetic. To be sure, *business* predominates with them, but for the most part they are not absolutely subdued to materialism.

There has been appointed a new Poet Laureate, a successor to Tennyson; his name is Alfred Austin.[548] The affair has excited great disgust, for he is a man of no distinction whatever; it seems to be a purely political appointment. The *Athenaeum* has absolutely ignored it. There was but one living successor to Tennyson, viz. Swinburne.[549] But his early erotic and republican writings made it impossible to offer him the title. However, the thing is now meaningless.

Get well again, dear Friend, and try to decide upon some hopeful course.

Yours ever,

GEORGE GISSING

[548] Austin (1835–1913) had been admitted to the bar in 1857, but gave up law to become a journalist in 1866. He was co-editor and then editor of the *National Review* from 1883 to 1895, and published twenty volumes of verse.

[549] In March 1895, the *Idler* asked GRG and several other writers to discuss their choice for the Poet Laureateship. GRG wrote: "By the weighing of reputations, how can the laurel be bestowed save upon Mr. Swinburne? Objections to him must be made upon side issues. We are told that Mr. Swinburne, in part, offends against the popular conscience; but the popular conscience has nothing to do with literary merit. We are reminded that the Laureate is an official of the Court; but (whether or no the view would influence those in authority) such precedent is well understood to be, nowadays, wide of the mark. Would we do formal honour to Poetry, he alone can be crowned whom competent criticisms and the general estimate uninvidiously hail. I have no space for specific eulogy. In certain granted aspects, Mr. Swinburne is great among the poets of the world, and I do not think this can be maintained of any other man whose title might, perchance, be pleaded. Much as I delight in what is given us by some of our younger poets, I assume that they, as yet, withhold from such competition. On the whole, ought we not to elect a Laureate, if only that the 'greasy citizen' may pause and marvel, and be for a moment disturbed with the surmise that there is yet a god who rivals Plutus?" ("Who Should be Laureate?" *Idler*, VII, 404–5).

Eversley, / Worple Road, / Epsom.

February 23. 1896.

My dear Friend,

It is good to have finished the labour of proof-reading. For my own part, I always find it torture. I am not at all sorry to know that the book is rather long; so much the more for me to read.

Now, that you have discovered, and actually taken, a little house all to yourself, is most excellent news. But what arrangements will you make about service? I am sure you will not be so thoughtless as to regard this with indifference. You absolutely must have someone to prepare for you at least one good meal every day; it is a *sine qua non*; the condition of even tolerable health. So I shall be anxious to hear of these details.

As for packing—nefandum! It is a horror to think of.

I heartily agree with you that Patriotism remains a virtue; in the nature of things there is no reason why it should not coexist with international amity. Yes, journalism plays the very worst part in international relations, and simply because of its being directed by an utterly selfish and reckless capitalism. The late troubles in S. Africa are of course due entirely to capitalist greed.[550] I cannot see any hope for peace, so long as these men of the money-market are permitted to control public life—as they now practically do. But, alas, we must remember that humanity is most imperfectly civilized. I greatly doubt whether a cessation of war is yet possible; the sincere lovers of tranquillity are too few, and moreover, the masses of mankind have to go slowly through a normal development. To be sure, there are people who hold that universal peace it not even desirable. And that *may* be the truth, from the point of view of general progress.

I am told that those two little books of mine are in great demand at the libraries; the reviewers, however, have been rather contemptuous about them. Your own remarks about "Sleeping Fires" were decidedly just. Whether you are not too favourably disposed to the other is a question.

[550] The government of the South African Republic controlled the railways and thus cut into the revenues of the British South Africa Company, which gave financial aid and advice to the rebels attempting to overthrow the Boer government. Cecil Rhodes, disappointed in his attempt to set up a customs union among all African states which would increase his profits, is supposed to have had a hand in planning the rebellion.

Very, very slowly, I shape the details of a new book.[551] I am afraid it will take me a long time.

By the bye, I have just read "La Débâcle." It seems to me a very ill-constructed book, but the work for the most part is wonderfully powerful. I was glad to find how little it contains of Gallic bitterness.

I shall be very glad if you find it possible to write another boys' story before your removal; I suppose it would be quite short. Thank heaven, the sun is drawing towards us once more, and this will aid your recovery from unhealthy conditions. Here in England the winter has been of a very extraordinary kind, hardly any frost, and a great deal of pale sunshine.

The other day I paid a visit to old Carlyle's house at Chelsea, which, as perhaps you know, is converted into a Carlyle Museum. Very interesting. And, in spite of all he might have said, the old fellow would not have been displeased to know that his dwelling was thus preserved and honoured.

Next week I mean to visit Meredith again.

> Ever yours, dear Friend,
> GEORGE GISSING

Eversley, / Worple Road, / Epsom.

March 8th. 1896.

Dear Old Friend,

So, here is the Book, and it even surpasses my hopes! I *knew* it would have much value; what I did not quite foresee was that you would be able to throw yourself so admirably into currents of life utterly alien to your mind and temper. This Book will be very widely read, in several countries—be sure of it! You have so treated an episode of colonial life (in itself very interesting) as to make it symbolical of the history of humanity. Your book abounds in sociological, ethical, international interest. At the same time, it is engrossing as a mere story. Again and again, for many pages at a time, I lost all consciousness of critical attitude, and simply forgot myself in the events of the narrative—and I assure you that this is an experience very rare with me nowadays.

---

[551] *The Whirlpool*, Lawrence and Bullen, April 1897.

The construction could not be bettered. You have so admirably subordinated persons and details to the homogeneous scheme. One closes the book with a sense of satisfaction, of repose after unutterable struggle—the true epic struggle between man and fate.

Your characters are, every one of them, individuals, very plain to see; and their variety is great. They range from Sir Austin to the half-savage *Eingeborene*—from Klotilde to Miss Dudgeon. Joseph Karnisen you have presented admirably, so as to balance the extravagant idealist; and his brother is too amusing to be altogether loathsome. Karl himself is a rich study, and, most important point, he remains the leading character throughout; he is never lost sight of amid the the [*sic*] manifold interests of the story.

There is humour (more of it, and truer, than in *Glück und Glas*); there is very deep pathos. Indeed, I know not what desideratum of an excellent work of fiction is lacking in this novel. This is my very strong opinion, which has grown and confirmed itself from page to page.

Now, as to the substratum of personal fact. I have marvelled that you actually went through these things. What a bit of life to look back upon! Of course I know it all much better now than I did from your letters at the time; it is infinitely more real to me. A wonderful experience! And how wrong it would have been to neglect the use of it! I repeat that the book is bound to have a very wide circle of readers. What about translation into English? Shall I recommend it to likely people? I only wish I could undertake the translation myself.

You have dealt very generously with "Sir Austin"; the original has no right to be offended.[552] Moreover, you have dealt generously with America, though, very rightly, you throw light upon the hateful side of American life. I feel pretty sure that you will soon receive applications from translators, at all events.

Well now, upon this book you might rest your reputation. Any man might do so. But heaven forbid that you should stop here. Go on! Write yet another big novel, for it is in you to write *many*. Let me know what the reviewers say about this book.

With the general results of your theme I am heartily in sympathy. The book is indeed "human," in the largest sense; very

[552] The "original" was Thomas Hughes.

tolerant, very noble. You draw the line admirably between Quixotism and true idealism. Karl's speech at the uproarious meeting is very fine. And what a capital fellow is Dr. Floyd!

Now if *I* had written a book on this theme, the flavour at the end would be bitterness. Not so with you. And you are on the side of all the great masters.

By the bye, there are a few misprints. On page 344 (l.10 from top) should not *Fibel* be *Bibel*? (I find there *is* a word *Fibel*, but did you mean this?). P. 351, l.6 from bottom—*Pantasiegebilde* instead of *Phant.* And p. 402, l.3 from bottom, should not *lasz* be *las*?[553]

I have not uttered a hundredth part of my thoughts about this book. I shall return to it in future letters. If I seem to you to be slow in writing, be assured that I have read the book *slowly*— very carefully; that is the reason of my delay. And most heartily I have enjoyed the reading. Well, out of all your terrible misery has come this work of art. Regret nothing!

I look at your portrait at the end of the book, and bid you be of good cheer. You have done a piece of work which you may well be proud of.

Ever yours, dear old Friend,
GEORGE GISSING

Nevin. / Caernarvon. / North Wales.

April 16. 1896.

My dear Friend,

Many serious disturbances have prevented me from writing to you for this long time.[554] I ought of course to have wished you good fortune in your change to the new abode. I heartily hope you are now settled there, and that already you feel benefit from the cessation of vile noises and ignoble neighbourhood.

---

[553] I have not been able to find a copy of *Das Sabinergut. Fibel* means primer or spelling-book.

[554] He had been having serious domestic troubles. In the following week, he took his son Walter to his mother's home in Wakefield, explaining to his brother: "The little lad will remain here, and be taught in the girls' school [Ellen and Margaret had started a little school]; I shall pay them £10 a quarter. His home has become utterly impossible. You cannot allow a hot-tempered child to grow up in an atmosphere of sordid quarrel; it

Possibly you have written to Epsom. I have been absent about ten days, and letters are not forwarded to me, as I came away in search of thorough mental quietude—a very difficult thing to obtain, at any time, for one of my nervous and impulsive temper. I went first of all to my people at Wakefield, and stayed a week; then, as the weather was promising, I came on into Wales; and here I am in a little hotel, in a very little town, seven miles beyond the last railway station. The scenery is glorious: a fine shore, and noble mountains for the near background. Such a place as this I wanted to find for use in my new book, and there, I hope, you will some day read a fuller description.[555] The London papers arrive here (if specially ordered) at 6.30 in the evening! But no newspaper of any kind can be purchased here. So for a little I forget the world.

But not you, old friend. I think very often of your book, of which already I have written to several people who are likely to appreciate it. By the bye, I forgot to tell you how glad I was to find poor old *Don*[556] alive once more. You have raised a worthy monument to the good fellow; many people will learn to love him.

You noticed, of course, that Tom Hughes died a few days after the publication of your book.[557] A very curious coincidence. The obituary notices, so far as I have seen them, preserve a discreet silence about "Rugby"; indeed that episode was very little to the poor man's credit.

I shall be here for another day or two, then I return to Wakefield. I dare say I shall be back at Epsom in about a week's time.

As I write, I hear the talk of a lot of men drinking in the next room. They are all Welsh, and it is a strange thing to hear this (to me) unintelligible tongue in my native island. The Welsh language has immense vitality. The people are becoming for the most part bilingual, but they are not likely to forget their Welsh

would be monstrous injustice. Had not this opportunity luckily offered, I should have sent him to strangers. I will not allow him to hear perpetual vilification of his father and all his father's relatives and friends—vilification utterly undeserved in each and every quarter" (To Algernon Gissing, 22 April 1896, Yale). The younger son, Alfred, born on 20 January 1896, remained with his parents.

[555] See *The Whirlpool*, Part the Second, Chap. II.
[556] The collie Bertz had taken to Tennessee with him.
[557] Hughes died 22 March 1896.

for centuries to come. Even in a town such as Liverpool, I am told there are 80,000 Welsh people, all habitually speaking Welsh in their own homes. Children in Wales *never* talk English, except when being taught it in the schools. Strange to think that these people have a better right in England than I have, and that my language is a modern, newfangled thing, compared with theirs.

Every word I wrote about your book was absolutely sincere; I think of it very highly indeed. When you are at peace, let me know what the German critics say.

Ever yours, dear Friend,
GEORGE GISSING

"Nos dawch!" I hear a voice say. It means "good night."

Eversley, / Worple Road, / Epsom.

May 9, 1896.

Dear Friend,

Thank you very much indeed for this picture you have sent. It is a most beautiful view; I wish it were possible for me to see the real thing. Well, some day, perhaps.

You are well out of that hideous neighbourhood from which you have escaped. The people must have been exceptionally vile. I like to think of you resting in the peace of your new home.

It is obvious that you must not bind yourself to any publisher. Our Society of Authors is always warning people not to do that kind of thing.

No, decidedly the *Dresdener Journal* did not in the least understand your *motif*. All that you say about it, I had already said to myself; it is perfectly plain and intelligible to any thoughtful reader. But how very rare it is for a reviewer to give proof of superior intelligence!

Well, I cannot of course speak as to the chances of the book with the German public; though I think it very strange if the publishers do not manage to sell a very good edition. In England, were it the work of an English writer, it most decidedly would have a success, quite independently of the Tom Hughes affair. Now I have spoken to certain people about it, but you cannot imagine how difficult it is to make men here take an interest in any foreign fiction except French and Norwegian. I am universally told that there is no public for translated novels—except those of Zola. But I may have something better to tell you on this point yet.

Zapp and Reissner are men whose good opinions of the literary merit of the book should certainly encourage you. The former was abundantly right in saying that the story is an epitome of human fate. I felt precisely the same thing.

So get on with your new work, and be of good courage.

The strange story about the tobacconist's wife is amusing, but at the same time rather alarming. For heaven's sake don't get involved in domestic tragedies! I hardly think you will find either strength or comfort in such a relation. Strange that you, who so steadfastly avoid disturbances, should be beset by this particular kind of trouble.

I have got to work again, quite seriously, and have done *three Chapters* of my new book, which may perhaps be called "Benedict's Household."[558] The theme is the decay of domestic life among certain classes of people, and much stress is laid upon the question of *children*. I hope to get it all done before the end of the autumn.

The American papers begin to write about me. A man had an interview with me the other day for the *Boston Transcript*.[559] He tells me that I am becoming "popular" over there. All I can say is, that I find no results of it yet. Martial said the same thing:

"Quid prodest? Nescit sacculus ista meus."[560]

The weather is wonderfully fine; it keeps up my spirits.

Ever yours, dear Friend,
GEORGE GISSING

[558] Changed to *The Whirlpool*.

[559] Joseph Anderson, the reporter, wrote a long review of the American edition of *The Unclassed* (New York, 1896), in which he said: "...'The Unclassed' reveals many, we are certain, of the sad and smarting experiences that have been Gissing's own, and there constantly comes through the confounding though pleasant thought that Waymark, the hero, and the interesting sad-eyed man in the portrait in the frontispiece are one and the same" (Boston *Evening Transcript*, 2 July 1896, p. 6).

[560] Martial, *Epigrammatrem*. XI. iii. 6.

Addressed: Herrn Eduard Bertz. / Neue Königstrasse, 71. /
Potsdam. / *Germany.*

Epsom.

May 20th. 1896.

Will you kindly get me (if possible) some information about
the terms and conditions of study at the *School* of *Music* at München.[561] No hurry. (I wish it particularly to be München.) I suppose
girls can attend there?

Also, please tell me how a boy would say in idiomatic German:
"An English gentleman, who speaks very funny German."[562]
I hope all goes well. Am working hard.

Yours ever,

G. G.

Epsom.

May 28. 1896.

Dear Friend,

I am very sorry indeed that I left your question about the
Hughes family unanswered. I think, in your position, I should
simply refrain from all mention of the book. It was your right to
write it, and it is public property; but it would not be in good
taste to speak of it, either one way or another, to Hughes's relatives. And you are not likely, I should think, to have much com-

---

[561] GRG was collecting material for *The Whirlpool*, in which the heroine
attends a Munich music school.

[562] Bertz translated the phrase as, "Ein Engländer, glaub' ich, und ein
schnurriges Deutsch ist's, das er verbricht!" (*The Whirlpool*, Lawrence and
Bullen, 2nd. ed., 1897, p. 69). When Bertz read the novel, he wrote to
GRG: "your treatment, the invention, the characters, the style, all is
masterly," but added, "I am less satisfied with my own part in the performance, indeed, I regret that you omitted to tell me the exact sentences
that went before the German words. As you spoke of a boy only, I had
imagined him to be of about fourteen. Now I find he is 'a little boy', which
means about nine years, I suppose; and in the mouth of such a little fellow
the word 'verbricht' is not childlike enough. Besides, I did not know that
the scene took place at Munich. If you meant to give the conversation in
the idiom in which it was spoken, you ought to have used the Bavarian
dialect which has a very distinct colour of its own. But these are things
which no English reader, at any rate, will notice" (E. Bertz to GRG
[? April 1897], first draft, Yale).

munication with them. There is nothing in the tone of your book
to make you ashamed; you simply keep silence *out of delicacy.*

These German notices are really excellent. They seem to be
very sincere. I rejoice that they notice the wide application of your
story, and that they speak so emphatically of your admirable
style. Most undoubtedly you have written a masterpiece. Never
mind the cliques; such work as yours can, and will, stand by
itself.

Very good, that again a story is finished. Boys' books are a
speciality of yours; you excel in that kind of writing, also.
Wonderful, this command over two such different styles. Get this
little book published quickly.

Hearty thanks for the German sentence, and for the trouble you
are taking about München. My book is a laborious one, but I
am not ill-pleased with it so far.

Alas! I don't like this behaviour of your mother's. She ought
not to use that tone with you. It is monstrous to press upon
anyone such a dubious experiment as that of marriage. Well,
well; take it quietly.

And bear also with the drawbacks of your house. They are
annoying, but you have made distinctly a change for the better.
And let us hope that better yet may come.

Yes, I quite understand the peculiar beauty of the Havel
scenery.[563] I should glory in those effects of colour. It is vastly
better for you to have this enjoyment than to be locked up in a
great town, where your spirits and health would soon fail. Evidently you are working well, and you may be sure that your book
will yet bring you all sorts of encouragement.

I write quickly and briefly, to answer the Hughes question. All
good be with you! A strange, strange life, this of literature—
isn't it?

Yours ever,
GEORGE GISSING

Apropos—would you *care* to send a copy of "Das Sabinergut"
to *Blackwood's Magazine*? Alone of English magazines it has an
article now and then on German novels. If you would think it
worthwhile to do so, I will joyously recommend the book to the

[563] The Havel river flows past Potsdam.

Editor.[564] Let me know, at your leisure, by postcard. The Magazine is pub[lished] at Edinburgh, Mess. Blackwood and Son—as you probably know.

(Letters are forwarded to me from Epsom)
Mablethorpe. / Lincolnshire.

August 3rd. 1896.

Dear Friend,

It is a long, long time since I wrote to you. The reason has been simply illness and depression and consequent inability to bring myself to anything at all—a curious nullification of the will, more decided than I have ever known. All my serious work has long been at an end. Two months ago I wrote a miserable short story for "Cosmopolis,"[565] and repented as soon as I had sent it; but the price was £20, and I could not afford to lose the money. The thing is so poor and empty, I shall not send it you. I am grievously ashamed to have it put so prominently before the public. Here I am at the sea-side, trying to recover my health. I dare say I shall stay for another week, but I find little pleasure. Indeed, every year I feel a most appreciable decline in my powers of enjoyment. Nothing gives me very much pleasure now-a-days, and I look forward to a time of very dreary impassivity.

Great heavens! I believe I never even thanked you for the München prospectus. It served my purpose perfectly.

I am reading your last letter, and with great interest I come upon the instance of artistic self-restraint which you mention. The story is very striking indeed, and of course you are entirely right about it. Yes, art must be typical; it does not deal in isolated manifestations—at all events, not in such as suggest a moral inference.

You mention Dowden's[566] address on Goethe. It excited universal surprise and indignation in England, and Dowden wrote to the papers, to say that these were not his *own* opinions, but

---

[564] William Blackwood (1836–1912). The novel was not reviewed in the magazine.

[565] "A Yorkshire Lass," III (August 1896), 309–26.

[566] Edward Dowden (1843–1913), professor of literature at Trinity College, Dublin, was president of the English Goethe Society at this time.

that speaking to a Goethe Society, he had deliberately taken the part of *advocatus diaboli*, for the sake of giving start to discussion. I suppose this explanation must be believed. For my own part, I need not tell you how utterly at variance I am with such a point of view. Goethe will of course always be one of my gods; most undoubtedly he had a considerable part in my later education.

Impossible to say anything about my book. I can't imagine when it will be finished, but it *must* be before very long. I have lost heart and hope—at all events for the present.

No doubt you have now finished the revision of your boys' story. I understand very well that you would not like to *devote* yourself to that kind of writing; but I think, also, that you will never wholly abandon it. Your interest in education accounts for your tendency (felt again and again) in that direction.

I do not study, I do not read; I simply loiter and rush and lose the precious weeks. A most grievous state of things; utterly contemptible. I have a suspicion that it is in part due to the relaxing climate of Epsom.

I shall hear from you presently.

Yours ever, dear old Friend,
GEORGE GISSING

Eversley, / Worple Road, / Epsom.

September 27. 1896.

Dear Friend,

Many thanks for the trouble you have taken in spying out those press notices. They are really good. I am so glad to see the stress that is laid upon your language—which shows that you stand out very distinctly, in this particular, among the writers of to-day. And indeed the scope of your artistic intention seems, on the whole, to be very well understood. The *Hamburgische Korrespondent* out to be ashamed of itself for not knowing you already. It is not by any means true that you lack, in the right sense of the words, "das Vermögen einer handlungsreichen Erfindung und straffer Concentration [*sic*]." Not a bit of it. Indeed, as for "Concentration," your power there I think particularly noticeable. The "Erfindung" that this critic desires, you do not aim at. And surely it is a strange confession to make, that the title did not at once suggest its meaning to him.

But you have every reason to be satisfied, as far as the reviewers are concerned. I wish you could hear good reports of the sale. And I still think you ought to send a copy to *Blackwood*, and let me write to the Editor about it.

I grieve to hear of your serious disappointment in your house, and I think with dread of your passing a long, hard winter amid such wretched surroundings. This question of housing is terrible, and so much depends on it. For heaven's sake don't allow yourself to get a severe cold, owing to draughts or dampness.

Yes, I am working very hard indeed, and I have written about 1/3 of my long book.[567] It *must* be finished before the end of this year. I don't think it will be altogether bad, and there is a most grave purpose in it. I write slowly, and have to re-write, and re-re-write, alas! I often marvel at my own stubborn patience. But it certainly does not surpass—nay, it does not equal,—your own.

A great row is going on here about the Armenians.[568] My chief interest in the matter is to observe a bit of medieval history going on in our own days. I wonder whether we shall live to see Constantinople pass out of the hands of the Turks. That would be the end of a long chapter in history, indeed. I have not yet lost hope of some day seeing Byzantium; it would be a pity if things went so rapidly that the Ottoman chapter had closed before I got there. Ah, there are grievous troubles ahead, I greatly fear.

Well, we have no part in them. Our business is to watch, and to picture—or at least to meditate; above all, to keep our heads above the dust.

Yours always heartily, dear Friend,
GEORGE GISSING

Addressed: Herrn Eduard Bertz. / Neue Königstrasse 71. / Potsdam. / *Germany.*

October 4. 1896.

I have written to the Editor of *Blackwood*, telling him to expect

---

[567] *The Whirlpool* was finished on 18 December 1896 (Diary).

[568] In August 1896 the Turks began a three day massacre of the Armenians. The European ambassadors forced the Turks to halt the persecution, but it precipitated a European crisis, for Britain threatened to turn her naval guns on Constantinople, in which case the Russians planned to seize the city and the Dardanelles.

a copy.[569] Will let you know what he replies. Think seriously of that project of removal to domestic surroundings.

Am working furiously.

Yours always,
G. G.

Epsom.

October 9. 1896.

Dear Friend,

I send you Blackwood's reply to me.[570] Of course do not return it. Many thanks for your last letter.

I am just about *half* through my book. It may possibly be called "The Whirlpool"—for it deals with the morbid activity of money-getters and pleasure-seekers. When you write again, tell me how this name strikes you.

Alas, the winter comes! For heaven's sake keep warm and well.

Ever yours,
GEORGE GISSING

Eversley, / Worple Road, / Epsom.

December 6. 1896.

Dear Friend,

One more week (or ten days at most) will, I think, see the end of my book. It has been a wretched struggle with ill health and evil circumstances;[571] but I have put into this novel a great deal that I really wanted to say, and that is always a satisfaction. I am afraid my health is getting to be a rather serious question, for I have had a bad cough for a long time, and now, in this vile weather, it is getting worse. When my work is done, I shall have a consultation with a doctor, and ascertain, once for all, what really is the matter with me.

But I feel ashamed to complain, when I think of the difficulties and hardships of every kind which you are facing. Evidently you are quite justified in your bitter feeling against the so-called critics.

[569] Of *Das Sabinergut*.

[570] GRG's note is written on the back of Blackwood's letter. See Appendix I.

[571] His troubles with Edith had increased to the point where he was determined to leave her.

The Neumann-Hofer story is of course very disgraceful.[572] Well, one can only pay as little attention as is possible to what these creatures say and do. They have a certain power, unfortunately; but I should not think they are able really to kill a book, which has in it the vital principle. As to Blackwood, I am of course unable to say who will read, or review, *Das Sabinergut* for him. My connexion with him is very slight, not at all personal. I can only *hope* there will be an honest notice.

Your letter from the Secretary of the Gesellschaft für Verbreitung von Volksbildung,[573] on the other hand, is greatly encouraging. Do not lose sight of this pleasanter aspect of things.

If you do indeed abandon all thought of pleasing the public, (not that you have ever much thought of it,) the probability is that your books will be more than ever read. I believe that success comes, and comes only, of writing from one's own mind. Even the *foolish* books that succeed are strongly marked by the foolish personality of their authors. There is no such thing as getting a public by *trying* to do so. But indeed, you have never prostituted your mind in that way.

I never see *Cosmopolis*, so did not read George Moore's article.[574] He is a most superficial man, whether as artist or critic. I quite agree with you in what you say of Stevenson.

Sometimes I wish for a little of the solitude of which *you* are so weary. I am beginning to know almost too many people; it threatens my leisure and quietness of thought. Except Kipling, I have now met every English writer of any standing, and with several of them I am on very good terms. I have found *Barrie*[575]

---

[572] Otto Neumann-Hofer, literary critic and editor of the Berliner *Tageblatt*. He had written an unsympathetic review of *Das Sabinergut*.

[573] Founded in 1871 to establish and foster popular libraries and community cultural centers.

[574] "Since the Elizabethans," *Cosmopolis*, IV (October 1896), 42–58. Moore said R. L. Stevenson was a graceful writer, but all he could do was to "compose pretty sentences on the subject of the colour of the seas and trees, to skim the surface of any secondary emotion" (p. 43). Bertz admired Stevenson, but GRG was not enthusiastic about his work or his personality. Later, he admitted to himself that he had once been jealous of Stevenson.

[575] Whom he met at an Omar Khayyám dinner on 20 June 1896 (*Letters*, p. 348). He described Barrie as "a very little, boyish fellow, without hint of ability, but simple and genial" (To Algernon Gissing, 23 June 1896, Yale).

are [sic] very genial fellow. There is a new man called *Wells*, whom I like very much. He has gone through great miseries, and declares that "New Grub Street" gives an absolute picture of his circumstances at one time; oddly enough, even the name of his wife was "Amy"—the same as that of Mrs Reardon.[576]

I long to have written my last line, that I may turn to something new.

> Yours ever, dear Friend,
> GEORGE GISSING

4 West End Villas. / Budleigh Salterton / Devon.

February 23. 1897.

Dear Friend,

This [sic] have been bad with me.[577] At last a medical friend took me to see a great London doctor, and he, a week ago, said I must at once go to the south coast of Devon or Cornwall. There is a decided weakness in one lung, and it was dangerous for me to remain at Epsom.

So here I am. But already I cough less, and have a better appetite. I shall probably stay here until the summer.

But your letter inspirits me. I am delighted to hear of this philosophical work, and of the quiet mind it has given you. The subject is *most* interesting, and your views will be valuable. Confound this eternal necessity of moving about! Is there really no possibility of getting a fixed abode?

[576] At the Omar Khayyám dinner on 20 November 1896, GRG was introduced to H. G. Wells. Mrs. Wells was Amy Catherine Robbins, his second wife, who had been a student in Wells's geology class in 1892. They lived together as man and wife for a few years and then married in 1895, after the first Mrs. Wells had obtained a divorce. See H. G. Wells, *Experiment in Autobiography* (1934).

[577] In a letter to Algernon, GRG said: "As you have guessed, no doubt, I have simply been driven from home—chased away with furious insult. I went first to Harry Hick at Romney. Yesterday, he came up to town with me, and took me to see Dr. Pye Smith, a great doctor. It appears that I have a decided weakness in one lung, just enough to make it dangerous for me to stay here through the spring. I have to go at once to South Devon. Every hope is held out of complete health, if I take care for a while" (17 February 1897, Yale). Dr. Philip Pye-Smith (18?–1914) was consulting physician to Guy's Hospital, London. GRG was suffering from a touch of emphysema, not tuberculosis ("Abstract of Notes by Dr. Henry Hick").

I thoroughly believe that you may not only earn money by philosophical work (of this kind), but I think it very likely that you may make a considerable reputation. You have only to raise your voice. "Herren = und Sklaven-Moral" is a fine title: most attractive. And of course the name of Nietzsche excites universal curiosity nowadays. Do you remember speaking to me about the man long before he became popularly known?

Give this a fair trial. Reissner's opinion (backed by money) is probably shrewd enough. I shall await reports of your progress very eagerly.

I hope to write again soon, when I feel able to give a better account of myself.

Yours ever, old Friend,
GEORGE GISSING

West End Villas, / Budleigh Salterton. / Devon.

April 16. 1897.

Dear Friend,

For many years, now, I have written my books with the consciousness that at all events *one* reader would understand them. Your encouragement is of great importance to me; you always see what I *mean*. Reviewers praise me, but very rarely understand my purpose. For instance, one paper has already said about "The Whirlpool" that it "chiefly tends to show *the importance in life of little things.*" I hope there will be better judgments presently. But thank you heartily for putting aside your own work to read and write about this novel.

I often thought of you surrounded with your 22 packing-cases of books! That is a terrible business. Over now, thank goodness. I am so glad you see your way to get on with philosophical work. (By the bye, I am sure that is a very good remark of yours, in this letter, about Nietzsche.)[578] You must not be hurried, but I shall wait anxiously for the result.

I think I am better in health; my cough is less troublesome.

[578] In his discussion of *The Whirlpool*, Bertz had written: "Several times I was struck with the likeness of the state of things, as you have reported it, to Nietzsche's ideals. For, though he believes himself, and his disciples believe him, to be a preacher *against* our time, in reality he is a mouthpiece of all that is worst in the *actual* tendencies of our present life"; and Bertz also acutely observed: "It is remarkable how greatly you are now inclined to pessimism in your delineation of women and marriage; that makes a

But I cannot climb a hill without terrible shortness of breath.[579] I shall stay here till the end of May, and then see my London doctor again.

At present I am studying the 6th. Century. I find that Gregorovius[580] frequently refers to a "Geschichte des Ostgothischen Reiches" by Manso (Breslau 1824) in 1 Vol.[581] Now, I wonder whether this is obtainable? If, in your intercourse with booksellers, you could hear of a copy at a reasonable price, I would gladly purchase it. I have got Opera Omnia of Cassiodorus;[582] 2 Vols. folio, Venice; and am reading through them with great delight. By the bye, in this edition the author is called Cassiodorius. I wonder how this difference of spelling arises. Nowadays, we always call the man Cassiodorus—do we not?

Everything is looking green now; but there is too much rain and wind for my liking. Yesterday I saw the first swallows. Well, well, I wonder how many more changes of the year I am destined to see. I *hope* for a good many, as I have still a lot of work to do; but I fear the best of life is over.

All good be with you, dear old Friend! I shall not be long before I write again.

Yours ever,
GEORGE GISSING

---

great difference from your earlier books; your realism is much more consistent or at least more pronounced than formerly. You are in no respect 'sicklied o'er' by the foolish affectation now in fashion elsewhere, of symbolism and mysticism. This novel, if any, deserves the praise of thorough honesty and sincerity" (E. Bertz to GRG, ? April 1897, first draft, Yale). See also 20 May 1896.

[579] About GRG's complaint Dr. Hick said: "He complained that he got short of breath when he walked, of course the emphysema would cause this to a certain extent, but as he wore two thickest Jaegar shirts, and a heavy tweed suit, and when he went out put on a muffler and a heavy Inverness cape, this caused the greater part of his difficulty" ("Abstract of Notes by Dr. Henry Hick").

[580] Ferdinand Gregorovius (1821–1891), German historian, author of *Geschichte der Stadt Rom im Mittelalter* (8 vols., Stuttgart, 1859–72).

[581] Johann Kaspar Friedrich Manso (1760–1826), *Geschichte des ostgothischen Reiches in Italien.*

[582] Flavius Magnus Aurelius Cassiodorus Senator (c. 490–c. 585), Italian historian, statesman, and monk, author of historical, political, theological, and grammatical works. He was a Syrian whose family held important civic posts in Scyllacium (now Squillace).

West End Villas. / Budleigh Salterton / Devon.

May 9. 1897.

Dear Friend,

Heartiest thanks to you for sending this admirable book![583] I see at a glance it is just what I wanted. A note informs me: "Die Handschriften schwanken zwischen Cassio*dorus* und Cassio-dor*ius*," which sets my mind at rest.

Now, you will of course let me know the price of the volume. As I might possibly have to ask you to use the same kindness in procuring one or two other German books, we must of course regard this as purely a matter of business. Please send a *postcard*. And—again to trouble you—will you kindly add upon that post-card; (1) the address of Tauchnitz (2) the proper way of writing to the firm—I mean, how to style them on the envelope, and how to begin the letter to them. For I am going to try to persuade them to take "The Whirlpool."[584] You will be glad to hear that it is selling far better than any other book of mine. The first edition of 2000 copies is just being exhausted, and a second 2000 is in the press.[585] Moreover, 1500 copies were printed for Australia.

I think I progress in health. At the end of this month, I shall go up to London, and see my doctor again.

In spite of hindrances, I doubt not that you are working on. Remember that, if you *can* complete your Nietzsche speedily, the present time is very opportune.

Always yours, dear Friend,
GEORGE GISSING

Addressed: Herrn Eduard Bertz. / Neue Königstrasse, 21. / Potsdam. / *Germany*.

[May 17, 1897][586]

Williams and Norgate[587] tell me that you need *not* re-purchase "Data of Ethics."[588] It constitutes Part I of the 1st. Vol. of "Principles."[588] You can procure:

[583] Manso's history.
[584] Tauchnitz did not accept the novel.
[585] Published in May 1897.
[586] Postmark.
[587] A London publishing house.
[588] Herbert Spencer; *Data of Ethics* came out in 1879; *Principles of Ethics* was published in 2 vols., 1892–93.

Parts II and III (price together 7 shillings)
and: Volume II (price 12 shillings 6 pence)
But only a limited number of Parts II and III were printed, and
only a few are left.
I will send Symonds's "Whitman"[589] very soon.

G. G.

Shall return to Epsom at end of May.

Addressed: Herrn Eduard Bertz. / Neue Königstrasse, 21. /
Potsdam. / *Germany.*
Epsom.

[June 9]
May 10th. 1897.[590]

Am sending "Walt Whitman." The doctor reports improvement,[591] and I shall work on hopefully. Will write at length very
soon. Am trying to get a little book done before the end of July.[592]

Yours,
G. G.

Addressed: Herrn Eduard Bertz. / Neue Königstrasse, 21. /
Potsdam. / *Germany.*
Epsom.

June 13. 1897.

I have been startled to learn that there is a German novel dealing
with the Ostrogoths, viz. "Der Kampf um Rom," by Felix
Dahn.[593] I can get this from a library, and shall read it soon. But,
after all, I feel sure that my own idea will be different; for I mean

---

[589] John Addington Symonds, *Walt Whitman: a Study* (London, 1893).
[590] A mistake in the month and day. "June" has been written beneath it
in Bertz's hand. The postmark reads June 9.
[591] Dr. Pye-Smith examined GRG on 1 June and ordered him to leave
London and to settle "anywhere in pure air provided it be on chalk or
sand" (GRG to Dr. Harry Hick, 2 June 1897, Yale).
[592] *The Town Traveller* (London: Methuen and Co., 1898). GRG had
started to write this novel on 8 June (Diary).
[593] Four vols., Leipzig, 1876–78. Dahn (1834–1912) was a classical historian. His *Prokopios von Cäsarea* was published in 1865, and *Die Könige
der Germanen,* in 20 vols., was brought out between 1861 and 1911.

18

to take the conflict between Christian ideals and the old Roman spirit; not the political question *as such*.

When you write again (no hurry) you might mention whether you have read Dahn, and whether his book is well known. He is the historian, the author of "Prokopios von Cäsarea," and "Die Könige der Germanen"—is he not? "Pereant qui ante nos nostra dixerunt!"[594]

Yours,
G. G.

Eversley, / Worple Road, / Epsom.

June 15. 1897.

My Dear Friend,

Thanks for your illustrated post card—a pretty idea.

I should be very glad to see the *Berliner Tageblatt*, as I cannot imagine how I come to be there.

I only sat to Rothenstein[595] the other day, and I think it will be some months before the publication of the portrait. But of course I shall give myself the pleasure of sending you a copy. I think it will be cleverly done. Rothenstein, a very young man, is well acquainted with the French artists and literary men. He used to live with Verlaine, for a time—hardly an enviable privilege, I should think.

"La Revanche d'Eve"—so the translator entitles "Eve's Ransom"—is announced to appear shortly in the *Revue de Paris*.[596] It seems strange to see my name in a list of Frenchmen—Daudet etc.

I am working very fruitfully at the 6th. Century, and have a glorious idea for a *novel*!!! I really think I begin to know that period. But it is a dead secret; I should not dare to mention such a purpose, till it was carried out. I am reading books by the score. Have gone most carefully, pen in hand, through the XII Books

[594] Not identified.

[595] William Rothenstein (1872–1945), noted portrait painter. Thomas Hardy had urged him to ask GRG to pose for his portrait, and the first sketch was made on 7 June 1897 (Wm. Rothenstein, *Men and Memories*, New York, 1931, I, 302). Of the two poses, one sitting, the other standing, GRG chose the latter.

[596] Georges Art translated the novel, which was finally published under the title *La Rançon d'Ève* from 1 April 1898 to 15 May 1898.

Variarum, of Cassiodorus—no slight work, as the Latin is difficult. I am now busy with topographers—Lanciani[597] especially. Gregorovius is of course of great help.

This is the outcome of a desire I have nursed for ten years.

At the same time I am writing a short story to be finished by end of July[598]—out of which I hope to make money.

I fear you are now beginning to suffer from the heat. Here it is tremendous. Of course I shall avoid all the Jubilee uproar.[599] London is hidden under wooden structures—a strange sight. Your work proceeds well, I hope. It is a great pleasure to me to know that you are absorbed in a subject that really suits you.

Hearty good wishes. Try—do try—to get some fresh air this summer.

> Ever yours, old Friend,
> GEORGE GISSING

No reply yet from Tauchnitz.

Castle Bolton / Seyburn, / Yorkshire.

August 19. 1897.

My dear Friend,

This is the fourth week that I have been living in Wensleydale— the finest of the Yorkshire dales. It is the valley of the River Ure (or Yore), in the north of the county. The bracing air of the hills and moorland seems to have done me much good. I shall be here till the end of August; then back to Epsom for September; then— I don't know the next step, except that it must be to a place where I can work hard.[600]

---

[597] Rodolfo Amadeo Lanciani (1846?–1929), archeologist, was professor of ancient topography at the University of Rome, and the author of several volumes on the history, life, and ruins of ancient Rome.

[598] *The Town Traveller* was finished on 14 July.

[599] Queen Victoria's Diamond Jubilee was celebrated in the summer of 1897.

[600] About the middle of June 1897 GRG had gone back to Edith, who was still in Epsom. At the end of July they moved to Yorkshire, as Dr. Pye-Smith had ordered. The Diary indicates that their life was as miserably unhappy as it had been when GRG fled from Edith in February. After a little family outing, GRG noted in the Diary: "Of course every thing spoilt by E.'s frenzy of ill temper. I merely note the fact, lest anyone reading this should be misled, and imagine a day of real enjoyment" (21 August 1897).

You, meanwhile, have been suffering both on your own account and that of others. A grievous catalogue, you send me! The only good to be seen in this broken time is that it *may* have benefited your health somewhat. Certainly your long walks must have been good for you. You are quite right to flee from the present impossible abode, and also quite right, I think, to warehouse your furniture. You will then feel really at liberty to look about.

As you are with Rehfeldt, I beg you to give him my kind regards, and the expression of my sincere sympathy with his sufferings in health. I hope he is now—as they say in Yorkshire—*mending*.

My "biography" of Dickens is not really to be a biography at all; the newspaper paragraph was misleading. I have simply undertaken to write a very small volume on Dickens, an "appreciation," for a series dealing with Victorian matters.[601] The editor is an old college-fellow of mine.[602] And in truth I shall enjoy the task; what is more, I shall enjoy sending the little book to *you*. It is to be finished by the end of the year.

The historical novel will involve a great deal of reading. Lecky[603] —whom you mentioned—I had already read with much care; he is very useful for that period. The "Kampf um Rom" I have also read, and find it will not affect my plans at all; for it deals with the *whole* of the Ostrogothic monarchy, and is written in an Epic way. Moreover, I am astonished at the liberties which Dahn has taken with history,—positive misrepresentations, here and there, for a romantic purpose.

I am just busy with a delightful book, Lenormant's "La Grande-Grèce."[604] I meant only to study the pages relating to the country of Cassiodorus, but find I must read it all. Of course it brings back to me my own days in Calabria.

What you say about the *Athenaeum* is only too true. I have read the paper for many years, and have often smiled at these

---

[601] *Charles Dickens: A Critical Study* (London: Blackie & Son, 1898).

[602] John Holland Rose (1855–1942) went on to Christ College, Cambridge, from Owens College. He was a university extension lecturer and in 1897 became editor of Blackie and Son's Victorian Era Series.

[603] William Edward Lecky (1838–1903), Irish historian and essayist. GRG probably had read Lecky's *History of European Morals from Augustus to Charlemagne* (2 vols., 1869).

[604] Three vols., Paris, 1881–84.

ridiculous incongruities. (By the bye, how did you like their notice of "The Whirlpool"?[605] Did you think it adequate?) These people are directed almost entirely by the personal bias of the moment— a very gross state of things for a *soi-disant* leading organ of criticism. As for Theodore Watts (he has lately added Dunton to his name),[606] my feeling about him is precisely yours. An essentially contemptible fellow—monstrously egotistic. For twenty years he has lived with Swinburne, and to Swinburne's glory he mainly devotes himself. Once I saw him at a public dinner, and found him a creature of dull, stolid aspect.

You shall hear of my arrival at Epsom. I *think* I shall manage to live through the winter in the neighbourhood of London, but the fact remains that I still have a slight cough—so things may turn out otherwise than I hope.

Indeed, I shall be heartily glad when you are released from that dreadful house of uproar.

Yours ever, dear Friend,
GEORGE GISSING

Eversley, / Worple Road, / Epsom.

September 13. 1897.

Dear old Friend,

I am sending news which will surprise (but not astonish) you. Rather suddenly, I have decided to go to Italy for the whole of the winter. I leave England on September 22nd.

My motives are several.[607] First of all, though my health seems greatly improved, I still have a little cough, and I want, if possible,

---

[605] "Mr. Gissing has often hesitated in his stories between the commonplace and the impassioned; yet even when he was most commonplace it has been easy to perceive how closely and faithfully he can reproduce the phenomena which have passed before his eyes, and how conscientiously he strives to place upon his canvas the figures and expressions which attract him. . . . But he shows a distinct advance in his art" (*Athenaeum*, 24 April 1897, p. 536).

[606] Theodore Watts-Dunton (1832–1914) added the surname of his mother, Susannah Dunton, to his in 1896. GRG met Watts-Dunton at the Omar Khayyám dinner on 13 July 1895.

[607] The most important one was that he felt he had to get far away from Edith, from whom he had again fled. His son Walter was still at Wakefield, and Alfred, the baby, was with Edith in London lodgings.

to get rid of this altogether. Secondly, I am weary, for the time, of England, and long unutterably for the glorious warmth and colour of the south. Thirdly, it is clear to me that my historical novel[608] will benefit greatly by studies made on the spot.

My plan is this. As I have promised to finish the little book on Dickens by the end of November, I go first of all to Siena—a tranquil place, which will not excite me, and where I can work steadily day after day. This task will, I hope, be finished in time to leave me a month or six weeks of fine autumn weather, and this I shall use in a journey of serious purpose. From Siena I go by rail to Rome, and from Rome I shall travel by carriage along the Via Appia, through Terracina, and turn off at length to Monte Cassino, where I hope to lodge for a day or two in the monastery of my old friend St. Benedict. Thence, to Naples, where I have to call upon Marion Crawford, the novelist, (he lives at Sorrento,) who, I hope, will give me letters of introduction to useful people in Calabria. Thus furnished, I take ship at Naples (the Messina steamer) for *Paola*, on the Calabrian coast, where these steamers call. (This is the town of S. Francesco di Paola, you know.) Thence I can travel by diligence, across the mountains, to Cosenza, where Alaric died. Here I touch the railway again, and with its help I mean to explore all (or nearly all) Magna Graecia, which may possibly yield me material for a book of travel-sketches. The Editor of the *Daily Chronicle*[609] has asked me to send him anything I think likely to suit the paper. I shall buy photographs, and make rough drawings, for the illustration of my proposed book.[610]

When really cold weather comes, I go back to Rome, and there make good use of the libraries for two or three months.

Now, does all this take away your breath? You see, I have come to the moment in my life when I must make a new start, intellectually and commercially. I *feel* that I am doing the right thing. Let me hear from you that you approve my projects.

A safe address for several weeks will be: Poste restante, Siena.

Of course I shall think of you much and constantly. You

---

[608] *Veranilda* (London: Constable, 1904). Published posthumously.

[609] H. W. Massingham (1860–1924).

[610] *By the Ionian Sea* (London: Chapman and Hall, 1901). The illustrations for the volume, based on GRG's sketches, were done by Leo De Littrow in color and in black and white.

shall hear from me often—if it is only a postcard. In returning to Italy, I am going *home* once more.

I hope you have enjoyed your stay with Rehfeldt. Do find a pleasant home before next summer, and then let me *come to see you*!

Wherever I am, you know me

Yours ever,

GEORGE GISSING

A copy of my "Human Odd and Ends" (short stories) shall be sent to you on its publication in the autumn.[611]

Addressed: Herrn Eduard Bertz. / Neue Königstrasse, 21 / Potsdam. / *Germania.*
Via delle Belle Arti, 18. / 30. piano. / Siena.

October 3. 1897.

Doubtless you received the illustrated cards from Göschenen, and from Milan. Shall send you some more later. I am very com-fortably settled with an Italian family, and am hard at work on my little Dickens book—very anxious to get it finished, and to think of other things. Siena is very quiet; of course of purely medieval interest. Last Sunday I saw the *head* of S. Caterina, exhibited for the benefit of a pilgrimage. Very impressive and strange—of course an undoubted relic.

I hope all goes well with you. It has been unendurably hot here; now the weather is cloudy and cooler.

Mil bei ricardi del amico tuo.[612]

G. G.

Siena. / *Via Franciosa, 8.*

October 29. 1897.

Dear Friend,

That I may not forget it, let me say at once that I received your illustrated post-card, in England, all right—with nothing extra to pay. The cards here at Siena are very poor, but I shall send you one before I leave.

---

[611] *Human Odds and Ends: Stories and Sketches* (London: Lawrence and Bullen, November 1897).

[612] "A thousand greetings from your friend."

Well now, I have had a rather troublesome time. About a week after I got into this house, I found that the landlady's husband was lying very ill,—they had not told me; he had been paralyzed for more than a year. A week later, he died. It was very painful, for this family was once rich, and is now falling into sad poverty. The man being dead and buried, they decided at once to go to a smaller flat, and the removal soon began. To-night I am writing for the last time in my old room; to-morrow I shall be at the new address—with which I head this letter. To be sure, I have had some new insight into Italian private life, and so far it was good; but I found it hard to get on with my work.

Notwithstanding, more than 3/4 of the Dickens book is done, and I really think it rather good. I have hope of being able to leave Siena on the 10th. of November, and I shall go straight to Naples, there to see Marion Crawford, and get letters of intro-duction for Calabria. I shall have to be very careful in the south. The newspapers make it clear that there is a good deal of bri-gandage now. But of course I shall do nothing foolish.

As for the noise of Italian towns; why yes, the silence of Siena is only comparative. There is much shouting and howling goes on day and night, and the carts make a great row in the narrow streets between the high houses. The country round about is *not* very interesting. I am sure many parts of Germany are much more beautiful. The hills (except a glimpse of the distant Apennines) have no beauty of form, and very little of colour. I feel a great desire to get away to the glorious south.

Living entirely with Italians, I make good progress with the language. I work, in thought, now and then at my historical novel. By the bye, when I said just now that I should go straight to Naples, I forgot that I am going to stop on the way, at Monte Cassino, where I hope to spend two nights in the Monastery. It will bring me nearer to old Benedict.

The paragraph from the *Potsdamer Zeitung* interested me very much. It was a daring thing to do, in your doubtful state of health. I hope you have got over the cold that followed. Indeed it is remarkable that you should so often have saved lives in this way.[613] I fancy very few people incur the trouble—and the danger.

[613] Bertz had apparently saved someone from drowning, and the rescue must have been reported in the Potsdam paper. In June 1880, when he was

It shows a great deal of moral and physical courage, undoubtedly.

I am distressed to know of your ceaseless trouble from noise. Ah! if you could but get a quiet abode!

The notice in the *Nord-Deutsche Allgemeine Zeitung* is very curious; I do not quite understand their point of view after all. But how absurdly late to review the book![614] Of course I am in perfect sympathy with your views as to treatment of the commonplace in art. *Your* way of treating it was anything but common, and this ought to be obvious to everybody. Well, well; it seems that the only way to achieve popular success is to keep on publishing incessantly, year after year, till you have forced people to know you. I confess I shall regret it if you never write another novel. But I am so anxious for the other work, too.

That man Lanzky[615] must be very interesting. By the bye, when I am at Rome, in the winter, I should like, if possible, to see Gabriele D'Annunzio.[616] He has a plan for establishing a theatre on the shores of the Lake of Albano, and is at present living there.

Ah, but Italy is in a bad state. Things cannot go on long like this. The country seems to be all but bankrupt, and I am afraid it contains very few honest men.

I shall send you a card before I leave here. Meanwhile—

> Ever yours, dear Friend,
> GEORGE GISSING

---

living in Middlesex, England, Bertz had rescued a boy from the river, Lea; GRG sent an account of the rescue to his sisters: "The other day a friend of mine was walking by the side of a river, where there were some boys bathing. One of these boys was at a little distance from the others, and my friend noticing something curious about him, soon saw that he was on the point of being drowned. Without waiting to throw away his hat and take off his gloves, at once he jumped into the river and succeeded in swimming to land with the half-drowned boy! I should like to have seen him as he walked home; he must have looked remarkably like a water-rat on its hind legs" (*Letters*, 20 June 1880, p. 75).

[614] *Das Sabinergut.*

[615] Paul Lanzky (1852–?), German critic, novelist, poet, and philosopher, who was living in Vallombrosa, Tuscany. Most of his work was published in Italian under the pseudonym of Panta Lambda.

[616] There is no record of a meeting between GRG and D'Annunzio (1863–1938).

Cotrone.
(i.e. *Croton.*)

December 2. 1897.

Dear Friend,

I have had a disagreeable experience—several days of illness here at old Croton. It is a terribly unhealthy place, and in my wanderings I got a fever, which complicated itself with a little lung-congestion. I have been in bed for five days, and have just risen for the first time. A bad place to be ill in! The doctor—a kind, genial fellow—ordered me (on the first day of fever) to eat a *bistecca* with a glass of Marsala!! Of course *bistecca* = beefsteak, and is always horribly tough. I managed to escape this ordeal, (which might have been fatal), and have since persuaded the good doctor (whose name is Sculco) that my peculiar constitution demands quite original treatment. I rapidly recuperate, as you know, and there is now little fever left. But it *might* have been a bad business. For the people here belong to the middle ages, in every sense of the word.[617]

I am very anxious to get away to Catanzaro, for that is situated 1500 ft above the sea, and is altogether more civilized. Here the food is very bad. One can only get milk of goats—generally high-flavoured; and sour butter made of it. The only eatable thing I have found at Cotrone is a melon.

The town stands on the site of the old Acropolis, jutting out into the sea. There are no ruins whatever of the city; only one column standing of the great temple of Hera on the Lacinian Promontory—you can see it from here, 5 miles distant.

I suffer (not only now, but always) from most troublesome *thirst*. It is poisonous to drink water, and there is really nothing to be had in these towns which will quench one's thirst.

I hope to be able to leave in two days. My hand is getting shaky, and I must not write more.

Yours ever, dear Friend,
GEORGE GISSING

[617] See *By the Ionian Sea*, Chapters VII to XI, for an extended description of Cotrone and his illness.

Addressed: Herrn Eduard Bertz. / Neue Königstrasse, 21. / Potsdam / *Germania.*

Catanzaro

December 9. 1897.

Hearty thanks for the interesting quotation in your letter. Card also received—wonderfully artistic. No illustrated cards are obtainable in Calabria—not even any photographs. Here at Catanzaro—in the glorious mountain air—I have quite recovered my health. Wonderful place! In a day or two I go on to *Squillace* (dear old Cassiodorus!) and then to Reggio. But you had better address: Ferma in posta / ROMA where I hope to be in about 10 days' time. There is no snow here yet; indeed, the climate of Catanzaro seems pleasanter in every way than that of towns along the coast. This is not an ancient city; it was founded in early middle ages. But in some of the villages round about, the people *still speak a sort of Greek,* and are called "i Greci." Their origin, of course, is Byzantine, not classic.

Shall be delighted to receive the *Preussische Jahrbücher,*[618] but I don't like you to have the expense.

Terrible days at Cotrone! And worse nights.

Yours ever,
G. G.

Good news about your book. Let me hear more at Rome.

Addressed: Herrn Eduard Bertz. / Neue Königstrasse, 21. / Potsdam. / Germania.

Cassino

December 15, 1897.

I passed last night in the great Monastery, on the mountain.[619]

---

[618] Containing an article, "Trunksucht, ein Symptom," by Sidney Whitman, who wrote: "Vor allen Dingen ist es doch die erste Aufgabe des phantasievollen Schriftstellers, zu fühlen und zu erkennen, was in der Luft liegt. So haben wir George Gissing, den Novellisten, der vielleicht von allen gegenwärtigen Schriftstellern hier am klarsten sieht—Erscheinung, Ursache und Wirkung. Kein Wunder, dass er skeptisch und verzagt auf die zum Gebrauch fix und fertigen Heilmittel blickt" (XC, September 1897, 421).

[619] Monte Cassino, built on a hill west of the town of Cassino, was founded in 529 by St. Benedict. GRG used the monastery as a setting in Chapters XXIV–XXVII of *Veranilda.*

Indescribable; I had no idea of it before. Unfortunately, no sun; heavy mist over the valley of the *Liris* (taciturnus amnis). But this was characteristic of old Casinum, so I do not grumble. Am delighted to have seen both Cassino and Squillace—the materials for my book are getting rich and abundant.

I leave this evening for Rome. Address: poste restante.

G. G.

Addressed: Herrn Eduard Bertz. / Neue Königstrasse, 21 / Potsdam. / *Germania.*
Via del Boschetto, 41. A. / Roma.

December 18. 1897.

Many thanks for your kind letter. All seems well with me again. A glorious journey, and it will make a good little book. I have a comfortable room here, and by straining from window can just see the Colosseum; I am on the north slope of the Collis Viminalis. Delighted to hear of your work. Shall soon write at length.

G. G.

Via del Boschetto, 41. A. / Roma.

January 13. 1898.

Dear Friend,

It is a very long time since I wrote you another more than a hasty card. Your letter to-day reproaches me. Hearty thanks for all the kind things you say about my short stories. They were all published in periodicals, but I had such a poor opinion of them, I never troubled to send them to you. I don't know what the papers are saying about them, and indeed don't care.

Unfortunately, I have been obliged to call upon several people in Rome, to whom I was introduced by London friends. And of course these are rich, aristocratic men and women, for whom I care very little. They waste my time. Why can one *never* find interesting people living in a poor way! Of course there are plenty of them; but for some years now I have never met with that kind of creature. I am always mixed up with wealth and fashion—and in the end, I suppose, it will become my natural atmosphere, in spite of my own poverty.

I could do with a little more money, to tell the truth. And it surprises me that my books do not sell better. Every month I have two or three letters from strangers, English or American; so it is plain that the books are extensively read. But the publishers' account is *nil*—after the first half-year. This means that I have to keep writing, writing, when I should like to rest. I have nothing to fall back upon.

Is it not a strange thing how a certain subject (artistic) is taken up by several men at the same time? I have heard of someone in England who is going to make a novel or a play out of the Ostrogothic story, and now an advertisement tells me that Sudermann has written a play—"Tejas"—on the last King of the Goths.[620] For my own part, I am reading a vast number of very solid books; just as if I were going to write a history of the 6th. Century. I work here at the Bibliotheca Vittorio Emanuele—a good library. At the same time I have to get my little travel-book written. So that my hands are full.

I did not tell you much about my experiences in the south, because you will read of it much better in the printed narrative.

My "Dickens" comes out on February 15. Of course you shall have a copy.

Your troubles have my fullest sympathy. I wish to Heaven some quiet and sympathetic people would take that empty flat. I suppose it is almost an impossible thing to happen. Yet there *might* come a decent—even an agreeable—family. Thinking of your own difficulties, I feel ashamed of what I have written above —grumbling about money. Of course I understand how difficult it is for you to write stories for money, and at the same time pursue your philosophical work. I don't see the way out of this difficulty; it can only be hoped that time will somehow help.

From the Italian newspapers I learn that old Zola is behaving in rather a fine way about that Dreyfus business.[621] He has courage.

---

[620] *Morituri (Drei Einakter: Teja—Fritzchen—Das Ewig-Männliche)* (Stuttgart, 1897).

[621] Alfred Dreyfus had been tried and convicted on 22 December 1894, but the case was still very much alive. Dreyfus's brother Mathieu had accused Esterhazy, a French army officer, of writing the treasonable papers. The French general staff protected Esterhazy, who was tried by a military court and acquitted. Then on 13 January, Zola published an open letter,

Certain it is—whatever be the truth—that the French nation is making a very base and disgusting figure before the world.

Every Sunday morning I give myself a holiday, and take a long walk. I am exploring the Caelian and the Aventine. These parts of Rome, in their utter quietness, contrast very pleasantly with the roar of modern life elsewhere. On the Aventine there are very few buildings; most of the land is cultivated. The Caelian, too, is most covered with gardens. I like to go to the church of S. Gregorio, which stands on the site of the house where Gregory the Great lived as a boy. Of course I am searching out all the oldest churches in Rome. Most of them are closed all the year round, except on the *festa*—the Saint's day.

To tell you the truth, I begin to know something about the 6th. century. I am now reading Dahn's "Prokopios von Cäsarea." Dahn is much better as a historian than as a novelist. His "Kampf um Rom" disappointed me extremely. He has taken astonishing liberties with history, and, to my mind, utterly fails to reproduce the time.

A delightful book is Giannone's "Storia del Regno di Napoli"[622] —including classical times. This book was *burnt* at Rome, soon after its publication, in the last century.

That reminds me; I have been to see the statue of Giordano Bruno, in the Campo dei Fiori. It is raised on the spot where Bruno was burnt—*"dove il rogo arse."*[623] Strange thoughts, as one stands there. Oh, what a terrible, and what a hateful thing, history is—from one side!

Very fine, warm weather here now. No need of fires. Windows open all day long.

But, alas! in Rome there is no music. Indeed, I am convinced that there is less music everywhere in Italy than there used to be. Naples is altering very much; since I first saw it, nine years ago, I note very great changes in the life of the city. The Italian nation

---

"J'accuse," in *L'Aurore*, which charged the general staff with obstructing justice and falsely condemning Dreyfus. Zola was brought to trial for his accusations on 23 February 1898, and was condemned to a year's imprisonment. He escaped the sentence by fleeing to England.

[622] Pietro Giannone (1676–1748), *Storia Civile del Regno di Napoli* (4 vols., 1723).

[623] "Where the pyre burned."

is being crushed by poverty, swamped in the ignobleness of modern life with none of its compensating luxuries.

Many thanks for your cards; I have received them all. They are wonderfully artistic. I will send you another from here very soon.

Always yours, dear Friend,

GEORGE GISSING

Hôtel Alibert. / Roma.

February 10. 1898.

My dear Friend,

I fear that, for once, you may have misunderstood me. Did you really think that I asked you to get a new house for *my* sake? No, no! Entirely for your own. To *me* it matters nothing where I am housed when I come to Potsdam. For, come I certainly shall, and it will rejoice me to shake hands with you again.

But --- !

I come to see *you*, and to see you only. I beg you to remember:

1) that, I am a wretched invalid, weak in body and mind.

2) that, I cannot *talk* German; nor even *speak* it with any comfort.

3) that, I dread the sight of strangers.

No, no. Let you and me pass one day together, one day more in this life; and let no one else intervene. Rehfeldt does not speak English, and to him I should only appear a stammering idiot. Let us say nothing to anybody, but creep about in secret, like two old fogies.

Seriously, I dread the thought of seeing anyone but you. I am sure you will not mind.

You see a new address at the head of this letter. I have been so ill, that in a day or two I am going to move to a hotel, where I can get my food without going out.[624] My health is now utterly ruined, I fear. Congestion, influenza, etc., have played the devil with me.

I long to be back in England. I shall never travel again.

---

[624] In his Diary, GRG wrote: "On Monday I move to: Hôtel Alibert, Roma, to be under the same roof with Wells, who is coming to Rome in a fortnight" (11 February 1898). Wells and his wife did not arrive until 8 March (Diary, 9 March 1898). After staying four weeks in Rome with GRG, Wells and his wife went on to Naples.

Let us hope there may come a few fine days in April, that I may travel northward as soon as possible.

All good be with you.

Yours ever,
GEORGE GISSING

Hôtel Alibert. / Rome.

February 20. 1898.

Dear Friend,

Many thanks for your kindness in sending this report. I went at once to the chemist's, and got a little bottle of *creosotal*[625]—which, by the bye, is already, it seems in common use. I shall pursue the treatment indicated, and give it a fair chance.

I will not write to Prof. von Leyden,[626] because I don't think he could say more (without a personal examination) than "Try!" And I shall not speak to a doctor here about it, because no doctor will allow you to use a remedy of your own suggestion. But, when I am in Germany, I should certainly like to consult the Professor.

But of course I should be glad to hear Rehfeldt's opinion of the matter.

Creosotal is a very thick oil, and therefore very difficult to take in *drops*. I shall do my best to make the doses exact, however. It is practically tasteless. Marvellous, indeed, if these few drops of colourless and tasteless stuff should have such an effect!

In a few weeks' time, I shall be able to judge whether there is any result. Just now my cough is very bad—but then I have had a cold. The weather is warm, and that ought to help me.

The medicine costs, here, about 2 Marks *a fluid ounce*. I don't know how that compares with the German price (2–3 Marks for 50 Grammes.)

I hope to send you my "Dickens" very soon.[627]

Thanks, again, dear old Man,

from Yours ever,
GEORGE GISSING

By the bye, ask Rehfeldt, some time, if the stuff should be taken *in water*, or alone.

---

[625] Creosote carbonate, a specific for tuberculosis, pneumonia, and bronchial disorders.

[626] Ernst von Leyden (1832–1910), director of a Berlin clinic, specialized in the treatment of tuberculosis, for which he advocated the use of creosotal.

[627] He sent a copy on 22 February (Diary).

Hôtel Alibert. / Rome.

March 8. 1898.

Dear Friend,

It is delightful that you find so much to praise in the "Dickens."
I myself had certain doubts about the quality of the work. However, I am told that it is selling well very well, and that there have
been many very laudatory reviews. Of course I shall be glad if
people in general recognize the fact that I am not confined to
novel-writing.

Naturally, you see more merit than the general reader is likely
to do; for you are able to sympathize with the thoroughly earnest
spirit in which I wrote the book. Well, once more I have to thank
you for pleasure and encouragement!

Now about the Creosotal. Please thank Rehfeldt very much
indeed, from me, for his detailed instructions. I am now carrying
these out, and the plain fact is, that in this last fortnight I have
grown wonderfully better. My cough has very greatly diminished,
and my appetite has enormously increased. I am very much
stronger. So I have every reason to hope for great results from
the continued use of the medicine.

Since *last* spring (a year ago) I had taken no medicine at all, and
my old prescriptions are in England. I was feeling very well, really,
until I came to Italy. And the truth is, that the northern climate
is much better for me—provided I live on dry soil. I shall return
with the resolve to live or die in England—and I really begin to
think that I have some years of life before me.

By the bye, before hearing the second time from you, I *did* write
to Prof. von Leyden, and I had a type-written reply, merely
repeating what I knew from that newspaper-cutting. However,
it also mentioned the best place (in Germany) for obtaining
Creosotal, and, when I am with you, I shall buy a good supply of
it. Here it is very expensive—as also is cod liver oil.

I fear you are suffering from cold, winterly weather. Here it is
very cloudy and rainy now, but fortunately quite warm.

I saw little of the *Festa* on March 4th.[628] It was really uninteresting. There is *no* national life in Italy, and the people showed not
the slightest enthusiasm. I fear evil times are coming for the
Latin race.

[628] Marking the anniversary of the Italian Constitution, ratified in 1848.

19

Zola's "Paris"[629] I have read in Italian, serially. The spirit is admirable, but the book seems to me inferior to most of his others. Well, he is a fine fellow, and I heartily agree with all you say of him.

Well, it will not be long now, I think, before we meet. I look forward eagerly to that time, and hope I shall hear much good of your work. Heavens! how we shall talk!

Ever yours, dear Friend,

GEORGE GISSING

Addressed: Herrn Eduard Bertz. / Neue Königstrasse. 21 / Potsdam. / *Germania.*

Hôtel Alibert / Roma.

[April 5, 1898]

March 5[630]

Am getting very restless, and anxious to be at work. Hope to leave Rome on *April 12* to travel to Berlin, with one night's rest at München. Could you tell me how I get from Berlin to Potsdam? Fear I shall not be able to let you know hour of arrival; yet I might *telegraph* from München perhaps. This will not be too soon for you.

The place where the Creosotal is bought is:

Dr. F. von Heyden Nachf., in Radebeul, bei Dresden.

Look forward with delight to seeing you. Hope to stop three days.

Ever yours,

G. G.

Addressed: Herrn Eduard Bertz. / Neue Königstrasse. 21 / Potsdam.

Hôtel Alibert. / Rome.

April 8. 1898.

Have only just heard from England about G[rant] A[llen]'s book.[631] It has not been very well noticed; charges of inaccuracy,

---

[629] *Le Ventre de Paris* (Paris, 1874).

[630] A mistake in the month, according to the postmark.

[631] *The Evolution of the Idea of God: An Inquiry into the Origins of Religions* (London, 1897). The review referred to was a scathing four-column criticism printed in the *Athenaeum* (20 November 1897, pp. 700–1).

plagiarism, etc. Difficult to know about the actual sale; probably not large. I tell you this—though of course I do not wish to damage G[rant] A[llen], who is a good fellow. Cannot learn about the notices and sale of the book in America.

Looking forward to our meeting next week.[632]

Yours,
G. G.

7 Clifton Terrace. / Dorking.

May 17. 1898.

Dear old Friend,

I am treating you very badly in keeping such a long silence—but I myself am being badly treated by circumstance. At last, I have found a lodging here at Dorking, some 25 miles from London. My one fear is that some idiot may discover my address, and make a newspaper paragraph of it. Of course I must hide myself, in constant fear of attack by that savage.[633]

I am now face to face with the serious necessity of earning money—for I have nearly come to the end of my means. I shall be working ceaselessly all the rest of the year. You shall have reports, and from you I hope to hear good news. I think very often of the delights of my visit to you. Splendid days, not to be forgotten!

I found my boy Walter in excellent health and spirits. Of the other little chap, I hear very seldom, and indeed I dare not think very much of him.[634]

All good be with you.

Yours ever,
GEORGE GISSING

[632] He left Rome on 14 April, spent four days in Potsdam with Bertz, and then returned to England on 20 April.

[633] His wife, who was determined to find GRG when he returned from Europe. She tried to force his family to give her his address and threatened to go to Wakefield, where Walter was being kept. Apparently GRG on his Potsdam visit had told Bertz about his problems with Edith, for this is the first remark about his personal affairs since the marriage in 1891.

[634] Walter was at Wakefield, but Alfred was still living with Edith.

7 Clifton Terrace / Dorking.

July 1. 1898.

Dear Friend,

Illness and toil and trouble! It is not my lungs that are now worrying me, but attacks of rheumatism, and the beginning of gout! What do you think? I have been seriously ordered to take bicycle-exercise, and I am just beginning to learn to ride the machine.[635] Perhaps this will do me good; I hope so.

Nothing settled yet about my wife and the little child. She does not know where I am, but is trying hard to discover, and threatens to give all possible trouble.[636] The Solicitor cannot persuade her to sign a deed of separation. Meanwhile, the people in whose house she is living have given her notice to quit, owing to her bad behaviour.

I cannot yet see any hope of a quiet termination.

But you—how does your work go on? I picture you in your beautiful room, working steadily at the great book.[637] If only I had your quietness of circumstance!

I rarely see anyone. As yet, I have written only one or two short stories. I cannot bring myself to any continuous effort.

However, I have agreed to write introductions for a new edition of Dickens, to be published by Methuen and Co.[638] Of course this will be easy work.

I am overwhelmed with anxiety about money, and see only difficulties in the future.

My boy Walter will come to the south coast for his holidays, and live with a friend of mine, a doctor.[639] I think I shall have him here for a day or two on his way back to Wakefield. My children

[635] H. G. Wells says it was he who "tried to make him a cyclist, for he took no exercise at all except walking, and I thought it might be pleasant to explore Surrey and Sussex with him, but he was far too nervous and excitable to ride" (*Experiment in Autobiography*, pp. 481–82). GRG went to Wells's home at Worcester Park on 2 July.

[636] In September Edith discovered where GRG was living and came to see him, bringing Alfred with her. She asked to be taken back, but GRG refused to discuss the matter and sent her back to London (Diary, September 7, 1898).

[637] *Der blinde Eros.*

[638] This was the "Rochester Edition" of Dickens, edited by F. G. Kitton.

[639] Dr. Harry Hick, living at East Romney.

will have strange thoughts of their father, when they grow up!
Let me have one line. I do hope you are well and active. Your
lakes must be glorious now, with their surroundings of wood and
meadow. I can hear the sound of the water, which I used to hear
from my bedroom window.

Ever yours, dear Friend,
GEORGE GISSING

7 Clifton Terrace / Dorking.

September 4. 1898.

Dear Friend,
Your letter is very seasonable. It does me great good. I was in
need of precisely this admonition. "The Town Traveller" was
written *more than a year ago*, and ever since I have been disgusted
with it. I doubt its popularity; I scarcely hope for it. For a long
time I have had in my mind a very serious book, and I hope soon
(when the weather is cooler) to get to work at it. You have helped
me greatly: I feel, now, that I shall be able to carry out my project.

In the book I am going to write, the question of Peace will be
involved. It is a love story, but with large issues—philosophic (I
hope) and cosmopolitan. The name (long in my thoughts) is to be:
"The Crown of Life."[640]

I don't know what to think of the Czar. It is so difficult to credit
an aristocrat with high humanity. But the declaration undoubtedly
has great importance.[641] As for the French affair, I rejoice. Zola
was right. We shall see the end of a hideous scandal.[642]

Have you seen Tolstoi's "Qu'est-ce que l'Art?" The French
translator—Halpérine-Kaminsky[643]—has sent me a copy, with a

[640] Published by Methuen and Co., 1899.

[641] On 28 August 1898, Czar Nicholas II proposed a conference of world
powers to discuss ways of preserving world peace and reducing armaments.
The declaration was made in Moscow to a gathering of international
diplomats who were attending the unveiling of a statue of Alexander II
(London *Times*, 29 August 1898, p. 3).

[642] Colonel Henry, the chief of the French intelligence service, on
30 August 1897, admitted forging the documents used to indict Dreyfus.
He was imprisoned, but almost immediately committed suicide. Mme.
Dreyfus filed a petition for a new trial on 3 September.

[643] Ely Halpérine-Kaminsky (1858–?), a Russian writer who became a
French citizen in 1890.

request for my opinion, which he says he will use in an article on the subject. Of course I have replied carefully. The man addressed me as "honoré confrère" and "cher maître"—so, you see, I really am getting some reputation in France. (By the bye, "New Grub Street" is to appear in *Les Débats*.[644])

Tolstoi is simply Ruskin. Art to be judged from the moral standpoint. The true judges of great art [are] the uneducated multitude. His spirit is noble, but I think his arguments unsound.

When you next write, tell me about the progress of your work. You say not a word of it.

Of course I am living in misery. That woman has been *assaulting* her landlady, and nearly got into the police-court.[645] It seems I cannot take the child from her; they say I have neither legal nor moral right. Well, I fear his life is sacrificed—my own fault. The marriage was *criminal*. (Yes, it was that girl of which you spoke in your last letter.)

I have undertaken to edit a new edition of Dickens's novels, and am to supply a long preface to each. This occupies me at present. But I must and will get on with my new novel.

Have patience with my long silences. I am heavily burdened. My affection for you is unchanged and unchangeable: whatever happens, you shall know.

All good be with you! I hope you are able to work.

Ever yours, dear old Friend,
GEORGE GISSING

The heat is terrible!

Dorking.

November 1. 1898.

Dear Old Friend,

Your postcards have found me in an unprecedented state of mind—namely, one of extraordinary happiness. I was just about to write to you, for I have a wonderful tale to tell.

[644] Translated by Mlle. Gabrielle Fleury. It was printed under the title *La Rue des Meurt-de-Faim* in the *Journal des Débats* from 23 February 1901 to 3 June 1901.

[645] "That woman in London was all but given in charge by her landlady for an *assault* the other day. She has gone off into other lodgings, and the solicitor is doing his best to get possession of the child—whose life is not safe, I fear" (GRG to Harry Hick, 10 August 1898, Yale).

Did I not mention to you that "New Grub Street" was being translated into French? The translator, Mlle. Gabrielle Fleury, being in England last July, called to see me about it. I was then staying with Wells, and learning the bicycle. We talked, and I received a very pleasant impression. A fortnight later, before leaving England, she came to spend a day at Dorking. Again we talked much, and again the impression was very favourable. She returned to France, and there followed a correspondence. From this correspondence it has resulted that Mlle Fleury has just being [sic] spending a week at Dorking, and—that next April we begin our life together as husband and wife!

The thing is a miracle, nothing less. Gabrielle is aged 29, beautiful, very intelligent, an admirable pianist. Her father is a confirmed invalid; her mother also in poor health; they are people in comfortable circumstances, living at Passy (Paris). She has a large circle of most interesting acquaintances: chief of them being Mme. Lardin de Musset, the sister of Alfred de Musset,[646] an old, delightful woman. Also, the widow of Georg Herwegh,[647] struggling to live on German lessons. Also Mme Darmesteter[648]—and many another. She possesses a very small income of her own, just enough to make her safe under any circumstances.

Well now, her mother knows the whole truth of the matter, and has given full consent. I have had a beautiful letter from her about it. Her father, being so ill (and hopelessly) is merely told that Gabrielle is going to marry an Englishman. Moreover, her French friends will learn the story in the same shape—simply a marriage in England.

As explanation of this rather extraordinary state of things, you must remember that I am at present almost as well known in Paris as in London, that French papers have abounded in flattering paragraphs about me, that *Le Temps* and *Les Débats* have disputed for the right of publishing "New Grub Street," that "The

[646] Hermine de Musset (1819–1944). She had been married to a M. Lardin, but after his death she resumed using her maiden name in tribute to her poet brother, Alfred (1810–1857).

[647] Emma Sigmund Herwegh. Her husband (1817–1875) was the German revolutionary poet.

[648] Mary Robinson Darmesteter (1857–?), widow of the oriental scholar James Darmesteter (1849–1894), and author of several novels, biographies, and volumes of verse.

Town Traveller" is being hurriedly translated by M. Art,[649] that all the periodicals eagerly accept translations of my short stories, and want my portrait and biographical notices. Of course all this has affected the mind of Mme. Fleury, a woman of great intelligence, well acquainted with English.

Next April, I shall meet Mme Fleury and Gabrielle at Calais, and thence we two go to Lausanne, for the purpose of consulting a certain doctor, a friend of Gabrielle (who, by the bye, is a splendid *alpiniste*!) as to where I had better permanently reside. We only know that it must *not* be in England; it will probably be in Switzerland.

There are difficulties and dangers; we know them and face them. My two children must not be neglected, and Gabrielle wants to have Walter with us; we shall see.

So there! For the first time in my life I am happy! And, if health does not fail me, I shall be happy for many a year.

Thank you for the two beautiful views. Yes, indeed they bring back to me my delightful walks at Potsdam. Well, we shall walk together again, be assured of it! If not in England, then somewhere on the Continent.

Delighted to hear that the book draws to its end. Your last letter troubled me a little, but I am hopeful now about everything and everybody.

Let me hear from you, with your opinion of this astonishing story.

Ever yours, dear old Friend,
GEORGE GISSING

7 Clifton Terrace. / Dorking.

January 17. 1899.

Well, my dear old boy, here is another book finished! I call it "The Crown of Life." It is first and foremost a love-story, but, blended with this, it contains a rather vigorous attack on militarism. I have had to say hard things of all countries. A strange thing that the writing of the book should be finished just when

---

[649] Georges Art, who had translated *Eve's Ransom*. His translation of *The Town Traveller* was not published.

the "Peace Crusade" is becoming active.[650] I planned the story more than a year ago. Still more oddly, Russia has a great part in it. But it is not the first time that my thoughts have anticipated public tendencies. Of course everyone will think I have sat down in a hurry to write an opportune book. If necessary, I shall contradict this charge with a prefatory remark.[651]

I have now to finish my Dickens Prefaces, before leaving England.

How is your own work getting on? I received your card at Christmas, and was glad of it, but I should have been gladder to have a word about your progress. However, I remembered that it was long since I myself had written. Indeed, I have been working fearfully, and the maddening eczema from which I have suffered all this summer made everything difficult. It often made me think of your similar ailment a year or two ago.

I suppose your winter in Germany has been much the same as here—very mild. I cannot remember such a January as this. To-day the thrushes and blackbirds are singing loudly, and the sun is shining with the warmth of spring—as indeed it has done on many days since Christmas. Probably winter will come in May—an evil state of things.

How is your health? Mine, I believe, steadily improves. I have had no lung-trouble this winter at all. By the bye, much interest is excited in England by the Consumption-cure of Dr. Walther at (I forget the name of the place) in the Black Forest. It seems wonderfully successful, and is simply open-air life with stupendous eating! No medicine at all.

You will be thinking of another migration. It is a terrible business, your packing of books each time. Did it ever occur to you what a very exceptional thing it is for men no better off than you and I to drag thousands of volumes after them from place to place (like a comet's train of light, as you once said)? There can be very few such cases in all Europe.

I am reading again at the 6th. Century, steadily accumulating

---

[650] The Peace Crusade developed in England as a result of Czar Nicholas's peace proposal made in August 1898. The aim of the crusade was to seek international cooperation in forwarding the Czar's program (London *Times*, 19 December 1898, p. 12).

[651] The novel was published without a preface.

material for my historical novel. Heaven knows when it will be written!

Wonderful how dull literature is just now! No book of importance ever appears in England, and very few, I think, on the Continent. Kipling has gone off into boys' books, of a blustering kind. That fellow has done terrible harm.[652] But of course he is only the mouthpiece of a tendency.

Let me know of your progress, dear friend, and believe me ever yours,

GEORGE GISSING

7 Clifton Terrace, / Dorking.

February 1. 1899.

Dear old Friend,

Your letter is very sad. I grieve over these miseries with you, and most heartily wish it were in my power to put an end to them. The rejection of that fiction[653] is maddening, after all your toil. I don't know what to say—except that it seems very clear to me that you have lost all heart (and how naturally!) for novel-writing. At all events, I am glad to hear that you do not propose to pack the books yourself this time. And I do, do hope that you will find your new home quieter. Oh, this ceaseless wandering! How sick of it you must be!

I want to ask you about a strange piece of information which has come to me from Paris. I am told that Sacher-Masoch[654] divorced himself from his first wife (a blameless woman) and married a second in a very extraordinary way—simply by going to Heligoland for the ceremony. The first wife still lives, and

---

[652] See 11 December 1899.

[653] *Der blinde Eros.*

[654] Leopold von Sacher-Masoch (1836–1895), German novelist, who divorced his first wife, Aurora Rümelin (1845–19?), in 1886, and then married Hulda Meister (1846–?), also a novelist. Madame von Sacher-Masoch was living in Paris, supporting herself by writing fiction under the pseudonym of Wanda Donajew, the name of the heroine in her husband's most famous novel, *Venus in Furs.* She had run away to Paris with a man named Rosenthal, who subsequently abandoned her. It was this escapade that gave her husband grounds for divorce. See Léopold Stern, *Sacher-Masoch ou L'Amour de la Souffrance* (Paris, 1933).

Gabrielle knows her very well, and has the story from her. Though at that time there was no divorce in Austria, Sacher-Masoch, in some unexplained way, was able to take a second wife—a German —in Heligoland; the thing was legal, and was proclaimed to all the world. What is the meaning of this? I am told that the thing could also be done at Hermannstadt in Hungary. Did you ever hear of such a thing? You would do me a very great kindness if you could tell me anything about it.

Mme Sacher-Masoch says also that something of the same kind exists in the Isle of Man. I am making inquiries about this.

Gabrielle's father died about a month ago, and we find ourselves great [*sic*] troubled by a difficulty about the money that is her own. You see, there will be complications about the legal signing of her name in future.[655]

Indeed, I am worried to death at present.

Prejudices? Good heavens, Gabrielle has no national prejudices.[656] She is the most sensible woman living. I hope some day, dear old boy, to see you in my own house.

Will write again soon. All good be with you.

Ever yours,
GEORGE GISSING

Addressed: Herrn Eduard Bertz. / Neue Königstrasse. 21 / Potsdam. / *Germany.*

Dorking.

February 11. 1899.

I have asked my literary agent,[657] but he does not know anyone who can translate from German *MS,* but he will continue inquiries. Many thanks for your letter. I feared that reply; but the evidence of her story given by Mme S[acher] M[asoch] is very astonishing. I am in correspondence with America on this subject.[658] G[abrielle] herself is perfectly prepared to meet all dangers; I only

---

[655] Gabrielle solved this problem by turning her property over to her mother, who then managed her daughter's legal and financial affairs.

[656] Towards the Germans.

[657] James B. Pinker (1863–1922).

[658] He had written to a Baltimore friend to see about getting an American divorce without having Edith learn about it. The plan was too involved, and he had to give up the idea (*Roberts,* p. 185).

feel it a simple duty to find some way of making her position easier, if possible. You were absolutely right in all you said about eczema; the doctors can do nothing whatever; diet and patience are the only help.

You shall hear again soon.

Always yours,
G. G.

7 Clifton Terrace. / Dorking.

March 31. 1899.

Dear Friend,

Your experience of mankind would justify a ferocious cynicism. Indeed, you go through great miseries, and if ever I hear from you that you are settled in a really comfortable home, I shall shout in jubilation. One reason, of course, why people use you so ill, is that *you* use *them* too well. One has to be hard and exacting, especially with all uneducated people. Gentleness, kindness, humanity, are never understood, and are repaid with contempt. I have proved it a thousand times.

For six weeks I have been very ill—an attack of influenza, followed by lung-congestion, pleurisy, and all sorts of things. Yesterday I went out for the first time. Happily, no signs of phthisis have come up during this illness. I have no cough, and do not lose weight. There can be very little doubt that, amid domestic peace, and in the air of the mountains, I shall soon be a very different man.

Of course all work suspended. However, before breaking down, I did something satisfactory. I planned out in detail my story of the 6th. century—settled all the names, etc.—and really got the book ready to begin upon. I even decided the title—"The Vanquished Roman."[659]

Zapp's book must be horrible;[660] I am glad I have not to read it. And I had no idea that the Duke of Clarence was in that morbid condition.[661] Heavens! What satire—the national lamentation at his death, with sermons and elegies and so on! But the world is compact of hypocrisy and ignoble subservience.

[659] Changed to *Veranilda*.

[660] Arthur Zapp, *Muttersohn* (Berlin, 1899).

[661] The Duke of Clarence died on 14 January 1892, of pneumonia following a severe attack of influenza.

Alas! My novel[662] is put off until September—partly because the present season is over-crowded with books, partly because "The Town Traveller" is still selling. I think it a mistake, the story being so opportune; but publishers are *always* making mistakes.

Did you see the malicious notice in the *Athenaeum* of "La Rançon d'Ève"?[663] It could be nothing but malice, as French people give high praise to the translation. To counteract that impression, I send you a copy of a literary journal[664] with a marked paragraph—which will interest you.

The actual date of my going abroad is still unsettled.[665] It will probably be at the end of April. We do not yet know the place where we shall live; it will be either in Savoy or Switzerland, high among the mountains.

I have written 6 Dickens prefaces, and publication will begin very soon.[666]

It is good that you are going to Rehfeldt's. There you will have a brief interval of rest and peace. By the bye, there is no reason why you should not speak to him, in confidence, of my private affairs—if you like. Give him my kindest regards.

Ever yours, dear old Friend,
GEORGE GISSING

In the paragraph about French translations I have marked with a G. those which have been made, or are to be made, by Gabrielle.

---

[662] *The Crown of Life.*

[663] "*Là Rançon d'Ève* (Paris, Calmann Lévy), M. Georges Art's rendering of 'Eve's Ransom' in French, results in very funny literature. Mr. Gissing's efforts in fiction are mostly characterized by a clearness and precision which are quite absent from the French translation. It is hard to see why this volume was selected for publication in Paris. It is not Mr. Gissing's best, it is rather dull, and it deals with most unconventional characters" (*Athenaeum*, 28 January 1899, p. 111).

[664] Not identified.

[665] He left England on 6 May, when he sailed on the 11:30 boat for Dieppe and then met Gabrielle and Madame Fleury at the Hôtel de Paris in Rouen (Diary). For Sunday, 7 May 1899, the Diary notes: "In the evening, our ceremony. Dear Maman's emotion, and G.'s sweet dignity."

[666] Twelve prefaces were finally written, but the edition was a financial failure, and only six were printed: *Pickwick Papers* (1899); *Nicholas Nickleby* (1900); *Bleak House* (1900); *Oliver Twist* (1900); *Old Curiosity Shop*, and *Master Humphrey's Clock* (1901); *Barnaby Rudge* (1901).

Addressed: Herrn Eduard Bertz. / 11 Alexandrinen Strasse. /
Potsdam. / *Allemagne.*

Hôtel des Terrasses. / St. Pierre en Port. / (Seine Inférieure) /
France.

Thursday.[667] [May 12, 1899]

We are spending a few weeks here on the coast of Normandy.
Glorious weather, and delightful scenery. So far everything has
gone well. Gabrielle wishes me to give you her kind regards, with
the hope that some day she may make your acquaintance. Absolute
perfection of mind and of character! The only other occupants of
this hotel are two grotesque Englishmen, with whom I hold no
communication; G[abrielle] and I speak only French. I do hope
that you enjoyed your holiday to the end, and that you have a
better prospect than you imagined. Let me hear from you, at above
address, if you can write during the next fortnight. Happily, there
is a piano here, and G[abrielle] makes glorious music. For the
first time in my life, I am at ease in mind. All good be with you!
Always affectionately yours,

G. G.

Poste restante / Trient. / Valais. Switzerland

July 23. 1899.

Dear Friend,

I am writing to you from a place called Samoens, in
Haute-Savoie, where we are passing a week to prepare ourselves for the higher altitude of Trient in Switzerland. If all
is well, we leave here for Trient on Wednesday, travelling along
the south shore of the Lake of Geneva. Trient is reached by
diligence from Martigny; it lies at a height of some 1300 m., with
glaciers near by. Here at Samoens the scenery is very grand, but
the weather has been hitherto terrifically hot, making it impossible
to walk far.

I was very glad to receive your letter at Paris. Let me hear soon
that the book of which you do not wish to speak in detail is going
on well.[668] By the bye, an intimate friend of Gabrielle is Mlle.

[667] A slip. The postmark reads 12 May 1899, which was a Wednesday.

[668] *Philosophie des Fahrrads* (Dresden: Reissner, 1900), based on Bertz's
experiences as a cyclist.

Funck-Brentano (a name which will sound very familiar to you),[669] and, in speaking with her, Gabrielle happened to mention that I had a German friend who was writing about Nietzsche.[670] This subject, it seems, has a special interest for Mlle. F[unck]-B[rentano], and she begged that the work might be finished and published as soon as possible!

In Paris I have met several interesting people. First among them I must mention Mme. Lardin de Musset, sister of the poet. She is a very old lady, but still in good health of mind and body. Gabrielle and I dined with her not long ago.[671] She inhabits an appartement near the Madeleine, and her rooms are made interesting with portraits of Alfred de Musset at various ages; there is also a fine bust of him, occupying a niche in the dining-room. She has a certain quiet stateliness of manner, a dignified repose, which tells of a by-gone time. Of course her reminiscences are endless. It was curious to hear that Balzac was a good deal of a gossip at times.

Another old lady whose acquaintance I have made is Mme. Herwegh, the widow of Georg Herwegh.[672] Though about eighty years old, she lives quite alone, in a very poor way, and supports herself by giving German and Italian lessons. I thought her rather an impressive person; she has great energy and courage. In her room is a fine portrait of Herwegh.

Mme Sacher Masoch I have not yet seen.[673] At present she is in Switzerland. Her life has been very miserable for many years, but now her son is doing well in a house of business in London, and probably things will be brighter for her in future.

Apropos, I must thank you for your newspaper cutting about

[669] Sophie Funck-Brentano, daughter of Theodore Funck-Brentano (1830–1906), French philosopher and sociologist; Bertz had met the Funck-Brentano's while he was in Paris in 1878.

[670] "Die neue Ethik," *Das literarische Echo: Halbmonatsschrift für Literaturfreunde*, II (15 October 1899), 90–4.

[671] "Thus, my first dinner in Paris is on the date of my marriage with G.—the 6th of the month" (Diary, 6 June 1899). The ceremony actually took place on Sunday, 7 May.

[672] The Gissings visited Mme. Herwegh on 5 July (Diary).

[673] GRG finally met her on 8 October: "In afternoon to call upon Mme Sacher-Masoch, the repudiated wife of the novelist, who married another woman in Heligoland. Has a son in business in London" (Diary).

Heligoland. It makes the whole matter quite clear. Of course Sacher Masoch had no intention of living in Heligoland, and therefore felt himself quite safe in committing perjury. I am very glad to have come to an understanding of this mystery.

When you were in Paris long, long ago, did you not form an acquaintance with Gabriel Monod and his family?[674] I remember your speaking of them. It is a strange thing that they are intimate friends of Gabrielle, and doubtless I shall meet them next winter. You probably know that Gabriel Monod is a strong Dreyfusard.

Yes, I should like to know Zola, but I do not know whether I shall ever have the courage to seek a meeting with him.

I have been doing a good deal of work in Paris. Among other things, I have half finished a little book describing my journey in Calabria—to be called "By the Ionian Sea." I hope my agent will succeed in getting it serially published first of all.

Our plans are rather uncertain, for they depend upon the health of Mme. Fleury. For the present it is settled that we are to spend next winter in Paris, and, in the spring, come to Savoie for at least a year. It has not been possible to arrange to leave Paris finally this year. At all events we are resolved to escape the Exposition, which will be a terrible affair.[675] What with the preparations for it, and the works for the new underground railway, Paris is in an extraordinary state of confusion—everywhere, in the west end, scaffolding and excavations.

I suppose my new novel will appear by the end of September,[676] and of course a copy will reach you as usual. It is arranged that G[abrielle]'s translation of "New Grub Street" shall begin in the Débats early next year.

You must have been suffering a great deal from the heat, I fear. I only hope it has not interfered with your work. For my

[674] Gabriel Jacques Jean Monod (1844-1912), French historian associated with the Ecole Normale Supérieure. Bertz said of the acquaintance: "I very much regret now that the time was too short for getting better acquainted with the Monod family who had so kindly welcomed me, for there, I feel sure, I should have moved among broad-minded and sympathetic people, such as I sadly [wanted ?], among that unruly group of eccentrics" (Bertz to Gabrielle Gissing, ? 1899, Yale).

[675] Construction of buildings began in March 1898 for the Paris International Exhibition, which opened officially on 14 April 1900.

[676] The Crown of Life was published in October.

own part, I am fairly well, and I hope that three months of the mountains will make a new man of me. Of course my life is very different from what it was in my old miserable loneliness. I still have to shake off the effects of that long wretchedness, and perhaps I shall never wholly attain to a cheerfulness like that of other men. But, after all I have endured, an extraordinary piece of good fortune has befallen me—a thing beyond all hope. Perhaps my life may end in a tranquillity unforeseen.

My dear wife wishes me to offer you her best and kindest remembrances. We speak of you often. May we all meet together some day.

Always affectionately yours,
old Friend,
GEORGE GISSING

Hôtel des Alpes. / Trient. / (Valais)

[August 1899][677]

Dear old Friend,

Gabrielle was delighted with the beautiful view of Potsdam, and with the reference to her in your letter. She is herself writing to you. Moreover, we are sending you a photograph of ourselves, taken here among the rocks.[678] Gabrielle is *coiffée en bandeaux*, which makes her look rather older than she really is; but I prefer that coiffure, because her hair was like that when I first saw her.

I am very glad indeed that you go on with your bicycling. It is not only the pleasure of the thing; but I am sure that it does your health a great deal of good. Indeed, I seem to notice that your letters are more cheerful in tone of late—probably a result of improved health. If I had inhabited a flat country, I should never have abandoned my bicycle; but Dorking was too hilly, and I fear the exercise did me harm rather than good.

You are very active just now. When your article "Die Neue [*sic*] Ethik" appears, I beg you to send me a copy, for I should greatly like to read it. By the bye, I have always forgotten to tell

---

[677] Written in Bertz's hand.
[678] "G and I have been photographed among the rocks by M. Laperriere, a Paris photographer who is staying here. Going to send Bertz a copy" (Diary, 21 August 1899).

20

you that Gabrielle knows German very well; she too would be delighted to read something of yours. So work on, and let us soon have the results of your labour.

Gabrielle once attended a course of lectures by Lichtenberger.[679] He was interesting and profound, but had a very bad delivery. Unfortunately, I do not know his book on Nietzsche. There are many such things that I should like to read, but in future my time for reading will be very small; naturally, now that my solitude has come to an end.

We have had very interesting society here. A really valuable acquaintance we have made is that of Ernest Bovet (a Swiss) professor of French at the University of Rome.[680] A fine fellow, with great energy; philosophic, at the same time, and an excellent talker in three languages—French, German and Italian. Gabrielle is very fond of his wife, and I hope we may some day be able to visit them in Rome. They come to Trient every year, as Mme Bovet is the owner of a great forest here.

On Thursday we are leaving Trient. It is beginning to be rather cold here in the evenings. We shall go first of all to Airolo, (Suisse) where our address will be *Hôtel Lombardi*—probably for a fortnight. But you shall have a card, of course. At Airolo, which is on the southern slope of the Alps, we shall find warmth again, and shall also get the grapes. But I think we shall be back in Paris before the end of September.

I climbed the other day to the top of the Col de Balme, and had a magnificent view; the whole chain of Mont Blanc and the valley of Chamonix. But I must not do much climbing; evidently my lungs are not strong enough for such fatigue.

I was pleased to hear of the honour received by Rehfeldt. Pray congratulate him from me, when you have an opportunity.

Curious that you should speak of Frau Berger. I have recently heard from her; she wants to translate "Eve's Ransom" for a Stuttgart firm.[681] But I think the work will be done by Mme Sacher Masoch, to whom, as a personal friend, we of course give the

---

[679] Henri Lichtenberger (1864–?), professor of German literature at the University of Paris, author of *La philosophie de Nietzsche* (Paris, 1898).

[680] Bovet was at the University of Rome from 1897 to 1901, and then returned to the University of Zurich.

[681] There is no record of a German translation.

preference. I have no idea why "New Grub Street" did not appear as a volume.

If it is possible to make Zola's acquaintance, I will certainly do so; for you know that I thoroughly agree with your view of his personality. But he must be a terribly busy man, and I shall take great care not to intrude upon him unreasonably. I, too, shall have to be working furiously all through the winter; for, the scoundrel English public will not buy my books, and my need of money will compel me to ceaseless production. I hope to see a few interesting men at Paris, and of course you shall know of all that happens.

Of course, in my case, the winter at Paris is an experiment; I cannot tell what the result will be upon my health. But I was very well there during the months of June and July, and I hope I shall be able to endure the winter season. However, in the April following we shall come to the mountains for at least a year. Gabrielle has an idea that she would like to spend a little time at Munich. We shall see. If ever we get there, could you not come to see us?

Meanwhile, always yours, old Friend,

GEORGE GISSING

P.S. Mme Fleury has a bad cold. In any case we shall have to remain here for a few days longer, perhaps a week. Let me know, by card, that you receive the photograph.

13 Rue de Siam. / Passy. / Paris.

October 22. 1899.

Dear old Friend,

You will by this have received my new book. In England it comes either very inappropriately, or just at the right moment. We shall see.

I am hard at work on another, to be called "The Coming Man."[682]

I cannot tell you how delighted we were with your last letters. My wife really rejoiced over them—as she will tell you herself. We wait impatiently for your article.[683] Of course the conditions under

---

[682] Published as *Our Friend the Charlatan* (London: Chapman and Hall, 1901).

[683] "Die neue Ethik."

which you wrote are quite understood. But we must have your *book* [684]—I shall not be satisfied till that is published.

On the whole, it is good, I think, that you have been writing some articles. One feels that one is getting something *said*, at all events. And evidently you have much benefited in health by bicycle exercise. I am not surprised; it is undoubtedly admirable for sedentary people. It tempts one to go out, when otherwise one would sit still.

Your panorama of Potsdam is on Gabrielle's piano, and makes a nice ornament—as well as constantly reminding us of you.

By the bye, if you have an opportunity, you might inquire about the *climate* (winter and summer) of München. It is a question with us whether Mme. Fleury's health will endure a sojourn there; we cannot leave her. I imagine that very good *pensions* exist, and not expensive. But do not trouble yourself specially about all this; there is plenty of time.

Mme Berger has given me trouble. After writing twice about "Eve's Ransom," she fell into silence, and, after a lapse of six weeks, I granted the right of translation to Mme. Sacher-Masoch (who writes under a pseudonym.) Now, the latter finds that the publishers will not accept the book, and I cannot help thinking that they have suffered some annoyance from this conflict of translators. But I suppose there would really be but a small public for translations of my books in Germany. People likely to read them at all would get the original. Mme S[acher] M[asoch] says that she frequently sees mention of me in the *Frankfurter Zeitung* I am surprised; I wonder who is so friendly disposed?

A friend of my wife's is translating "Eve's Ransom" into Italian, but where it will appear is by no means certain. [685] At Trient, we made the acquaintance of a M. Bovet (a Swiss) professor of French at the University of Rome, and he promised to inquire for me among Italian editors. Bovet is a most interesting man, whose special study is the Romance literature. He writes both in French and Italian. A very vigorous personality.

Do you know a cheap German Bibliothek published by one Meyer—said to be cheap and better than Reclam? If so, you might mention the fact to me.

[684] *Philosophie des Fahrrads.*
[685] There is no record of an Italian translation.

Gabrielle has just been reading Doistoievsky's "Le Crime et le Châtiment"[686] with great delight. It is a marvellous book, indeed. I think nothing very noteworthy has recently appeared in Paris. Prévost's "Les Vierges Fortes" [*sic*] was dull.[687]

My agent Pinker is trying to serialize "By the Ionian sea."[688] Doubtful whether he will succeed, I fear. People don't like me as an author, though they speak of me with a certain respect. One must struggle on.

All good be with you. Never force yourself to write, when you have not time.

Ever yours, old friend,
GEORGE GISSING
(*Over*)

October 30th.

I read your "Die neue Ethik" last night. This review of the latest opinion interests me very much. I notice the *maturity* of your tone. But I shall write to you again on the subject.

Of course you received "The Crown of Life."

13 Rue de Siam. / Paris.

December 11. 1899.

Dear Friend,

I wonder whether you actually have a copy to spare either of "Glück u[nd] Glas," or of "Das Sabinergut"? The fact is, I did not want you to have to buy one. But of course I am anxious that Gabrielle should become acquainted with your work; and, as the date of the coming of my library is still uncertain, depending on several contingencies, I should be glad, in truth, to have either of the two books now. But on no account ought you to purchase a copy. Rather than that, we will wait.

You are doing too much, I fear. The account you give of your work is appalling. Do be prudent. I quite agree with you that cycling is *not* compatible with very hard intellectual work. Still, it

---

[686] Translated into French by Victor Derély, Paris, 1884.

[687] Marcel Prévost, *Les Vierges fortes. Frédérique* (Paris, 1900).

[688] The book was published serially in the *Fortnightly Review*, from 1 May to 1 October 1900.

doubtless did you a great deal of good, and I heartily hope you will be able to renew it when the blessed spring comes round again.

The quotation you give from Foerster's[689] article really startled me. Why, great heavens! the man evidently thinks that those words of Harvey Rolfe are spoken seriously; whereas they are *in bitterest irony*. Now, this will never do. As Dr. Foerster evidently reads my books, I am going to write him a very serious letter, to put myself right in his opinion. Can I address to him simply at Zürich University? If you know his real address, will you have the great kindness to send it me on a post card.

This matter is of grave importance to me. No man living more abhors the influence of Kipling than I do; and I cannot endure to have it thought that I glorified him in "The Whirlpool." *You,* of course, knew that that passage was ironical? Rolfe speaks with a throwing-up of the arm; he puts himself into the position of a Jingo, and mouths Jingo words![690] I thought the meaning was unmistakable to any intelligent person.

As you say, it is a very good sign indeed that my books are thus quoted.

No; the novel I am now writing is not, after all "The Coming Man." I worked for a month at that, then put it aside, as it was not quite clear in my mind. Instead, I took up another attractive subject—the restless seeking for a *new religion*, which leads people into Theosophy, Spiritualism, and things still more foolish. The title I have chosen is "Among the Prophets." I feel sure I can make this a striking and rather an exciting book.[691]

You are quite right about the defect, from the popular point of view, of "The Crown of Life." In England, the book is exciting no attention whatever. It was very coldly reviewed, and will evidently soon cease to be spoken of at all. This is worse luck than has befallen any book of mine for several years. Of course the moment of publication was most unfortunate. If—as I proposed—it had

[689] Friedrich Wilhelm Foerster (1869–?), a tutor at the University of Zurich.

[690] Harvey Rolfe's speech satirizes the glorification of imperialism in Kipling's *Barrack-Room Ballads*. See *The Whirlpool*, Chap. XIII.

[691] "Among the Prophets" was never published. According to Mr. Alfred C. Gissing the manuscript was destroyed.

been published last spring, it would have had a very much better chance.

However, I see that it has been quoted by Robert Buchanan, in an article in this month's "Contemporary"—he copies a passage in criticism of the influence of newspapers.[692] But Robert Buchanan has very little reputation nowadays. His article is a violent attack upon Kipling, and I strongly approve it. Indeed, nothing too severe can be said against the brute savagery of Kipling's latest work. I wish you could read "Stalky and Co."[693]—you, who take such an interest in education and boys' books! Doubtless you will see reviews of it. Such a book ought to be burnt by the hangman! It is the most vulgar and bestial production of our times.

Many thanks for your careful answers to my various questions. If indeed you can some day come to Paris, it will be a joy to both of us! We must look forward to that.

Under the circumstances, you certainly would not have been justified in writing a review of "The Crown of Life." Your hands are much too full, and I should have reproached myself seriously if I had been the cause of thus adding to your burdens. No, no; let us be patient, and each get on quietly with his own work.

The first volumes of *my* edition of Dickens are just published— "Pickwick." It is beautifully illustrated. Some day I hope you will have a chance of seeing the prefaces I have written. Unhappily, publishers do not give copies with the same freedom as in the case of one's novels.

Are you suffering from the cold? Here it is terrible. This interferes so seriously with one's work. The winter is always a time of darkness within as well as without; I regard it always as a semi-death.

Gabrielle is very pleased with your kind remembrance.

Ever yours, old Friend,
GEORGE GISSING

[692] "The Voice of 'The Hooligan,'" *Contemporary Review*, LXXVI (December 1899), 774–89. Buchanan quotes a discussion on the newspapers' misuse of the great power in their command from Chapter XIX of *The Crown of Life*.

[693] Published in 1899.

By the bye, your reviews in *Das litterarische Echo* have given me one or two ideas for the book I am writing.[694]

Do you know by name Fräulein Schirmacher?[695]—a feminist. We have made her acquaintance lately. Very interesting woman. I have read a book of hers called "Halb"—a feminist novel, rather good.

No meeting with Zola. It seems too difficult. I am rarely able to go visiting.

Kindest regards from Gabrielle, who always has great interest in your letters.

Addressed: Herrn Eduard Bertz. / Alexandrinenstrasse. 15. / Potsdam. / *Allemagne.*

13 Rue de Siam. / Paris.

December 18. 1899.

Hearty thanks for the copy of "Glück u[nd] Glas." Arrived yesterday. G[abrielle] will read it at once, and I myself shall go over it again, to revive the old days. Very glad of your letter, hope your view of Foerster is correct. Probably. I feel ashamed that you should take trouble about my book, but of course if you really feel disposed, I am very grateful.[696]

Ever yours,

G. G.

13 Rue de Siam. / Paris.

December 31. 1899.

Dear old Friend,

Every good wish for the New Year! On the whole, I cannot but think that you are more enjoying your life now than in the years gone by. You are very active, which is always a good thing— provided the activity be congenial, and your health is certainly

---

[694] The reviews were on Heinrich Driesmans, *Die plastische Kraft in Kunst, Wissenschaft und Leben* (Leipzig, 1898), and Peter Sirius, *Tausend und Ein Gedanken* (München, 1899).

[695] Käthe Schirmacher (1865–?), a German writer living in Paris. She published *Halb* in 1893.

[696] Perhaps Bertz had volunteered to answer Foerster's article on *The Whirlpool.*

better. I often wonder whether we shall ever meet amid circumstances of real tranquillity. Fate owes us a year or two of peace before the end. We must wait and hope.

Most unfortunately, just when she was beginning "Glück und Glas" Gabrielle was attacked with influenza, or something of the kind, and she is still unable to do anything. Meanwhile, I am using the opportunity to re-read your book—a chapter or two each day. How it brings back the old times to me! It holds my interest very firmly, and the probability is that I appreciate its "atmosphere" better than when I first read the book. After novels of restless modernism, this has an idyllic calm which really does one good. Ah, those peaceful South-German homes! I see them in a light of warm, soft sunshine. I feel the wish to sit with good old Krausz[697] in his quiet library, and forget all the "questions" of to-day. I assure you, it is a book that does good to the nerves, a tranquillizing book.

Many thanks to you for that little packet of Catalogues. I am glad to know of these series of very cheap publications.

You are working on, of course, and to me it is a great satisfaction to know that certain dates are fixed for the appearance of what you write. But of course—no foolish excess of toil! If that reviewing proves too much for you, it must stop. I understanding [sic] the temptation of having all those new philosophical books put at your disposal; but they must not injure your health, or put a stop to your more serious productivity.

I have been turning over the pages of "Sartor Resartus." Do you not agree with me that it is one of the most *important* books of the century? If only Carlyle had more closely adhered to that doctrine of philosophic idealism! His influence would probably have been deeper and more lasting. But in "Sartor" he wrote one of the world's eternal volumes. It is a sort of Bible.

Tolstoi, I fear, is dying.[698] Him I esteem more and more; his tendency is of vast importance in such a noisy, greedy time as ours. The future will see him in a clearer light than he appears in now.

Of course I am heartily at one with you in loathing this war-fever

[697] Pastor Krausz, a character in Bertz's *Glück und Glas*.
[698] Tolstoi died in 1910.

which has possession of the English.[699] It is a grievous retrogression. And does it not amaze one, the perpetual assumption in newspaper-writers that all the nations of the world are eager to fly at each other's throats! We know so well that not *nations* at all, but greedy *syndicates* and the like, are the cause of this barbarism. The people follow like sheep and like sheep go to slaughter. One groans, often, in heaviness of heart.

I see that an English translation of a book on Ethics by Prof. Paulsen is being very well received in England.[700] Of course you know it.

I get on, slowly, with my "Among the Prophets." Winter is always an unfavourable time for my work; the sky depresses me grievously. I hope to have finished before the spring.

Once again, all good wishes, in which I am joined by Gabrielle. She hopes soon to be able to let you hear about "Glück und Glas." Let us hope, hope, hope for the new year, and then for the new century.

> Ever yours,
> GEORGE GISSING

Addressed: Herrn Eduard Bertz. / Alexandrinen strasse. 15 / Potsdam. / *Allemagne.*

> January 12, 1900.

Dear friend, I perfectly understand, and thoroughly approve, your decision to postpone writing about my book. It was a pain to me to think of you adding this to the immediate pressure of your work. I shall be very eager indeed to see the book which is so nearly ready; you are in good spirits and hope! Gabrielle is much better, and has already read "G[lück] u[nd] G[las]." Oh yes, she would like to say something about it to you, presently; for certain things in it have struck her very much. Of course I have carefully explained to her the relation it bears to your present mode

---

[699] In the early months of the Boer War, which broke out on 12 October 1899, the small English force met several defeats; the result in England was a surge of nationalistic feeling and a deep interest in the war.

[700] Friedrich Paulsen (1846–1908), professor of philosophy at Berlin. The book was *System der Ethik* (2 vols., Berlin, 1889), translated into English by Frank Thilly (London, 1899).

of thought. My "Among the Prophets" goes on slowly, though I am trying hard to get it finished soon. But the state of the book-trade in England is alarming just now, and it is possible I shall have great difficulties before long.[701] I reply quickly, lest you should misunderstand my silence. Letters from both of us will come very soon. Many thanks for your kind remembrances to G[abrielle], who returns them heartily.

> Ever yours,
> G. G.

13 Rue de Siam. / Paris.

January 22. 1900.

Dear Friend,

I wonder whether you know a book called "La Cité Moderne," [sic] by Jean Izoulet (prof. de philosophie au lycée Condorcet)—pub[lished] at Paris (Alcan) 1894?[702] I fancy you would find it very interesting and remarkable. It is an ethical treatise on the basis of sociology. Socialism, in the ordinary sense, it strongly opposes (he makes a distinction between l'élite and la foule) yet its object is to show the unity of mankind, and to deduce all morality from the principle of association. This will give you no idea of the book, if you do not know it. I wish it might be possible for you to lay your hands on it, as I cannot help thinking that it contains much which would please you. Izoulet evidently has a wide culture. He often quotes Goethe and English poets. The style is of geometrical clearness, yet there are passages which strike me as very fine. A large book, nearly 700 pp.

I am drawing slowly to the end of "Among the Prophets." It does not greatly please me.

You will know that Ruskin is dead.[703] The last of England's really great men. If he had been capable of watching events, how

---

[701] "Just as I was hoping to earn a little more money comes this scoundrelly war, and the ruin of the book trade" (GRG to Ellen Gissing, *Letters*, 2 January 1900, p. 368).

[702] Jean Bernard Joachim Izoulet-Loubatière, *La Cité moderne. Métaphysique de la sociologie*. Dyce Lashmar, the anti-hero of Gissing's *Our Friend the Charlatan*, constructs his "biosociological" theory from the principles suggested and discussed in *La Cité moderne*.

[703] He died on 20 January 1900.

he would have scorned the time that could exalt such a man as Chamberlain![704] Indeed, I suppose it is the first time in English history that a man so thoroughly ignoble has obtained the position of a leader. Of course you are right in saying that *Finance* is the enemy. But the world will go its way.

I hope you will escape the universal influenza. Be careful in the evil month of February.

> Ever yours,
> GEORGE GISSING

I copy a typical passage from Izoulet:
"L'Europe est en révolution, non pas depuis 1789, non pas même depuis la Réforme, mais depuis la fin du 13e. siècle.

"Et cette vaste et profonde Révolution, c'est le retour du *dualisme au monisme,* ou de la *transcendance* à *l'immanence:* ....

"C'est à dire que, par dessus la crise médiévale, la moderne humanité d'Occident renoue la tradition avec l'antiquité, et rallie la grande voie du genre humain."
> — Livre III. Chap. 14.

Addressed: Herrn Eduard Bertz. / Alexandrinen strasse. 15 / Potsdam / ALLEMAGNE
Paris.

> February 21. 1900.

Dear Friend,

We are thinking of you and your work. Hope soon to have good news.[705] Have you escaped influenza? Doubtless you received our letters some time ago.

You will be glad to hear that "By the Ionian Sea" has been accepted for publication in the *Fortnightly Review.* This is a step in advance.

I have finished "Among the Prophets," and am now turning my thoughts again to "The Coming Man."

---

[704] Joseph Chamberlain (1836–1914), a retired Birmingham screw manufacturer, who led the Liberal Unionists in Parliament and served as Colonial Secretary. He was the father of Neville Chamberlain.

[705] That Bertz had found a publisher for his book.

"The Odd Women" is being translated into German by Herr Von Oppeln-Bronikowski,[706] of Berlin. He seems to be very capable—and a gentleman.

Yours ever,
G. G.

13 Rue de Siam. / Paris.

March 11. 1900.

Dear Friend,

Do be careful. You will be having an attack of writer's cramp, if you don't mind. The copying must have been a hideous task, but thank heaven it is really done. I await with the utmost curiosity "Philosophie des Fahrrads"; beyond doubt, it will be a most remarkable book. The payment is ridiculous; is it final? I should think it very likely indeed that such a book may excite a good deal of attention. You wrote it quite spontaneously—which is a great thing.

Now about the English Literature. I wish you could treat the subject at greater length, but not impossibly this Chapter may lead to something else.[707] I have written to England for information about books, and you shall hear as soon as possible. I have not read Mrs Oliphant's History,[708] but I remember that it was noticed rather severely, as a very perfunctory work. I hope to be able to mention more useful books in a few days. No, I don't remember any work of that kind by a *man* named Oliphant;[709] I have asked about it.

As you say, two books are quite enough for one year. Of course I want to read the ethical book, but I should not like to think of you toiling at it now. Plainly, you ought to have a rest. I am sorry

---

[706] Friedrich von Oppeln-Bronikowski (1873–1936), German historian and biographer. He had also translated the works of Stendahl and Maeterlinck.

[707] Bertz was writing a chapter on English literature for Wilhelm Spemann's *Das goldene Buch der Weltlitteratur* (Berlin, 1900).

[708] Margaret Wilson Oliphant, *The Literary History of England in the End of the 18th. and the Beginning of the 19th. Century* (3 vols., London, 1882).

[709] Bertz might have meant James Oliphant, author of *Victorian Novelists* (Glasgow, 1899).

you are obliged to turn at once to reviewing. But it is very probable that, after this year, you will find it better to give that up.

It is a great pity that Ruskin should be misrepresented by collections of "aphorisms."[710] I fear one could easily make a large collection of foolish and hasty sayings from his voluminous work. But, on the other hand, nothing would be easier than to collect a great number of most admirable passages. Ruskin must be considered as a prophetic force. The value of his *theories* is often very doubtful, but his *spirit* cannot be too highly esteemed. And as a writer of prose, he stands in the very front of English literature. No one, since the great Elizabethan time has written such English. In our century the only prosaist to be spoken of together with him is Landor, whose best pages are glorious. De Quincy, too, as you know, has a great deal of noble prose, but, mentally, he is on a somewhat lower level.

Your domestic worries are very grievous. Poor old Frau Sommerfeld![711] I fear she was horribly incompetent, and I heartily hope that her successor gives you more satisfaction. Of course it is monstrous that your time and strength should be wasted in domestic labour.

Send me any question you like whilst you are engaged on the Eng[lish] Lit[erature] work; I will do my best to answer at once.

At the beginning of April I shall have to go to England for a short time. It is almost impossible to do all one's business by correspondence, and then too I find it necessary to collect some material for my next novel. Of course you shall know all about dates presently. In the middle of May, we hope to go to Savoy, to pass about four months at S. Gervais. In that way we shall avoid the horrors of the Exhibition. Mme Fleury will go with us. I hope to have at least one month of holiday at S. Gervais but for the most of the time I shall be working. I think my next book will be "The Coming Man." At present I am reading the typewritten copy of "Among the Prophets," and it gives me very little satisfaction. I'm afraid—to tell the truth—that it is rather poor stuff.

[710] *John Ruskin, Thoughts.* Chosen and arranged by Henry Attwell (London, November 1900).
[711] Bertz's housekeeper.

By the bye, a recent novel of my brother's has been remarkably well reviewed. Perhaps you have noticed it in the Athenaeum— "A Secret of the North Sea."[712] I am very glad, for the poor fellow has been going through dire struggles lately. I have not read this book, but I fancy it must be very good.

I feel a certain gratification at the fact that my "Ionian Sea" is to appear in the Fortnightly. When they will begin the publication, I don't know, but it is to be some time this year, and *not* in successive numbers. They are to pay £120 for the serial rights. I hope to publish it afterwards in a volume with illustrations. With more leisure, I could have made the thing better. But the terrible money question haunts me ceaselessly, and I am never able to work with a really calm mind.

Do you happen to know what is the period during which (under the Berne convention) an author has the right to make translators pay? I have been astounded to discover that my agent, Pinker, is absolutely ignorant of the subject. There is no hurry about this; I ask only out of curiosity.

On the 18 August of this year, the works of Balzac fall into the *domaine public*. French copyright lasts fifty years after the author's death. I wish we had such a law in England. (It is for 42 years after publication, or 7 years after author's death—whichever be the longer period.)

Gabrielle is always delighted to hear from you, but she begs that you will not write just yet; you are far too busy, and indeed this excess of writing becomes really dangerous. Take care!

I shall be curious to have your opinion of "Stalky." I fancy it is an infamous production. Of course Kipling is only an instrument of fate, but, as such, he is doing incalculable harm to the human race. At present he is at the Cape, and I see that he has just taken upon himself to telegraph to an Australian newspaper, calling for a fresh supply of horses for the war! However,

---

[712] London: Chatto, January 1900. After praising the book, the reviewer said: "It is only necessary to add that a slight acquaintance with current literature will readily distinguish between Mr. Algernon Gissing's work and that of Mr. George Gissing. We cannot here point out the numerous elements of contrast in their respective writings" (*Athenaeum*, 10 February 1900, p. 173).

we must not forget that, in his early days, he did some very strong things.

Affectionate regards to you from us both.

Ever yours, dear Friend,
GEORGE GISSING

With regard to *American* literature, note the recent rising of a strong school of historical romance.

Addressed: Herrn Eduard Bertz. / Alexandrinen strasse, 15 / Potsdam / *Allemagne.*
Paris.

March 17. 1900.

I have an unsatisfactory reply from London. There is mention of a little book on Victorian novels by *George Saintsbury,*[713] but nothing else. I am writing again.

Yours,
G. G.

13 Rue de Siam. / Paris.

March 28. 1900.

Dear Friend,

Herewith a satisfactory list of books on Victorian literature. Henry Morley's Volume is, I think, in Tauchnitz,[714] but not worth much. No one of them is known to me by actual reading so I cannot give much advice.

I shall be anxious to hear that you have got over your cold. I heartily hope it did not prove to be anything worse.

The payment for your book is, I think, disgraceful. But why, why, *why* did you not have a regular agreement? One can *never* trust a publisher. I feel sure he[715] would have agreed to pay you at least twice the money. I entreat you never to do such a thing again. Always stipulate for a certain sum.

I am very anxious indeed to see the book.

If all goes well, I shall leave here on Monday next (April 2)

[713] *Corrected Impressions: Essays on Victorian Writers* (London, 1895).

[714] *Of English Literature in the Reign of Victoria with a Glance at the Past* (Leipzig, 1882). This was volume 2000 in Tauchnitz's "Collection of British Authors."

[715] Carl Reissner published Bertz's *Philosophie des Fahrrads.*

and pass one month in England. I have a great deal to do there—
to visit relatives, to get material for new books, to talk with my
agent, and all sorts of thing [*sic*]. First of all I shall go straight to
Wakefield, so that, if you do not hear from me again, my address
after April 2 will be: 9 Wentworth Terrace. / Wakefield.

I hope I shan't get any harm by the change of climate. It is
certain that the *dryness* of Paris suits me very well, for, though
the winter has been a bad one, I have scarcely had a cold, and very
little cough. I wish I could have delayed my visit to England, but
we hope to leave Paris before the end of May for the mountains.
Of course that depends on Mme. Fleury's health, which is extremely uncertain.

You are overburdened with work. How I wish it were possible
for you to have a really good holiday! If ever a man needed and
deserved a rest, it is you. I wonder whether the gods will grant
us a few quiet days together, once more, before the end of all
things?

With regard to "Stalky and Co.," I should like to know whether
it is *true* as a picture of English schoolboys nowadays? To be sure,
one must remember that the school described is *military*. But
there have been a good many protests from English schoolmasters.
Imagine this book surviving into a remote century, and being
accepted as a picture of our civilization!

Gabrielle sends her kindest remembrances. She will be glad to
read your book.

Ever yours,
GEORGE GISSING

Do not trouble to acknowledge receipt of this. Send a card,
presently, to Wakefield. But, by the bye, if you do so, do not
mention on the card anything relating *to Paris*. Of course it has
to be kept secret from my family.[716]

Addressed: Herrn Eduard Bertz. / Alexandrinen strasse, 15 /
    Potsdam.
9 Wentworth Terrace. / Wakefield.

April 6. 1900.
To my surprise, I have come into brilliant weather. Shall stay

[716] GRG had not told his mother and sisters in Wakefield of his relationship with Gabrielle.

21

here till Wednesday, then go on to Lincoln (which I want to use in a book).[717] If necessary, address still to Wakefield. Please send your book to Paris; G[abrielle] will be delighted to have it. Let me know any way in which I can be useful *re* English Literature. Hope all goes well.

Yours, GEORGE GISSING

13 Rue de Siam. / Paris.

May 7. 1900.

My dear Friend,

On reaching Paris,[718] I was seized with a severe attack of inter-costal rheumatism, which kept me in bed for two days. Mean-while, I happily had your book to read, and it helped me greatly. Before speaking of it in detail, let me explain to you the position of affairs in our house. The flat has been let to strangers for the summer, and, in consequence, we have to go into the country on the 25th. of this month, exactly. We are going to St. Honoré-les-bains, near Nevers, a beautiful place at the foot of the Morvan hills, where we have taken a villa till the end of October. I will send you the precise address. Meanwhile, a great deal of packing and arranging has to be done; it must needs be done slowly, owing to the weakness of Mme. Fleury, who of course goes with us.

Having told you this, I can turn to speak of your very interesting book. In one respect it has surprised me, being far more practical than I had expected. Indeed, it is a *guide* to the use of the Bicycle. But of course it is also far more than that. As you told me, you have put into this book a great deal of your mature thought on the gravest of modern subjects.

First of all, the practical details. In reading you, I reviewed all my own experience as a cyclist, during that summer at Dorking, and found all sorts of little things which I had had occasion to think about. The great question of health preponderates. You know that I rather fear I did myself harm by the exercise, and simply because I exaggerated it—the point on which you give such useful

[717] He spent five days at Lincoln, taking notes for *Our Friend the Charlatan*, which he had tentatively called "The Coming Man."

[718] GRG spent the last two days in April with H. G. Wells at Sandgate before returning to France on 1 May 1900 (*Letters*, p. 369).

warning. Then again, I never had a cycling costume, which was a great mistake. I used to get drenched with perspiration, and of course caught colds and rheumatism and liver-complaint; and I don't know what. By the bye, your remarks on the trouble experienced by Germans about their costume are very curious. I was surprised to hear of the prohibition to enter a law-court in cycling garb. In England, nothing has ever been said about *man's* dress; the only objection is to *women* in knickerbockers etc.

On p. 88, you object to the use of the term *gentlemen* riders, *gentlemen* cricketers etc. Now, so far as this involves snobbery, I too dislike the word. But it occurs to me that, in our day, more good than harm may be done by insisting on the distinction of those who play a game for its own sake, and those who do so for money. One of the characteristics of the *true* gentleman (no one knows it better than you) is his scorn of self-interest in matters where that has no legitimate place, and I confess I think it necessary, nowadays, to accentuate this nobler characteristic. As Tennyson says, the word *gentleman* is "defiled by every charlatan, and soiled by all ignoble use";[719] but the *thing* still exists, and one would try to preserve it.

p. 93. Very curious, that *Automatism*, and quite news to me.

p. 99. Very good the phrase *ein gewiszer Urwald-zustand des Geistes*, and of course absolutely true.

About the action of the mind, during riding. Do you know, I found myself constantly working hard upon the next chapter of my novel! This was doubtless because I rode in Surrey lanes, where there was no danger. But it is clear that in no respect did I get the full benefit of cycling.

p. 104. Too true, the political results of the sporting spirit in England. And—as you see—how terribly difficult to keep it within bounds, anywhere! Again and again you have to return to *media tutissimus*; but is it to be hoped that men will ever learn that lesson.

Extremely interesting, all your *personal notes*. I wished there had been more of them. "Nicht die Ideen herrschen, aber die

[719] *In Memoriam*, CXI: And thus he bore without abuse
The grand old name of gentleman,
Defamed by every charlatan,
And soil'd with all ignoble use.

Stimmung ist verinnerlicht; sie schwebt hoch über dem Leben."
I think that admirable, as observation and expression.

Indeed, Chapter VI is especially good. It is both wide of scope,
and deep of insight.

p. 160. Wir können daher den Satz aufstellen etc. Yes, this is
the truth, indeed. Here you have hit the nail on the head. All
difficulties in the endless controversy are solved by keeping in
mind this simple key to the truth about woman's nature.

p. 182. Very legitimate, your deductions from the principle that
a cyclist is of necessity keenly aware of his human rights. But,
by the bye, would it not be a cause of great public inconvenience if,
as you propose, cyclists were allowed to use the side-walk (Bankette)? What about pedestrians? I am afraid they would altogether
be driven into the road. I am told that in Belgium special tracks
for cyclists are made, *between* the road and the pedestrian's sidewalk. This, of course, is the ideal state of things. In your last
chapter (p. 230) you seem to say that *abroad* there is more liberty
to cyclists in this respect. Is it really so? Certainly not in England,
and I think not in France. Your argument on this subject is very
full, and I do not pronounce emphatically against it, but the fact
remains that the bicycle is a *wheeled* vehicle, and, as such, seems
to call for a track apart from that of pedestrians. Granting that
mere *proscription* has no force, I should feel disposed to say that,
if the sidewalk is thrown open to cyclists, pedestrians have certainly
the just claim to some other track of road. The point is that a
feeble person, walking, should not be compelled to keep all his
eyes about him to avoid collision with wheeled vehicles. However,
you end by granting that the demand for use of the Bankette
applies only to a temporary state of affairs, and this of course is
the best way of regarding the matter.

In reading you, I have often smiled to find a stronger spirit
than I expected against *den alten Schlendrian*! The fact is, I grow
very conservative in my ways of thought—a curious thing for a
man of my experience, and in my peculiar position. You, I fancy,
are decidedly more progressive in your habit of mind.

Of course your last chapter has a far wider significance than
would appear to the casual *cyclist* reader. It implies a whole social
philosophy. "Ein werdendes Recht" is that of Humanity—not
merely of the Radler. I am struck by your pithy statement of the

upshot of Nietzsche's teaching; obviously it is the truth of the matter; Nietzsche must be regarded as a Man-worshipper in the larger sense. The kernel of your own philosophy is in the passage at the foot of p. 228, "Durch sein Alter allein" etc. Yes, yes, yes; *Entwickelungsfreiheit!* Whether we like it or not, that is the principle of life on this world, and, with you, I cannot help thinking that on the whole it promises for *some day* a true ethical Culture. How far ahead, one dare not conjecture.

Well, to a certain extent you may say: Liberavi animam meam! This book has a significance, as everything of yours must needs have. It well rewards the reading, and I thank you for it.

Whilst in England, I saw Pinker, my agent, twice, and had long talks with him. He thinks it indispensable to get my books out of the hands of L[awrence] and B[ullen], who do nothing with them.[720] But to whom they are to be transferred remains uncertain. However, Pinker is an excellent man of business, and will act for the best.

The first part of "By the Ionian Sea" appears in the May *Fortnightly.* You will read it when it comes out as a volume.

I have a short story to write before I leave Paris—that is to say, if I can get hold of one.[721]

I cannot tell you how glad I was, old friend, to have such good news from you about your easy circumstances this year. Let me know what you are going to do. I heartily hope that you will manage a good holiday. For my own part, I *must* write "The Coming Man" whilst I am at St. Honoré, and that will leave me little leisure. You, too, have a terrible lot of work on hand. But remember that your health is more important than the immediate results of publication.

Gabrielle will have to read your book at St. Honoré. She is overwhelmed with domestic work, as you may suppose. But the quiet days will come, and you shall hear from her.

All good be with you!

Yours ever, dear Friend,
GEORGE GISSING

---

[720] They held the copyrights of *Denzil Quarrier* (1892), *The Odd Women* (1893), *In the Year of Jubilee* (1894), *Eve's Ransom* (1895), *The Whirlpool* (1897), and *Human Odds and Ends* (1898).

[721] "The Scrupulous Father," *Cornhill Magazine*, X NS (February 1901), 175–87.

Villa des Roses. / St. Honoré les bains. / Nièvre. / France.

August 5. 1900.

Dear Old Friend,

Gabrielle was delighted with your long and kind letter. At the moment I dreaded the least letter-writing; now, as I begin to see the end of my book, I feel able to send you a line. If all goes well, I shall finish "The Coming Man" this month. It is perhaps amusing; I rather think so.

Your English Literature must have given you severe labour; I rejoice to know that it is finished. Of course you have been suffering from the heat, like everyone else. I worked all through it, but for several days sat dressed only in a cotton shirt and drawers, with bare feet! The slightest additional garment was unendurable.

Chapman and Hall are going to publish "By the Ionian Sea" after it has run through the *Fortnightly*. They want to have it well illustrated, and are trying to find an artist who can make use of the elementary sketches I brought back with me.[722]

The newspapers lately have made me ill.[723] It is to be feared that never again in our lifetime shall we see peace and quietness. Of course the outlook of literature is very gloomy. There seems little hope for anything but books which deal with questions of practical interest. No *great* writer can be looked for, I am quite sure, nor, indeed, any great artist of any kind. A period of struggle for existence between the nations seems to have begun, and indeed it will obviously soon be a struggle for the very means of life. This may very well result in a long period of semi-barbarism, until— perhaps by immense slaughter, perhaps by famines and epidemics —the numbers of the human race are once more reduced.

I am reading Holm's History of Greece.[724] How it refreshes one to go back into those times when *the world was large*! It is little enough now, in every sense of the word.

It will amuse you to learn that Ollendorffs have just bought from

[722] See 13 September 1897.

[723] "The barbarisation of the world goes merrily on. No doubt there will be continuous warfare for many a long year to come. It sickens me to read the newspapers; I turn as much as possible to the old poets" (GRG to Clara Collet, *Letters*, 8 July 1900, p. 371).

[724] Adolf Holm, *The History of Greece from Its Commencement to the Close of the Independence of the Greek Nation* (4 vols., London, 1894–1898).

me (for 300 francs) the right to translate "The Unclassed."[725] Why they paid, I do not know, as of course the book is long ago in the *domaine public*. The old "Unclassed"! It was written a lifetime ago.

Of course I knew that your book would have appreciative notices; I should like to have seen those by Bölsche[726] and Burckhard.[727] As for the sale, why, I have almost ceased to think of a great sale as possible in the case of any book which is quite serious in spirit. Fashion gives vogue to a few writers of the better kind, it is true, but in general the selling book is the all but worthless book. Still, we must not feel sure that your book will not find a public. In its nature, it will continue to be of interest for a long time, and then, you (like me) would be more than content with a sale considerably less than that enjoyed by Hall Caine or Marie Corelli!

I am grieved to hear of Rehfeldt's illness, especially as it put an end to your hopes of a much-needed holiday. Indeed, I don't know how you go on in this way, year after year, without proper rest and change. You must have an immense reserve of strength—obviously much more than I have, for I soon break down.

How annoying, about the "Hamburger Nachrichten"![728] Yet, as it is not certain that they will decline, I shall continue to hope for better news. At all events the novel will come about as a book, and I shall read it.

Fiction seems to be dead in France. Nothing of the slightest importance has appeared for a long time, putting aside "Fécondité"[729]—a book I dare not read, for I have grown to abhor Zola's grossness. Science is swallowing up the arts. It is rather humiliating to have to live by story-telling in a time which condemns one to mediocrity.

[725] No record of a published translation.
[726] Wilhelm Bölsche (1861-?), a minor poet but an influential critic. Bölsche reviewed *Philosophie des Fahrrads* in *Das litterarische Echo* (II, 15 June 1900, 1249–54) as a feature article on the first page of the magazine.
[727] Max Eugen Burckhard (1854–1912), Austrian writer and critic, who said: "Wenn eine Philosophie des Fahrrads überhaupt zu schreiben wäre, so hat Bertz sie geliefert" (*Wiener Abendpost*, No. 12, 1900).
[728] Bertz wanted to have his novel, *Der blinde Eros*, printed serially in a newspaper before bringing it out as a volume.
[729] *Les Quatre Évangiles. Fécondité* (Paris, 1899).

You are getting on, no doubt, with your ethical work, and you will tell me more about it presently.

Gabrielle sends kindest regards and wishes. All good be with you!

Ever yours,
GEORGE GISSING

Addressed: Herrn Eduard Bertz. / Alexandrinenstrasse. 15 / Potsdam / *Allemagne.*

Villa des Roses / St. Honoré les bains. / Nièvre / France.

September 6. 1900.

Dear Friend, I have been wanting to write to you day after day, but cannot get the time. My book is finished, but I have a lot of little things to get off hand. Hearty thanks for the photograph, which is excellent. Gabrielle is much pleased with it. I quite agree with you that you must not do that ethical chapter unless you can sign it yourself, and write it frankly from your own point of view.[730] It would be waste of time. You are working terribly hard, and I am so afraid that you will overtax your strength. Do not dream of writing letters just now. The summer has been most interesting: we have need of a little tonic weather. Here it is still hot. I wish I could get away from my desk a little, but that will depend on the terms I am able to make for "The Coming Man." Of course life is as difficult with me as ever, from the money point of view; and likely always to be so. I can imagine that you had not much delight in the article on Automobilism;[731] thank heaven it is done!

Gabrielle sends her kindest regards.

Ever yours,
G. G.

Villa des Roses / St. Honoré les bains. / Nièvre / France.

September 30. 1900.

Dear Friend,

I am delighted to see, from your last letter and card, how well

---

[730] "Spruchweisheit," *Das litterarische Echo*, III (March 1901), 818–22.

[731] "Automobil und Radsport," published serially in *Zeit* (a Viennese weekly paper), between January and June 1901.

things are going with you. Yes, it is good that your cycling book has been taken seriously by the medical and educational papers. Of course it was only written for serious people—the mere sportsman would find little in it to his mind. Now I trust, you will often find the opportunity of saying what you really *want* to say. "Oui, répondit Pococurante, il est beau d'écrire ce qu'on pense; c'est le privilège de l'homme."

By the bye, what did Goethe really mean by those words of his—"Was man in der Jugend" etc?[732] Is it a general expression of optimism? Common experience *seems* flagrantly to contradict it. I should like to know your own real opinion some day.

Now I will tell you what I am doing. "The Coming Man" is trying to get serialized; Pinker (my agent) thinks he will succeed in doing that. (By the bye, I am delighted to hear that there is still hope for the serial publication of *your* novel.) The difficulty is that I cannot wait long. My pinched circumstances are always the cause of much loss to me. "By the Ionian Sea" is to appear (Chapman and Hall) next spring; they promise to have it well illustrated. Pinker has sold the copyright *for seven years* (a good plan) for £130. Not much, but then the book is not a novel. The *Fortnightly* paid me the same sum for serial rights.

I am now writing a little book which has been in my head for many years. It is to be called "An Author at Grass"—rather a good title, I think.[733] I imagine an author who has led a long Grub Street life, and who, at the age of fifty, is blest with a legacy which gives him £300 a year. Forthwith he goes down into Somerset, establishes himself in a cottage, and passes the last five years of his life in wonderful calm and contentment. During this time he keeps a diary—not a formal day-book, but occasional jottings of his experience and thought and memories. I, at his death, am supposed to publish selections from this *Nachlasz* [*sic*]. Behold the title-page:

[732] "Was man in der Jugend wünscht, hat man im Alter die Fülle" (Motto for the second part of Goethe's *Dichtung und Wahrheit*). For GRG's discussion of this phrase, and his interpretation of it, see *The Private Papers of Henry Ryecroft*, "Autumn," Chapter VII. See 15 February 1903.

[733] Published in book form as *The Private Papers of Henry Ryecroft* (London: Archibald Constable and Co., 1903).

An Author at Grass.

_____

Extracts from the private papers
of Henry Ryecroft.
Selected
by
George Gissing
"Hoc erat in votis."

— —

Now it strikes me that this book will rather please you. I divide it into four sections: Spring, Summer, Autumn, Winter. I hope there will be some good bits of English, and some decent thoughts. In any case, it is a great rest to my mind after so much fiction of the ordinary sort. Indeed the thing is doing me good.

Let me know your opinion some day.

We shall go back to Paris about the end of October, probably stopping on the way to see some of Gabrielle's relatives at Nevers. Well, this Summer, thank heaven, I have not wasted. I am in better health than for a very long time. Our garden is full of grapes, apples, pears, plums, and this diet is beneficial, no doubt.

It is good news that your Nietzsche brochure will appear after all.[734] I shall be eager to read it. But most of all am I glad to think that you see a chance of a holiday next Summer. Indeed it is high time. If possible, do not work too hard through the winter.

Gabrielle sends her kindest remembrances, with many thanks for yours.

Ever affectionately,
GEORGE GISSING

St. Honoré les bains.

October 24. 1900.

Dear old Friend,

I grieve to hear of your illness, and of all the annoyance it has caused you. It is strange that even the doctor cannot understand

[734] Bertz had two articles on Nietzsche published between July and December 1900. One was "Friedrich Nietzsche," printed in the Hamburger *Nachrichten*, and the other, "Nietzsche in seinen Briefen," appeared in *Zeit* (Vienna). Probably both of these articles composed the Nietzsche brochure.

this swelling of the foot. I suppose it is not in any way connected with your bicycle exercise? Well, I earnestly hope that it will prove to be only local. There is no doubt that for a long time you have overworked yourself; I wish it were possible to put an end to that bad state of things. But I know all the difficulties, and should be the last to preach on such a subject.

We hope to leave St. Honoré on Saturday, but we do not return straight to Paris. About a week will be spent at Nevers, with some of Gabrielle's relatives. It will be better, therefore, if you do not address to Paris until about the 4th. of November. After that I hope we shall be settled again.

Well, I have finished "An Author at Grass," which makes a little book of about 45,000 words—to use the common method of description. As a bit of English, it is better than anything I have yet done—of that I feel no doubt. As to its reception by the public, that is another matter. I have expressed very freely my views with regard to the present tendencies of English life; but, at the same time, I have put into relief the old English virtues—so there will be things pleasant as well as disagreeable.

On settling again, I shall begin at once upon another novel, which is now growing in my head. The fact of the matter is, people seem to be forgetting me—readers, I mean—and I shall have to publish rapidly, to put myself *en évidence* again. My old books (those in Bullen's hands) have a very small continuous sale; some of them (*The Odd Women, The Unclassed*, and one or two others) are bought to the extent of twenty-five or thirty copies a year (each). Of course this is ridiculous, but it is better than absolute cessation of sale. Whether the sale will ever increase, who knows? Bullen has now gone out of publishing, and for the moment nothing can be done.[735] Pinker is doing his best, however, to find some decent publisher who will purchase Bullen's interest, and take over the books. Of course my great disadvantage is that no periodical takes any particular interest in me; I am seldom spoken of nowadays.

It is freezing here now, but the sun shines brightly. I suppose we shall have a long and severe winter, which is not a pleasant

---

[735] Bullen had dissolved his partnership with H. W. Lawrence, but he had not left the publishing business permanently.

prospect with coals risen to such a price. I fancy the world is becoming very uncomfortable, as well as very foolish. The two things naturally go together.

Well, all good be with you! We two, at all events, shall continue to understand each other. I hope to hear of your great improvement. Yes, yes, if you *could* devote yourself to your real work, I should be glad—but I don't wish you to do so as a result of broken health.

Always affectionately Yours,
GEORGE GISSING

13 Rue de Siam. / Paris.

December 26. 1900.

Dear Friend,

With great pleasure I received the volume—"Das Goldene [*sic*] Buch der Weltlitteratur,"—and of course I turned at once to your section of it.[736] It seems to me that you have done this bit of work very well indeed; and how difficult it was to do at all any man of letters can understand. You have compressed a wonderful amount of information into a short space; yet, it is not mere *pemmican*; you have managed, in an astonishing way, to preserve the qualities of your style, notwithstanding the demands of brevity. Of course I was mainly interested in what you had to say about the novelists, and I thought it very good. On Charlotte Bronte and George Eliot you are excellent; but so you are on all. Performed as a task, this turns out an admirable bit of work. I wonder whether any conspectus of English literature anything like so good exists in German. The American part, also, is very well done, and must have given you a great deal of trouble.

As to what you have said about me, I am more than satisfied.[737] Thank you, old friend!

[736] Bertz had written one section on English literature and one on American literature.

[737] "Hardy. Gissing. Meredith. Die drei bedeutendsten unter den lebenden englischen Romanschriftstellern sind George Meredith, Thomas Hardy und George Gissing.... Den sozialen Roman vertritt seit 1880 George Gissing (geb. 1857), der Begründer des modernen Naturalismus in England. Er ist der erste, der die englische Arbeiterklasse aus voller Kenntnis realistisch und ohne tendenziöse Färbung darstellte. Seine Chrakterzeichnung [*sic*] ist fein und mannigfaltig, seine Naturempfindung sehr lebendig, sein Blick umfassend, die Weltanschauung stark pessimistisch. Mit gleicher Wahrheit

Well now, we are entering upon another new year, and may it be for you, in great part, a year of rest. You have worked enormously—there is no other word for it, and I should be really relieved to think of you as reposing. I am often very uneasy about your foot. Gabrielle and I talk of the matter frequently; your last news did not tend to set our minds at ease. I wonder whether *season* has any appreciable effect upon the foot? Do not be tempted, by the bye, to think of this as only a local ailment; I feel quite sure that it must have some larger significance, which I hope the doctors will discover before long—for it is better to know *à quoi s'en tenir*. What what [*sic*] Rehfeldt's final opinion? You must suffer very much indeed from the necessity of keeping a reclining posture; for I suppose you find it impossible to write under those circumstances. Remember that I shall be grieved, rather than pleased, if you send me *long* letters whilst you have so little time to spare. Always let me know how your health goes on, but do not write at length except when you feel thoroughly able to do so.

By the bye, I was amused at my portrait in the *Goldene* [*sic*] *Buch*. I had forgotten its existence. Why, it must be some fifteen years old? Yours is excellent, I was glad to see.

This *Buch* will enable me to learn more about contemporary German literature, which I very much wished to do. But, alas! I have so little time for reading. I have begun—really begun— "The Vanquished Roman"; the first two pages are written. It has taken me a month to make an elaborate plan of the whole story— which of course is a most important thing. I really think I can make an interesting book. One thing is certain—I know my period. Few people, I imagine, are so well acquainted with that bit of Italian history—political, civil, ecclesiastical. Lately I have found useful books in the Bibl[iothèque] Nationale. Well, now for the actual writing, which will take practically all my time and all

---

dringt er in das Seelenleben des Volkes und der höchsten Bildung. Er gestaltete nach einander die verschiedenen Probleme der modernen Kultur zu typischen Bildern: die Psychologie des Sozialismus in 'Demos', die untersten Schichten Londons in 'The Nether World', die Schriftstellernöte in 'New Grub Street', die Frauenfrage in 'The Odd Women'. Er hat auch ein vorzügliches Buch über Dickens geschrieben, das als Kritik der alten Schule durch die neue ästhetisch von groszem Interesse und als gerechte Würdigung für beide Teile ehrenvoll ist" (pars. 361-63).

my thoughts. The beginning is fearfully difficult, for I have to find a new style.

In the spring, I too shall have something to send you—"By the Ionian Sea." Chapman and Hall have found an illustrator, and they talk of making a really handsome volume. Well, you shall have it, of course, as soon as it is published. As for my novel, we find that the title "The Coming Man" has already been used. I think it will be called "The Young Man Eloquent." Pinker has not yet settled about its publication, and I fear I shall not get such good terms for it as for my last. The truth is, you know, people are rather forgetting me, and I shall have a hard struggle to keep myself alive, with all my expenses. It is a disagreeable thing to feel that, at my age, I am beginning to lose even what little public I had.

I believe the publication of "New Grub Street" will begin in *Les Débats* in a few weeks. It is to be called "La Rue des Meurt-de-faim!" Gabrielle's translation is excellent.

Happily for me, I have no disturbances from England—that is to say, no material disturbances. My lawyer[738] pays that terrible woman £104 a year, and she makes no trouble. Of course I am often driven almost mad in thinking of the poor child who remains in her hands—but I can do nothing.[739] Walter goes on very well at Wakefield. It will soon be time to think of what he is going to do in life—a terrible difficulty, of course. Well, I can only work.

Gabrielle sends her very kindest regards. She is always much occupied in looking after her mother, who remains in the same state—the heart disease (or rather, disease of the arteries) going its slow way. She sees a few friends from time to time, but I have time to see no one at all.

All good be with you in 1901. I cannot help thinking that you still have many years of good work before you. We think of you always.

Ever yours,
GEORGE GISSING

[738] Brewster.
[739] Edith was still in lodgings in London with Alfred; Miss Orme, a former member of the Lawrence and Bullen staff, was supposed to keep her under surveillance.

13 Rue de Siam / Paris.

March 17. 1901.

Dear old Friend,

Gabrielle is down again with the influenza; she has it regularly twice every winter—a confounded nuisance. Of course it is not immediately serious, but sometimes ill results come from it, and the fact that both her parents have suffered from heart disease of course makes one anxious. On this account, she is not able to reply herself to your kind letter. We are both worried about your ailment; but it is at all events very good news that you will feel able, this summer, to give particular care to your health. I very urgently recommend you not to change this intention. You do not know what good might result from a real holiday—such as you have not had for years; nay, when *did* you last take a holiday? I am very glad, on all accounts, about the *Hamburger Nachrichten*.[740] Heaven be thanked, the volume will be in my hands this year!

Concurrently with *your* feuilleton, *ours* is running in the *Journal des Débats*. What will be done with the thing in volume form, we do not yet know, for publishers want to see the complete translation, and the only copy is that in the hands of the printers.

A week ago, we had a visit from H. G. Wells and his wife, who returned through Paris from a short stay at Genoa.[741] Wells is wonderfully prosperous. He has built himself a beautiful house on the cliff at Sandgate (near Folkestone), where, sitting at his ease, he communicates with London by telephone! That kind of thing will never fall to me.

However, my two books are getting printed. The novel (after several changes of title) is to be called "Our Friend the Charlatan" —not bad, I think. I hope it will be out before May. Also in the

[740] In which *Der blinde Eros* was being published serially.

[741] Thirty-one years after the visit, Wells wrote: "When a year or so later, Jane and I, returning from an excursion to Switzerland, visited him in Paris, we found him in a state of profound discontent. The apartment was bleakly elegant in the polished French way. He was doing no effective work, he was thin and ailing, and he complained bitterly that his pseudo mother-in-law, who was in complete control of his domestic affairs, was starving him. The sight of us stirred him to an unwonted Anglo-mania, a stomachic nostalgia, and presently he fled to us in England" (*Experiment in Autobiography*, pp. 489–90).

spring will appear "By the Ionian Sea." Chapman and Hall, who publish both books, (it reminds one of old days) are making the travel book a veritable *édition de luxe*. They have found an artist who, out of my rough sketches, is making a few beautiful pictures, some of which are to be in colour, some in black and white. Of course you will have a copy, but I shall give away only very few, as the price will no doubt be high. You, I think, have *all* my publications; the only person living who has a complete set.

Meanwhile, I work steadily at "The Vanquished Roman." It will not have the success of "Quo Vadis,"[742] but I think it will be found picturesque and interesting. As soon as I can finish it (during the summer) I shall take the MS. myself to England.

Many thanks for your kind messages. Mme Fleury is just as usual; she cannot go out, and is anxious for the fine weather to return. I suppose we shall go into the country about the end of May, but the place is not yet decided.

Do get rid as soon as possible of all that heavy reviewing; it is terrible work, and wears you out.

Kindest regards from us all.

> Ever yours, dear friend,
> GEORGE GISSING

13 Rue de Siam. / Paris.

April 24. 1901.

Dear old Friend,

I am really alarmed. This will never do. Get your doctor's advice immediately, I entreat. It is *almost certain* that bicycling must cease—you have warning in two directions. Go at once to the doctor.

I am just doing the same thing, for my emphysema[743] troubles me much, and I dare not let this summer go by without doing something decisive. It is criminal to neglect any possible means of health.

Better translation "Dispensation" by "Ordnung," I think.

I can say no more; your letter has disturbed me. Forthwith cease cycling, and get advice.

[742] Henryk Sienkiewicz, 1896.
[743] A chronic lung disease, rarely fatal.

Our affectionate regards to you. Gabrielle is always uneasy about your health.[744] Let us know that you are prudent.

Ever yours,
GEORGE GISSING

I shall of course send you both my books on publication.

Spade House / Sandgate.

June 20. 1901.

Dear Old Friend,

You will wonder what has become of me. Things have been happening. Some three weeks ago, I decided to come to England, for a few days, on business. Gabrielle accompanied me, and we spent a delightful week here at Sandgate in the house of Wells.[745] I benefited so much that it was decided I should prolong my visit; the poor girl was obliged to go back on account of her mother. Well, I was next persuaded to consult a London doctor,[746] and he spoke of my health in the gravest way. He said that, evidently, in France I was being starved.[747] Steadily I had been losing weight, and my lung was getting into a dangerous condition. To pass the summer in France probably meant death next winter.

Well, what could I see. I knew only too well that the French food did not suit me—but of course it is a very delicate subject (complicated with the mother-in-law difficulty). My friends here opposed themselves, tooth and nail, to my return to France. I had to yield to reason—why should I die, if I can help it?—and I have now decided to enter an English Sanatorium for the next two months. I go there in a week's time.

Of course there results a great deal of misery. I don't yet know what Gabrielle will—or can—do. I earnestly hope we shall find some way of releasing her from slavery to her invalid mother, which is most grievously affecting her health—but it is extremely difficult.

I am not well enough to write much. How are *you*? Have you

[744] She wrote a solicitous note to Bertz beneath GRG's message: see Appendix II.
[745] See Introduction.
[746] Dr. Harry Hick took him to see the London specialist.
[747] See Introduction.

received "The Charlatan" and "By the Ionian Sea." Alas! I was not able to inscribe them—you will forgive the omission. Let me hear of you—address to Sandgate. I will write again from the Sanatorium.

Probably, after great tumult, we shall come to a period of calm.

Ever yours,

GEORGE GISSING

East Anglian Sanatorium[748] / Nayland / Suffolk.

June 22. 1901.

My dear Friend,

I go to the above address on Monday, and know not how long I shall stay. That depends on my health. I have to gain weight, and to repose, for my right lung is now seriously threatened with tuberculosis[749]—but I have taken the thing in time. At the end of the summer I hope to be in France, but I shall not dare to live again in Paris. Everything must remain uncertain.

A thousand thanks for your most kind letters. That about "The Ionian Sea" has been a joy to me. Well, the book was half written to please *you*—and I seem to have succeeded. Reviews of that and of the novel are very laudatory. Perhaps success is coming. It need do so, for my expenses are of course very heavy.

You know that Gabrielle came over with me to Sandgate. She passed a week here with the Wells's, and a couple of days at the house of my agent, Pinker, near Wimbledon—a very delightful time. Everybody liked her. She has now just gone with her mother to: Châlet Feuillabois. / Couhard. / près Autun / (Saône et Loire.) A letter from you would always gladden her. Of course she is in much distress about the necessity of our temporary parting.

[748] This was Dr. Jane Walker's establishment.

[749] Morley Roberts suggests that Dr. Hick sent GRG to the sanatorium because he thought "a prolonged course of feeding and rest was the one thing he required, [and] induced him to go to a sanatorium in the east of England. At this time Lake [Hick] had practically no belief whatever in the man being tuberculous, but he used Maitland's [GRG] firm conviction that he was in that condition to induce him to enter this establishment. It was perhaps the best thing which could be done for him. He was looked after very well, and the doctor at the sanatorium agreed with Lake in finding no evidence of active pulmonary trouble" (*Roberts*, p. 199).

No, I cannot ask her to leave her mother, but I think it possible that Mme. Fleury may live for some years, and this makes a very difficult situation. Gabrielle is not a wife, but a garde-malade. In health, I could just support this, but it broke me down, and, as an invalid, I have to seek nursing elsewhere. Gabrielle's health is being ruined—a miserable state of things. Well, there's no help.

We must take a country house (*not* an accursed flat!) where some measure of privacy, at all events, is obtainable.

If you write to Gabrielle, try to impress upon her the (surely obvious) fact that nothing on earth could keep me away from her but fear of utter ruin to my health. I *must get well*, that I may face the hard life which is before us. As I have said, I hope to go back before the end of the summer. In any case, I shall go back then to see Gabrielle, and settle everything.[750]

The report as to your health is less alarming, but it is plain that you must take every care. Yes, throw up the reviewing altogether; I am sure you ought to.

Oh, how remote that American life of yours![751] It gave me a sort of shock to be reminded of it. At the time (I remember) I gave you up for lost—that terrible typhoid!

I have not much strength; a very little writing fatigues me greatly. Still, I get better, and am steadily gaining weight. Every kind remembrance to you.

Affectionately ever,
GEORGE GISSING

---

[750] GRG's friends thought he should not return to France unless particular arrangements about his diet were accepted by Mme. Fleury, but, according to Morley Roberts, the suggestion was never made, "although I undersand [*sic*] it was discussed by some of his friends. It appears that a year or so afterwards when he was talking to Miss Kingdon [Clara Collet], she told him that it had been thought possible that he might not return to France. This he received with much amazement and indignation, for certainly he did go back, and henceforth I believe the management of the kitchen was conducted on more reasonable lines. Certainly he recovered his normal weight, and soon after his return was actually twelve stone" (*Roberts*, p. 200).

[751] See Introduction.

Sanatorium.

August 7. 1901.

Dear Friend,

On Saturday I leave here, and travel straight to Autun. I hoped to have seen my people at Wakefield, but the weather is so uncertain, and I am afraid to risk journeys in the north. With such impediments, life is not very cheerful.

Well, I am decidedly better, and—most important—have learnt how to take care of myself. What to do for the winter, I can't yet decide, but we must not live again in Paris. Altogether, it is a very troublesome state of things.

How are *you*? Let me know at Autun. I do hope you are able to cycle and enjoy the summer.

I must now begin to work—for pauperdom stares me in the face.

Madame Fleury is not well, I fear, and Gabrielle is anything but cheerful.

Ever yours,
GEORGE GISSING

Autun.

September 8th. 1901.

Dear old Friend,

You know already that I have returned to France, after my Sanatorium experiment. On the whole, I benefited considerably by that treatment, and chiefly in acquiring the habit of living, day and night, with windows open. This, I am sure, I should never have ventured to do, without the Sanatorium example; and even now, indeed, I don't see how I am to continue through the winter, for it will be impossible to write when one is suffering from cold. Where I shall pass the winter, is not yet decided. We stay here till the 15th. October, and then I shall go to Paris to consult our doctor.[752] In any case, residence in Paris is impossible. Of course this involves us in great difficulties—especially the money question.

Meanwhile, I am doing a little work—about two hours every morning. I am engaged upon "An Author at Grass," which I am

---

[752] Dr. Anatole Chauffard, professor in the Faculté de Médecine de Paris, whom GRG had consulted in the spring.

considerably altering and improving. I hope it will be finished before I leave here.

We have been very glad to receive the two illustrated cards. It was good news indeed to hear that you are able to go upon a bicycle tour; but I beg you to be careful; do not injure yourself by over-exertion. You do not tell us at what date you return to Potsdam; no doubt, if you are still absent, this letter will be forwarded. Let us know the result of your sheet-baths[?], and general treatment. Of course you have been altogether over-worked with that detestable reviewing, and I hope you will never again undertake anything of the kind.[753] We look anxiously for the novel;[754] it will be very curious to see fiction from your pen after this long time, and to compare it with the last.

My two books have had considerable *literary* success, but I do not suppose they have brought much money to the publisher—who purchased the copyright for 7 years. This will be the case to the end—much praise and little money.

"Quid prodest? Nescit sacculus ista meus."[755] When I shall be able to finish "The Vanquished Roman" there is no saying. I can only write it in my own library, so that this winter it will have to lie aside. And, indeed, I am rather discouraged by the multitude of Roman novels now appearing. You will see that even Hall Caine has turned to that subject.[756] My book was conceived many years ago, and ought to have been written then. I almost fear I have waited too long.

Gabrielle and I are reading the history of Port Royal by Sainte-Beuve.[757] Do you know the book? It is long—5 volumes—but very full of interest, and enlightens me on a subject of which I knew little or nothing.

I wish you could see this remarkable little city of Autun. It is most picturesquely situated, and consists almost entirely of very old buildings, including about a dozen monasteries. There are considerable Roman remains—a good deal of the original wall, with two fine gates. And all around are very beautiful hills, in places

---

[753] Bertz was reviewing for Joseph Ettlinger's *Das litterarische Echo*.
[754] *Der blinde Eros*. The preceding one was *Das Sabinergut*.
[755] Martial, *Epigrammatrem*. XI. 6.
[756] *The Eternal City: A Novel* (London, 1901).
[757] *Port-Royal* (5 vols., 2nd. ed., Paris, 1860).

well wooded. It seems to be a very healthy situation. I sleep well here—a great thing. Unfortunately, it is seldom that I have a good appetite; I have to force myself to eat quantities of food.

My book on "Charles Dickens" is coming out in a new edition— as the introductory volume to a large edition of the novels to be published by a Scotch house.[758] I have thoroughly revised it, and it is to have illustrations. I don't know what the price will be.

Well, I hope to have good news of you soon. Gabrielle sends kindest remembrances and best wishes.[759]

Always yours, dear Friend,
GEORGE GISSING

Addressed: Herrn Eduard Bertz. / Alexandrinenstrasse, 15. / Potsdam. *Allemagne.*

Autun.

[September 24, 1901]
Wednesday.[760]

Dear Friend, hearty thanks for the book. I began reading it at once, and will only now say that it holds me with a genuine interest; so far, I think it psychologically of great interest, and dramatically very strong. I will write at length in a few days, when Gabrielle and I have both finished the book. As a *story* it is the most interesting you have yet written, and it would not at all surprise me if it had a popular success. Gudula is excellent![761] But no more at present. Rain, rain, rain; hope it is better with you. I grieved to hear about your foot. Gabrielle's kindest regards.

Yours ever,
G. G.

Couhard. / Autun.

September 25. 1901.

Dear Friend,

It seems to me that you decidedly under-value *"Der Blinde [sic] Eros."* I do not say that it is your best novel, but I think it is your

---

[758] The Gresham Publishing Company, Glasgow, planned an "Imperial Edition" of Dickens's work, but the project was never accomplished.

[759] For the note she included in this letter, see Appendix II.

[760] A slip. 24 September 1901, the date on the postmark, was a Tuesday.

[761] The heroine of *Der blinde Eros.*

best *story*. The very simplicity of the theme helps to its dramatic effectiveness. In this, Gabrielle agrees with me; we both find that you have never so well succeeded in holding the reader's interest, page after page, chapter after chapter. Indeed, I could not too highly praise the book from this point of view, and I fancy you will hear much to the same effect from your German reviewers.

Then, the characterization. Johannes is good—very good. In him, you have done a most difficult thing: you have depicted a man who is at once philosophical and virile—a student who yet has blood in his veins. I sympathize very strongly indeed with him, throughout. In his sufferings, he never becomes weak or puling; Edmund's praise of him at his death is well merited. On pp. 259, 260, his behaviour is admirable—and the scene was no easy one to write—experto crede! Indeed, I do not know where to look for a parallel to your skill in this portrait. It is work of the ripe mind and practiced hand.

Gudula—excellent! Here I feel I am a very competent judge, for I know this kind of woman very well indeed. Her whims and her follies are very finely exhibited—quite without exaggeration. At moments the reader *feels* her own self-justification—which is good and right. She is entirely human, and delightfully detestable! Very good indeed, her letter on p. 166.

The betrothal and marriage of these two, however monstrous, are shown as things natural, inevitable. Fate is at work; we feel its pressure—we see the gulf ahead. Never a moment of improbability. Thus things happened; thus they *must* have happened.

Chapter XV is terrible. It reminded me of all you have yourself suffered from noises. Impossible to describe the torture more vividly. Of course it has its humorous side, as it ought to have. I roared over the *sneezer*! And I was so glad that you insisted on the fact that of course it was an *excessive* sensibility in Johannes which caused his worst sufferings at that time. The bowls [*sic*] towards the end of his life make a more tragic impression.

Apropos, what excellent comedy on p. 342. That, I suppose, is your own observation. Surely the Herr Konrektor must walk the earth!

To conclude, the atmosphere of the book is very fine. Here— as in all your work—one lives with a mind born to the noblest idealism. Your view of life is ever exalted; it does one good. One closes the book with a sense of profound peace. Delightful, to me, is your picture of Gansweide, and of scholastic life at its best; it tranquillizes even while it charms.

Gabrielle agrees with every word of this, and joins her thanks to mine for the book you have given us. She bids me thank you, also, for your delightful letter in German. It will not be long before she writes again.

But you send bad news about your foot. I don't like that continued swelling. However, it does not seem to cause you much inconvenience at present, and I can only hope that it will disappear in time.

With regard to Ettlinger,[762] you have done the right thing. If the man is offended, he is grossly unreasonable, and it means, I suspect, that he is annoyed at losing good work which cost him very little money. Go on quietly with your ethical work, and, after it, let us have the book on French philosophers as soon as possible.

No, no, you must never buy the "Rochester" Dickens. It is ugly in form, and all the good of the prefaces you will find in my "Charles Dickens." The publisher[763] is horribly mean. He sends me only one copy.

I am very glad to hear of the *Allg[emeine] Zeit[ung]* review of *Phil[osophie] d[es] Fahrr[ads]*. That book must have greatly extended your reputation.

Well, I have finished "An Author at Grass," and must now think how to spend my winter. Every thing is yet uncertain.

Hearty greetings to you from us all. Enjoy the fine autumn weather. By the bye, *"Der b[linde] E[ros]"* brought to my mind the days at Potsdam, and our walks about.

All good be with you!

Ever yours,
GEORGE GISSING

---

[762] Joseph Ettlinger.
[763] Algernon Methuen (1856–1924), founder and head of Methuen and Co.

Addressed: Herrn Eduard Bertz. / Alexandrinenstrasse, 15. /
    Potsdam. / *Allemagne.*
Villa Souvenir / Arcachon. / Gironde. France.

December 8. 1901.

Dear old Friend,

I have been driven away by the cold weather, and, by Chauffard's advice,[764] am at Arcachon, where I shall have to pass the
winter. G[abrielle] is with me, but cannot stay long. My disease
is taking the form of serious emphysema; I cannot breathe in cold
air. Happily, I am able to work, but it is difficult on a *chaise
longue* in the open air. How are you? G[abrielle] sends her kindest remembrances, and will let you have news before long. Did I
tell you that I am doing an abridged edition of Forster's Dickens
for Chapman and Hall?[765] It will gladden you to hear that "An
Author at Grass" will probably appear in the *Fortnightly* before
publication in volume.[766]

Yours ever,
GEORGE GISSING

Villa Souvenir. / Arcachon. / Gironde.

December 27. 1901.

My dear Friend,

I must not let a new year begin without sending you my good
wishes—among them the hope that *you* may live to do a great
deal of the work you want to do (no man does *all.*) *I,* for my part,
hope to see yet another year or two of fair health before I go
hence. Tranquillity I must not expect; the circumstances of my life
are too fatally complicated.

The word tranquillity reminds me how glad I am that, after all,
you are to keep an independent abode. I trembled for you, when
I heard of that project. Most certainly the relations between you

[764] Dr. Chauffard found a lesion in GRG's lung and an increase in the
emphysema; he prescribed immediate removal to a warm climate, rest in
the open air, and a strict diet (Gabrielle Gissing to Bertz, ? 1901, Yale).

[765] John Forster, *The Life of Dickens.* Abridged and revised by George
Gissing (London, 1902).

[766] The *Fortnightly Review* printed *An Author at Grass* in four parts:
Part I, 1 May 1902; Part II, 1 August 1902; Part III, 1 November 1902;
Part IV, 1 February 1903.

and your mother will be better if no such change is made. So you are now writing your ethical book; of that also I am glad. Get on with it steadily and courageously. I know that the literary people who come to see you, though they take a certain tax of time, yet help to keep you in spirits. One *cannot* labour on without recognition; it is very precious, even to the least conceited or egoistic.[767]

As you say, work on a *chaise longue* is no easy thing. Nevertheless, it has to be done, and I am getting steadily on with my abridged edition of Forster. Whether I shall be able to do any original writing here, is another question. However, you will be pleased to hear that "An Author at Grass" is definitely accepted for the *Fortnightly*. As you will understand when you see the book, I feel deeply interested in its fortunes.

Well, I improve in health—but very slowly. I can now walk a couple of miles without fatigue. The climate here is good; too much rain, indeed, but seldom any cold, and at times a day of glorious sunshine. The great pine forest stretches about us to a length of 80 miles, and I really believe that its odours have a bracing quality. In cold air I should soon be seriously ill, for the worst part of my disease is the emphysema—i.e. sclerosis of the lung, which cold at once makes worse. Don't be gloomy about me. I feel a great deal of vitality in me yet, and am *never* downcast by fear—unless it be fear of beggary.

I suppose I shall be here till the end of April. Where we then go to, there is no means yet of knowing. It is terrible to have to pay that Paris rent all this time.

All good be with you.

> Ever yours,
> GEORGE GISSING

[767] On New Year's Day 1902 Bertz replied: "One cannot labour without recognition, you say. Well, it is agreeable at least if one is not compelled to do it. In my own case, all those visitors I told you of, meant personal good will rather than literary recognition. My novel, certainly brought me very little of that. I gave away nine copies. Of those, one (Rehfeldt!) was not acknowledged at all; among four of which simply the receipt was acknowledged, three men told me that they had no time to read the book; from two [ladies?] I only heard that they liked it, and only of the remaining two the receivers spoke kindly and with interest, i.e. yourself and Zapp" (To GRG, first draft, Yale).

Villa Souvenir. Arcachon. / Gironde. France.

February 24. 1902.

Dear old Friend,

It is long since I had your last kind letter. Time has gone rather drearily with me, for the weather has been bad, and the days on a chaise longue did not lend to cheerfulness. No less than 20 times in the month of January, the thermometer was below freezing point. This climate is probably very healthy, but, in winter, it is certainly less agreeable than that of Devonshire or Cornwall. However, I think I have made some progress; I feel stronger. I have managed to finish my abridgment of Forster's Dickens, and to plan a new novel.[768] My "Vanquished Roman" must be postponed. Too much has been written of late, in the form of fiction, about things Roman. But, if I live, I shall still write the book.

Apropos of that, I remember very well the passage you quote from Cassiodorus, containing the word *modernus*. I feel rather proud, you know, of my familiarity with that forgotten author.

By the bye, English publishers no longer send reviews to authors. This graceful habit has ceased since the establishment of press-cutting agencies.

I grieve, indeed, at the necessity in which you find yourself of passing yet another year in an abode so displeasing to you. It is a lamentable thing that your humble and reasonable ambition, to live in quietness, seems impossible of attainment. Yet I cannot but hope that a day will come when the true home will be found. Of course the nervous strain under which you live doubles or trebles the effort necessary for your work.

And now I have some grave personal news to send you. About three weeks ago, I had a letter from Miss Orme (the London friend, you remember, who has frequently been of help to me)[769] telling that she had received a visit from a police inspector, who came to inform her that Mrs. Gissing had been arrested by the police for serious ill-treatment of her little boy.[770] Moreover, on examination, the woman had been found to be *insane*, and had been removed to an asylum. Well, this has surprised nobody.

[768] *Will Warburton. A Romance of Real Life* (London: Constable, 1905).
[769] Sarah Orme. See Introduction.
[770] Alfred.

Miss Orme always believed that she was not in her right mind. Happily, the landlady of her lodgings had the good sense and humanity to interfere (after many warnings) to protect the poor little child. I need not tell you that, on the whole, I regard this as a good thing for the poor woman herself, who was merely leading a brutal life, causing everybody connected with her a good deal of trouble. She will now be taken care of in a proper way, at less expense to me than before. Little Alfred, who has been in Miss Orme's care, is to be sent, to recover his health, to a farm-house in Cornwall,[771] where he will be close to the residence of a sister of Miss Orme. My mind, on *that* score, is enormously relieved. I always felt myself guilty of a crime in abandoning the poor little fellow. He will now have his chance to grow up in healthy and decent circumstances. I cannot tell you how greatly I am relieved. Indeed, I believe that this event is already having a good effect upon my health.

And now the question arises of our future abode. We must quit Paris, and Chauffard strongly advises *le pays basque*, somewhere, that is to say, on the French slope of the Pyrenees. The removal will be a most troublesome and costly business. Were it not for Mme. Fleury, I should (as things now are) go and settle in Devonshire or Cornwall, for the climate is equally good, and the old question of food still troubles me.[772] But we cannot take Mme Fleury out of her own country. It is a grave decision, to settle so far away from England, where I can get no books without buying them. Well, you shall hear again about this presently.

Gabrielle's kindest remembrances. We hope you have got through the winter well, so far.

Ever yours,
GEORGE GISSING

Can you tell me about Otto Seeck's book—"Der Untergang der antiken Welt,"[773] 2nd. vol. just noticed in *Athenaeum*. I should like to know the *price*.

---

[771] At Mabe, between Falmouth and Penryn.
[772] See Introduction.
[773] *Geschichte des Untergangs der antiken Welt* (6 vols., Berlin, 1895–1920). The second volume was reviewed in the *Athenaeum* on 22 February 1902, p. 236.

Addressed: Herrn. Eduard Bertz. / Alexandrinenstrasse, 15. /
       Potsdam / ALLEMAGNE.
Arcachon.

                                March 18th. 1902.
Dear Friend, I am told that the Oxford Dict[ionary] says of
altruism that the word was invented by Comte, and first used
in England by G. H. Lewes, 1853. This does not advance you.
I suspect that Comte may have used this word in correspondence
etc., and not in his books. Many thanks for information about
Seeck. The book must be very interesting, but, having regard to
its doubtful features, and still more in view of my present poverty,
I don't think I should be justified in buying it. In any case, not
just now; for I am already embarrassed by the number of volumes
which I brought to Arcachon; sending them about the country
is very expensive. I hope to be able to give you definite news about
our future movements before long. Yes, the pays basque is very
remote, and I shrink from the thought of taking all our possessions
such a distance. Never was a more difficult situation. Little Alfred
is safe in Cornwall, at a farm, with a good school in the neighbourhood, and friends at hand to keep an eye on him. Affectionate
regards from both of us.

                                      Yours ever,
                                      G. G.

Addressed: Herrn Eduard Bertz. / Alexandrinenstrasse, 15 /
         Potsdam / ALLEMAGNE.
42, Quai. / Ciboure. / St. Jean de Luz / (Basses Pyrénées.)
                                    April 25. 1902.
Dear old Friend, I left Arcachon yesterday, very glad to get away,
for it has been terribly dull. Gabrielle is in Paris, making arrangements for our departure at the end of June. After all, we have
decided to take a chalet for a year (furnished) at St. Jean de Luz,
where I now am. The place is indescribably beautiful: a grand sea,
noble mountains, most picturesque and quiet little town. Very
curious to hear the people talking Basque. I hope soon to find a
house, and then return to Paris. It is high time to get to work,
indeed; but little can be done till we are settled here. My doctor at
Arcachon says there is considerable improvement, but just the

same necessity for great care. However, I am twice as strong as six months ago—and that is something. I shall be here for at least a fortnight, so let me have a card from you, with news. You are rejoicing, I know, that the winter is over. How is your health? How does work get on?

Ever yours,
G. G.

13 Rue de Siam / Paris.

June 3. 1902.

Dear Old Friend,

Have you noticed that Macmillans are publishing a new edition of *The French Prisoners*? It is mentioned towards the end of "Our Library Table" in the *Athenaeum* of this week.[774] By all means write to Macmillans, and demand a copy. Strange revival of old days, to see that!

I grieve with you over your trouble with the brutal neighbours. They are incredible. Well, well, you must escape as soon as you can. As regards your work, too, I see you are much worried just now. I quite understand the difficulty; the work you planned was enormous. Do try to give the results of your long thoughts and reading in some briefer form. I shall bitterly regret it if you do not, in one way or another, discharge your mind of its serious message. (True, you found an opportunity for uttering yourself to a certain extent in the cycling book.)

Alas! I never received the *article* you say you were forwarding to me.[775] Was it lost in the post?

I spent about a month at St. Jean de Luz, and settled everything. I took—not a whole villa—but half a dozen good rooms in a house inhabited by a very quiet family; the year's rent is 1500 f. Thither we go on July 2nd. The address is: / Villa Lannes. / Place de la Mairie. / Ciboure. / St. Jean de Luz.

It will be a difficult matter to preserve my health through this month of June and all the horrors of the removal. We have found

[774] Macmillan first published Bertz's *The French Prisoners* in 1884 (see Introduction). The new edition was advertised in the *Athenaeum* for 31 May 1902, p. 691.

[775] "Sport," *Die neue Zeit*, No. 413, 1902.

a very cheap little flat at Boulogne-sur-Seine, where furniture, books etc. will be in safety—with the possibility of living there for a short time if necessary. But I assure you that, if I make the progress I expect at St. Jean, I shall not be in a hurry to come back to Paris.

I have finished correcting the proofs of my edition of Forster's Dickens. At present I can of course do nothing. But I have a novel ready to begin as soon as I get to Ciboure again.

I earnestly hope that your throat trouble is now at an end. As for the foot, well, I know not what to say; but it seems to me plain that you ought not to undergo much physical fatigue.

Gabrielle sends her kindest remembrances. She will write you a long letter from the slope of the Pyrenees.

Chauffard, by the bye, says I am better in general health, but, as to lungs, very much the same. Clearly, if I am to overcome this disease, I shall only do so in the course of a *long* residence in a very favourable climate. St. Jean did me immense good—for so short a time. Arcachon—alas!—did me next to no good at all.

Ever affectionately yours,
GEORGE GISSING

Addressed: Herrn Eduard Bertz. / Wippra i. / Harz / (bei Sangerhausen) / *Allemagne.*

Villa Lannes. / Ciboure. / St. Jean de Luz / France.

——— (Sufficient address.)

July 25. 1902.

Dear Friend, Gabrielle is delighted with your card this morning. Beautiful panorama! We reproach ourselves much with not having written to you already, but will do so on Sunday next. All goes well with us; weather generally cloudy, but at times fine and hot—as to-day. We hope you are thoroughly resting. I am slowly getting to work, but can only write for a couple of hours a day. Nevertheless, I am very much better.

Letter, then, on Sunday.

Ever yours,
G. G.

Villa Lannes / Ciboure. / St. Jean de Luz.

July 27. 1902.

Dear Old Friend,

You received my postcard, I hope. Now to let you know more in detail the state of things with me.

I was a little afraid of the heat, so far south; but hitherto it has been very endurable. The weather changes about every 36 hours; there is frequent rain (though never a *damp* atmosphere, strangely enough), and the sky very often over clouded. In fact, it is an improved climate of England in the warmer parts. And the landscape has few if any southern characteristics. The light is of course more limpid than in the north, but it does not recall Italy—nor even the Riviera. For health one could not do better than here, I think. And indeed, I feel steady progress towards strength. The excellent dairy produce, and abundance of fine fish, are of course valuable points.

I write every morning from 9 to 11.30 or 12, and then put aside my work for the day. This is a poor account, for a man who used to write his 8 or 10 hours daily, but I am not sure that it is not better from every point of view. I have more time to *meditate* my chapters, and lose less by the necessity of recommencing.

Then, I am achieving a very old ambition of mine. You know that Don Quixote was always one of my favourite books. Twelve years ago, I bought a copy in Spanish, saying that some day I perhaps might find time to learn the language. And that I am now doing. Already I have got through 8 chapters of the Don, and each day I read an increased number of pages. The language has strong peculiarities—I mean the Spanish; one sees the enormous effect of Visigothic and Arabic conquests. In no other of the Romance tongues is the Latin so *harshly* corrupted. Sometimes you have the feeling that Spanish has been formed by utterly barbarous people; as, for instance, in coming upon the word *milagro*, which means *miracle*. Italian is wonderfully pure in comparison. Well, it is vastly interesting, and I rejoice to find myself face to face with dear old Cervantes, one of the most glorious brains and souls that ever existed. Though I know the book so well, the re-reading makes me marvel at the vigour of imagination which stamps every page of it.

I am delighted to think of you at your ease in a beautiful mountain country. Undoubtedly it will do you good to have a little society, and your report suggests that the people are pleasant. It is a great thing to combine this with as much privacy as one desires. Do stay as long as possible; it will be pure gain, I feel sure, from every point of view.

So the new edition of "The French Prisoners" seems satisfactory to you. By the bye, you may always be proud of have [*sic*] written that book. It was a remarkable linguistic feat, and the story had very distinct literary quality. I remember it as though I had read it yesterday.

Thank you for sending me your article. I read it with pleasure, and also with that sort of surprise which still comes upon me when I think of you in connection with sports. Yet you have thoroughly justified yourself in handling such matters, and I was delighted to hear that your cycling book maintains—even extends —its reputation. But I want very much to see some of that more abstract writing to which you have devoted so much time. It will enrage me if you never see your way to complete a book of the purely philosophical kind.

I suppose you carried books with you to Wippra. Here at Ciboure I have with me about fifty volumes, carefully chosen, including those which I take everywhere: Homer, Horace, and so on. For the present, Spanish gives me enough work for afternoon and evening, but I want to go straight through the Iliad once more. I always keep an eye on my Sixth Century, but it is plain to me that I shall not get that book written just yet. Long idleness has made the money question rather a grave one, and for the present I must do what I can do pretty easily.

All good be with you, dear old friend. Let me hear that you are gathering strength and courage. I will not be too long silent.

Ever yours,

GEORGE GISSING

Villa Lannes. / Ciboure. / St. Jean de Luz.

October 26. 1902.

Dear Friend,

We were grieved to hear that your holiday at Wippra did not end so pleasantly as it began. You know, it is very difficult for us

23

bookish people to live long on easy terms with ordinary people of the world. But it is all behind you, now, and I hope you think no more about it. Except for some of its news, Gabrielle was very glad to have your letter. She reads the German character very easily.

I wonder whether you have received the copy of my edition of Forster's Dickens, which I sent some few days ago? Probably I shall have a note speaking of it before long. To tell you the truth, I felt a good deal of hesitation about cutting down such a biography as Forster's; it savours of philistinism. But people do not read the book nowadays, calling it too long. And, if I had not undertaken the task, someone else would have done it far less reverently. We are having fairly good weather now, though it rains a great deal. Our only grave trouble in the house arises from the *underground* kitchen, which is so cold and damp that our servant is constantly ailing, and I fear lest she should get permanent damage.

Gabrielle is very well indeed, and her mother better than for a long time. I, however, have recently had a slight attack of bronchitis, and of course I have to be abominably careful. On the whole, the climate seems to suit me very fairly. I work every day from 9 to 12, and am getting on gently with my new novel.

The curious production which is appearing, at long intervals, in the *Fortnightly*, under the title of "An Author at Grass," will presently be published in volume form as "The Private Papers of Henry Ryecroft." I shall be very anxious to hear your opinion of this thing. I suspect it contains the best literary work I can hope to turn out. People have written to me about it from various parts of the world; it seems to be found interesting.

Meanwhile, my reputation in England steadily increases; I receive invitations to become President of literary societies etc., and many proofs of extended recognition. But the old contradiction is still in force—my fame brings me no money, my books have only the smallest sale. I suppose I am a notable victim of the circulating-library system. My books are read only from the libraries. And so, no doubt, it will be to the end.

My time is up; I have to go and lie down for an hour or two. Gabrielle sends her affectionate regards. All good be with you.

Yours ever, old friend,
GEORGE GISSING

Villa Lannes, / Ciboure. / St. Jean de Luz.

November 16, 1902.

My dear Friend,

Our letters crossed. You will know that your German letter
was perfectly intelligible—though, for my own part, I am bound
to confess that the Latin characters are vastly easier reading. I have
often wondered at the facility with which you continue to write
long English letters, the English quite excellent. For all that,
if ever you feel that the effort is wearying I entreat you to write
in German instead, for you have quite enough fatiguing work
without adding a laborious correspondence. As for your con-
versational English, at our last meeting[776] it was admirable; but
I know how necessary practice is, and perhaps some day you
will find it convenient to talk with some Englishman. If only
you could find a man in himself interesting.

I fear that your objections to my abridged Forster are well
founded; but, as you say, I could not make the book different
in these respects without adding too much. On the money question, I have spoken very plainly. Yes, far too much talk of money
goes on in the "literary" world of our time. The *Spectator*, reviewing this volume, wished I had added a statement of Dickens's
entire gains from his books[777]—an unworthy remark from such a
paper. Of course the fact of the matter is that, from of old,
authors have been cheated by publishers, and there is now a
loud cry for the redressing of this ancient injustice. Unfortunately,
it is not always a Dickens who gets satisfactorily paid; the richest
authors, to-day, are generally the least important, as everyone
knows.

My "Author at Grass" is appearing, each 3 months, in 4 parts,
in *The Fortnightly*. Early next year, it will be pub[lished] in a
volume, entitled "The Private Papers of Henry Ryecroft." The
publishers thought this a better title for a book essentially grave.

Well now, I am very glad to hear that you have settled the
removal question, and I earnestly hope the new quarters will be

---

[776] In April 1898.

[777] "One thing would have added no little to its interest; that is an
account, so far as it might have been possible to give it, of the total circulation of Dickens's works, and of his literary profits" (*Spectator*, LXXXIX,
18 October 1902, 576).

an improvement. I grieve that you have to find more money for rent; but there is always the hope that it will come naturally with increased acceptance of your work. Most certainly it is better for you, in the higher sense, to write books than a number of articles, and very likely it would be better in pecuniary results also. In any case, write "In Luthers Heimat."[778] That seems to be very promising from every point of view, and assuredly it will be a delightful book to read. One word of suggestion. *Don't be too thorough!* Don't trouble too much, I mean, about erudition; but make the volume above all one of personal impressions and views. Put into it much more of your own thought than of mere historical fact. I am convinced you have already *quite enough* material.

So you enjoyed "Tess" and "Jude." I prefer the former; but neither of them appeals to me like Hardy's earlier books, when the idyllic spirit was unaffected by fierce pessimism. "Jude" I shall never be able to read again. It is powerful, yes; but its horribleness does not, I feel, faithfully represent the life it pretends to depict. The end of "Tess" I think an entire artistic mistake. But I greatly admire Hardy, and am very sorry he will write no more fiction. His verse (a volume or two recently pub[lished])[779] has but small value.

We get on very well here. I am working at a novel called "Will Warburton," and feel a little stronger than in the summer. Mme Fleury keeps as well as she can hope to, and Gabrielle decidedly improves in health. It is really a good climate; changeable, rainy, but much sun. Once or twice we have been into Spain. Some day we must get to Roncesvalles, which is quite near. Then, we have pleasant acquaintances, English and French. The most interesting of them is an Oxford Don, named Butler Clarke,[780] who passes the greater part of the year here, and has done so since he was a boy. He is a great authority on Spanish—has written a history of Spanish Literature, and so on. Lives quite alone; has a fine library, which he has invited me to use as my own.

---

[778] See 3 November 1892, *et passim*.

[779] *Poems of the Past and Present* (London, 1901).

[780] Henry Butler Clarke (1863-1904), a student of Spanish literature and history, held a Fereday fellowship at St. John's College, where he usually stayed for one term each year, spending the rest of the time at his home in St. Jean de Luz.

I have now read 3/4 of "Don Quixote"—glorious book! The vocabulary is very difficult, but I can at length read with ease. It is an acquisition. I wonder whether Butler Clarke (an Orientalist also) will tempt me to have a peep at Arabic? I fear I am too old. Gabrielle's kindest regards. We talk of you much.

Ever yours,
GEORGE GISSING

Villa Lannes. / Ciboure. / St. Jean de Luz.

February 15. 1903.

Dear old Friend,

Your letter gladdens me. It is infinitely good of you to give so much time always to comment upon my books. Of course it is very pleasant indeed to know that you think "Ryecroft" on the whole achieves what I aimed at. The book has grown very slowly, and was written with gusto.

There is some force in your objection to the picture of such tranquillity of mind in a quite solitary man aged only 50. I might reply, perhaps, that these "extracts" from his journal merely give the *best* aspect of his life during those years, for he only took up the pen when he was in a thoroughly good mood. Still, I prefer to regard his happiness as quite possible, and I will tell you why. Had he been merely a booklover, I admit that the picture would be improbable, but a booklover who is at the same time a passionate lover of nature can, I believe, more easily and happily live quite alone than any other kind of man. Ryecroft, it's obvious, was at no time fond of *much* society, and at 50 he *was* (as you say) decidedly cool of temperament. Books and nature, taken together, I think suffice to a man of that stamp.

I fear you are right on the military service question, but it has such a very hateful side that one is driven to strong speech about it.[781] I lament the lot of the "poor devil" who makes soldiering his trade; but I lament still more the lot of quiet people whose lives are, or may be, made miserable by the accursed spirit of war, and in that mood I spoke.

Again, you are certainly right in your last thought on Goethe's

[781] See *The Private Papers of Henry Ryecroft*, "Spring," Chapter XIX.

sentence.[782] Undoubtedly it is ironical. I ought to have seen that more clearly. My attention has been drawn to the fact in a letter from a Cambridge Don, Dr. Ward,[783] the historian—who was once my professor at Manchester.

Well, well, once more we are brought close together by this talk about our common thoughts, and so much the better. You, I doubt not, were right in declining to settle at Wippra, and of course I am even glad to hear of your need of, and pleasure in, human intercourse. At 50, I do not think you so old a man as Ryecroft; for I am convinced that you have still a great deal of work to do. It is my earnest hope that in your new quarters (once the horror of removal over) you will be really comfortable, really quiet. You excite my envy in speaking of the "cedar bureau." My nomad life allows no luxury of that sort, little even of common comfort, and I suffer much from the lack of my books. You must now have a splendid library. How I wish we could both look in upon you some day!

I have nearly finished "Will Warburton"—a light, fanciful book.

Made my peace with the world, you think? Why, only in a literary sense. The troubles about me and before me are very grave, and any day I might find the world very much my enemy. My need of money grows rather serious, for though we live very economically indeed, I earn so little, so little! Last year my income was not quite £300, all told.

Did you see in the Athenaeum about that astounding American edition of Dickens, one set of which is to cost £20,000?[784] I am connected with the affair, having written the Preface to "Copperfield," and I have just *signed* 300 copies of the last sheet of the said preface. I only asked £20 for this bit of writing, and I suspect I might have got very much more.

[782] "Was man in der Jugend wünscht, hat man im Alter die Fülle."

[783] Adolphus William Ward (1837–1924), master of Peterhouse, Cambridge. He had been a professor of history and of English language and literature at Owens College from 1866 to 1897. While at Owens College, GRG won Dr. Ward's English poem prize. GRG sent Dr. Ward a copy of *Ryecroft*.

[784] "The 'Autograph Edition' of Dickens, just begun, is an elaborate enterprise which deserves a note. The set will be completed in fifty-six volumes, too bulky to be pleasant to handle. There will be upwards of

Do you know much about the Shakespeare-Bacon controversy? It is growing rather important, and very astonishing facts (?) are being set forth by the Baconians. I don't believe—*can't* believe —their theory, but the matter distresses me. I wish to heaven some decent Shakespearean scholar would *answer* these people. It will certainly have to be done, before long. One can no longer merely smile at them.

Lovely weather here for nearly two months now. You, I fear, suffer from cold and gloom. Gabrielle sends her kindest greetings. We shall think much of you at the time of your removal—though that is still rather far off. I feel pretty well—except for a severe attack of sciatica, which has tortured me for weeks. Your foot, I hope, is quite well now?

Ever yours, old Friend,
GEORGE GISSING

Villa Lannes. / Ciboure. / St. Jean de Luz.

April 5. 1903.

Dear old Friend,

We are delighted to have your two cards, and much pleased with the appearance of your abode. No noises overhead! May you long continue there in peace.

I ought to have long ago answered your last letter. But I have suffered severely from Sciatica (Ischias) which is making me quite lame, so that at length I am confined to the house. The doctor is doing his best. How could you suppose that I should misinterpret your remarks on Ryecroft? You are always too indulgent. Remember that, after all, "Ryecroft" is a fictitious personality. Though, by the bye, a lot of English readers are stupidly believing that the man really existed, and I receive letters inquiring about "his works," the most comical of all being one from a parson, who

---

5,000 full-page pictures by every known illustrator of Dickens, besides new ones specially drawn by such artists as Messrs. Harry Furniss and Gordon Browne, Hugh Thomson and H. M. Brock; and a brilliant set of literary people are writing introductions. Mr. George D. Sproul is the publisher. He also announces a 'St. Dunstan' edition, costing about 20,000£., which we suppose the new millionaires will cable for as an advertisement of their resources" ("Literary Gossip," *Athenaeum*, 24 January 1903, p. 116).

asks, gravely, whether "the late Mr. R's" housekeeper is in need of a situation? He sends me a stamped envelope for reply. You will have seen from the advert[isement]s in the *Athenaeum* that the book has now reached a third edition. Of course more of a success than anything I have yet published.

It grieves me horribly to hear of the continued trouble in your feet. Certainly the toil and worry of removal will not have been beneficial. At this rate we shall both of us be cripples before long. *Ma, speriamo!*

No, shall you really be obliged to abandon the Luther book? I am vexed at that. But you have not yet, I think, finally decided the matter. I did so hope this would give you the opportunity for a notable personal utterance. Do not be too much influenced by Reissner;[785] publishers are often quite wrong about the chances of a book. In the quiet of your new home, I do not doubt that new confidence will come to you.

Very curious and interesting, that glimpse of your family circle, with the total of centuries! But, as for your own age, do not be troubled too much by appearances. You always seem to me to have a great deal of vital energy, and abounding freshness of mind, and the fact, which you mention, that you have *not* made your peace with the world, is significant of vigour. For the matter of that, *my* reconcilement with the state of things is rather literary than actual; as a matter of fact, I am sadly ill at ease in the world. But I fear that I am losing combative force, and so, in a very important sense, am older than you.

Gabrielle is not quite up to the mark just now, or she would write; she suffers too much from neuralgia. It's probable that we shall go for the summer to Bagnères de Bigorre, in the Pyrenees, and I hope we shall all be better for it.

I get on well with Spanish, and have lately read several volumes of a very remarkable series of historical novels by Perez Galdòs, which deal with the history of Spain in the Napoleonic era.[786] Heaven be thanked, I now read the language with ease, but it has cost a good deal of labour, for the vocabulary is tremendous, and so many words are of Arabic origin. It seems to me now very

---

[785] See 29 September 1893.

[786] Benito Perez Galdòs (1843–1920) published 46 volumes of historical novels under the title *Episodios Nacionales*.

strange that I never made this effort before. I suppose I literally never had the time.

I must stop; Ischias is making me groan as I bend over the table. Gabrielle sends you her best thanks and kindest regards. She is making fair progress with Italian. It seemed better for her to take up that than Spanish.

Old Morley Roberts was here for a day or two a month ago. He does not exactly flourish, but makes a decent living by his (rather inflammatory) books. We talked of you, and the old days— ah, the old days! Do you remember Margarette Terrace?[787] Why has that just come into my mind? Shall I ever see it again?

Ever yours, old friend,
GEORGE GISSING

Addressed: Herrn Eduard Bertz. / Waisenstrasse 27. / Potsdam /
Allemagne.
Ciboure.

[June 2, 1903][788]
Tuesday.

Dear Friend, I have been so unwell, that I am just going away for a week to Cambo-les-Bains near here. You shall hear again very soon. Many thanks for your letter. Delighted to hear of your quietness. Would it be possible for you to order your bookseller to post to me directly the foll[owing] 3 books, pub[lished] by F. Duncker, Leipzig?

Ammiamus Marcellinus.	(2 Mark)
Eugippius, Leben d. heiligen Severin.	(1 Mark)
Prokop, Vandalenkrieg	(1 M. 2d)

All are German translations, in the series "Die Geschichtschreiber der deutschen Vorzeit." I should be very glad, at some time, to have a complete *list* of this series, up to date. Of course I will send you money when I know cost of postage. I hope this will not give you much trouble.

Ever kindest remembrances from us both.

Always yours,
G. G.

[787] Where Bertz lived for a time while in London.
[788] Postmark.

Ispoure. / St. Jean Pied de Port / Basses Pyrénées.

June 27, 1903.

Dear Friend,

I can write only a few lines—am too weak and pain-ridden. Sciatica worse than ever. We go on Wednesday to above address, where benefit is hoped from change of air.

Many thanks for your kind attention to my request. The 3 volumes arrived yesterday.

Procop.	1.20
Eugipp.	1 —
Amm. Marcell	1.50
Postage	50
	————
M.	4.20

So I send a Mandat postal for 5 francs.

I earnestly hope my health may improve at Ispoure, for I am getting weak to a dangerous degree. Of course I cannot work, yet I *must* work soon. I fear the climate here has been altogether too relaxing for me. I don't know whether I shall dare to face another winter without more complete change.

I hope you will never have sciatica. It is particularly bad from 11 p. m to 3 a. m; I cannot lie in bed because of the pain. Cambo did me a little good, so I continue to hope.

I will write a decent letter as soon as I see the results of the change.

Kindest regards from Gabrielle.

Ever yours, old friend,
GEORGE GISSING

Ispoure. / St. Jean Pied de Port. / B[asses] P[yrénées]. / France.

July 10. 1903.

Dear Friend,

It is a most unfortunate thing that you should be suffering so from the heat in your new abode. Indeed, you had never thought of that possibility. Here, until a day or two ago, the weather has been extraordinarily cool—indeed, like a northern spring; but the heat has now come upon us. However, the nights are always very fresh, a great thing. I can only hope that a change of weather will very soon give you relief. Of course it is a most serious thing for you to be driven out of the house every evening. If you had some pleasant way of spending this time, it would not be so bad. But let us hope for a change of weather.

I was unable to say in my last how much obliged I felt to you for the 3 volumes—to-day I am feeling better, (though yet I cannot sleep,) and have more strength to write. Alas! I cannot afford the books of which I have need, and there is another grave difficulty—the impossibility of accumulating heavy volumes whilst I lead this nomadic life. But, if you should ever see a cheap and portable copy of the *Epistles of St. Jerome*, or those of *Pope Gregory I* (the Great), be so kind as to let me know of it. My studies centre more and more in the period of transition from classical Rome to the Roman middle age—it has a vast fascination for me.

I am at last seriously working on my 6th. Century story, and hope to make something good of it. I have greatly improved my original scheme. But I live in fear of breaking down. My sciatica is very slightly better—oh, the torments of the last half-year! But I am afraid it is insomnia that will kill me. I do not know what it is to sleep for more than 2 or 3 hours in a night.

We are very comfortably established here. The situation is not high (only 300 mètres above the sea) but the air is very pure and tonic. All around are beautiful panoramas of mountain scenery—beautiful, not grand; to anyone who knows the Alps, the Pyrenees are rather tame. But the universal greenness refreshes one's eyes, and the tranquillity of the country life is good for the nerves.

I am indignant at the thought of your acting as a guide to strangers in Potsdam. For this, your time is far too precious. Of course it is pleasant to be sought out because of your reputation, but you must not allow too much encroachment.

Gabrielle is fairly well, though a little neuralgia troubles her now and then. Mme. Fleury seems to me much better than a year ago. If all goes well, we may perhaps try the experiment of remaining here all thro' the winter. Moving is a horrible business.

I have had sent me a German novel—"Jörn Uhl" by Frenssen,[789] which seems to be rather good. Do you happen to know whether

[789] Gustave Frenssen (1863–1945), (Berlin, 1901).

the Roman and Greek novels of Karl Eckstein[790]—"Der Mönch vom Aventin"—"Kyparissos" etc.—are well done?
Our love to you.

Ever yours,
GEORGE GISSING

Ispoure. / St. Jean Pied de Port. / B[asses] P[yrénées]. / France.

October 4. 1903.

Dear old Friend,

Heaven be thanked, I have just got past the middle of my book. Did I mention that it was to be called "Veranilda"? This is the name of the Gothic heroine. The writing is very laborious, but gives me great pleasure as each chapter is finished. Of course I am often troubled with doubts, thinking the whole thing a mere worthless effort of the imagination. Yet it *may* be more than that, for I sometimes feel that I have got hold of the spirit of the 6th. Century. I shall be extremely curious to hear how it strikes you.

In point of health, I am decidedly better. Since we came here, I have slept well, had an excellent appetite, and never had the slightest fever. I made a great mistake in passing a whole year at St. Jean de Luz, which really did not suit me at all. Another grave mistake was the winter spent at Arcachon. Thus does one waste the precious years of so short a life.

How long we shall stay here, is uncertain, but we shall probably go away at the end of the year. Of course there is no society here, and one feels at last that it is necessary to talk with someone. One of our vague projects is to go next spring to Geneva, and see how that suits us. Do you know anything particular about Geneva—for instance, whether there is a good public library? The need of books is becoming a very serious matter for me. Gabrielle tells me that Geneva is better in many ways than Lausanne, because of all sorts of taxes on foreigners at the latter place, which at the former do not exist; otherwise, as regards climate and situation, no doubt Lausanne is preferable. We shall see; we shall see.

"Veranilda" ought to be finished by the end of the year. Yet

---

[790] GRG means Ernst Eckstein (1845-1900), author of *Der Mönch vom Aventin* (Berlin, 1893) and *Kyparissos* (Berlin, 1895).

there are the hazards of the cold weather before me, and its manifold discomforts. If possible, I want to publish this book before "Will Warburton."

Gabrielle writes to you about "Jörn Uhl."[791] It was a stranger who sent me the book, a Mrs Upward,[792] resident at Brussels, who began by writing to me about my "Ryecroft." You will see that the thing has been a grave disappointment, and Zapp is obviously quite right.[793]

Such little time as I have for reading is given to old Gregorovius, a book more and more delightful to me. For half an hour every day Gabrielle reads Italian aloud, our book at present being the memoirs of Luigi Settembrini,[794] a Neapolitan revolutionist of the middle of the 19th. Century. Very interesting!

How have you got through the summer? How does your work go on? Not too many interruptions from importunate tourists, I hope.

By the bye, I never told you of a four days' excursion we made not long ago into Spain, by way of Roncesvalles. We got as far as Pamplona. It was delightful—a wonderful change in so short a distance. Spain is Spain everywhere; Navarra breathes of Don Quixote. Oh, if you could see Maritornes in the flesh! If you could *smell* the inns! I got on better with colloquial Spanish than I had expected. Pamplona is marvellously picturesque, very oriental.

All good be with you.

Ever yours, dear friend,
GEORGE GISSING

From: Gabrielle Gissing
Addressed: Herrn Eduard Bertz / 27 Waisenstrasse / Potsdam / *Allemagne*
Ispoure / St Jean Pied de Port / BP

Sunday
[December 27, 1903]

Dear Friend,

I have a terrible piece of news to tell you: my dearest G. is dying

[791] For Gabrielle's note, see Appendix II.
[792] Not identified.
[793] Arthur Zapp probably reviewed the book.
[794] Settembrini (1813–1877) worked for Italian unity in the 1830's. A two-volume edition of his memoirs, *Recordanze*, edited by F. de Sanctis, was published in 1879–80.

des suites of a bronchio-pneumonia from which he suffers since already 3 weeks. Every hope of saving him must be abandoned and his end is now awaited at every moment. He is delirious since 7 days. and speaks about his *Veranilda* which he leaves un-achieved, with just 5—the 5 last chapters missing! This idea adds to the dreadful sorrow I have. You will share it I know.

Affectionately yrs
GABRIELLE G

Monday. Died today th[is] afternoon.

APPENDIX I

Addressed: George Gissing, Esq
From: William Blackwood
45 George Street / Edinburgh

8th. October 1896

Dear Sir

I was obliged by your letter of the 4th inst, and have to thank you for kindly bringing your German friend's novel under my notice. I had the pleasure of receiving it this morning, and I shall be glad if I see my way to giving it a favourable notice in the next article on German fiction in the Magazine.

I wonder what you have been busy with lately. Have you nothing that you think would suit Maga? I shall always be glad to hear from you when you write anything you would like me to consider.

With best regards believe me

Yours very truly
WILLIAM BLACKWOOD

APPENDIX II

Gabrielle Gissing to Eduard Bertz.

[24 April 1901]

Cher Monsieur et ami, il y a longtemps que j'aurais voulu répondre à votre aimable lettre, reçue au milieu d'une troisième atteinte d'influenza, mais, depuis, les santés ont été si peu satisfaisantes chez nous que mon temps a été fort tristement pris. Je suis bien peinée de vous savoir tojours si mal en train et je partage l'opinion de George que la bicyclette doit vous être très contraire. Quel ennui, n'est ce pas, de se voir entravé toujours dans ce qu'on a de plaisir à faire? Je veux espérer néanmoins que ce beau temps vous apportera quelque amélioration. Au revoir, cher monsieur et ami, ma mère vous envoie ses meilleurs compliments. Croyez-vous votre bien affectionnée,

GABRIELLE GISSING

Gabrielle Gissing to Eduard Bertz.

[8 September 1901]

Cher Monsieur et ami, merci [de] vos aimables lignes. Je suis heureuse de voir que votre santé est assez remise pour vous permettre des excursions à bicyclette. Le pays d'où vous écriviez parait ravissant. Seriez-vous assez bon pour me rappeler comment on dit en allemand: "Le temps va *s'éclaircir?*" Nous avons discuté cela, avec Georges, sans pouvoir nous mettre d'accord. Et puis—je me permets de vous exprimer le plaisir que vous me feriez en m'écrivant désormais *en allemand?* J'ai perdu presque toutes mes occasions d'entretenir mon allemand, que j'ai travaillé avec tant de zèle jadis, et bien lu, et je serais très fâchée de le perdre tout à fait.

J'envie beaucoup vos talents de bicyclette ici où il y aurait de charmantes courses à faire et où, privée de ce mode de transport si rapide et si commode, je ne vois presque rien, n'étant guère plus propre à la marche que Georges. Nous allons tout doucement, ensemble voir la ville et les souvenirs de son passé, les restes de ses murailles romaines, à demi revêtues de lierre, et de clématite, si pittoresques par endroits, mais les environs nous échappent. Il y a pourtant, non loin, les ruines d'un château ayant appartenu à Bussy-Rabutin et d'où Mme. de Sévigné a daté plusiers de ses lettres, que j'espère voir avant de repartir.

Ma mère se joint à moi pour vous dire les voeux que nous formons en faveur de la continuation de votre meilleur état de santé. Croyez-moi, cher Monsieur et ami, bien affectueusement votre.

GABRIELLE GISSING

George va certainement mieux, toutefois il est loin d'être *guéri*, et doit se soigner sans relâche, de peur d'une rechute. J'ai été bien ennuyeuse et sans sujet.

Gabrielle Gissing to Eduard Bertz.
Ispoure

9 October. 1903

Cher Monsieur,

Malgré tous les ennuis domestiques qui m'absorbent en ce moment et me prennent le meilleur de mon temps, je veux vous envoyer aujourd'hui, après si longtemps, mon affectueux souvenir et vous dire moi-même mon impression du livre de Frenssen "Jörn Uhl" que George vous a raconté que j'etais en train de lire. Mon avis est tout à fait celui de M. Zapp: c'est extrêmement ennuyeux, difficile à lire, long plus que de raison, et mal composé, ou plutôt pas composé du tout. L'auteur ajoute bout à bout une quantité d'épisodes concernant des personnages qu'on voit apparaître pour la première fois sans qu'on puisse, par la suite, s'expliquer ce qu'ils étaient venus faire dans le récit. Enfin j'ai cru ne jamais arriver à la fin du volume tant j'en étais excédée. Et, à vrai dire, je n'ai fait que parcourir, feuilleter le dernier tiers pour en prendre idée; la lecture suivie m'en était devenue fatigante; je préférais, en outre, consacrer le peu de temps dont je dispose à une œuvre plus digne d'intérêt. Je me suis en effet mise à l'Histoire de Rome à travers le Moyen Age, de Gregorovius, et j'en suis enchantée.

Je ne sais si George vous a fait part de son sentiment sur le pays basque que nous aimons comme pays et comme climat mais non comme habitants en général. Cette race basque à idées primitives et à d'immense orgueil, est à coup sûr fort intéressante à étudier et à voir en passant, mais les rapports quotidiens avec ses individus manque [sic] d'agrément au plus haut point.

Au revoir, cher Monsieur et ami. Avec les souvenirs de ma mère, recevez l'expression de mes affectueux sentiments.

GABRIELLE GISSING

INDEX